PENGUIN BOOKS

ENEMY AT THE GATES

William Craig (1929–97), a native of Concord, Massachusetts, was educated at Columbia University. His first book, *The Fall of Japan*, was a documentary account of the last weeks of the Second World War in the Pacific. His first novel, *The Tashkent Crisis*, a thriller about espionage and international politics, was published in 1971. *Enemy at the Gates* is the culmination of five years of research, during which he travelled extensively on three continents, studying documents and interviewing hundreds of survivors of Stalingrad.

ENEMY
AT THE GATES

The Battle for Stalingrad

BY WILLIAM CRAIG

PENGUIN BOOKS

PENGUIN BOOKS

Published by the Penguin Group
Penguin Books Ltd, 80 Strand, London WC2R ORL, England
Penguin Putnam Inc., 375 Hudson Street, New York, New York 10014, USA
Penguin Books Australia Ltd, Ringwood, Victoria, Australia
Penguin Books Canada Ltd, 10 Alcorn Avenue, Toronto, Ontario, Canada M4V 3B2
Penguin Books India (P) Ltd, 11 Community Centre, Panchsheel Park, New Delhi – 110 017, India
Penguin Books (NZ) Ltd, Cnr Rosedale and Airborne Roads, Albany, Auckland, New Zealand
Penguin Books (South Africa) (Pty) Ltd, 24 Sturdee Avenue, Rosebank 2196, South Africa

Penguin Books Ltd, Registered Offices: 80 Strand, London WC2R ORL, England

www.penguin.com

This edition first published by Hodder & Stoughton Ltd 1973
Published as a Classic Penguin 2000
10

Copyright © William Craig, 1973
All rights reserved

Printed in England by Cox & Wyman Ltd, Reading, Berkshire

To my wife Eleanor
whom I cherish

Prologue

When I was a child I discovered an exciting fantasy world in the pages of history books. At seven I marched to the walls of Jerusalem beside the Crusaders; at nine, I memorized Alfred Lord Tennyson's glorious paean to the immortal men of the Light Brigade as they charged at Balaklava. Two years later, uprooted from familiar surroundings when my family moved to another city, I discovered a kindred spirit in the lonely figure of Napoleon Bonaparte as he languished in exile on Saint Helena Island.

The bombing of Pearl Harbor on December 7, 1941, added a new dimension to my interest in historical figures and events. My own relatives were plunged into the global conflict, and I followed their exploits with a daily diary of World War II. As the self-ordained Boswell to the Allied forces I neglected my Latin declensions to record the ominous details about Wake, Guam, Bataan, and Corregidor. On entering the eighth grade in the fall of 1942, I became an amateur cartographer, drawing meticulous maps of places like Guadalcanal and New Guinea—even a city called Stalingrad, deep inside Russia. Because of my passionate interest in Napoleon, because I knew of the rout of his *Grand Armée* on the vast snow-covered plains of czarist Russia, I quickly developed an interest in the German attempt to conquer the Soviet Union. It occurred to me that the same fate might await the Nazi panzers as they moved resolutely into the heartland of the USSR.

During October and November of 1942, I spent more and more time away from my studies to read everything I could find about this Soviet city on the edge of Asia. The reports told of fighting in sewers, cellars, office buildings, and I tried desperately to imagine such horrible moments in men's lives. For a thirteen-year-old boy brought up in a peaceful land, such images were difficult to conjure.

In February 1943, the German Sixth Army surrendered and our newspapers carried pictures of the astonishing Russian victory. One particular wirephoto of captured Field Marshal Friedrich von Paulus caught my attention. His face was deeply lined; his eyes spoke of nightmares he had witnessed. This once-proud German officer was now a broken man.

The memory of that picture remained with me over the years.

During the next quarter century, an avalanche of books spewed forth from both Soviet and German presses about Stalingrad. Some were personal narratives, others historical treatises. The Russians wrote proudly of their incredible victory. Frequently, however, they distorted facts in order to conform to political realities. Stalin's name disappeared from accounts of the battle; so did those of Khrushchev, Malenkov, and Marshal Georgi Zhukov. Thus the Russian side of the story was shrouded by official secrecy.

The telling of the story from the German side suffered a different distortion. Few German authors examined the myriad complexities that led to the loss of Sixth Army at Stalingrad, nor could they, since they were denied access to Russian sources. And the memoirs of the German generals who participated in the battle were filled with controversial statements, personal vilification, and censure. Furthermore, the Germans never gave credit to the Red Army for its dogged defense of Stalingrad and brilliant counterattack that defeated what, until then, had been the finest army in the world.

By now I had become an author and historian and, still captivated by that picture of a beaten Paulus, I embarked on a personal investigation of what had happened at Stalingrad. To be successful in this venture, I had to do what no one had done before: study the official records of both the Russian and Axis forces engaged in the conflict, visit the battlefield and walk the ground for which so many men had died, locate survivors of the battle—Russians, Germans, Italians, Rumanians, Hungarians—and get their eyewitness accounts, their diaries, photographs, and letters. It was not an easy task.

First I met with Ernst von Paulus, the field marshal's only surviving son, at Viersen in West Germany. Looking strikingly like his father, Ernst spoke for hours about the man who had endured so much: the loss of his entire army, his years of captivity in the Soviet Union, the twilight of a broken life in Dresden, where Paulus spent his last days composing rebuttals to those critics blaming him for the tragedy at Stalingrad.

Then I went to Stalingrad, the city that had destroyed Paulus's career and reputation. A casual visitor there finds that Stalingrad is once again an industrial giant in the Soviet Union. Its broad boulevards are rimmed with banks of flowers. Sparkling white apartment houses form miles of comfortable oases in a sea of busy factories and workshops. The city's inhabitants move energetically along downtown streets. At one intersection, a crowd gathers around a new sedan to admire it; at night, couples stroll the Volga embankment and watch the lights of passing steamers and barges. In so peaceful a setting it is almost impossible to imagine that two nations fought a titanic battle here only thirty years ago.

Evidence of that cruel struggle is sparse. At a grain elevator, an irregular line of bullet holes can be seen across the concrete face of the silos. On the wall of the bustling Univermag Department Store, a plaque notes that the German Sixth Army surrendered there in 1943. Further north, on Solechnaya Street, a television antenna sprouts up from an apartment house where another sign describes a fifty-eight-day struggle for the building during the fall of 1942. As I stood there reading it, children ran across a grassy courtyard that once had been filled with mines and dead soldiers.

At the small Volgograd Defense Museum near the main railroad station, justifiably proud officials showed me memorabilia of the conflict: the tattered and bullet-riddled greatcoat of a Red Army officer, hundreds of red-white-and-black flags displaying the swastika that had been taken from famous German units, guns, official orders, captured diaries and letters. On all the walls were brightly painted dioramas of battle scenes.

But only at Mamaev Hill, rising from the center of the city, can one begin to understand the enormity of what really happened there. As I walked the 336 feet to its summit, I passed through a forest of sculptured tableaus recalling the Russian triumph: a figure of Gen. Vassili Ivanovich Chuikov, the one man who could be termed "the Savior of Stalingrad"; a woman holding tight to a dying boy; men firing their weapons at enemies trying to drive them into the Volga. At the top of Mamaev, I gazed upward in amazement at a 170-foot high statue of "Mother Russia." A cape flies back from her shoulders, and her right hand brandishes a sword. The face is contorted as she exhorts her countrymen to victory. In a circular rotunda at her feet is a mass grave containing the mortal remains of ten thousand of her sons gathered together from the battlefield; their names have been inscribed on the rotunda's walls. Funereal music sounds constantly in the stillness. From the middle of a concrete slab covering their resting place, a giant carved arm thrusts defiantly upward. In its clenched fist, a gleaming torch pierces the gloom.

From a winding ramp, visitors gaze down onto the tomb. No

one speaks. The hush of death follows them out into the brilliant sunlight where Stalingrad seethes with renewed life. The trenches have been filled in. Barbed wire has disappeard from the hillside. All the rusted tanks and guns have been removed. Even German grave markers have been pulled from the earth. Almost every physical scar of that terrible war has been erased. But the mental scars remain and, around the world, men and women who were at Stalingrad in 1942 still flinch at the memories of those awful days.

There is the Stalingrad factory worker whose eyes narrow in hatred as he recalls enemy planes machine-gunning civilians on a crowded Volga pier; a former Soviet officer who speaks haltingly as he describes the terrible cries of his men after they had been ambushed and slaughtered in the fields west of Stalingrad; a Russian émigré in Haifa, Israel, who sobs his grief at the memory of a baby smashed against a wall by drunken German soldiers.

In an opulently furnished home in Rome, an eminent Italian surgeon shudders as he explains the various stages of cannibalism that occurred in the prison camps of Siberia after the battle ended. His wife listens in horrified fascination as the doctor recalls that the most sophisticated cannibals ignored corpses more than a day old. They preferred the warm blood of freshly killed soldiers.

A Russian woman, now the wife of a prominent American musician, has only one searing recollection. Eighteen months after the fighting ended, when her refugee train stopped at Stalingrad, the stench of thousands upon thousands of corpses still lying in the rubble made her want to vomit.

It is the same with the Germans. In a suburb of Hamburg, when a strapping Luftwaffe officer unlocks bitter images of beatings by Soviet prison guards, he suddenly breaks down completely and begs me not to question him further.

In Cologne, a woman who has been waiting twenty-seven years for the return of her husband, reported missing in action, asks me a question. Her eyes glassy with tears, she says: "Do you think I should go to Stalingrad and look for him?" I think of her unbelievable devotion to the memory of a man long since written off as a casualty by government archivists, and can only shake my head numbly and say: "No, I don't think it would help."

She had known what my answer would be. Smiling bravely, she rose and made tea for the two of us.

The catalogue of bitter memories increased in scope as I met with hundreds of men and women who survived the holocaust of Stalingrad. I was deeply upset by what they told me, and I had to remind myself time and again that I had to listen to these tales of horror because the stories were vital to a valid reconstruction of the conflict.

Most appalling was the growing realization, formed by statistics I uncovered, that the battle was the greatest military bloodbath in recorded history. Well over a million men and women died because of Stalingrad, a number far surpassing the previous records of dead at the first battle of the Somme and Verdun in 1916.

The toll breaks down as follows:

Conversations with official Russian sources on a not-for-attribution basis (and it must be remembered that the Russians have never officially admitted their losses in World War II) put the loss of Red Army soldiers at Stalingrad at 750,000 killed, wounded, or missing in action.

The Germans lost almost 400,000 men.

The Italians lost more than 130,000 men out of their 200,-000-man army.

The Hungarians lost approximately 120,000 men.

The Rumanians also lost approximately 200,000 men around Stalingrad.

As for the civilian population of the city, a prewar census listed more than 500,000 people prior to the outbreak of World War II. This number increased as a flood of refugees poured into the city from other areas of Russia that were in danger of being overrun by the Germans. A portion of Stalingrad's citizens were evacuated prior to the first German attack but 40,000 civilians were known to have died in the first two days of bombing in the city. No one knows how many died on the barricades or in the antitank ditches or in the surrounding steppes. Official records show only one stark fact: after the battle ended, a census found only 1,515 people who had lived in Stalingrad in 1942.

As these grim statistics emerged, I began asking the survivors the most important questions of all: what was the significance of the battle?

In 1944, Gen. Charles de Gaulle visited Stalingrad and walked past the still-uncleared wreckage. Later, at a reception in Moscow, a correspondent asked him his impressions of the scene. "Ah, Stalingrad, *c'est tout de même un peuple formidable, un très grand peuple,*" the Free French leader said. The correspondent agreed. "*Ah, oui, les Russes . . .*" de Gaulle interrupted impatiently. "*Mais non, je ne parle pas des Russes, je parle des Allemands. Tout de même, avoir poussé jusque là.*" ("That they should have come so far.")

Anyone with an understanding of military problems must agree with de Gaulle. That the Germans had been able to cross more than a thousand miles of southern Russia to reach the banks of the Volga River was an incredible achievement. That the Russians held them at Stalingrad, when almost every Allied strategist thought the Soviet Union was on the verge of collapse, is equally extraordinary.

Battered for more than a year by the Nazi juggernaut, most soldiers in the Soviet Army had become convinced the Germans were unbeatable. Thousands of them streamed into enemy lines to ask for succor. Thousands more bolted from the front lines and ran away. In unoccupied Russia, the civilian population fell victim to the same despair. With millions dead or under German control, with food, clothing, and shelter in increasingly short supply, the majority of the Russian people had begun to doubt their leadership and their armies. The surprising victory over the German Sixth Army at Stalingrad changed that negative attitude. Psychologically buoyed by this magnificent triumph against the "Nazi supermen," both civilians and military braced for the grueling tasks ahead. And though the ultimate destruction of the Third Reich would prove to be a long and costly struggle, the Russians never again doubted they would win. After Stalingrad, they moved resolutely westward, straight to Berlin, and the legacy of their arduous passage into the heartland of Germany remains with us to this day. For the Soviet Union, the path to its present role as a superpower began at the Volga River, where, as Winston Churchill described it, "the hinge of fate had turned. . . ."

For the Germans, Stalingrad was the single most traumatic event of the war. Never before had one of their elite armies succumbed in the field. Never before had so many soldiers vanished without trace in the vast wilderness of an alien country. Stalingrad was a mind-paralyzing calamity to a nation that believed it was the master race. A creeping pessimism began to invade the minds of those who had chanted *"Sieg Heil! Sieg Heil!"* at Hitler's rallies, and the myth of the Führer's genius slowly dissolved under the impact of the reality of Stalingrad. In furtive conversations, men once too timid to move against the regime began to make concrete plans to overthrow it. Stalingrad was the beginning of the end for the Third Reich.

After spending four years intensively researching the battle of Stalingrad from both sides of no-man's-land, I found that the mosaic of the story changed with the passing days—as does all history. The brilliant German offensive to the Volga paled in relation to the inspired defense of Stalingrad by the Russians. Beyond that, most gripping of all, was the gradual moral and physical disintegration of the German soldiers as they realized they were doomed. In their struggle to cope with the unthinkable, lies the ultimate drama of the event.

Brutality, sadism, and cowardice are undeniably prominent in the story. Jealousy, overriding ambition, and callousness to human suffering occur with shocking frequency. Man aspires to greatness, but all too often his hopes are submerged by the primitive instinct to survive at any cost. What happens is not pleasant reading. No book that deals with widespread slaughter can be. At Stalingrad we are witnesses to monumental human tragedy.

William Craig
Westport, Connecticut
November 8, 1972

ENEMY
AT THE GATES

Chapter One

Parched by the blazing sun of summer, the grassy plain of the steppe country is light brown in hue. From the vicinity of Lugansk in the west to Kazakhstan in the east, the barren tableland stretches more than six hundred miles across southern Russia. Only a few rectangular patches of cultivated farmland, *kolkhozi*, relieve the desolation and, from them, ribbons of road run straight to the horizon.

Two majestic rivers, running roughly north to south, scour the land. The erratic Don gouges a convulsive path to the city of Rostov on the Sea of Azov. Farther east, the mighty Volga bends more gently on its way to a rendezvous with the Caspian Sea at Astrakhan. Only at one place do the rivers run parallel to each other, and here they are forty miles apart. After that brief attempt at union, they flow relentlessly on their lonely journeys to different destinations, giving but brief respite to the harsh terrain. Otherwise, the suffocating heat of the region cracks the ground and paralyzes life.

It has been that way for centuries on the steppe. But on August 5, 1942, a malevolent presence intruded on the timeless scene. From the west, from the far-off Ukraine, came giant pillars of dust. The whirling clouds advanced fitfully across the prairie, slowing only for short periods before moving on toward the east and the Don River barrier. From a distance they resembled tornadoes, those natural phenomena that plague the open areas of the earth. But these spiraling clouds hid the German Sixth Army, an elite legion dispatched by Adolf Hitler to destroy the Soviet Army and the Communist state led by Joseph Stalin. Its men were supremely confident; during three years of warfare, they had never suffered defeat.

In Poland, the Sixth Army had made the word *blitzkrieg* ("lightning war") a synonym for Nazi omnipotence. At Dunkirk, it helped cripple the British Expeditionary Force, sending the Tommies back to England without rifles or artillery. Chosen to spearhead the cross-channel invasion, the Sixth Army practiced amphibious landings until Hitler lost enthusiasm for the assault and sent it instead to Yugoslavia, which it conquered in a matter of weeks.

Then, in the summer of 1941, the Sixth Army began its Russian campaign and completely mastered the enemy. It quickly "liberated" several million square miles of the Ukraine and attained a level of professional excellence unmatched in modern warfare. Increasingly arrogant about their successes on the battlefield, its soldiers reached the conclusion that *"Russland ist kaputt."* This conviction was buttressed by propaganda emanating from the Führerhauptquartier (Field Headquarters of the OKW). For with the unleashing in late June 1942 of Operation Blue, the knockout blow, Adolf Hitler had promised his soldiers an end to the war.

Most Germans on the steppe agreed with their Führer's prophecies of triumph, especially when they noted the slackening resistance of the Red Army. Now, on this stifling August morning, the Sixth Army prepared to spring another trap. Two battered Soviet armies, the First Tank and the Sixty-second Infantry, lay penned up against the cliffs that dominate the western bank of the Don.

Fingers of steel had already reached out on either side of the Russians. Packs of German Mark III and Mark IV tanks, coated with dust, roamed the land. From hundreds of turrets, tank commanders issued curt orders to gunners who swiveled their weapons around to fire on targets of opportunity.

Terrified Russian soldiers, lacking faith in their officers and in the Red Army itself, rushed to join a swelling throng of deserters. The Germans herded them into ragged columns that marched west, away from the sounds of war. The Russians were happy. Capture meant they had survived.

The Germans had little time to care for their prisoners. In regimental and divisional command posts, senior officers drew new lines on maps, wrote out new directives and gave them to couriers who gunned their motorcycles past jammed lines of trucks moving men and supplies ever closer to the Don River. Inside the transports, infantrymen tied handkerchiefs over their faces to ward off the clouds of dirt that engulfed them. Their gray green uniforms were coated with steppe soil; their eyes were bloodshot. They were miserable, but since they were winning, morale was high. Strident marching songs drifted out from the lorries as the motorcyclists roared by.

When the couriers reached the main line of resistance, they handed messages to weary battalion and company commanders, some of whom had not rested for more than thirty days. Their appearance reflected the strain of constant combat: faces were pinched, their once-neat uniforms stuck to their bodies and held the accumulated grime of the steppe. Helmets were a monstrous hindrance, a magnet for the sun that beat on them and sent perspiration pouring down inside their collars.

Still the officers shrugged off the discomfort and shouted new commands to their bedraggled men. The *landsers* stubbed out cigarettes, shouldered rifles and machine pistols, and fell into the inevitable columns pointing east, always east into the heartland of the Soviet Union.

Contrary to popular belief at the time, German armies were far from total mechanization. In Sixth Army alone, more than twenty-five thousand horses moved guns and supplies. They were everywhere: huge Belgian draft horses, small Russian *panjes,* not much bigger than donkeys and native to the steppe. Their flanks heaved from exertion, and their eyes rolled as they bucked in fear at sudden explosions. The marching soldiers stepped in the manure and cursed violently at this additional affront to their sensibilities.

But they marched on and quickly reached the edge of no-man's-land where burned and gutted tanks stood mute, their treads twisted crazily and gun barrels snapped off. Amidst this desolation, the troops dug shallow foxholes and waited for the signal to attack.

Russian shrapnel sprayed the newly arrived; human debris collected quickly. Medics loaded the wounded into ambulances, which raced toward field hospitals located safely in the rear. Trucks, tanks, and motorcycles pulled to the roadside to let the "meat wagons" pass, while inside, attendants bent over mutilated bodies strapped tightly onto stretchers.

At the field hospitals, the atmosphere was almost tranquil. Only the gravediggers disturbed the hushed quiet as, behind the hospital tents, they methodically lowered one coffin after another into the ground. Army chaplains intoned appropriate prayers, then an honor guard fired quick volleys into the air. Moments later, a team of men began hammering wooden crosses into the ground at the head of each grave, marking by name, rank, and unit, the soldier who was now buried beneath foreign soil. A passing courier noticed that groups of cemeteries were spreading across the steppe like clumps of wild mushrooms.

Three miles from the front, a battery of 150-millimeter *nebelwerfers,* those fearsomely squat, six-barreled mortars mounted on rubber-tired gun carriages, was strangely silent. Throughout the morning, as the gun crews huddled in slit trenches to escape the terrible back blast of their weapons, the mortars had spat series of 78-pound high-explosive shells toward an unseen foe. Now out of ammunition, the men were relaxing and their commander, Lt. Emil Metzger, squatted in the shade of a truck. Taking a pad of paper from his jacket pocket, he began to scribble a message to his wife in Frankfurt: *"Liebe Kaethe. . . ."*

How could he break the news that he had decided to give up his first furlough in two years so that one of his friends could go home in his place and get married? As he pondered the question, Emil paused to rub the stubble of his three-day-old beard. He was proud of what he had accomplished since that day back in 1933 when he had first joined the fledgling Reichswehr for a twelve-year hitch, because he "wanted to do something for the Fatherland." During the invasion of Poland in 1939, Metzger's aggressiveness, his gymnast's quickness and ability to withstand physical hardship, had earned him promotion to sergeant. The next year he and his men had fought across France and were hardened by the horrors they saw on the roads surrounding Dunkirk. He now wore the Iron Cross Second Class, and was an officer. It was a far cry from the apprenticeship that he had been supposed to serve while learning the career of master butcher. Patriotism had not been his only reason for joining the army. His other reason for enlisting was that he was sickened by the killing of animals.

Emil wondered if he should confide in his letter that his curly black hair was suddenly touched with gray. His brown eyes crinkled at the corners as he recalled the dance at which he had met Kaethe Bausch. They had married shortly afterward, in a brief span of time between fighting in 1940, and they had spent only four nights together before he had gone off again to battle. It was difficult to find the proper, soothing words to explain why he was not coming home, but he was sure Kaethe would understand. There was no reason for her to worry. According to the latest rumors the war was nearly over. The Soviet Army had been routed; one more battle should end the killing. In closing, he said, "I should be home for Christmas."

He sealed the letter and handed it to an orderly to mail just as the supply truck pulled up with a fresh stock of shells. Tying a handkerchief across his nose and mouth, the lieutenant ordered the battery to join the line of march. They were headed, Emil had been told, for a place on the Volga River called Stalingrad.

Other men shared Emil Metzger's optimism. At Sixth Army Field Headquarters, thirty miles west of the fluid front, officers read maps and mentally subtracted two more armies from the Russian Order of Battle. It was obvious that when the German tanks linked up, the last escape route to the Don would close and the rabble trapped within the pincers would cease to exist. Now what concerned the strategists was the plotting for the next phase of the offensive: fording the Don and moving forty miles further east to the Volga.

The original plans for Operation Blue did not call for the capture of Stalingrad. In fact, the city was not even a primary target for attack. As originally conceived, the strike force was to consist of two groups of armies, A and B. Army Group A, under the command of Field Marshal List, included the Seventeenth and First Panzer armies; Army Group B, under Fedor von Bock, boasted the Fourth Panzer and Sixth armies, which were to be aided by the Hungarians in support of their rear echelons. The army groups were to move eastward on a broad front to the line of the Volga River "in the area of" the city of Stalingrad. After "neutralizing" Russian war production in that region by bombing and artillery fire, and after cutting the vital transportation line on the Volga, both army groups were to turn south and drive on the oil fields of the Caucasus.

But in July, the Führer himself had subtly altered the scope of the campaign after German intelligence reported that the Russians had few reliable divisions on the west bank of the Volga. Boat traffic on the river had not increased, which indicated that the

Soviet High Command was not yet pouring reinforcements into the city from the Urals or Siberia. Furthermore, the Armed Forces High Command (OKW) determined that the defense lines between the Don and Volga were primitive at best, though it appeared that some Russian work battalions were out on the steppe, throwing up hasty antitank fortifications. Thus, Hitler concluded, the Red Army was not about to make a major stand at Stalingrad, and he ordered Sixth Army to seize the city by force as soon as possible.

In his cramped, field-gray tent, the commander of the Sixth Army, Col. Gen. Friedrich von Paulus, was rejoicing quietly. A cautious man, who disdained public emotion, he relaxed for a few moments by listening to Beethoven on a gramophone. Music was the best catalyst for his moody, introspective personality. Tall and darkly handsome, the fifty-two-year-old general was the classic example of a German General Staff officer. Apolitical, trained only to do his job in the army, he left diplomacy to the party in power. He thought Adolf Hitler an excellent leader for the German people, a man who had contributed greatly to the development of the state. After watching him evolve the strategies that conquered Poland, France, and most of Europe, Paulus was awed by Hitler's grasp of the technical aspects of warfare. He considered him a genius.

His wife did not share his beliefs. The former Elena Constance Rosetti-Solescu, Coca to her friends, a descendant of one of Rumania's royal houses, had married Paulus in 1912 and borne him a daughter and twin sons. Both boys now served in the army. She detested the Nazi regime and told her husband he was far too good for the likes of men such as Keitel and the other "lackeys" who surrounded Hitler. When Germany attacked Poland, she vehemently condemned it as an unjust act. Paulus did not argue with her. Content with his role, he merely carried out orders. When, in the fall of 1940, he brought home maps and other memoranda related to the planned invasion of Russia, Coca found them and confronted Paulus, saying a war against the Soviet Union was completely unjustified. He tried to avoid discussing the matter with her, but she persisted.

"What will become of us all? Who will survive to the end?" she asked.

Attempting to calm her fears, Paulus had said the war with Russia would be over in about six weeks' time. She was not appeased. Just as she had feared, the new campaign dragged on past the six-week deadline and into the awful winter of 1941 on the Moscow front. Yet despite the setbacks, despite the horrendous losses suffered by the German Army because of the climate and ferocious Russian resistance, Paulus retained one unshakable belief: Hitler was invincible.

In January 1942, when his superior, Field Marshal Reichenau died suddenly, Paulus finally got his life's desire: command of an army in the field. The two men could not have been more dissimilar. Reichenau, an ardent Nazi, had been coarse in manner and unkempt in appearance. Paulus was impeccably groomed at all times. He even wore gloves in the field because he abhorred dirt; he bathed and changed his uniforms twice a day.

Despite such glaring differences, Paulus had sublimated his retiring manner to the volatile Reichenau. A master of detail, fascinated with figures and grand strategy, he handled the administration of the Sixth Army while Reichenau led charges at the front. In return, Reichenau treated Paulus like a son and always trusted his judgment. The two men agreed on all but one important policy. It marked the great gulf between them in heritage and philosophy.

Reichenau had been a ruthless believer in Hitler's thesis of racial supremacy and had supported the Führer's infamous "Commissar Order," which ordained the killing of all captured Russian political officers without benefit of trial. He even went a step further by introducing within Sixth Army Command what came to be known as the "Severity Order." It read in part:

> . . . The most important objective of this campaign against the Jewish-Bolshevik system is the complete destruction of its

sources of power and the extermination of the Asiatic influence in European civilization. . . . In this eastern theatre, the soldier is not only a man fighting in accordance with the rules of the art of war, out also the ruthless standard bearer of a national conception. . . . For this reason the soldier must learn fully to appreciate the necessity for the severe but just retribution that must be meted out to the subhuman species of Jewry. . . .

Reichenau's insistence on "retribution" had resulted in monstrous crimes. After the front-line troops of Sixth Army divisions passed through towns, a motley collection of homicidal maniacs came in their wake and systematically tried to eliminate the Jewish population.

Divided into four *Einsatzgruppen* (special extermination squads) across Russia, they numbered approximately three thousand sadists, who had been recruited mostly from the ranks of Himmler's police forces, the Schutzstaffeln, or SS (Elite Guard) and Sicherheitsdienst, or SD (Security Service). Others wandered in from punishment battalions and psychiatric hospitals. At a training center in Saxony they had been taught to use the rifle and machine pistol and told explicitly what to do with them in the Soviet Union. Dressed in black uniforms, they traveled by truck convoy, and terrified villagers soon referred to them as the "Black Crows."

Reichenau had helped the *Einsatzgruppen* as much as he could. Anxious to conserve ammunition, he even suggested each Jew be finished off with no more than two bullets. The mass killings affected the attitude of many Sixth Army soldiers who witnessed the Black Crows at work. Given free rein by their commanders, they enthusiastically helped exterminate the Jewish population. At times, soldiers in bathing suits and other casual off-duty attire snapped photographs of executions and sent them home to families and friends. A picnic atmosphere prevailed around ditches filled with bodies.

Those Germans who had protested the killings were ignored. Nothing interfered with the campaign of extermination. Nearly a million people died before Friedrich von Paulus assumed control and ended the genocide—at least in his sector—by rescinding both the Commissar and Severity Orders.

As commander of the Sixth Army, Paulus was victorious in his first major battle when, in May, the Russians had tried to upset German plans at Kharkov by attacking first. The Sixth Army was instrumental in rallying the Wehrmacht from near disaster and trapping more than two hundred thousand Russians in a giant envelopment. Congratulations poured in from old comrades, some of whom now assiduously courted his favor. It was clear to them that he was marked for greater responsibilties within the German Army's High Command. Later, when Operation Blue appeared to be sweeping the Russians away like chaff in the wind, Paulus's career expectations assumed even more gigantic proportions. Still fastidious, always the epitome of the cool, thinking machine, he traveled the barren steppe, seeking a last confrontation with the enemy.

An excellent cadre of staff officers made the task of running Sixth Army immeasurably easier. The chief of staff, Gen. Arthur Schmidt, was new but, like Paulus, he was a master of the smallest detail and promised to take much of that tedious work load upon himself. A thin-faced man with bulging eyes and a sharply pointed chin, Schmidt did not fit the traditional mold for German staff officers. Born in Hamburg to a merchant family, he had served in World War I as a soldier. Afterward he stayed through the convulsions of postwar politics and emerged as an officer under Hitler's reborn Reichswehr.

He was autocratic, overbearing, and had a nasty habit of interrupting conversations when the subject bored him. Many officers disliked his imperious manner. Some resented his rapid rise in rank and responsibility, but as he assumed his job under Paulus, Schmidt ignored his critics. Sharply different in temperament and tastes, the two men thought alike on military matters. As a result, the Sixth Army was functioning like a smoothly running watch.

Then there were the field commanders, including such men as Gen. Walther Heitz, head of the Eighth Corps, a "bull," who had been in charge of the funeral procession for Chancellor Hindenburg, and now was a veteran professional who enjoyed soldiering and fox hunting. Walther Seydlitz-Kurzbach, of the Fifty-first Corps, the infantry arm of the army, was the stubborn, white-haired scion of a noble family in Prussia, a highly competent tactician, and only the fifty-fourth German to earn the coveted Oak Leaves to the Knighthood of the Iron Cross. Edler von Daniel, a hard-drinking womanizer, had been brought from peaceful occupation duty in Normandy to lead the 295th Division. Hans Hube, a severely wounded veteran of World War I and the only one-armed general in the German Army, had persevered to become commander of the famous 16th Panzer Division, now hurrying to forge a link around the Russians at the Don. Hube was known as *"Der Mensch"* ("The Man") to his troops.

Thus Sixth Army was a model of military brilliance, and in his camper, Friedrich von Paulus reflected on the good fortunes of past weeks and wrote an effusive letter to a friend in Germany, ". . . We've advanced quite a bit and have left Kharkov 500 kilometers behind us. The great thing now is to hit the Russian so hard a crack that he won't recover for a very long time. . . ."

In his enthusiasm, Paulus neglected to mention several nagging concerns. The dysentery he had first picked up in the Balkans during World War I was plaguing him. And on the strategy level, his left flank was worrisome. There, well to the north along the line of the tortuous upper Don, the armies of the satellite nations —Hungary, Italy, and Rumania—were struggling to hold the left flank while Sixth Army moved east. He was relying heavily on the strength of these puppet forces to blunt any enemy attack coming from that direction.

The armies Paulus worried about were moving slowly. Farthest toward the northwest, soldiers of the Hungarian Second Army had begun to dig in along the upper Don. To their right, men of the Italian Eighth Army were preparing to occupy a long stretch of looping river line running toward the east. The Italians not only had been given the job of containing any Russian threat from across the river, they also served as a buffer between the Hungarians and the Rumanian Third Army, which was to hold the territory from Serafimovich to Kletskaya deep in the steppe. The German High Command had inserted the Italians between the other two armies to avoid conflict between ancient enemies, who might forget the Russians and go at each other's throats.

That rivalry was hardly an auspicious omen. It underlined the Germans' desperate manpower situation, for the three satellite armies had been brought together in a haphazard manner. The Hungarian and Rumanian forces were staffed mostly by political officers who were unschooled in warfare. Both armies were riddled by corruption and inefficiency. The lowly soldier had it worst of all. Poorly led and poorly fed, he endured outrageous privations. Officers whipped enlisted men on the merest whim. When action got dangerous, many officers simply went home. One private wrote his family that even his priest had deserted in a moment of crisis. Worse, they were equipped with antiquated weapons: antitank guns were almost nonexistent; rifles were of World War I vintage.

Many similar conditions prevailed in the Italian Army. Dragooned into service far from their homeland, wary of the bond between Hitler's Nazi Germany and Mussolini's Fascist state, the troopers grumbled unhappily as they marched through shattered Russian towns and villages. These men had not come on any crusade for *lebensraum* ("space for living"); they moved toward the Don because Benito Mussolini bargained for Hitler's favor with the bodies of his soldiers.

The Italians had sent their best units into the Soviet Union. Proud military names such as the Julia, Bersaglieri, Cosseria, Torino, Alpini, graced the shoulder patches of troops struggling through the enervating heat. Their fathers had fought along the

Piave and Isonzo rivers against the Austrians during World War I, and Ernest Hemingway immortalized their battles in *A Farewell to Arms.*

Some of the Italian soldiers questioned the reasons they were fighting for the Nazi cause. At a railroad siding in Warsaw, twenty-one-year-old Lt. Veniero Marsan had seen its harsh realities for the first time. From a train window, he watched a long line of civilians passing by. Apathetic, forlorn, each wore the yellow Star of David. Then Marsan saw the cruel-faced guards with guns, cocked and ready to fire. A chill rippled along his spine and, long after his train had rocked on into Russia, he brooded about what he had witnessed.

For other Italians, the expedition into the steppe had different connotations. Crack Alpini soldiers guided mules along and kept their mountain-climbing gear under canvas. The nearest mountains were in the Caucasus, far to the south, and Hitler had decided to conquer them without the Italians. Shaking their heads in amazement, the elite Alpini trudged along the flat plains wondering why they were in Russia at all.

But twenty-seven-year-old Lt. Felice Bracci was delighted with the great adventure. He had always wanted to explore the steppe country of Russia, to gaze on its timeless beauty. A recent university graduate, Bracci joined the Young Fascist League and went from there directly into Mussolini's army.

In his first battles in Albania, he was wounded and decorated for defending an outpost. When offered the choice of going to Libya or Russia, the decision was difficult to make: he wanted desperately to see the pyramids. Finally choosing the steppe, he now led a company of men eastward to the Don.

Dr. Cristoforo Capone did not share Bracci's cultural interests, but that mattered little. He, too, was pleased to be part of the Russian expedition. The seventh of nine children, he was the "rogue" in his family. Constantly good humored, he delighted everyone who met him. In his division, the Torino, the prankster, was easily the most popular man among soldiers trying to conquer homesickness.

When the news came of the birth of his first daughter, Capone got permission for a month's leave. With a last joke and a smile, the happy doctor waved goodbye to his friends and left the line of march for a reunion in Salerno. He hoped to be back in time for the finish of the "walkover" campaign.

In the meantime, his comrades plunged doggedly ahead, dragging their antiquated cannon and rifles, singing songs of Sorrento and the sunlight. On their hats they wore bright green-and-red cockades; in their hearts they longed for home.

Chapter Two

Deep in a Ukrainian pine forest, outside the town of Vinnitsa and five hundred miles west of the German troops near the Don—on the same morning that Friedrich von Paulus wrote glowingly of the future to a friend—Adolf Hitler climbed the steps of a log cabin and swept into a starkly furnished conference room. Seating himself on an iron chair at the head of a map table with his back to a window, he listened carefully to the latest intelligence reports as they were explained by his chief of staff, the bespectacled, trimly mustachioed, Gen. Franz Halder.

The meticulous Halder had no love for the man he served. He acted deferentially toward his Führer and accepted frequent tirades with the calm of one resigned to his fate. Before and during the war, Halder had schemed with other officers to overthrow Hitler and replace him with a monarchy. The dissident group was too timid and vacillating to initiate the coup, however, and watched passively as the German Army scored triumph after triumph under Hitler's almost mystical leadership. By the summer of 1942, Halder was a captive in thrall to a despot.

For weeks, though, he had reminded Hitler that the signs of

Russian disintegration were illusory, that the enemy was not "*kaputt*." Halder believed that the campaign in the previous winter had bled Germany white. The equivalent of eighty divisions, nearly eight hundred thousand men, were buried beneath the soil of Russia. Despite carefully doctored tables of strength, the majority of the German divisions were 50 percent under strength. And while more than a million besieged Russian civilians had starved to death during the nightmarish winter of 1941, Leningrad still clung to life. Moscow also remained as the nerve center of the Soviet state. Of more significance, the oil fields in the Caucasus pumped life-giving petroleum products to the Soviet war machine.

As a result, Hitler had become obsessed with the importance of petroleum products to a mechanized state, and he had devised Operation Blue expressly to strangle Russia's oil production and, thereby, her potential to wage modern war. To promote the offensive, he had flown to Poltava on June 1, and, surrounded by deputies such as Paulus, he put on a brilliant oratorical display that mesmerized everyone. Predictably, the generals failed to make any rebuttal to his proposal, which completely ignored German shortages in manpower and equipment and concentrated only on the abysmal state of the Red Army.

Thus, Operation Blue had begun when the Fourth Panzer Army struck on June 28, due east toward the rail junction of Voronezh. Two days later, Paulus's Sixth Army followed suit, covering the Fourth Army's right flank and engaging Russian forces pulling back in disorder. Almost immediately, the Fourth Army ran into difficulties. Originally, Hitler planned to bypass Voronezh in hopes of trapping the Soviet armies on the open plains. But when German armor easily penetrated the outskirts and commanders radioed for permission to seize the rest of the city, Hitler vacillated, leaving the decision to Army Group B's commander, Field Marshal Fedor von Bock. Amazed at being given a choice, Bock hesitated briefly, then sent two tank divisions into Voronezh.

The Russians had rushed in reinforcements, quickly pinning the Germans down in savage street fighting, and soldiers in the

Fourth Army soon referred to Voronezh as a "cursed town." Meanwhile, Hitler raged. The main Russian armies were slipping away, down a long corridor to the southeast between the Don and Donets rivers. Hitler demanded that Bock catch the Russians. The marshal tried, but the Russians withdrew rapidly, taking most of their trucks and tanks with them.

To General Halder, this successful withdrawal was ominous. It meant the Soviet High Command still was retreating according to plan. But once again, when he told Hitler his fears, the Führer laughed aloud. Arrogant in his belief that the Russians were reeling, confused, and ripe for slaughter, the Führer began to tinker with the delicate balance of his own forces. He separated the army groups, sending Group A off at a right angle into the Caucasus while Group B drove straight ahead across the steppe toward Stalingrad. Worse, Hitler stripped the Fourth Panzer Army from Group B and attached it to the Caucasus operation. That left Paulus's Sixth Army alone, driving on into the hostile depths of the Soviet Union.

By his action, Hitler had weakened each army group and left them vulnerable to Soviet counterstrokes. The move also caused consternation within German Army Headquarters. Halder could not believe the Führer would commit such a blunder. Stunned, he went to his quarters and poured his agonized feelings into his diary: ". . . The chronic tendency to underrate enemy capabilities is gradually assuming grotesque proportions. . . . Serious work is becoming impossible here. This so-called leadership is characterized by a pathological reacting to the impressions of the moment. . . ."

When Hitler pivoted an entire army across another's path, he had defied the military maxim that any interference with the delicate internal functions of a massed body of troops frequently leads to chaos. And on the steppe roads of Russia, the Sixth Army stopped dead while swarms of vehicles and men from the Fourth Panzer Army cut left to right across its line of advance. Enormous traffic jams developed. Tanks of one army mingled with those of the other; supply trucks got lost in a maze of contradictory signposts and directions handed out by irate military policemen. Worse, the Fourth Army took the bulk of the oil and gasoline meant to fuel both armies.

By the time the last Fourth Army tank had disappeared to the south, Paulus was commanding a stalled war machine. His supply lines were tangled, his tanks were without fuel, and he watched impotently as Russian rear guards vanished into the eastern haze. Furious at the delay, he began to wonder openly whether the enemy might now have enough time to organize a formidable defense line beyond the horizon.

Only Hitler remained unruffled. He scoffed when Halder showed him an intelligence estimate of more than a million Russian reserves still uncommitted behind the Volga. Jubilant at the easy capture of Rostov, the gateway city to the Caucasus, on July 23, he executed another series of orders which reflected his growing confidence in an early victory. He transferred Field Marshal Erich von Manstein and his five divisions from the Crimea north to Leningrad—at the very time their strength was needed to guarantee success in the oil fields. He also uprooted two elite panzer divisions, the Leibstandarte and Grossdeutschland, from southern Russia and sent them off to France, because he was suddenly fearful of an Allied invasion from across the English Channel.

Again, the bewildered Halder tried to instill a note of caution. At another briefing, he pushed a worn map across the table and drily explained that it showed where the Red Army had defeated Denikin's White Army in the Russian Civil War of 1920. Halder ran his fingers along the line of the Volga near the old city of Tsaritsyn. The architect of the victory, he added, had been Joseph Stalin and the city was now called Stalingrad.

Temporarily sobered by Halder's obvious reference to the possibility of history repeating itself, Hitler had promised to keep a close watch on the progress of the Sixth Army and to pay particular attention to its flanks. In the last days of July, he moved swiftly to strengthen Sixth Army's exposed position on the steppe. Completely reversing himself, he told the Fourth Panzer Army to turn around again and rejoin the drive to the Volga.

Rushing toward the Caucasus, the Fourth Army's panzers suddenly stopped dead and turned northeast. "So many precious days have been lost," General Halder fumed in his quarters. But at least he was happy that Paulus now had a friendly army coming up on his right flank. Perhaps, thought Halder, the delay had not given the Russians the grace period they needed.

By the evening of August 5, intelligence pouring into Vinnitsa tended to sustain that hope. Halder briefed Hitler that Sixth Army's pincers were about to close on two enemy armies. And the Fourth Panzer Army confirmed the capture of Kotelnikovo, a key rail center, just seventy-three miles southwest of Stalingrad. Barring any unforeseen obstacles, Fourth Army anticipated a quick thrust to the Volga.

At dinner that night, Adolf Hitler gloated over the situation. His strategy had been vindicated; he told everyone that the Soviet Union was about to collapse.

Chapter Three

While Hitler spoke of triumph, the streets of Moscow were totally dark. But behind drawn curtains in his Kremlin office, the premier of all the Russias, Joseph Stalin, was following his normal work schedule, which began in late afternoon and ended near dawn. The lynx-eyed Stalin had pursued this timetable for years. And from these sessions had come orders that brought terror to his people and subversion to nations around the world.

He was a tyrant who once had studied for the priesthood, a revolutionary who robbed banks to support the Bolshevist cause, a glutton, and a near drunkard. Upon the death of Lenin, he assumed total control of the Soviet Union. Those who served him endured his rages in silence; those who crossed him died violently.

Stalin never forgot or forgave. He once told a Russian writer that Ivan the Terrible had not been ruthless enough because he left too many enemies alive. Stalin did not make the same error. Nearly twenty years after he broke with Leon Trotsky, one of his agents penetrated the exiled dissenter's security screen in Mexico and drove an alpenstock through his skull. From Stalin's office, emissaries emerged to slay thousands of Red Army officers in the 1937–

1938 purges. It was on his orders that more than ten million *kulaks*, farmers and landowners who balked at turning over their properties to the new Communist state, were killed. And it was from this apartment that the directive went out to sign the Nazi-Soviet nonaggression pact in August 1939, which Stalin believed gave him time to prepare for the inevitable war with Germany.

In this decision, Stalin had trusted an equally cynical dictator, even when spies like Richard Sorge and a man called Lucy told him the exact date Germany proposed to attack the Soviet Union. Branding the information provided by these agents as part of a British plot to draw Russia into war, Stalin put his faith in Hitler's word.

It had been a colossal blunder. The Nazi invasion brought the Soviet Union to the brink of disaster and Stalin went into shock. Ten days passed before he rallied enough to resume command of his shattered armies and it was none too soon. By October 1941, Hitler had swallowed most of European Russia. In December, now only seven miles from Moscow, German scouts trained their binoculars on the turrets of the Kremlin. But the Russians held and the crisis eased.

Stalin regained his equilibrium and learned from past mistakes. When the spies who had warned him about Hitler's plans for invasion continued to send a torrent of vital information to Moscow, he paid closer attention. Operating out of Paris was Leonard Trepper, called the "Big Chief," who ran a spy network known to German secret police as the "Red Orchestra," because of its nightly radio chorus across Europe. Trepper, a Polish Jew, had been planted in France before the war. There he cultivated an influential circle of German businessmen and military leaders from whom he extracted masses of information. Hounded by German radio sleuths, who tracked his transmitters with special directional equipment, Trepper still survived. But his time was growing short.

Other spies were relatively invulnerable. In Switzerland, a Hungarian Communist named Alexander Rado ran both a publishing business and a spy ring. One of his agents, Rudolf Rossler, was probably the most valuable weapon the Soviet Union possessed. The shy, bespectacled Rossler, code-named "Lucy," had contacts inside the High Command of the German Army. His sources, never identified to this day, provided him with almost every decision made by the Führer. Rossler had passed both strategic and tactical battle plans on to Moscow, usually within twenty-four hours of their having been approved. His communiqués were worth many divisions to Stalin.

Thus, Moscow knew explicit details about Operation Blue: the names of the divisions involved in the attack, the number of tanks to be committed to battle, plus the operation's ultimate goal of severing the Volga River lifeline and capturing the oil fields of the Caucasus. As the offensive progressed, Lucy also had forwarded each major shift in tactics, from Hitler's indecision about taking Voronezh to his startling insistence on splitting his armies on the steppe.

Yet Stalin was hesitant when Lucy told of Hitler's confusion at Voronezh. The premier had always believed that the Germans intended to take Moscow from the south, and therefore might be using the drive toward the Caucasus as a feint to draw Russian reserves from the capital. But when Lucy's torrent of "inner strategy" continued to accurately forecast the German Army's course across southern Russia, Stalin began to base Russian defense plans on Lucy's confidences.

While Hitler chased two hares at the same time, Stalin, on July 13, had agreed to a plan set forth by his general staff (STAVKA) to withdraw Soviet units as far as the Volga, thereby forcing the Germans to spend the coming winter in open country. Almost a week later, when STAVKA received the astonishing news that the German Army groups had begun to split their forces on the steppe, Russian strategy changed again. Until this time, little consideration had been given to making a determined stand on the west bank of the Volga. Now Stalin made a decision of momentous significance. He sent an order to members of the City Soviet (city council) in Stalingrad to prepare for a seige. As of July 21 they were to organize the entire population in a frantic effort to build a fortified ring around the outskirts of the city while STAVKA tried to beef-up the small military garrison.

No one realized it at the time, but this decision to "stand fast" would change the course of history.

A few days later, on the night of August 1, Stalin had made another attempt to strengthen Stalingrad. Near midnight a Red Army staff car pulled up to the entrance of the Kremlin's private quarters, and a squat, gray-haired officer eased slowly out of the back seat to limp painfully into the building. At the door to the premier's office, forty-nine-year-old Gen. Andrei Ivanovich Yeremenko put down his cane, braced himself, and walked briskly into the room.

Stalin greeted him warmly. Shaking Yeremenko's hand, he asked, "Do you consider yourself recovered?"

Yeremenko said he felt fine.

Another general interrupted, "It looks like his wound is still bothering him, he's limping."

Yeremenko shrugged off the remark, so Stalin let the matter drop. "We shall consider that Comrade Yeremenko has fully recovered. We need him now very badly. Let's get down to business."

Stalin spoke to the point. "Due to the circumstances around Stalingrad, prompt action must be taken to fortify this most important sector of the front . . . and to improve control of the troops." Stalin went on to offer Yeremenko command of one of the fronts in the south. The general accepted, and Stalin sent him to STAVKA Headquarters a few blocks away to be briefed about the situation on the steppe.

Yeremenko spent the better part of August 2 studying the maps of Stalingrad and the surrounding area. As he stared at the topographical details of the forty-mile strip of land between the Don and Volga rivers, he concluded that in order to attack Stalingrad the Germans would have to concentrate most of their strength in that narrow "bridge" where the Don and Volga come closest to each other. And he wondered whether that type of deployment might offer the Russians a chance for a successful counterattack from the flanks.

After selecting the nucleus of a staff, he went back to Stalin for another conference. This time, the premier seemed more nervous and preoccupied. Puffing absently on his pipe, Stalin listened while his army chief of staff, Marshal Alexander Mikhailovich Vasilevsky, briefed him on the day's activities. When the marshal concluded, Stalin turned to Yeremenko and asked: "Is everything clear to you, comrade?"

Yeremenko spoke up against the idea of two Russian fronts in the same region, especially since their boundaries met in the exact center of Stalingrad. To him, trying to coordinate the defense of a city with another commander equal in responsibility would be "utterly confusing, if not tragically impossible."

Stalin left at that point to take some phone calls from the south. When he returned, he was subdued and obviously worried. Picking up Yeremenko's protests about dual fronts, he said firmly: "Leave everything as it was outlined. . . ." Stalin told Yeremenko to take over the Southeastern Front and hold back the German Fourth Panzer Army coming toward the Volga from Kotelnikovo. Unhappy with this assignment, the general asked if he could lead the Stalingrad Front, comprising the northern part of the city and beyond to the Don, because he wanted to attack the German flank in that region.

Stalin broke in brusquely, "Your proposition deserves attention, but in the future . . . now the German offensive must be stopped." Stalin had sounded annoyed and when he paused to fill his pipe with tobacco, Yeremenko mended his fences by agreeing with his commander in chief. As Stalin saw him to the door, he warned Yeremenko to take drastic measures to enforce discipline at the front. Now, on the night of August 5, Joseph Stalin paced his office waiting for further news from the steppe. Yeremenko had phoned from Stalingrad. He had sounded optimistic, but Stalin knew that sixty miles to the southwest, German tanks were brushing aside scattered Russian resistance and charging toward the city.

Unless Yeremenko stopped them, Stalingrad would fall in a few days.

Chapter Four

The city that Hitler had never planned to capture, and that Stalin had never intended to defend, lay sweltering under the summer sun. No rain had fallen for two months and, day after day, the temperature soared well above one hundred degrees. Worse, the humidity that typifies a river town was totally enervating. When the wind blew, it always came from the west—hot, dusty, bringing no relief. The citizens of Stalingrad were accustomed to being uncomfortable and they joked about how the heat made the concrete sidewalks bulge and buckle upward, splitting the slabs into giant fragments. As for the shiny asphalt roads, all one could do was watch the mirages rising from the wide boulevards in the center of town.

Few people in this cauldron knew their city was about to become a battlefield, but the tragedy of war had always menaced the region. In the year 1237, the Golden Horde of the Great Khan had crossed the Volga at this perfect fording point, ravaged the territory, galloped on to the Don, and then swept westward into European Russia, stopping their invasion just short of Vienna and the Polish border. During the thirteenth and fourteenth centuries,

Moscow began her own expansion into Asia; the region became a border post from which Russian soldiers sallied forth to fight the Mongols. When the czar decreed the area safe for settlement in 1589, he established a trading center called Tsaritsyn. In Tartar language the name was pronounced "sarry-soo" and meant "yellow water."

Though the location was safe enough to settle, it never knew peace. Russian brigands wreaked havoc on the citizenry as they plundered their way north and south along the length of the Volga. The geographical key to bringing the wealth of the Caucasus to Moscow and Leningrad, the heartland of Russia, as well as being the east-west gateway to Asia, Tsaritsyn was a place for which men would always do battle.

The legendary cossack leader, Stenka Razin, took the city in 1670 and held it during a bloody siege. Just over one hundred years later, another cossack named Yemelyan Pugachev, decided to challenge the power of Catherine the Great and stormed Tsaritsyn in an effort to free the serfs. The rebellion ended as could be expected. The czarina's executioner cut off Pugachev's head.

Still the city prospered, finally taking its place in the industrial revolution when, in 1875, a French company built the region's first steel mill. Within a few years, the city's population had grown to more than one hundred thousand and, during World War I, nearly one-quarter of the inhabitants were working in its factories. Despite the boom, the city reminded visitors of America's wild west. Clusters of tents and ramshackle houses sprawled aimlessly along the riverbank; more than four hundred saloons and brothels catered to a boisterous clientele. Oxen and camels shared the unpaved streets with sleek horse-drawn carriages. Cholera epidemics scourged the population regularly as the result of mountains of garbage and sewage that collected in convenient gullies.

It was almost predictable then that the Bolshevik Revolution would bring Tsaritsyn to its knees. The fighting for control of the region was unusually bitter and Joseph Stalin, leading only a tiny force, managed to hold off three generals of the White Army. Finally driven from the city, Stalin regrouped his forces in the safety of the steppe country, fell on the flanks of the White Army in 1920, and won a pivotal victory in the revolution. To honor their liberator, a jubilant citizenry renamed the city Stalingrad, but words alone could not repair the damage wrought by war. The factories had been rendered useless, famine struck down tens of thousands, and Moscow decided the only way to save the area was to return it to its industrial state. It was a wise decision. The new industrial plants soon were exporting tractors, guns, textiles, lumber, and chemicals to all parts of the Soviet Union. During the next twenty years, the city grew by leaps and bounds along the high cliffs of the western bank of the Volga. Now half a million people called it home.

When General Yeremenko first looked down on Stalingrad through the window of the plane bringing him to battle, he thrilled at the sight. Hugging the serpentine bends of the Volga, the city looked like a giant caterpillar, sixteen miles long and filled with smokestacks belching forth clouds of soot that told of its value to the Soviet war effort. White buildings sparkled in dazzling sunlight. There were orchards, broad boulevards, spacious public parks. During the drive from the airport through the city, Yeremenko felt himself overwhelmed by the power and charm of the rawboned metropolis.

The general's underground command post was located in the city's heart, only five hundred yards away from the western shore of the Volga in the north wall of a two hundred-foot deep, dried-up riverbed called Tsaritsa Gorge. A superb location for a head-quarters (some said that it had been built years before on explicit orders from Premier Stalin himself), the bunker had two entrances: one at the bottom of the gorge and the other at the very top, leading into Pushkinskaya Street. Each entrance was pro-

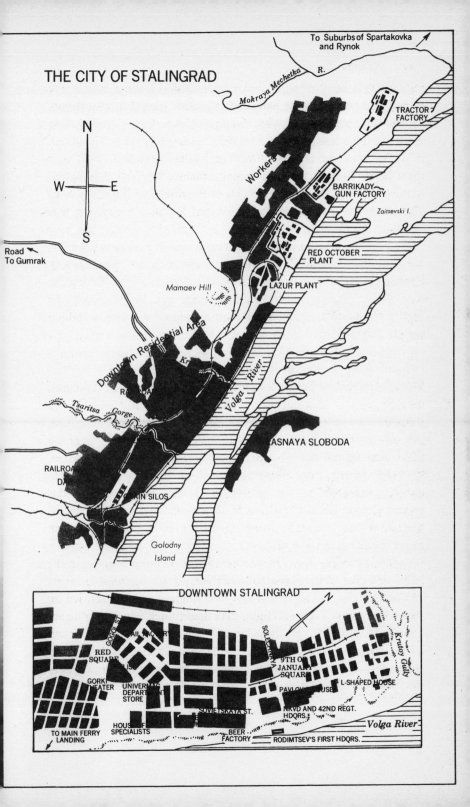

THE CITY OF STALINGRAD

To Suburbs of Spartakovka
and Rynok

Mokraya Mechetka R.

Workers

TRACTOR
FACTORY

BARRIKADY
GUN FACTORY

Zaitsevski I.

Road
To Gumrak

RED OCTOBER
PLANT

Mamaev Hill

LAZUR PLANT

Downtown Residential Area

Kr

Volga River

R

Tsaritsa Gorge

ASNAYA SLOBODA

RAILROA
D

RAILROA
D

AIN SILOS

Golodny
Island

DOWNTOWN STALINGRAD

GOGOL ST.

RAIL FACT

RED
SQUARE

GORKI
THEATER

UNIVERSI
DEPARTMENT
STORE

SOLECHNAYA

9TH OF
JANUARY
SQUARE

Krutoy Gully

PAVLOV HOUSE

L-SHAPED HOUSE

SOVIETSKAYA ST.

NKVD AND 42ND REGT.
HDQRS.

Volga River

TO MAIN FERRY
LANDING

HOUSE OF
SPECIALISTS

BEER
FACTORY

RODIMTSEV'S FIRST HDQRS.

tected from bomb blasts by heavy doors, plus a series of staggered reinforced partitions, or baffles. The interior was lavish by Russian military standards. The walls were paneled with an oaken-plywood surface; there was even a flush toilet.

In his comfortable office, Yeremenko immediately began to familiarize himself with his domain. On the desk lay a huge contour map, marked in pencil to show the demarcation line between his Southeast Front and the Stalingrad Front to the north, commanded by Gen. A. V. Gordov. The boundary ran straight as an arrow from the town of Kalach, forty miles west at the Don River, to the same Tsaritsa Gorge where Yeremenko sat. The longer he examined the artificial border, the more he fumed at STAVKA's inability to realize that the dual-front concept was absurd. Worse, he had already spoken with General Gordov and discovered him to be as insufferable as he was reported to be. In the best of times a difficult man, under pressure Gordov became a tyrant, humiliating his staff, inciting open revolt among subordinates. Now faced with Yeremenko, a rival for power, he was evasive, uncooperative, and unpleasant. But since there was no point waiting for STAVKA to admit its mistake and reassign command responsibilities, Yeremenko tried to come to grips with his own immediate assignment.

He lingered over the map, searching its symbols for clues to a defensive strategy. Between Kalach and Stalingrad there was only steppe country—flat, grassy terrain that was perfect for German panzers. He next eliminated the assorted farms in the region, the *kholkozi*, where he knew thousands of Stalingrad's citizens were finishing the job of snatching a bumper wheat harvest from the invaders. The farm crews out there had been straining under the brutal sun while Stuka dive-bombers machine-gunned them and set fire to trains filled with grain. Nevertheless, nearly twenty-seven thousand fully loaded freight cars had already rolled away to safety in the east. Behind them came nine thousand tractors, threshers, and combines along with two million head of cattle, bawling plaintively as they pounded toward the Volga and a swim to the safety of the far shore.

The "harvest victory" was the only one that Yeremenko could savor. Four rings of antitank ditches being dug twenty to thirty miles west of Stalingrad offered little hope. Neither did the "green belt," a twenty-nine-mile arc of trees planted years before to ward off the effects of dust clouds and snowstorms. Only a mile wide at its thickest point, it could not withstand the concentrated fire of heavy artillery.

Yeremenko's attention wandered southward, down the map to the rail center of Kotelnikovo, seventy-three miles away. Captured by the Germans on August 2, the city controlled the main road to Stalingrad. The German line of march was obvious: through Chileko, where the Siberian 208th Division had just been decimated by the Luftwaffe, and on to the towns of Krugliakov and Abganerovo. At the latter location, Yeremenko paid closer attention to swirling lines on the contour map indicating hills rising to elevations of from two to three hundred feet. The hills followed the main road the rest of the way to the congested suburbs of Stalingrad. With mounting excitement, he noted deep ravines cutting across the region from east to west and concluded that it would have to be in this twenty-mile strip of hill country that he would try to halt the German advance.

Deep in his heart, however, Yeremenko knew that eventually he would have to fight for Stalingrad block by block and street by street. So, as he pored over the map, he embarked on a peculiar mental exercise: replacing the map's impersonal symbols with his own images of rock formations, houses, and streets, he strove to understand the battleground he had inherited. The southern part of Stalingrad became a jumble of white wooden homes, surrounded by picket fences and flower gardens. This was Dar Gova, a residential zone just below some light industrial development that crowded close to the Volga—a sugar plant and a massive concrete grain elevator that looked like a gray dreadnought on a prairie sea.

A short distance north of the elevator, the Tsaritsa Gorge cut its two hundred-foot deep scar in the earth before it ran due west for several miles into the steppe. Just above this dividing line was

Gordov's territory, over which Yeremenko had no jurisdiction. But he kept on with his studies, because he intended to be ready when STAVKA came to its senses.

Here was the heart of the city. It encompassed more than one hundred blocks of offices, stores, apartment buildings, and was bounded on the east by the central ferry landing—the only major crossing point on the Volga—plus a promenade along the Volga shore. To the north, it was cut off from the next section of the city by another deep ravine, the Krutoy Gully, and on its western flank was another drab community of single-storey frame houses. Yeremenko sensed immediately that this whole central section of the city could become a fearsome line of defense. Reduced to rubble by gunfire, the fallen bricks and mortar would provide perfect cover for Russian infantry.

The center of town also contained Railroad Station Number One. For months trains had passed through it carrying refugees from other battlegrounds: Leningrad, Odessa, Kharkov. Crammed into cattle cars, when the trains stopped in Stalingrad they jumped off to find water and barter for food with merchants lining the platforms. While they haggled for fruit and bread, the penniless among them stole whatever they could behind the vendors' backs. But in early August, the motley traffic from other fronts had to share train space with thousands of Stalingrad natives who suddenly had been ordered eastward into Asia by official decree. Now the terminal was swollen to the bursting point with tearful relatives embracing children, old men, and women, amid choked promises to write and keep well. The shrill whistles of the locomotives finally separated the groups. With a last wave and forced smile, a new flood of refugees joined the trek into the vast interior of Russia.

A half block east of the station, the men responsible for the city's evacuation occupied a five-storey office building on the west side of the shrub-lined Red Square. Across the square, beside the cavernous post office, the newspaper Stalingrad *Pravda* ("*Truth*") still printed a daily edition and distributed it to an anxious readership. Under the guidance of the chairman of the City Soviet, Dmitri M. Pigalev, and other members of the council, it published information about air raid drills, rationing, as well as battle reports from the front. To ward off panic, it reported only that the Red Army was scoring impressive victories west of the Don.

Close by, the squat, ugly bulk of the Univermag department store guarded the northeast corner of the square. Once a showroom for fashions from sophisticated Moscow, its counters now held only essential items: underwear, socks, trousers, shirts, coats, and boots. In the Univermag's gloomy basement warehouse, reserve stocks had sunk to an alarmingly low level.

At the south side of the square, the Corinthian-columned Gorki Theater still hosted a philharmonic orchestra that played regularly in an ornate auditorium festooned with graceful crystal chandeliers hovering over a thousand velvet-backed seats. The theater represented the pinnacle of perfection for Stalingrad's citizens who resented the city's reputation as a provincial pretender to culture.

North of Red Square, soldiers clucked horse carts along wide boulevards, past row after row of sterile, white brick apartment houses that looked like barracks. Automobile traffic was minimal and exclusively military in nature. In the evenings, the streets would be filled with pedestrians strolling beneath maple and chestnut trees lining the sidewalks. Many strollers whistled tunes from *Rose Marie,* which had played for weeks at a downtown theater.

Occasionally, a public garden separated the housing complexes. On Sovietskaya Street, a bank interrupted the residential pattern. A flour mill intruded along Pensenskaya Street. Closer to the Volga, in a library facing the river, a prim matron handed out copies of books by Jack London, a favorite author of the young people.

Neighborhood stores tucked into corner lots competed for business. "Auerbach the Tailor" offered soldiers in ragged uniforms a dingy shop in which quick repairs could be made. Swarms of flies pestered women as they picked over watermelon and tomatoes at open-air markets. Beauty parlors were crowded with girls on off-duty time from war work at the factories.

In the Tsaritsa Gorge, Andrei Yeremenko had already scanned the intersection at Solechnaya Street to assess its military significance. He also examined labyrinthine side roads, off the Ninth of January Square. What really fascinated him was that immediately to the north of Krutoy Gully, the buildings abruptly gave way to a grassy, rock-studded slope rising to a height of 336 feet. This was Mamaev Hill, once a Tartar burying ground and now a picnic area. From there, a casual observer could see most of the city. The view was breathtaking. To the west, there was an uninhabited stretch of steppe country, badly broken by *balkas* (deep, dried-up riverbeds) and, on the distant horizon, a line of homes and a few church steeples.To the north was the awesome network of industrial plants that had made Stalingrad a symbol of progress within the Communist system. Almost at the base of Mamaev were the yellow brick walls of the Lazur Chemical Plant. They covered most of a city block and were girdled by a rail loop resembling a tennis racquet. From the Lazur, trains puffed north past an oil-tank farm on the bluff beside the river, then on to the Red October Plant with its maze of foundries and calibration shops, from which poured small arms and metal parts. Further north, the trains passed the chimneys and towering concrete ramparts of the Barrikady Gun Factory, whose outbuildings ran back almost a quarter mile to the Volga bank. There a row of workers' homes languished in an unfinished state. Around the yards of the Barrikady, hundreds of heavy-caliber gun barrels lay stacked, awaiting shipment to artillery units at the front. Beyond the Barrikady loomed the pride of Russian industry, the Dzerhezinsky Tractor Works. Once the assembly point for thousands of farm machines, since the war it was one of the principal producers of T-34 tanks for the Red Army.

Built in eleven months, the tractor factory had opened officially on May 1, 1931, and, when it was completed, it ran for more than a mile along the main north-south road. Its internal network of railroad tracks measured almost ten miles; many work-shops had glass roofs to permit a maximum use of sunlight. Ventilation ducts, cafeterias, and showers had been added to the plant to make the workers' lives more pleasant and productive.

On the other side of the main road, paralleling the eleven miles of industrial park, a special, self-contained innercity had sprung up to accommodate families of factory employees. More than three hundred dwellings, some six-stories high, housed thousands of workers. Clustered around carefully manicured communal parks, they were only a few minutes' walk from summer theaters, the cinema, a circus, soccer fields, their own stores and schools. Few factory personnel living in this compound ever wanted to leave it. The state had provided almost every basic necessity and the model community that Stalin had fostered was a showpiece of the Soviet system.

From his mental perch on Mamaev, Andrei Yeremenko was not unduly concerned about the view north into the "economic heart" of Stalingrad. Even the most powerful field glasses of an artillery observer, should he chance to be a German, would not be able to penetrate as far as the tractor works, or past it to the uppermost boundary of Stalingrad, the Mokraya Mechetka River.

What alarmed Yeremenko about Mamaev was its staggering vista to the east—down the shimmering Volga, which was jammed daily with hundreds of tugs, barges, and steamers, whistling at each other in riverboat language and trailing wreaths of smoke as they navigated the channels between barren Golodny and Sarpinsky islands. The route they traveled, a vital artery of the Soviet war machine and necessary to any intended defense of Stalingrad, was completely exposed to the whims of the army that possessed the hill. Furthermore, the far shore, which was as flat as a billiard table and stretched into infinity, lay open to observation; so was its lush meadowland, once an amusement park for vacationers who went there to dance or to swim at the pearl-white beaches and to spend weekends at the cottage village near the shore. Now the meadowland was deserted. But through it, in time of need, must come the soldiers, ammunition and food for the relief of Stalin- grad. And from Mamaev, an enemy could easily track every boat that left it.

Finished with his exercise, Yeremenko wearily pushed his map away and began issuing orders. Now, more than before, he was determined to dig in firmly along the line of hills that began near Abganerovo. Proper antitank defenses there should delay the German advance. But first he had to scrape up enough manpower for the job.

Above his bunker, a flaming red sun had set; the night air was uncomfortable and muggy. Civilians walked down to the relative cool of the river embankment, where a crowd of evacuees waited for a ferry to arrive from the opposite bank. In a waiting room beside the ferry pier, men and women filled pots of boiling water from giant copper kettles. Some used the water to wash clothing, others to make "tea" from dried apricots or raspberries. It was all they had left.

Chapter Five

The dawn of August 7 engulfed the steppe country with a rush of blazing color and burning heat. In the gullies and hollows just outside the thatched huts of the village of Ostrov, twenty miles west of the Don River, Russian soldiers stretched and rubbed their eyes.

Tall, broad-shouldered Maj. Nikolai Tomskuschin faced a special personal dilemma. When, on July 15, he was ordered to take his artillery regiment onto the steppe to protect Sixty-second Army Headquarters, his superior had told him, "In the event of encirclement, save your men before your equipment." But on July 28, Tomskuschin heard another command, this time from Radio Moscow and Premier Stalin, who told the Red Army to hold at all costs. "Not one step back" was the ultimatum Stalin issued.

As his men ate breakfast, German planes appeared overhead and Tomskuschin called Sixty-second Army Headquarters for further guidance. The line was dead. "Hello! Hello!," he shouted. No one answered. The major dropped the phone and ran to find someone on the staff who could give him new orders. But he was stunned to find that Sixty-second Army Headquarters had disappeared. His commanders had fled to Stalingrad.

Trained for years to obey and serve, he hurried back to his regiment. In the next hours, German tanks blew up most of his .76-millimeter guns; Stuka dive-bombers burned the steppe grass around him with incendiary bombs. In desperation, Tomskuschin dispatched a messenger to the rear, to the bridge crossing the Don at Kalach, where he hoped there was some sort of headquarters. While he waited for orders, the blinding disk of the sun beat down, the Stukas hovered and dove. Casualties soared; by late afternoon more than four hundred men lay dead or wounded in the grass. The messenger never returned.

At twilight, Tomskuschin gathered his aides. "Assemble the men after dark," he told them. "Head for the Don. Take everyone and everything that can move."

He had made his compromise between conflicting orders.

In the sudden cool of nightfall, the men formed up and shuffled off to the east. Conversation was forbidden. Even so, weapons clanked against mess tins, and the troops cursed loudly when they stumbled. As the moon peeped fitfully through the clouds, Tomskuschin listened for suspicious sounds. Occasionally a rifle popped, but it was always far away, and the major whispered his troops on. Suddenly the darkness burst into a thousand lights, and tracer bullets ripped into the column from both sides of the road.

"Ambush!" Tomskuschin screamed. "Run, run to the river!"

The regiment stampeded into the darkness, but Tomskuschin stayed behind. It was quiet now, except for moans from the road, and he crawled into the high grass to await the dawn.

Lying under a brilliant canopy of stars, he thought of his family, safe in Sverdlovsk behind the Ural Mountains. He had not seen them for more than a year, since the war began and swept him to this wretched field. He thought, too, about his military career, irrevocably ruined since he had chosen to move back against Stalin's orders. While he had no regrets about disobeying a senseless order that conflicted with his duty to his men, he had no illusions about the fate awaiting him back at headquarters. His offense was punishable by death.

As dawn streaked the sky, the major rummaged in a pocket for his wallet and took out wrinkled pictures of his wife and son, six-year-old Vladimir. He held the photos a long time before he put them down and reached for his pistol. As he raised the gun and fingered the trigger, the image of Vladimir seemed to rise up before him. He hesitated, wanting desperately to hold the boy in his arms. Even imprisonment in Germany might be better than destroying his last chance to see the child. He eased the pistol back in the holster.

The Germans found him in the high grass. *"Ruki verkh!"* they shouted; he raised his hands meekly in surrender. They took his wallet and ring, but they did not abuse him and he rode away from the battlefield on top of a German tank. Tomskuschin was not afraid. In fact, he felt invigorated. He had a dream to realize someday, back behind the Urals where little Vladimir watched for his return.

In the aftermath of the battle around Ostrov, the German Sixth Army counted its booty: "more than fifty-seven thousand prisoners, more than one thousand tanks destroyed."

As a result, General Paulus saluted his men with a special message: "The Russian Sixty-second Army and great parts of the First Tank Army are destroyed. . . . Thanks to a brave advance . . . the possibility of this victory was set. . . We proudly think of the fallen . . . on to the next task set by the Führer. . . ."

Despite the fantastic success of Paulus's forces in crushing the last Russian resistance west of the Don, the most immediate danger to Stalingrad was the Fourth Panzer Army, which was swinging northeast to join the assault on the city. Any advance they made would be along a major highway and rail line, and they had no rivers to cross.

It was logical then, that the commander of the Fourth Panzer Army, horse-faced "Papa" Hoth, should relish his new assignment. His scouts had already worked their way to within twenty miles of Stalingrad's outskirts and with luck, Hoth hoped to beat Paulus into the city. Even the latest intelligence reports of stiffening Soviet resistance at the low range of hills crossing the railroad and highway near Abganerovo just south of the city did not worry him. He was confident he could not be stopped.

Most of the Russian stragglers retreating toward Stalingrad would have agreed with this estimate of the situation. Disillusioned, desperate, they had been reduced to fighting each other for scraps of food and water—especially water, which was scarce on the barren steppe. At precious watering holes they found another enemy had been there before them: the Kalmucks, natives to the region and intensely anti-Communist, had thrown dead animals into the wells. The poisoned water quickly killed unwary drinkers.

One retreating Russian soldier, curly-haired Lt. Hersch Gurewicz, forgot his thirst as he dove into a ditch for the third time that day. The Stukas were back, like prehistoric birds, circling impudently, searching for carrion below. Gurewicz was exhausted. Chased by the Germans for more than a year, he had begun to wonder where it would all end. Just twenty-one years old, a native of Mogilev near the Polish border, he had first joined the Red Army in 1940 during the war with the Finns. Then, his mother had been a Communist party member, working for the military. His father taught violin at the Rimsky-Korsakov School of Music in Mogilev. The German invasion had brought death to both his mother and sister, who were tracked down and slain as partisans; his father and brother disappeared into the army and Hersch had been unable to locate them since.

Now in the ditch fifty miles southwest of Stalingrad, Gurewicz was a hardened veteran. He could tell by the sound of a shell whether it was close or meant for someone behind him; he knew the exact moment to run for cover when bombers began to hurtle down out of the sun. He knew other things, too, like the price of desertion. He had seen the "Green Hats" of the NKVD instilling their special brand of discipline. The NKVD first appeared on the battlefield in July when Joseph Stalin made the Red Army a scapegoat to appease public indignation and fear about the German advance across the steppe. Stalin's Order Number 227 had unleashed a reign of terror. At countless roadblocks, the Green Hats inspected papers, asked curt questions, and shot anyone suspected of running from the front. Thousands of corpses lined the roads as a warning to those contemplating such desertion.

Gurewicz had seen mounds of bodies at the checkpoints, but they did not shock him for he had seen worse. The previous winter, fighting as a partisan, he had entered the town of Rudnia just after the Germans left. The body of a woman lay in the street. She was blonde, young, and must have been pretty, but her arms, extended upward, had no hands, and her legs had been cut off above the knees. Someone had slit her torso from navel to crotch with a knife or bayonet. Around the corpse stood a crowd of people crying loudly. One man spoke up in trembling indignation.

"This was our schoolteacher," he said, weeping. "She taught our children."

His stomach churning, Gurewicz had turned away.

Once when the Germans caught him, he had learned of their savagery firsthand. Trapped in an ambush, he was marched for miles with a rope around his neck as an object lesson to villagers. A sign pinned to his chest read: "I am a Russian Partisan." Later, at Gestapo headquarters, he passed into the hands of specialists, two blond officers in black uniforms, who pulled him into a room where another partisan had been strapped onto a table. While Gurewicz watched, a German turned a lever and the table moved apart in sections like a rack. A terrible scream burst from the man's throat and his leg bones snapped through his skin. The lever turned again and his arms ripped apart in jagged tears. When the man fainted, his torturers shot him dead.

Gurewicz then went to his own chamber of horrors, where he was pushed into a chair and his head was forced back. An interrogator hovered over his face and slowly threaded a thin wire up his nose. While Gurewicz tried to retch, the wire entered his lung, jerked horribly and he fell unconscious.

He awoke lying in the snow, his hands tied to a horse's tail. He dimly heard someone shouting, then a slap and the horse reared and galloped off at full speed. Snow flew in his face. He gasped for breath. The horse bucked through drifts and smashed Gurewicz into the ground again and again. His head cracked against something solid, he felt a searing pain, then nothing.

Incredibly, he regained consciousness between the crisp sheets of a hospital bed in Moscow. He was alive only because his partisan comrades had followed him to Gestapo headquarters and ambushed his tormentors. Yet every night in the weeks that followed, Gurewicz dreamed of wires and broken bones and a schoolteacher with severed limbs. The nightmares always left him spent and fearful. But through it all, he never broke and cried.

Returning to duty he became an officer in the Red Army, and went to an advanced infantry training school at Krasnodar in the Caucasus, at that time far behind the front lines. But the summer of 1942 quickly brought German tanks to the edge of the city and forced Gurewicz and his fellow students into an authorized retreat to the Volga. Now on the dusty road to Sety, he cringed as the Stukas nosed over into their dives. The concussions from explosions swept over him and pounded the breath from his body. One blast caught a cadet out in the open and ignited Molotov cocktails that were strapped to his back. A human torch, the soldier danced convulsively, his back exploding in brief orange puffs as the gasoline fed on his body.

Ignoring the planes, Gurewicz ran from the ditch to help. Kneeling over the charred, sizzling body, he saw a monstrous sight: the man's chest had burned away, exposing the entire rib cage and his furiously pumping heart. The man he once had known was no longer recognizable. His face had melted. Gurewicz stared in horror. Another bomb exploded nearby and there was a sharp pain in his back. But he remained kneeling beside the blackened lump in the road until the heart contracted one last time, and stopped.

Only then did he leave what remained of his friend. Bleeding heavily from his own shrapnel wounds, he went on to Sety for first aid and then rode an ambulance through Stalingrad to a recuperation center across the Volga. As his back healed slowly, he began to badger doctors about releasing him to active duty. They told him to be patient. The summons would some soon enough.

To save his southern flank, Yeremenko ordered his retreating soldiers to hold at Abganerovo, while he reinforced them with whatever fresh troops he could find. The last antitank guns that he could locate on August 9 were ordered to dig into the hills overlooking the highway and the railroad; fifty-nine tanks were sent on a suicidal attack. It was not much of a holding action, Yeremenko knew, but it might at least buy a day's time.

Meanwhile, along his Don River flank to the west of Stalingrad, the bridge at Kalach was the key to the situation. Thus, Col. Pyotr Ilyin received orders directly from Yeremenko to hold or destroy the bridge. The men of Ilyin's 20th Motorized Brigade were hollow-eyed with fatigue. Running low on both guns and ammunition, they dug in at an orchard on the outskirts of Kalach and listened quietly as Ilyin explained that they were to be a rear guard. Ilyin tried to assure them that other Russian divisions would protect their flanks, that with this added support they could hold their position on the river. Few men in the brigade believed him, and he was thankful that none of them deserted that first night.

Across the Don all was silent. From their positions on the low, flat east bank, Russian soldiers could not see past the lip of the three-hundred-foot bluff across the river that was controlled by the Germans. Ilyin sent scouts across the river where they trained binoculars on enemy troop concentrations, and for several days an uneasy quiet descended on that part of the steppe. Ilyin took advantage of the situation to carefully dig in his few artillery pieces and the last of his machine guns at strategic points. Then he waited.

On the morning of August 15, the scouts tumbled back down the palisades on the far shore and screamed: "They're coming!" Behind them, German soldiers suddenly lined the cliff. On Ilyin's orders, sappers blew the explosive charges they had placed under the bridge. It heaved into the air with a shattering roar. When the smoke cleared, the western section had fallen into the river and the eastern part was on fire. Ilyin had gained some time.

Behind the protection of the high bluffs on the opposite shore, the Germans plotted new tactics and twenty-eight-year-old Capt. Gerhard Meunch made the rounds among his men. Recently made a battalion commander in the 71st Division, an extraordinary promotion for one so young, Meunch wanted to make sure his troops understood that he cared about them. He listened patiently as they griped about the heat, the food, and the lack of mail. Finally satisfied that they appreciated his interest, he went to an observation post at the edge of the Don cliff. Below lay Kalach, a cluster of old houses with an apple orchard on the outskirts. Beyond it, in the hazy distance, Meunch could see almost to Stalingrad.

In the apple orchard across the river, Colonel Ilyin had just learned that the other Russian divisions protecting his flanks had melted away, and he was left alone to hold the German Sixth Army at bay. To complicate matters, Ilyin was unable to raise anyone in Stalingrad headquarters by radio for instructions.

As if sensing his dilemma, the Germans came for him right away. At point-blank range, Ilyin's gunners blew apart their fleet of rubber boats. But more than twenty-five miles upstream, Sixth Army engineers under Maj. Joseph Linden, a bookish-looking technician from Wiesbaden, had thrown two pontoon bridges across the Don. Faced only by scattered resistance, the engineers quickly secured a bridgehead on the eastern shore, and Paulus ordered three divisions toward the three-hundred-foot spans. Hundreds of tanks plowed up the roads and fields on their way to the river. They stopped on the western side of the Don while the cautious Paulus tidied up his lines, refitted his armor, demanded more quartermaster supplies, and coordinated more Luftwaffe bomber support from improvised steppe airfields.

Filling their mess tins at field kitchens, German troops now spoke openly about furloughs back in Germany and civilian jobs awaiting them after a final thrust to the Volga. Their mood was jubilant, their expectations heady.

On the evening of August 22, two men stood in a garden near the German bridgehead and talked urgently of the next day's work. One of them was Gen. Hans Hube, of the 16th Panzer Division. A courier handed him a dispatch. Hube read it quickly and said, "The balloon goes up at 0430 hours tomorrow, Sickenius."

Colonel Sickenius acknowledged the news and Hube dismissed him.

"Till tomorrow, Sickenius."

"Till tomorrow, Herr General."

Hube paused, touched his only hand to his cap, and remarked, "Tomorrow night in Stalingrad!"

Forty miles to the east, signs had been posted on trees throughout Stalingrad exhorting the citizens. "Death to the Invader!", they read. But few civilians knew exactly where the enemy was.

In the Tsaritsa Gorge, Andrei Yeremenko agonized over the obvious buildup going on in Paulus's sector. Intelligence showed that the Germans were planning another classic pincer movement with Sixth Army acting as the left arm and Hoth's Fourth Panzers as the right. And though he had been able to stall Hoth temporarily in the hills around Abganerovo, Yeremenko knew he had too few reserves available to cope with such a combined attack.

On the political front, at least, he had scored an impressive victory. A new-found friend, Commissar Nikita Sergeyevich Khrushchev, had proven a reliable ally in recent days as Yeremenko argued about the dual command problem with STAVKA on the BODO line, the direct telephone link to the Kremlin. Khrushchev was Stalin's political emissary to the military council in the Tsaritsa command post, and he had backed Yeremenko fully in his campaign to realign divisions of authority. Finally, on August 13, Stalin had given Yeremenko supreme responsibility for both fronts and demoted the irascible General Gordov.*

Now in complete charge of Stalingrad's defense, Yeremenko had to cope immediately with another unexpected problem; the city's garrison commander had disappeared, leaving chaos behind. Without a local leader, the city's forces floundered. Their confused state was most noticeable in the streets. Military vehicles were getting lost and accidents proliferated at intersections as drivers jockeyed for the right of way and drove far faster than regulations allowed. Since discipline was broken, hundreds of Russian garrison troops were beginning to desert to the far side of the Volga.

With all his problems out on the steppe, General Yeremenko struggled to restore order within his own house.

The thunder of tank motors shattered the early morning darkness of August 23, and from the steppe, lines of German panzers moved awkwardly to the bridges that crossed the Don. They maneuvered carefully onto the pontoon tracks and gingerly picked their way to the far side. Trucks followed, carrying infantry, am-

---

* During this period, Stalin was entertaining British Prime Minister Winston Churchill, who had flown to Moscow with depressing news: the Allies would not be able to launch a cross-channel invasion in 1942. On hearing this, Stalin was furious, but he was mollified somewhat when Churchill, accompanied by Averell Harriman, disclosed plans for the invasion of North Africa (Operation Torch), which was scheduled for that coming November.

munition, food, medicine, and fuel. The movement attracted the attention of the Russians, who fired artillery in the general direction of the noise. But their aim was erratic, and the panzers and support troops quickly assembled into three fan-shaped combat groups on the eastern side of the river. At a signal, they roared across the steppe, beneath a stunning, sudden dawn. The sky was gray, then brilliantly orange and red and violet, and finally a yellow gleam that seared the tankers' eyes, and made them marvel at the beauty of the Russian prairie.

Lt. Hans Oettl was ecstatic as he saw the sky turn into an azure blue, untrammeled by clouds. For Oettl, a twenty-two-year-old former city employee in Munich, the Sunday morning was absolutely perfect. Even the enemy was cooperating. Only sporadic gunfire intruded from the flanks as the tank column headed toward the Volga. He watched in fascination as Stukas dove on unseen positions to silence the opposition. When the planes returned, the lieutenant waved gaily at them, and they responded by sounding their sirens in acknowledgment. Marveling at the technical cooperation within his army, Oettl patted his pet goat in satisfaction. He had found Maedi wandering alone on the steppe, put a red ribbon around her neck, and kept her ever since as an affectionate friend. Now Maedi stood beside her master while his tank column whirled by through dense clouds of dust.

Wheels and treads loosed billowing clouds of grime. Most men tied handkerchiefs over their mouths and wore goggles. At the tip of the spearhead, radio operators of the 16th Panzer Division kept Sixth Army Headquarters informed of each kilometer they clicked off.

At Golubinka, Sixth Army's new command center on the west bank of the Don, General Paulus read a dispatch: "9:45 A.M. Russians seem surprised about attack and not too strong between Rossoshka and Don. . . . In north we count on heavy resistance. . . ."

But resistance in the north, on the tank group's left flank, was almost nonexistent. The panzers pushed ahead easily and Hans

Oettl continued to relish the beauty around him. It was the most beautiful day he had seen during the war.

Noon passed and the panzers kept driving eastward into the haze. The sun turned from its zenith and dropped behind tank commanders standing in their turrets. Their faces were caked with dirt but they were happy; within a short time they expected to see the Volga. Some officers reminded themselves that the river was more than one thousand miles from Germany.

Behind the 16th Panzers, the 3rd Motorized Division tried desperately to keep pace, but slowly fell behind as the dust clouds blinded the drivers. Further to the rear, the 60th Motorized Division was in a hopeless snarl, with horns honking and tempers flaring. A man stepped from the side of the road and faced a column of trucks. Pointing a pistol directly at the first vehicle, he yelled, "If you don't let us through, you'll get it right in the tires!"

The astonished soldier pulled over to give Dr. Ottmar Kohler the right-of-way. Kohler, a brilliant, acerbic surgeon, had served with the division since its formation in Danzig in 1939. He was fed up with delays. He believed his place was up front with the wounded. For months he had been promoting a plan whereby doctors could treat seriously wounded men within minutes of their being hit instead of sending them far to the rear for aid. In so doing, Kohler had gone against Wehrmacht traditions, but he was convinced he was right. That attitude was indicative of his personality, which now brought him to the middle of the road with a drawn gun. Impatient with incompetence, he acted without hesitation to correct the situation.

Kohler waited until his unit reentered the line, then jumped into a motorcycle sidecar and waved his driver on. Blinded by the sun, the man drove straight into a hole. Kohler smashed his head against the driver's helmet, felt something in his face pop and cringed in agony. Feeling his mouth, he diagnosed the ailment immediately: a broken upper jaw. Nauseated from the pain, he swigged down some cognac and ordered the driver to catch up with the rest of the medical detachment.

At Golubinka, a clerk made a notation in the war diary of the Sixth Army: "1:00 P.M. Still further confirmed the enemy was surprised. . . ."

The advance continued into the afternoon. Tank commanders tensed when they saw church steeples and white houses on the horizon. Clutching their throat microphones, they told their crews: "On the right is Stalingrad." The men clambered up for a look at a montage of homes, *balkas,* and smokestacks that passed beside them, and cheers echoed along the column. Then shells erupted around the lead tanks and they buttoned up for a fight.

The Stukas came back and tanks fired point-blank into gun emplacements. Tankers who dismounted and stood over the blasted holes saw bits of calico and cotton dresses, arms and legs, and female torsos tossed carelessly about. They went back to their vehicles and told everyone that the Russians had sent women to fight them. The march to the Volga continued. Some of the tankers were sick to their stomachs.

The sun was low in the west when the first German tank came to a halt at the edge of a sheer cliff overlooking the Volga. Lt. Gottfried Ademeit, the son of a minister, stared in awe across the river. He could see almost a hundred miles into the mysterious flat land on the other side. As he put it, he "was looking into the heartland of Asia."

When Hans Oettl arrived, he hopped down from his vehicle and joined the rush to bathe in the river while his goat, Maedi, feasted on the lush vegetables in the fields. German soldiers, officers and men, stripped and plunged into the cold water. Afterwards, recalling the scene, Oettl wondered openly why it had to be that war was the only way he could see such a magnificent natural wonder.

Behind the main column, late-arriving soldiers entered the

suburbs of Rynok, just north of Stalingrad, and followed tramcars down the trolley tracks. When passengers looked back and saw troops dressed in strange uniforms, they panicked and jumped off the trains. The Germans laughed and left the Russians alone for the time being.

By 6:00 P.M., the German Sixth Army held a small stretch of the Volga north of Stalingrad. Hundreds of trucks and tanks moved up in support while radio operators of the 16th Panzer Division transmitted the news back to headquarters. It had been another fantastic day for General Paulus.

Chapter Six

Most of Stalingrad had been asleep when the Germans crossed the Don. In the tractor works, men and women from the night crew were preparing sixty tanks for final assembly when, at 5:00 A.M., someone rushed in with news of the enemy breakthrough. Amid a babble of noise, supervisors called a meeting to organize defense lines around the factory.

To the south, deep inside the Tsaritsa Gorge, Andrei Yeremenko woke up to a barrage of frantic telephone calls from threatened outposts along the German line of march. Surprised at the audacity of the narrow thrust toward the Volga, the general quickly routed sleepy staff officers from beds all over town and ordered breakfast for himself from the bunker's kitchen.

Only five hundred yards away, at Red Square, black loudspeaker boxes crackled to life and advised citizens of the possibility of air raids. Few people paid any attention to the message since the only German air activity in recent days had been made by reconnaissance planes. The City Soviet chairman, Pigalev, broadcast the warning, but did not mention the German tanks now heading for the northern part of the city. He feared the news would sow panic among the population.

Mrs. Vlasa Kliagina did not hear the loudspeakers because she had left home early to drop her infant son, Vovo, at a communal nursery. Then she and her daughter, Nadia, joined a neighborhood volunteer group at the southern suburb of Yelshanka where, at 7:30 A.M., with the temperature climbing into the high nineties, she continued to work on a primitive line of antitank trenches. Mrs. Kliagina had no idea that General Paulus was about to burst into the city from a completely different direction.

Less than two miles from Yelshanka, in the suburb of Dar Gova, an assistant station master, Constantin Viskov, collapsed into bed. He had just finished a grueling twelve-hour tour of duty, shuttling troops, refugees, and supplies through Railroad Station Number One. As Viskov fell into a deep sleep, his wife tiptoed about doing housework.

By 9:30 A.M., activity in the Tsaritsa Gorge accelerated as hundreds of soldiers passed in and out of the underground bunker's two entrances. Plagued by phone calls, Yeremenko had not yet touched the breakfast on his desk. He was speaking now to the deputy comander of the Eighth Air Force, who relayed shocking news, "The fighter pilots flying reconnaissance have just returned. They said that a heavy battle is going on in the region of Malaya Rossoshka [twenty-five miles northwest of Stalingrad]. Everything is burning on the ground. They saw two columns of approximately one hundred tanks each and, after them, compact columns of trucks and infantry. They're all moving into Stalingrad."

Yeremenko told him to get as many planes as possible into the air.

The phone rang again: this time it was Nikita Khrushchev calling from his downtown apartment. When Yeremenko told him the news the commissar said he would come over as soon as he could. At 11:00 A.M., he was in the bunker, listening intently to Yeremenko's briefing. Shocked at the extent of the German drive, Khrushchev shook his head. "Very unpleasant facts," he said. "What can we do to keep them from Stalingrad?"

Yeremenko told him how he was trying to juggle forces to

the northern part of the city and they discussed the problem of finding more reinforcements for the threatened suburbs. Everyone in the room was subdued, fully conscious that this might mean the fall of Stalingrad. They talked in low tones about the impact of such a calamity on the rest of the country. His hands sweating, Yeremenko tried to remain calm in front of his colleagues.

When Major General Korshunov called with a report that the Germans had just burned a huge supply depot out on the steppe, Yeremenko lost his temper. Disgusted by Korshunov's hysterical tone, he shouted, "Carry on with your job. Stop this panic." Then he hung up abruptly.

Two generals walked into the bunker to announce that a new pontoon bridge, the only one connecting Stalingrad with the far shore, had just been completed. Yeremenko thanked them for working so hard, then told them to destroy it. The officers stared at each other in astonishment, wondering if Yeremenko suddenly had gone crazy. He repeated his instructions. "Yes, yes, I said to destroy it. And quickly!"

When they still failed to react, he warned them that the bridge must not fall into German hands. The two generals left to carry out this draconian measure.

Near the mouth of the Tsaritsa Gorge, boredom and the noontime humidity had brought out dozens of swimmers like Lt. Viktor Nekrassov who, with a friend, dove into the sun-streaked water and floated lazily in the current. Launches and steamers struggled past and Nekrassov swam in their wake, listening contentedly to the guttural rumble of their diesel engines. When he tired, Nekrassov climbed from the water onto a pile of logs, where he stretched out to soak up the sun.

With his eyes screwed up tight to shut out the brilliant light, he tried to imagine how the Volga compared with the Dnieper at his home in Kiev. The lieutenant decided that his river had been peaceful, a joyous place for children, and that the Volga was totally different, filled as it was now with clamorous boat traffic. Another thing bothered Nekrassov. Few bathers in Stalingrad smiled these days.

As he dozed on into the afternoon, Nekrassov thought more and more about the Germans on the steppe and he wondered what would happen to Stalingrad when the enemy finally reached the Volga. He could see himself crouching in the scrub grass on the far shore while German shells blasted up huge fountains of water.

Fifteen miles north of Nekrassov's lumber pile, the nightmare he envisioned had already begun.

Machinist Lev Dylo had just met his first Germans. He tried to run, but was thrown to the ground and manhandled. One soldier snatched his watch. Others prodded him to his feet and marched him across a field. Dylo waited until he saw a deep ravine, then plunged into it and escaped. The Germans did not shoot.

Dylo ran two miles to the tractor works and burst in on his superiors.

"They're here. Hurry!" he shouted, but the factory supervisors had already been alerted. The first battalions of workers' militia, some wearing uniforms but most in civilian clothes, were marching out to man barricades along the Mokraya Mechetka River.

In factory courtyards up and down the main north-south highway in Stalingrad, political commissars and foremen processed thousands of workers for duty. They told each group, "Whoever can bear arms and whoever can shoot, write your names down." Those who signed got a white armband, a rifle, and a bandolier of ammunition before they moved off in platoons to the riverbank. Workers not selected went to the settlement houses to alert relatives of those who had gone into the lines.

Pyotr Nerozia hurried home from one of these meetings at the Red October Plant to say good-bye to his family which was being evacuated that afternoon across the Volga. He arrived too late and found only a note saying that his wife and children had already left for Uralsk. Though relieved that they had gotten off safely, Pyotr felt a sudden loneliness. The stillness of the house bothered him and he left for a walk. Near the aviation school, he stopped in a field, picked up a watermelon, then turned and went back home. In the kitchen he started to fry two eggs.

When another air raid alert sounded, Nerozia turned off the stove, left the two eggs in the pan, and went to the battalion headquarters of his workers' fighting detachment.

The air raid siren that Nerozia reacted to was just another in the series of false alarms that Stalingrad residents had endured during the day. By late afternoon, the center of the city had lapsed into apathy. Incredibly enough, despite the presence of Yeremenko's nerve center in the Tsaritsa Gorge and the unusual military traffic on roads leading north to the factory area, most people in the downtown part of the city remained completely ignorant of the crisis.

Lt. Viktor Nekrassov had finally gotten up from his comfortable log heap and, with his friend, wandered over to the main library at the river's edge. In the quiet and cozy reading room, he sprawled into a wicker chair and begn to thumb through a magazine containing short articles on Peru. At a long table, two young boys laughed out loud at a book of drawings about Baron Munchhausen. On the wall, a big clock struck each quarter hour. After a while, Nekrassov and his frend got up and left.

Loudspeakers were spewing yet another warning across squares, intersections, and side streets. The voice minced no words: "Attention. Attention. Citizens, we have an air raid! We have an air raid!"

As if to underscore that it was not just another drill, antiaircraft guns around Red Square banged loudly in frenzied cadence. Small black puffs marched across the clear blue sky; automobiles quickly screeched to a halt. Tramcars let off passengers who stood mute for a moment, shaded their eyes and looked into the sun to gauge the danger point.

Then they saw them, the lead groups of more than six hundred German planes, coming from beyond the Don. Like strings of gulls, flying in perfect V's, the Stukas and Ju-88s droned over the sun-drenched city and tipped over into their dives. Their bombs fell into the crowded downtown residential area and, because of the long drought, flames spread like wildfire. In seconds, Stalingrad was ablaze.

Concussions blew down most of the houses on Gogol and Pushkin streets. Outside a cinema, a woman was decapitated as she ran along the sidewalk. The city waterworks building collapsed from a direct hit. The telephone exchange fell in on itself; all regular phone communications blinked out. The screams of trapped operators came up through a jumble of broken switchboards and control panels.

At Stalingrad *Pravda*, on the northern side of Red Square, bombs smashed the outer walls and brought survivors streaming out to seek safety in a nearby cellar. In the meantime, the loud-speakers on Red Square tonelessly asked people to shoulder arms and fight the invader.

On Medevditskaya Street, every house burned briskly. When firemen arrived, they saw a hysterical woman running down the middle of the road, while clutching a baby tightly to her breast. One of the men jumped out, grabbed her and pushed her down into a trench. A bomb went off, killing the man as he tried to get down beside her.

On Permskaya Street, Mrs. Konstantin Karmanova returned home after seeing her two older sons march off with their factory unit. As she and her sixteen-year-old son Genn turned into the street, they saw the whole block burned out except for their own home, a one-storey brick dwelling. Mrs. Karmanova ran inside to save what she could. She grabbed a bundle of papers left by her husband when he went off to war: some of them dated back to

1918 when he fought as a Bolshevik for Tsaritsyn. Rushing into the backyard, she dug a hole and buried the documents and some silver heirlooms. Around her, houses continued to burn.

In Dar Gova, railroad man Constantin Viskov woke from his drugged sleep to hear bombs crumping down near the train station. As he jumped out of bed, his wife handed him a package of food and kissed him good-bye. Viskov raced away through smoke and fire toward the terminal.

The first bombs fell as Pyotr Nerozia unlocked the safe at battalion headquarters. His superior, a woman named Denisova, rushed in and told him to send guns to the tractor factory. After issuing orders for their transfer, Nerozia reminded himself to go home and pick up some food.

Outside the headquarters, the city shook in agony. Smoke pouring through the windows choked him, and suddenly he was thirsty. Comrade Denisova grabbed at his arm and pointed to the main hospital, which collapsed while they watched. Running over to help the patients, they shepherded a group on to the nearby children's clinic. But it caught fire immediately and the invalids inside were roasted to death.

Nerozia then went off to assemble a workers' detachment at the Factory Krasny Zastava. It was a mass of flames. He moved on to the City Soviet at Red Square, but it, too, had flared and broken under a string of bombs. He ran ahead to the Metro, a cavernous underground air-raid shelter, now crammed with screaming and suffocating people. Nerozia balked at going into this hellhole and, remembering the food at home, circled back to his own street where his house was still standing.

Going to the bedroom he found his parrot squawking for attention as it hopped frantically about its cage. Taking the trembling bird in his hands, he held it at the window and released it into gray clouds of smoke. The parrot flew off and flitted nervously from tree to tree.

Nerozia watched his pet for a moment, then ran back to the kitchen and filled a bedsheet with farina, wheat grain, dried bread, and a bottle of vodka. When he finished he gazed wistfully at the stove where his two fried eggs lay under a coverlet of fallen plaster. With a final shrug, he hoisted the sack of rations onto his shoulder and left his house for the last time.

At 7:00 P.M., during the height of the bombing, the City Soviet leaders managed to function from an improvised network of cellars. They sent out orders to continue publication of *Pravda* and Mikhail Vodolagin, a thick-lipped, bespectacled member of the Central Committee, hurried over to *Pravda* headquarters on Red Square and found the entire building a shambles. A few hundred yards away, he stumbled on the newspaper staff, cowering in a basement and too stunned to work.

Vodolagin commandeered a car and went north toward the tractor factory, which he knew had a printing press. The trip normally took twenty minutes, but with German planes overhead and bodies and debris clogging the main road, the passage was torturous. To Vodolagin's right, liquid fire from ruptured oil tanks passed down the slope and spilled into the Volga. To his left, the lower slopes of Mamaev Hill were covered with the bodies of picnickers.

After two harrowing hours, Vodolagin arrived at the nearly deserted tractor works. He found his printing press, collared a militiaman who said he knew how to set type and, as plaster fell from the ceiling, he started to bring out a special issue of *Pravda*.

Close to 9:00 P.M., with the Stukas and Ju-88s still overhead, Mrs. Vlasa Kliagina hurried back from digging ditches in Yelshanka. She was anxious to find her daughter, Nadia, who had gone home early to be with little Vovo. At a roadblock, Mrs. Kliagina fretted impatiently until a soldier finally waved her through into her own neighborhood, crackling from a hundred fires.

She ran along Sovietskaya Street and turned into Karl Marx

Gardens where thousands of people huddled around benches. Homeless, crying, many had already lost relatives. Mrs. Kliagina searched for her children, but did not find them in the crowd.

When she came to her own home, her heart sank. It was a smoldering ruin. She called out several times but no one answered and she fled down Komsomolskaya Street. A friend saw her there, sobbing incoherently, and shouted that Nadia was safe in a nearby cellar. At that moment, her daughter ran out and told her mother that Vovo had vanished. Mrs. Kliagina refused to believe her and broke away, screaming, "Vovo! Vovo! Where are you?" She never saw him again.

In his diary that evening, the aggressive, flamboyant Luftwaffe general, Freiherr von Richthofen, summed up the results of his pilots' operations over the stricken city, "A sudden alert sent out by VIII Air Corps put the whole of Air Fleet Four into the air, with the result that we simply paralyzed the Russians. . . ."

It was true. The city's pulse slowed, numbed by the blows that had killed nearly forty thousand people.

Close to midnight, with the Tsaritsa Gorge completely ringed by fire, a bone-tired General Yeremenko picked up the BODO conference phone to speak with Stalin. Within minutes, the premier was on the line, listening as Yeremenko confessed that the situation was very bad, so bad that city officials wanted to blow up some of the factories and transfer the contents of others across the Volga. The general stressed, however, that both he and Commissar Khrushchev opposed such a move.

Stalin was furious.

"I do not want to debate this question," he shouted. "The evacuation and mining of the plants will be interpreted as a decision to surrender Stalingrad. Therefore the State Defense Committee forbids it."

With this order, Stalin left Yeremenko to cope with the Germans knocking at the city gates.

Chapter Seven

According to the tactics devised by General Paulus, the three German divisions crossing the steppe on Sunday, August 23, were supposed to forge a forty-mile-long corridor from the Don to the Volga. This barrier of steel would seal off Stalingrad from the north and prevent reinforcements from filtering down to the aid of the city. In theory, the plan was sound. In practice, it required perfect coordination among the participating units.

By midnight of August 23, the 16th Panzer Division on the outskirts of Stalingrad had outrun its support. Twelve miles to its rear, the 3rd Motorized Division halted for the night. Another ten miles back, the 60th Motorized Division had bogged down in a giant traffic snarl. Completely separated from each other, the three divisions became a chain of "islands" dropped in the middle of a hostile sea. Until these islands joined into a solid land bridge extending outward from the main body of the Sixth Army, each would be extremely vulnerable to Soviet counterattacks.

While the Russian Military Council in Stalingrad dispatched the workers' militia to trenches north of the tractor works, Gen. Hans Hube ordered his 16th Panzers into a circular defense perimeter, a hedgehog, with the division's heavy artillery covering a 360-degree front. At the same time, Hube issued instructions for an immediate attack if there was any opportunity to take advantage of tactical surprise.

At 4:40 the next morning, his gun batteries opened a furious barrage on Russian positions around Spartakovka and the Mokraya Mechetka River. Shortly afterward, panzers of Combat Group Krumpen roared out from the hedgehog onto the softened targets only to run into withering fire from hastily fortified Soviet trenches.

In a miracle of overnight organization, Russian militia had dug interlocking strongpoints and assimilated the rudiments of modern warfare. Now, dressed in work clothes or Sunday finery, they crouched behind mortars and machine guns and challenged the finest tank army in the world. When Combat Group Krumpen staggered under their hail of shells, the Russians even opened a counterattack, sending unpainted T-34 tanks straight from the factory assembly lines at the Germans. The situation suddenly reversed, General Hube radioed Sixth Army Headquarters for information about his tardy supporting divisions.

They, too, were under heavy pressure. The 3rd Motorized at the town of Kuzmichi, had just captured a Soviet freight train bulging with American Ford trucks and Willys jeeps, but it had to turn into its own hedgehog formation to face a reckless onslaught by the Russian 35th Guards Division, which was pouring down from the north to widen the gap between the 3rd and 60th Motorized to the west. Led by packs of tanks, Red Army soldiers spilled across the steppe and descended on the flanks of both divisions.

Unaware of the situation, Dr. Ottmar Kohler tended to his patients at a makeshift hospital along a railroad siding, twenty-five miles west of the Volga. He was still in great pain from the broken jaw he had sustained the day before in the motorcycle accident. Unable to eat properly, he was living on chocolate and cognac. To keep his loose upper jaw in place, Kohler worked with a piece of cork clenched in his mouth.

As the surgeon concentrated on an operation, a soldier yelled into the operating room, "The Russians have broken through!" Kohler kept working and, when he finished, went to the door to see several Soviet tanks squashing German vehicles only a hundred yards away. The sight brought a roar from his throat. Spitting out the cork, he screamed, "Load the wounded!"

At that instant, concealed German antiaircraft guns fired ear-splitting salvos directly at the enemy tanks, which blew up, and scattered flaming fuel and bodies across the ground. The shooting increased as other Russian tanks came to duel with the German artillery.

Rooted to the doorway, Kohler noticed a German sergeant and his six-man squad walking unconcernedly around the corner of the hospital. Trailing their guns in the dirt, the soldiers came up to him and the sergeant asked, "What the hell's going on around here?"

In reply, the astonished Kohler asked his own question, "What the hell are you going to do about it?"

The sergeant shrugged in indifference, and begged to be allowed to rest. When Kohler looked into the man's eyes, he held his temper, for it was clear to him the soldier had just undergone a harrowing experience. In the midst of the earthshaking shelling, he ordered food and rum for his guests.

They stretched out against a wall and watched the battle escalate. Hundreds of Russian troops were marching toward them across a grassy field. Their arms linked together, they were singing songs in loud harmony. When the sergeant stopped eating he wiped his hands on his uniform and told Kohler he was ready for orders. The doctor suggested that the squad do a little fighting and asked the name of the sergeant's commanding officer. "Captain Holland," he said, adding in a hollow voice that Holland's head had just been shot off by a Russian tank.

Kohler knew now what haunted the sergeant so he left him alone, jumped on a pile of manure and trained his binoculars on the incredible parade coming at him from the meadow. Behind him a German staff car careened into the yard and an officer standing in the back seat hollered, "Just what in hell is going on around here?"

Used to that question by now, Kohler merely waved a greeting. "Come up on my manure pile and see for yourself."

Giving the officer his glasses, he pointed to the enemy infantry. The man swore in delight, handed back the binoculars, raced to his car and sped off toward an artillery command post.

Kohler fixed his attention on the marching soldiers, whose songs drifted toward him on the balmy summer breeze. As the doctor stared in horrified fascination, geysers of earth suddenly blossomed among them and jagged holes appeared where men had been moments before. Kohler watched as the steppe grass turned red and the singing was replaced by the shrieks of the dying.

Sickened by the slaughter, the doctor lowered the glasses, climbed down off the dung heap and went to care for his own wounded. Bending over the operating table, he carefully put another cork in his mouth to keep his throbbing jaw in place.

Twenty miles southwest of Ottmar Kohler's dispensary, Sixth Army commander, Friedrich von Paulus, read the radio messages from his three divisions on the steppe and lost his initial exuberance over the "lightning" victory of the previous day. He now faced the chilling prospect of losing one or more of these units unless he could send enough reinforcements and supplies to help them forge that barrier of steel to the Volga. As a precautionary measure, Paulus alerted the Luftwaffe to begin dropping ammunition and food into the most distant of the islands, General Hube's 16th Panzer hedgehog at the outskirts of Stalingrad. Meanwhile, the general wondered how he was going to take that city in the next twenty-four hours, as Hitler expected him to do.

At dawn, the city of Stalingrad looked as though a giant hurricane had lifted it into the air and smashed it down again in a million pieces. The downtown section was almost flat, with nearly a hundred blocks still engulfed by raging fires. With the waterworks broken, firemen could only try to care for the victims of the holocaust.

On a street beside the black walls of the NKVD prison, a rescue team worked feverishly to extricate a young woman, Nina Detrunina, whose legs had been pinned under tons of masonry. Their job was complicated by the ominous creaking of the prison walls, weakened dangerously by a near miss. While men and women gingerly removed brick after brick, a doctor knelt to give morphine to Nina, who smiled gratefully at her saviors. Not long after the last of the stones had been removed and Nina was taken to a hospital, she died from internal injuries.

In a deep *balka*, a group of naked adults wandered helplessly through the smoke. Inmates from the insane asylum, they were unable to comprehend the new nightmare in which they existed. On flame-blackened sidewalks, Komsomol boys and girls helped people pick through bodies to find their kin. When anyone recognized a family member, the volunteers acted quickly to ease the shock by embracing the survivor.

One woman did not need their solace. She spent hours turning over the bodies, rejecting them and moving on until she found her infant, who had been mangled by a bomb. The woman stooped, gathered the remains in her arms, and rocked the baby tenderly for some time. As a Komsomol worker edged closer to comfort her, he heard the woman speaking to the dead child. In a scolding tone, she asked: "How am I going to explain this to your father when he comes home from the war?"

Komsomol director Anastasia Modina spent most of her time rounding up hundreds of orphans, most of whom just sat beside the bodies of their parents and stared at the mutilated figures. Some children spoke to the dead, trying to rouse them. Others smoothed the victims' torn clothing as if to make them all better. Anastasia went to the children, took them by the hand, and led them away to the evacuation shelter at the Volga. Some balked at leaving the bodies of their parents, but she talked to them and they listened while tears ran down their faces. Eventually, most of them reached up to the lady with the soothing voice. But a few steadfastly refused to move from the cadavers. Anastasia left them alone; she had too many others to care for.

At the main ferry, thousands of frightened civilians milled restlessly around the pier while grim-faced NKVD police tried to hold them in check. Many were leaving loved ones behind, either dead in their homes or working as essential personnel in the factories. On the embankment under the cliff, the evacuees scribbled notes and tacked them to trees or the sides of buildings:

> Mama, we are all right. Look for us at Beketovka.
> >   Klava.
> Don't worry, Vanya. We have gone to Astrakhan. Come to
> us.   Yuri.

Out on the Volga, battered tugs and steamers steered carefully around the northern tip of Golodny Island and edged in toward the landing. Docked amid a cacophony of whistles, they heeled over badly from the weight of passengers running up the gangplanks. When the boats cast off and reversed course for the far shore, the departing Stalingraders waved sorrowfully at the retreating shoreline of the city they had once called home.

Overhead, German reconnaissance planes wove back and forth, noting the chaotic scene at the ferry and radioing the information back to their bases at Morosovskaya and Tatsinskaya on the steppe.

A quarter mile west of the central landing on the Volga, Andrei Yeremenko juggled his reserves to contain Gen. Hans Hube's 16th Panzers in the northern suburbs. When Col. Semyon Gorokhov stepped ashore with his six thousand-man brigade, he thought he was supposed to take them to fight on the southern fringes of the city. Instead, Yeremenko sent him north to the tractor factory to build a line girdling that plant. Another group, marines from the Soviet Far East Fleet, piled into a convoy of automobiles for a breakneck trip past Mamaev Hill to the trenches along the Mokraya Mechetka River, a mile above the tractor works. The marines rode to battle with their rifles sticking out the car windows.

One traveler to the factory complex was Georgi Malenkov, Stalin's personal watchdog in Yeremenko's headquarters. If the general was nervous with Malenkov peering over his shoulder, Nikita Khrushchev was more so, for he and Malenkov were bitter rivals in the murderous world of Kremlin politics.

Khrushchev knew that he had lost favor with Stalin because of his partial responsibility for the disastrous spring offensive at Kharkov which had resulted in the loss of more than two hundred thousand Red Army troops.* A master of intrigue himself, he realized that Malenkov would gladly report any of his mistakes to the premier.

Malenkov had gone to the tractor factory, where under a broiling sun, his face flushed and hair hanging in wet strands, he exhorted the plant personnel to hold on until more help arrived. He spoke with great fervor while the pounding guns from the battle around Spartakovka to the north punctuated his sentences.

After Malenkov finished speaking, the workers dispersed to the cavernous shops. Inside one of the rooms, Mikhail Vodolagin had finally brought out the emergency edition of *Pravda*, 500 single-sheet copies that he rushed out to the population with instructions to pass them on after reading. The main point of Vodolagin's special issue was to instill a sense of continuity, a feeling that the city was still functioning and would survive. He made an urgent appeal for everyone to stay calm and not to give in to panic. His editorial

---

* Khrushchev has claimed that he called Stalin's *dacha* to ask permission to call off the Soviet offensive, and that Malenkov relayed Stalin's order to continue the attack.

    Marshal Zhukov denies this in his memoirs, charging that, in reality, Khrushchev urged Stalin to ignore warnings of disaster and press the assault.

proclaimed: "We will destroy the enemy at the gates of Stalingrad."

While the fledgling publisher moved his printing operations further south, to the less-threatened Red October Plant, civilian militia and regular troops rushed past the tractor factory toward the Mokraya Mechetka River where German combat groups were trying to overrun the stubborn Russian amateurs. The only German success had been the capture of the trans-Volga ferry terminus for the railroad to Kazakhstan. Around the approaches to the factories of Stalingrad, they had met constant and bloody rebuffs.

One Russian woman, Olga Kovalova, dominated a section of the defenses protecting the tractor factory. Stalking the line, her head wrapped in a gaily colored kerchief, she screamed invective at militiamen whom she found derelict, clumsy, or incompetent. The men were used to her rough language. Olga had worked with them for twenty years, during which time she had become the first woman steel founder in the Soviet Union. Gruff and earthy, she had earned their respect and devotion.

Her battalion commander, Sazakin, heard Olga badgering the workers and tried to get her out of the dangerous sector. "Olga," he implored, "this is no place for a woman. Go back where you belong."

When she failed to respond, he ordered her to leave. Olga turned, fixed him with a malevolent stare and answered: "I'm not going anywhere."

Sazakin threw up his hands and left her alone. Hours later, he spied a colorful splotch of clothing in a clump of high grass and went to investigate. He found Olga lying on her back, the bright kerchief smeared with blood. Her left eye was missing. She had been dead for some time.

Once again the Germans tried to stampede the civilian population. The Stukas came back to bomb the jammed embankment beside the main ferry landing. With no place to hide, the masses there weaved back and forth like a pendulum, first close to the cliff wall for shelter and then out again when the Stukas dove past. Clusters of bombs found them and the shoreline was slippery with blood. Medical teams pulled the dead from the footpaths as the living pushed each other on to the boats that were to evacuate them. But the Stukas were sighting on them, too; they dropped to hundred-foot altitudes and machine-gunned the vessels.

In the hazy sunlight of the warm afternoon, the Volga erupted in a chain of fierce explosions, and several boats of the rescue fleet broke apart and sank with almost no survivors. The surface of the river was soon dotted with bodies, bobbing lazily in the current that carried them downstream to a rendezvous with the Caspian Sea.

There was no change in the pattern of fighting during the next three days. The Germans tried to consolidate their gains; Yeremenko's troops fought desperately to hold their positions to the north and south of the city, but it was becoming increasingly clear that drastic measures would have to be taken if Stalingrad was to be saved. The pressure of the German assaults was wearing down the defenders.

Late in the evening of August 27, a Red Army staff car sped from Moscow's Vnukovo Airport across the city to the Kremlin. Inside sat Marshal Georgi Konstantinovich Zhukov, a barrel-chested, forty-six-year-old peasant. No stranger to crisis, in 1939 Zhukov had faced a surprise Japanese attack at the Khalkin Gol in Manchuria and won a tremendous victory over the vaunted Kwantung Army. That triumph earned him promotion at a time when Stalin was killing fifty percent of his Red Army officer corps in an orgy of paranoia. In September 1941, when Nazi tanks ringed Leningrad, Stalin sent him there to mastermind the defense. Zhukov raged around that city, executing derelict officers, sacking generals, molding a rigid discipline which helped the people of Leningrad brace and hold.

Later, Zhukov again plunged into battle, this time in front

of Moscow, where enemy panzers had broken through on the road from Smolensk and precipitated a disorderly evacuation of the capital by many government employees: Zhukov toured the lines, rallying demoralized divisions and creating an elastic defense which, when aided by the advent of a brutal winter, crippled the Wehrmacht west of Moscow.

Now Stalin needed his special talents in the struggle for the Volga. Surrounded by members of STAVKA, the premier greeted Zhukov somberly and filled him in on developments around Stalingrad. Then he ordered the marshal to take personal charge of overall strategy in that crucial region.

During the dinner that followed, Stalin outlined the temporary measures he had introduced to harass the enemy. He was bringing elements of three armies—the First Guards, the Twenty-fourth and Sixty-sixth—against the fragile blocking corridor the Germans had created from the Don to the Volga. But these piecemeal attacks had proven ineffectual, Stalin admitted: he wanted Zhukov to find a workable solution. Before the two men parted, Stalin told him he was giving him a new title, Deputy Supreme Commander of the Red Army, which made Zhukov second only to Stalin in rank.

As the marshal prepared for his trip, he could not know that the first problem he would have to solve was the accelerating breakdown in morale among Russian troops. Few Russian soldiers believed the Germans could be stopped short of the Volga. Defeatism infected the conversations of both headquarters staffs and enlisted men. The Germans themselves were amazed at the torrent of prisoners coming into their lines. OKW in East Prussia received a cable from Sixth Army stating that the battle value of enemy soldiers was judged to be very poor: "Many deserters, some even coming in . . . with their tanks."

Inside the perimeter of the newly arrived Soviet 64th Division, stationed twenty-five miles due north of Stalingrad, morale was particularly bad. A German air raid had leveled the field hospital, killing many of its nurses and doctors. Wounded men back from the battlefield told horrifying stories of enemy superiority, and these tales spread fear among the inexperienced troops. They started to slip away singly, in pairs, and finally, in large groups.

With the division on the verge of dissolution before ever seeing combat, its commanding officer acted decisively to curb the epidemic. Calling a general assembly of regiments, he stood before them and berated them for shirking their duties to the Motherland. The colonel charged his men with the same guilt as those who had already run off and told them he intended to punish them for cowardice.

His harangue ended, the colonel moved purposefully to the long lines of massed soldiers. A pistol in his right hand, he turned at the end of the first row and began counting in a loud voice: "One, two, three, four." As he reached the tenth man, he wheeled and shot him in the head. As the victim crumpled to the ground, the colonel picked up the count again: "One, two, three. . . ." At ten, he shot another man dead and continued his dreadful mono- logue: "One, two. . . ."

No one bolted. Nurses standing beside the formation sucked in their breath at the macabre scene. The colonel's mournful voice stabbed at the troops, ". . . six, seven. . . ." Men mentally guessed their place in line and prayed the colonel would finish before he got to them. When the last bullet in the revolver thudded into a man's brain, the commander shoved the pistol back in his holster and walked away.

An officer bellowed, "Dismiss!"

The order ricocheted across the parade field, and soldiers broke from formation and scattered in all directions. Behind them six of their comrades lay in a neat pattern on the grass.

Less than twenty miles south of this grotesque ceremony, the Germans clinging to the 16th Panzer Division hedgehog at the Volga faced annihilation. A Fourteenth Corps officer put it suc- cinctly when he complained to Paulus: "If this situation continues,

I can name the exact day when . . . we . . . will cease to exist."
He was complaining about the supplies that were still blocked by
Soviet interference.

A five-hundred-car freight train finally broke past Russian rail
blocks on August 28, to deliver ammunition and food to the surrounded tankers. Its timely arrival saved the fiery General Hube
an embarrassing moment. He had just agreed with irate staff members to pull back from the Volga and try to reach Sixth Army's
main lines back at the Don. In five days of fighting against the
factory workers of Stalingrad, Hube had not been able to reach
the tractor plant. But now, replenished with artillery and mortar
shells, the general turned his heavy weapons back on the militia
holding the *balkas* at the northern border of the city.

In his underground bunker at Tsaritsa Gorge, Andrei Yeremenko
scanned his maps, which told an ugly story. On his right flank,
he had held Hube at bay with a motley collection of civilians and
military units. But Stalin's attempts to interdict the German corridor had failed, and the 3rd Motorized Division had finally linked
up with the 16th Panzers to seal off an eighteen-mile stretch of
steppe running from the Don to Stalingrad. Also, the 60th Motorized Division bringing up the rear was about to complete the
junction of the German islands and completely block any further
penetrations by Soviet troops coming down from the north to
reinforce the city.

In the center of Yeremenko's front, the main body of Paulus's
Sixth Army was massing for a broad sweep over the steppe from
Kalach east to the very heart of Stalingrad. And to hold this region,
Yeremenko could count at best twenty-five thousand combat soldiers, the remnants of the battered Sixty-second Army, which was
virtually destroyed in the Germans' pincers in early August beyond
the Don.

Over on his left flank, southwest of the city, Yeremenko
looked with some satisfaction at the defense line he had engineered

in the low hills from Abganerovo on to Tinguta and Tundutovo. The line had brought German general "Papa" Hoth to the verge of apoplexy as Russian antitank guns pummeled his armor and decimated his grenadiers. But Yeremenko could not afford to relax about the situation there. In recent hours, his Intelligence had noted an ominous series of complicated troop movements behind the German lines. Opinion in the Tsaritsa Gorge was divided, but Yeremenko guessed that Hoth had lost patience with frontal assaults and was attempting to outflank the hill line, creating another pincers with Paulus in order to trap both the Sixty-second and Sixty-fourth Red Armies outside Stalingrad. If he succeeded, the battle for Stalingrad would end within days.

Yeremenko was right, but only to a degree. Hoth had lost patience with the discouraging and costly direct approach to Stalingrad. With a swollen casualty list preying on his mind, he formulated a radical maneuver, a sideslip around the enemy. Pulling his tanks and armored infantry out of the line by night, he regrouped them thirty miles to the west. To confound Russian spies, he replaced the withdrawn divisions with new units to maintain a semblance of continuity.

But Hoth's plans were not as grandiose as Yeremenko envisioned, at least not in the beginning. The horse-faced general merely wanted to roll up the Russian hill system from the flank and, given extraordinary luck, perhaps pin the Russian Sixty-fourth Army against the Volga south of Stalingrad.

On the evening of August 29, Hoth unleashed his panzers north through Abganerovo and onto the steppe for twenty incredible miles. The thrust confirmed Yeremenko's opinion that Hoth intended to meet Paulus out on the steppe, and he quickly authorized the painful withdrawal of his divisions from their positions south and southwest of the city. Unlike previous Soviet command decisions of the first months of the war, this one would save whole armies for another day, even though it entailed the possible loss of Stalingrad.

The retreat wrought terrible confusion. At 10:00 P.M. that

same day, the Russian 126th Division received its order to pull back. When some regiments left ahead of others, a headlong flight began. Flanking divisions melted into the night. On the morning of August 30, the German 29th Motorized Division intercepted thousands of enemy soldiers wandering the steppe. The commander of the Russian 208th Division surrendered with his entire staff. Trucks, tanks, and hundreds of artillery pieces dropped into German hands without a fight.

"Papa" Hoth had unlocked the door to Stalingrad. Astounded at the sudden Russian collapse, he revised his goals and now sought what Yeremenko had mistakenly believed he always planned to do. He sent his panzers north to meet Paulus's tanks coming from the corridor to the Volga. Army Group B Headquarters informed Friedrich von Paulus of the golden opportunity offered by the bold gambit: "In view of the fact that Fourth Panzer Army gained a bridgehead at Gavrilovka at 1000 hours today, everything now depends on Sixth Army concentrating the strongest possible forces . . . and launching an attack in a generally southerly direction. . . ."

Inexplicably, Paulus did not move. Harried by the suicidal Russian attempts to break his thin corridor to the Volga, he refused to rush troops south for a linkup. Crucial hours passed. Another urgent cable went out to Paulus. Again he failed to respond. And while the German High Command tried to move its pincers, Andrei Yeremenko pulled back more than twenty thousand Russian soldiers on the steppe between the Don and Stalingrad.

Ever since he had ordered the destruction of the bridge at Kalach, Col. Pyotr Ilyin had held his position in the orchard on the southeastern edge of the town. With his ammunition running low, and only a hundred men left in his command, he had been unable to keep the Germans from crossing the Don by boat. During this period he had not received any new orders, but on the night of

August 28, the Stalingrad radio finally contacted him. A hesitant voice from Sixty-second Army Headquarters asked, "Is that you, Comrade Ilyin? Where are you?"

"Yes, it's me. We're in Kalach."

"In Kalach? The Germans are there." The voice was incredulous.

Ilyin tried to explain how he was still holding out, even though Capt. Gerhard Meunch's battalion had forded the Don and seized the old part of the town. The voice on the radio told him to wait a minute. Ilyin listened to the static, then the voice on the radio came back with another question: "Tell me, Comrade Ilyin, where is your command post?" Realizing the voice was trying to trap him, he immediately pinpointed his location, and was showered with congratulations for fighting so well. Then headquarters broke off the conversation.

Three nights later, as Yeremenko began disengaging his troops from the steppe, the voice called Ilyin again and told him to give up the orchard and make a run for the Volga. Within hours, his brigade stole out of Kalach in a thirty-eight-truck convoy. When the Germans sensed movement in the dark, they blazed away at the sound and Ilyin stood in the road, exchanging shots with Meunch's battalion. Then he leaped into a car and rode off safely to Stalingrad.

On September 2, Paulus finally agreed to the southward drive toward Hoth, and within hours, the jaws of the pincers snapped shut. But Paulus had waited too long. Most of the Russian troops on the steppe had escaped into Stalingrad, and his seventy-two hours of indecision had given the enemy another chance to fight. Now the battle would be in the streets of Stalingrad, where *blitzkrieg* tactics were useless.

Chapter Eight

On September 3, Joseph Stalin sent a telegram to Marshal Zhukov at Malaya Ivanovka on the western bank of the Volga, fifty miles due north of Stalingrad:

> The situation at Stalingrad has deteriorated further. The enemy stands two miles from the city. Stalingrad may fall today or tomorrow if the northern group of forces does not give immediate assistance. See to it that the commanders of forces north and northwest of Stalingrad strike the enemy at once. . . . No delay can be tolerated. To delay now is tantamount to a crime. . . .

In the five days he had been at the front, Zhukov had not yet performed a miracle, but he was attempting to coordinate Russian infantry attacks with meager air and tank strikes. Such an effort needed time. This Stalin would not allow him. When Zhukov called him, pleading for a delay until ammunition arrived in sufficient quantities, Stalin gave him until September 5. On that day, Zhukov launched "human wave" assaults, which crashed into the left flank of the German corridor from the Don to the Volga and immediately foundered. At nightfall, the German corridor was still intact.

Zhukov phoned Stalin with the bad news. After describing the carnage, he mentioned that Paulus had been forced to transfer some reserves from the outskirts of Stalingrad to contain him.

Stalin was elated. "That's very good," he said. "It is of great help to the city."

When Zhukov cautioned that the Russian success was illusory, the premier dismissed it, saying, "Just continue the attacks. Your job is to divert as many of the enemy forces as possible from Stalingrad."

With that Stalin hung up.

Adolf Hitler, the other grand chessmaster in the fateful game, paced the fragrant pine woods of Vinnitsa in growing frustration. He could not understand why the goals of Operation Blue had not been met. General Paulus had hit the Volga on August 23, but Stalingrad had not yet fallen. And in the Caucasus, where Army Group A strove for the prized oil fields, something else was going wrong.

Ever since the Germans had turned the corner at Rostov on July 23, and burst into the land mass between the Black Sea and the Caspian, the Russians had played a skillful game of will-o'-the-wisp, drawing the Nazis further and further from their supply bases. The German grenadiers of the First Panzer and Seventeenth Armies crossed parched desert, fields of six-foot-high sunflowers, and, on August 9, finally came to the foothills of the Caucasus Mountains where they captured the oil center of Maikop, only to find it burned to the ground by retreating Russians. Hitler then urged his commanders on toward Grozny, Batum, and Baku. Along the way, they acquired new allies: Moslems, Circassians, natives who rejected Communist rule. Still the Germans never trapped a large body of the Red Army. By September, with supply lines sluggish, their march toward the chief oil centers slowed. When Army Group A's commander, Marshal List, recommended regrouping, Hitler went into a tirade and threatened to fire him.

In the daily staff meetings with his "conscience," the stubborn

Gen. Franz Halder, Hitler bridled under repeated warnings about weak flanks and poor communications both at Stalingrad and in the Caucasus. He began to think about replacing Halder, too.

The situation deteriorated further on September 7, when Gen. Albert Jodl returned from a hurried trip to the Caucasus headquarters and heartily endorsed List's idea of ending all attacks until Army Group A was resupplied with men and matériel. Hitler exploded at this defection by a trusted aide. He screamed at Jodl, who also lost his temper and shouted back stinging reminders of Hitler's various directives that had brought the operation to its present sorry state.

His face blotched and his eyes feverish, the Führer stormed out of the meeting. From that moment on, the breach between him and the Wehrmacht generals widened irreparably. Until the end of the war, whenever he stayed at the OKW, Hitler took almost all his meals alone, except for the companionship of his dog, Blondi.

While the leader of the Third Reich sulked at Vinnitsa, his pawns in the Fourth Panzer Army were storming the southern outskirts of Stalingrad. After meeting Paulus's Sixth Army on the steppe just outside the city, "Papa" Hoth wheeled his divisions eastward for a drive to the Volga that hopefully would split the Sixty-second and Sixty-fourth Soviet armies. But the moment his tanks rolled off the steppe into the congested, hilly suburban towns of Krasnoarmeysk and Kuperosnoye, Hoth faced a different kind of war.

Gone were the lightning ten-mile advances. Now Hoth settled for only a mile or two each day. When the panzers bogged down in narrow streets, Russian soldiers doused them with Molotov cocktails. From windows, enemy snipers picked off whole squads of unwary foot soldiers. Artillery, once used to decimate unseen targets miles away, was now employed to rip out the guts of buildings just fifty yards in front of stalled German divisions.

The cost was frightful. Werner Halle, a corporal in the 71st Regiment of the 29th Motorized Division later wrote in his diary,

"During this period we were frequently without company commanders or even platoon leaders . . . each one of us, this may sound hard but this was the way it was, could easily guess that he might be the next to go. . . ."

On the evening of September 9, Halle and his men received a warm meal, their first in many days. The next day, he stood on the slopes leading down to the Volga at Kuperosnoye and marveled that he had made it to this huge river. After sending word back of his triumph, he dug in quickly to await a violent Soviet reaction to his presence.

Halle's arrival at the Volga marked the final isolation of the Russian Sixty-second Army. Already cut off in the north by the German Sixth Army's push to the Volga on August 23, it was now penned into a salient around the suburb of Beketovka and was about to absorb the full weight of Friedrich von Paulus's main body, drawn up at the western rim of Stalingrad. The Sixty-second Army was now the only combat force left to deny Stalingrad to more than two hundred thousand invaders.

In the Tsaritsa Gorge, traffic around the Russian Military Council bunker was unusually light. Civilians who commented on the hushed atmosphere were unaware that Gen. Andrei Yeremenko had moved out, across the river to Yamy. Yeremenko's reasons for leaving were legitimate. He had trouble communicating with his armies over phone wires, which were constantly being cut by enemy fire, and German mortars were shelling the Tsaritsa Gorge itself. Only a few days before, flames from a burning oil dump had poured down the gorge and almost incinerated the headquarters.

When Nikita Khrushchev phoned Stalin to explain why they wanted to leave, the premier fumed, "No, that's impossible. If your troops find out that their commander had moved his headquarters out of Stalingrad, the city will fall."

Khrushchev kept repeating the arguments until Stalin relented: "Well, all right. If you're certain that the front will hold and our defenses won't be broken, I'll give you permission. . . ."

The headquarters staff crossed the Volga on September 9, and before he left, Khrushchev called in bald-headed Gen. F. I. Golikov and told him to stay as liaison with Gen. Alexander Ivanovich Lopatin, commander of the sacrificial Sixty-second Army. Golikov turned "white as a sheet" and begged Khrushchev not to abandon him. "Stalingrad is doomed!" he begged. "Don't leave me behind. Don't destroy me. Let me go with you." *

Khrushchev brusquely ordered Golikov to pull himself together, then stalked out of the bunker to catch the ferry to the far shore.

---

* Later, Golikov complained bitterly to Stalin about his treatment at Khrushchev's and Yeremenko's hands. The premier very nearly cashiered Yeremenko on the spot. Only when Khrushchev told Stalin about Golikov's cowardly behavior was the situation clarified.

Chapter Nine

General Golikov's hysteria reflected the increasing tendency among Soviet personnel to quit the city. While Golikov was forced to remain because of a direct order from Khrushchev, thousands of Russian officers and men sought safety on the eastern shore of the Volga. Some forged false papers; others hid on the ferries. All were desperate enough to chance a fatal encounter with NKVD police. But even the Green Hats were now leaving.

At his nearly deserted bunker in the Tsaritsa Gorge, General Lopatin tried valiantly to rally his dispirited soldiers. But the Sixty-second Army he commanded existed in name only. Having been badly battered west of the Don, its survivors had straggled into Stalingrad to seek refuge, not combat. Its front extended from the tractor factory to the grain elevator and it was ill-prepared to withstand the full weight of the oncoming Germans. An armored brigade possessed just one tank. An infantry brigade counted exactly 666 soldiers, of whom only 200 were qualified riflemen. A regiment which should have mustered 3000 troops listed 100. The division next to it, normally 10,000 strong, had a total of 1500. On the southern fringe of the city, the once great 35th Guards Division carried 250 infantry on its rolls.

With these statistics confronting him, General Lopatin lost confidence in his ability to save Stalingrad. When he confided his fears to Yeremenko, he lost his job.

Across the Volga, in the woods at Yamy, Yeremenko and Khrushchev held a hurried conference to choose a successor. Sifting the names of candidates, they quickly agreed that one general, Vassili Ivanovich Chuikov, the deputy commander of the Sixty-fourth Army, was best qualified for the job. A peasant whose career included work as a bellhop and shop apprentice before the Bolshevik Revolution, Chuikov had joined the Communist party in 1919 and within months became leader of a regiment during the Civil War. Six years later, at the age of twenty-five, he graduated from the prestigious Frunze Military Academy and went on to command an army in the Russo-Finnish War of 1939–1940. When Hitler invaded the Soviet Union, Chuikov was stationed in Chungking, China, reporting the palace intrigues around the "Fascist" Chiang Kai-shek. Not until the spring of 1942 did he return to Russia, where, for the past six weeks, he had worked in General Shumilov's Sixty-fourth Army as it fought the German Fourth Panzer Army on the steppe southwest of Stalingrad. Despite the constant retreats before the massed enemy tanks, Chuikov never succumbed to defeatism. Strong-willed, imbued with a belief in himself, he heaped scorn on those who lost heart. Argumentative to a fault, he readily chastised anyone who disagreed with his ideas about military matters.

His abrasive personality went hand in hand with his pugnacious appearance. Broad-shouldered, stocky, he had a jowly, seamed face. Tousled black hair fell into his eyes, and his smile revealed a row of gleaming gold teeth. Chuikov cared little about his dress, so ordinary and unkempt that he was frequently mistaken for the average foot soldier.

Yeremenko and Khrushchev felt that Chuikov's dynamic manner far outweighed any deficiencies in temperament. Precisely because he was decisive, tenacious, and a brilliant improvisor on the battlefield, they believed that he was the right man to send into Stalingrad. Yeremenko phoned Stalin on the BODO line to get approval for the appointment, then called the general to Yamy for a conference.

On the evening of September 11, Chuikov appeared at the main ferry landing in Stalingrad. While waiting for a steamer, he wandered into a first aid station and immediately became furious at what he saw. Men with grievous wounds were lying on the floor, their blood-soaked bandages unchanged for hours. Unfed, they continually asked for water.

When Chuikov asked "Why?" of doctors and nurses, they shrugged their inability to cope with the staggering input of casualties. The reply seemed logical so Chuikov watched an operation, then went out to his jeep and sat brooding about the wounded until the ferry came in and transferred him to the far shore.

At 10:00 A.M. on September 12, he saluted Andrei Yeremenko and said: "*Tovarishch* commander, General Chuikov has arrived according to your order."

Yeremenko greeted him warmly and offered to share breakfast. When Chuikov refused, the two men talked about general conditions in the Stalingrad area. Outside, an occasional German shell exploded in the nearby trees.

"Vassili Ivanovich," Yeremenko got to the point. "I asked for you in order to offer you a new position. . . ." Though he had anticipated the new post, Chuikov looked genuinely startled as Yeremenko stared intently at him for a reaction, ". . . the position of commander of the Sixty-second Army. What do you think of that?"

Chuikov responded immediately, "*V etom otnoshenii . . .*" ("In this respect"), and Yeremenko remembered that Chuikov was fond of using this phrase in conversation, ". . . the appointment, of course, is extremely responsible."

Yeremenko broke in, "The situation of the Army is very tense, and I am happy you realize the heavy load you bear."

Chuikov nodded. "I think that, in this respect, I will not let you down."

Satisfied with Chuikov's responses, Yeremenko took him to

see Khrushchev, who was quickly convinced that Chuikov meant to stand fast in Stalingrad. The meeting broke up on the implicit understanding that Front Headquarters would not deny Chuikov help when he asked for it. Then the new commander of the Sixty-second Army left to collect his belongings before the return trip to the west bank of the Volga.

On the same day, Gen. Friedrich von Paulus flew more than five hundred miles west to Vinnitsa in the Ukraine. There he spent hours with Adolf Hitler and discussed his chief concern, the left flank along the Don. Paulus asked the Führer to give him some "corset" units, a reserve for the puppet armies still moving into position. Hitler was most cordial and promised to look into the problem immediately. When he pressed Paulus about Stalingrad, the general told him the city should fall in a matter of days.

That evening Paulus dined with his old friend Franz Halder. Over good wine, they talked of the successful summer steppe campaign, and Paulus repeated his fears about the weakness of the puppet armies on his left flank. Halder told him he intended to keep after Hitler on the subject and the two men parted on an optimistic note.

Meanwhile, the three top men in Soviet military affairs were also in conference. Joseph Stalin, Georgi Zhukov, and Alexander Vasilevsky pored over the critical news coming from the battlefields. They noted that in the Caucasus, German Army Group A was beginning to slow down in its drive for the oil fields. But Stalin, still unsure that he had the strength to contain the enemy there, summed up the problem by saying, "They want to get at the oil of Grozny at any price." Without pause he added, "Well now let's see what Zhukov has to say about Stalingrad."

Zhukov did not have good news. His northern forces could not break the German corridor from the Don to the Volga. Stalin went to a map and studied his list of reserves in other sectors while Zhukov and Vasilevsky stood to one side and discussed in hushed tones the possibility of an alternative solution, another way out.

Suddenly Stalin snapped, "What other way out?"

Both generals were shocked by his keen hearing. Stalin continued, "Look, you had better get back to the general staff and give some thought to what can be done at Stalingrad and how many reserves we will need to reinforce the Stalingrad group. And don't forget the Caucasus front. We will meet again tomorrow evening at nine."

While Stalin and his brain trust maneuvered in Moscow, Vassili Chuikov came ashore in Stalingrad to assume command of the Sixty-second Army. A rabble ran to meet him. Old men and women, little children crowded around; faces black with grime, they were a pathetic sight. The whimpering children begged for water, and that bothered Chuikov most of all, for he had none to give them.

He drove off to the Tsaritsa Gorge to meet his staff, but the headquarters was empty and he had to ask soldiers in the streets for directions to the new command post. Someone told him it was on Mamaev Hill and, driving there through the wreckage from the bombings and shellings of previous days, he was appalled at the flimsy antitank defenses. From his own experience, Chuikov knew the Germans would roll over them in seconds. He noticed something else: Though it was still summer, every leaf had fallen from the trees.

Reaching the southeastern slope of Mamaev, Chuikov climbed upward and stumbled upon the new headquarters, just a wide trench with a bench of packed earth along one wall and a bed and table on the other side. The roof was made of brush covered only by a foot of dirt.

Two people were in the dugout, a woman telephone operator

and Gen. Nikolai Ivanovich Krylov, a heavyset man with a serious face. Since Krylov was arguing heatedly on the phone, Chuikov slipped his identification papers onto the table and waited while Krylov glanced casually at them. When he finished his call, the chief of staff of the Sixty-second Army reached out and shook hands with his new superior.

Still very upset about his telephone conversation, Krylov explained that he had just been speaking with an officer who had moved his own headquarters back to the edge of the Volga without permission. "In other words," Krylov said, "[his] . . . command post is now behind us. It's disgraceful. . . ."

Chuikov agreed and sat down. He needed time to grasp the situation; so, for the moment, he did not intrude on Krylov's activities.

Toward midnight, the general who had arbitrarily relocated his command post arrived with his deputy. At this point, Chuikov asserted himself as army commander and berated the man, "What would your attitude be as a Soviet general, in command of a military sector, if one of your subordinate commanders and headquarters left the front without your permission? How do you regard your own action? . . ."

The general and his deputy hung their heads and did not reply. Chuikov kept lashing out at them, accusing them of cowardice. Before dismissing them, he demanded they return to their former position by 4:00 A.M. Then the outraged Chuikov went back to a study of the tactical maps. The arrows on them pointed to disaster. Less than half a mile away, troops of the German 71st and 295th divisions were about to lunge toward the vital main ferry linking Stalingrad with the far shore.

At 6:30 A.M. on September 13, the enemy attacked and, with communications among his ground units frequently cut by explosions, Chuikov had great difficulty in maintaining control of the battle. By late afternoon he had "almost completely lost contact with the troops." But the Germans still had not been able to break into the downtown section of Stalingrad.

Exposed to incessant gunfire on Mamaev, and deprived of normal telephone and radio circuits, Chuikov suddenly told everyone in the crowded trench to pack up and leave for the Tsaritsa Gorge bunker, so hastily abandoned in recent days.

Following their orders of the night before, Marshals Vasilevsky and Zhukov were again closeted with Stalin. After shaking hands with them, an unusual thing for the premier to do, Stalin launched into an attack on his Allies, "Tens and hundreds of thousands of Soviet people are giving their lives in the fight against Fascism, and Churchill is haggling over twenty Hurricanes. And those Hurricanes aren't even that good. Our pilots don't like them."

Without pausing, Stalin asked, "Well, what did you come up with? Who's making the report?"

"Either of us," Vasilevsky said. "We are of the same opinion."

Stalin looked at their map and asked, "What have you got here?"

"These are our preliminary notes for a counteroffensive at Stalingrad," Vasilevsky answered.

Zhukov and Vasilevsky then took turns explaining their idea: after breaking through both the German flank defenses a hundred miles northwest of the city along the Don River, and fifty miles south of the city around the Tzatza chain of salt lakes, two Russian pincers would then meet near the town of Kalach. Hopefully they would trap most of Paulus's Sixth Army in the forty-mile-wide land bridge between the Don and Volga.

Stalin objected, "Aren't you extending your striking forces too far?" When the marshals disagreed with him, he said, "We will have to think about this some more and see what our resources are."

While they argued the merits of the bold plan, General Yeremenko called from Yamy on the BODO line and Stalin listened intently to the news that the Germans were entering Stalingrad from the west and south.

When Stalin hung up, he turned to Vasilevsky. "Issue orders immediately to have Rodimtsev's 13th Guards Division cross the Volga and see what else you can send across the river tomorrow."

The three men parted with this warning from the premier. ". . . We will talk about our plan later. No one except the three of us is to know about it."

On the morning of September 14, the German 71st Division entered downtown Stalingrad on a two-mile-wide front. Captain Gerhard Meunch personally led the 3rd Battalion, 194th Infantry Regiment, as it tried to cross several city blocks and gain the river front. Until now, his men had suffered mostly from the heat or occasional Russian rear guards, and Meunch thought their chances of reaching the Volga before nightfall were excellent.

But once they reached the congested avenues of the city, casualties rose sharply. From third- and fourth-floor windows, snipers riddled the columns, and hidden light artillery blew gaps in the ranks. The Germans found few places to hide, for they always had to force the battle and dig the enemy from the ruins of buildings.

Still, by 2:00 P.M., the Third Battalion had closed to within a few hundred yards of the main railroad station just off Red Square, and Meunch received orders to seize the ferry landing at the Volga. Despite mounting losses, he was still confident. His men had captured several Russian couriers running through the' streets with handwritten messages. Sensing that the Soviet Sixty-second Army's telephone communications had broken down, and that it was now increasingly dependent on isolated small groups to contain the Germans, Meunch assumed that his depleted battalion could manage the last half mile toward their goal.

Meunch's estimate of enemy problems was amazingly accurate. General Chuikov was in a desperate situation. Back again in the underground bunker at Tsaritsa Gorge, he had just been told that the 13th Guards Division would come to his aid and cross the river that night. But in the meantime, he had to find enough troops to hold the main ferry landing. Without the ferry, the center of Stalingrad was sure to fall.

Around 4:00 P.M., Chuikov called in Colonel Sarayev, the NKVD garrison commander. General Krylov had already warned Chuikov about Sarayev's attitude: "He considers himself indispensable and does not like carrying out the army's orders."

When Sarayev arrived in the bunker, Chuikov sized up his guest and dealt with him bluntly, "Do you understand that your division has been incorporated into the Sixty-second Army and that you have to accept the authority of the Army Military Council?" When Sarayev grumbled and looked annoyed, Chuikov made the ultimate threat. "Do you want me to telephone the Front Military Council to clarify the position?"

Faced with a reprimand or worse from Yeremenko and Khrushchev, Sarayev caved in and humbly answered, "I am a soldier of the Sixty-second Army."

Chuikov sent him to organize his fifteen hundred militiamen into squads of ten and twenty in strategic buildings in the heart of the city. These "storm groups" were his answer to the German superiority in troops, artillery, and planes—especially planes. Throwing away the Red Army textbook on tactics, he was substituting an idea he had first conceived on the steppe, where he watched enemy *blitzkrieg* tactics against the Sixty-fourth Soviet Army, and became convinced that he could not compete against German firepower. He countered by creating a series of minifortresses, commanding various street intersections. The small storm groups could act as "breakwaters," funneling Nazi panzers into approach roads already registered on by Russian artillery. When the tanks lumbered along these predictable routes, they would face a murderous fire from heavy weapons. With the tanks bogged down, the storm group could then deal with German infantry, exposed behind the flaming armor. And by fighting at such close range, the storm groups also eliminated the threat of the German Luftwaffe. Afraid to bomb their own troops, the Stukas and Ju-88s would be unable to attack the Soviet strong-points.

A mere half mile northeast of Chuikov's bunker, a group of NKVD soldiers braced for the final German thrust to the river. Drawn up in an arc around the main ferry, the sixty soldiers waited for their commander, Colonel Petrakov, to return from a scouting mission along Pensenskaya Street. To figure out where the enemy was trying to break through, Petrakov and two aides walked as far north as the Ninth of January Square. The roar of small-arms fire was rolling over them from a distance, but they had neither seen a German nor heard any close-range shooting. The square was deserted, and Petrakov stood beside an abandoned car to assess his situation.

Submachine-gun bullets suddenly whistled through the car windows, forcing Petrakov to duck for cover. Almost instantly German shells exploded up and down the square and he was knocked unconscious. Rescued by his men, he awoke in a tunnel at the edge of the Volga where he lay under an overcoat and heard that the Germans had rushed for the river and taken a series of buildings near the shore. From the House of Specialists (an apart-ment house for engineers), from the five-storey State Bank, and from the beer factory, the Germans were hollering: *"Rus, Rus, Volga bul-bul!"* ("Russians will drown in the Volga!").

Petrakov staggered to the tunnel entrance and looked out at the river for some sign of the 13th Guards Division. But the time for their crossing was still hours away and he had to keep the Germans from the ferry until then.

When a small Russian boy wandered into the tunnel, the curious Petrakov asked his name. "Kolia," he replied and told the colonel that the enemy had sent him to spy on Russian strength between the House of Specialists and the Volga. Petrakov smiled and asked Kolia to tell him instead about the Germans. Kolia knew exactly who his captors were: the 1st Battalion, 194th Infantry Regiment, 71st Division, commanded by a Captain Ginderling. Protecting Gerhard Meunch's left flank, Ginderling was also trying to sweep to the main ferry before dark.

As dusk approached, Ginderling sent his troops from the beer factory toward the ferry pier, just 750 yards away. Petrakov's sixty men formed a skirmish line around the landing, fighting hard although their ammunition was dangerously low. Suddenly a motorboat appeared from across the Volga carrying cases of ammunition and grenades. Resupplied, Petrakov's NKVD soldiers now prepared to counterattack. The colonel had found a .76-millimeter gun on a side street, and while he tried to learn its parts, he issued the order to move out when he fired the fifth shot from his new artillery piece.

Petrakov aimed the weapon at the State Bank, loaded the first shell very carefully and shot directly into the cement building. As he readied another round, a launch chugged in behind him carrying men of the 13th Guards. But the Germans had seen them, too, and the launch was quickly surrounded by explosions.

Bracketed by gunfire, Colonel Yelin, commander of the Guards' 42nd Regiment, jumped off the boat into knee-deep water and ran up the embankment. When he met Petrakov, and heard that he was firing at the State Bank, Yelin angrily told him to stop because his own men were about to storm the building for hand-to-hand combat. The situation was still perilous, but no Russian was aware of one significant fact: the Germans attempting to drown them in the river were themselves on the verge of collapse.

Near the railroad station, Captain Meunch counted his ranks and realized that the one day's fighting in Stalingrad had cost him most of his battalion. Almost two hundred of his men lay dead or wounded on the streets leading to Red Square. Now the railroad station was an even more deadly obstacle. Although the Russians had not yet occupied it in strength, Meunch was instinctively afraid of it. Hidden inside its vast network of tracks, cabooses, and freight cars, a small group of snipers could tear his reduced force to pieces.

He decided to bypass it and called in an air strike. It came quickly. But the Stukas missed the target and dropped their bombs in the midst of Meunch's troops.

As darkness fell, the captain assembled his battalion in the U-shaped, unfinished Government House where, from the terrace, he first saw the Volga. He made another head count and found he had less than fifty men left to take the ferry. Recognizing that his 3rd Battalion no longer had the power to accomplish that on its own, Meunch told his soldiers to take cover and settle in for the night.

Barely five hundred yards from Meunch's U-shaped building, the 13th Guards were now ashore in strength. Two regiments and one battalion from another regiment made it across the Volga through the shellfire, landed, and ran up the gradual incline directly into battle. In the dark, the Russians got lost and stumbled over the wreckage of previous days, but they managed to form a defense line before dawn.

On Mamaev Hill, squads and platoons dug frantically into the side of the former picnic grounds. But the German 295th Division had already taken the crest where two green water towers provided a sheltered command post. The noise on Mamaev was dreadful. One Russian soldier likened it to two steel needles pressing in on his eardrums and reaching into the brain. The sky was ripped by explosions that turned faces a dull red, and to Colonel Yelin it seemed everyone was about to die.

Somehow the Russians managed to hold the hillside. Casualties were enormous. Yelin had to send in men piecemeal to fill holes torn in the line. Soldiers never knew their comrades' names before dying together in the scooped-out ground.

At his headquarters, Chuikov tried to gauge the situation on the hill, but could not because of contradictory information. He also had other problems. His command post along the Tsaritsa Gorge was under siege. At the Pushkinskaya Street entrance, messengers and staff ran in and out. Some men entered just to escape the bullets and shells tearing through the air. The heat in the bunker was unbearable. Drenched with sweat, several times Chuikov walked out into the fresh air to maintain his equilibrium. German machine-gunners fired close to him, but he did not mind. The bedlam inside the shelter seemed worse.

From the meadowland on the far shore of the Volga, the commander of the 13th Guards was about to cross into Stalingrad. Thirty-six-year-old Gen. Alexander Ilyich Rodimtsev was no stranger to war. Under the pseudonym "Pavlito Geshos," he had gone to Spain in 1936 and fought with the Loyalists against Franco. Named a Hero of the Soviet Union for that exploit, he now paced the river's edge and could not believe what he saw. On the western bank, Stalingrad burned brightly in the sunrise of September 15; the boats carrying his troops to the city were being chopped to pieces by artillery fire. While Rodimtsev watched, one craft was suddenly engulfed in smoke and then an ear-splitting explosion spread out from it for a hundred yards. When fountains of water fell back into the river, the boat and its sixty-five occupants had vanished.

Rodimtsev and his staff boarded their own launch and crouched below the gunwales as it backed slowly into the current. Shrapnel beat against the wood and geysers of spray washed over them from near misses. But the launch made it to the main ferry and Rodimtsev jumped off and ran north a quarter mile to his command post in Colonel Petrakov's old tunnel, a poorly ventilated corridor with a ceiling formed from old planks. As dirt showered down on him from explosions, Rodimtsev met his advance party and learned that the Germans seemed to be trying to seize three miles of riverfront, from Tsaritsa Gorge up to Mamaev Hill. Anxious to report to Chuikov, the general took five staff officers with him, ran down the embankment to the ferry landing, then cut west for a half mile into the underground bunker in the gorge. In that brief journey, shells killed three of his companions.

Chuikov embraced the dirt-covered Rodimtsev and made him sit down while the guards commander quickly briefed him on the status of the reinforcements. Most of his division was already across, but they were short about two thousand rifles. After Chuikov arranged to fill this need from army reserves, he asked Rodimtsev how he felt about the terrible assignment he had been given.

"I am a Communist," he replied. "I have no intention of abandoning the city."

Chapter Ten

Soldiers scurried about in a harsh light of raging fires and bursting flares that illuminated the scene like mid-morning on a summer's day. Vassili Chuikov anxiously prowled around the Pushkinskaya Street entrance of his bunker to get a breath of air. Spotting an officer, he called out, "Lieutenant, where are your men?" Anton Kuzmich Dragan told the general that he commanded the 1st Company, 1st Battalion, 42nd Regiment, 13th Guards. Chuikov gave him a terrifying order, "Hold the main railroad station."

Dragan dutifully assembled his troops and moved toward the concrete terminal just west of Red Square. They came under vicious crossfire from several buildings and Dragan realized that the Germans were in the station ahead of him. But he kept on, creeping to the left, moving closer to the terminal. After a series of whispered instructions, Dragan and his men rushed the building. Grenades exploded, machine-gun tracers split the darkness and suddenly the Germans were gone. The Russians swiftly scattered into the maze of freight cars and cabooses and waited for the dawn. They had no idea that the Germans around them were suffering sixty percent casualties.

When the Germans burst into the residential section of the city, they came too fast for some civilians. The ferries had evacuated most of the population, including Anastasia Modina and her orphans, stationmaster Viskov and his wife, and *Pravda* editor Vodolagin, but some three thousand inhabitants still remained.

In the suburb of Dar Gova, the advance caught hundreds of these noncombatants in their homes. Among them was fifteen-year-old Sacha Fillipov and his family. While his parents and ten-year-old brother stayed inside their house, the diminutive, frail Sacha went out to fraternize with the enemy. A master cobbler from his training at trade school, Sacha introduced himself to German officers occupying a nearby building and offered his services to them. Amused at the thought of someone so young and delicate having such a skill, the Germans promised him work soling army boots.

Sacha returned home that night with the news that he was going to work for the enemy. He did not tell his parents that he had also contacted Russian intelligence officers and arranged to spy on German headquarters in Dar Gova.

Mrs. Katrina Karmanova was also caught by the swift German advance. She had lingered at home for days, carrying valuables to the backyard for burial. Silver, jewelry, family heirlooms, all were dumped into a hole and covered over. Now, with her son Genn, she listened to the sounds of machine guns at the end of the block and knew she had waited too long to leave.

An artillery shell exploded on the roof, setting the house on fire; she and Genn ran next door and hid behind a sofa in the parlor. Grenades popped outside and then a fiery string of tracer bullets flew through the room.

Genn suddenly cried out, "Don't be afraid, Mother. Please pull the bullet out of my arm!"

With trembling fingers, Mrs. Karmanova picked at the metal and finally removed it. Ripping off a piece of her slip, she fashioned a crude bandage and then shouted: "Let's get out or we'll be killed."

They ran into the street and fell into a zig-zag trench beside Russian soldiers and civilians. A little girl lay huddled up, her body punctured with shrapnel. She screamed and screamed: "Find my mama before I die."

Mrs. Karmanova could not bear it. As she crouched under a hail of bullets and tried to block out the sounds of the dying child, she saw a family dart from shelter and run toward the river. At the same moment, a German sniper tracked them and quickly killed the son, the father, and then the mother. The sole survivor, a little girl, paused in bewilderment over her mother's body. In the trench, Russian soldiers cupped their hands and hollered, "Run! Run!" Others took up the cry. The girl hesitated, then bolted from the corpses into the darkness. The German sniper did not fire again.

Throughout the night, Mrs. Karmanova and Genn stayed in the trench. A few yards away, rescuers frantically tried to save several soldiers buried alive by a shellburst. At dawn on September 16, during a temporary lull, she and Genn jumped up and ran to the Volga. The Germans let them go.

In their wooden cottage, eleven-year-old Natasha Kornilov and her mother were not as lucky. Wounded days previously by bomb fragments, they lay helpless while German soldiers broke down the front door and stood over them with machine guns. The woman thought they were about to be raped, but the Germans ignored them and ransacked the house for pots, pans, food, even bedding.

When they left, Mrs. Kornilov scrawled the word "Typhus"

on a board and had Natasha put it up on the door. The ruse back-fired. Within hours, a German medical team saw the sign and set fire to the supposedly plague-ridden home. As flames danced around her, Natasha dragged her crippled mother into the back-yard and into a concrete storage shack. There, under a thin blanket on the cold floor, the Kornilovs listened to the gunfire from the direction of Red Square and wondered whether anyone would come to their rescue.

On September 17, with Germans pressing in from north and south of the Tsaritsa Gorge, Vassili Chuikov had to seek a new home. All during the day, while bullets ricocheted off rocks and shells exploded outside the Pushkinskaya Street entrance to the bunker, the headquarters staff of the Sixty-second Army scrambled away toward the main ferry. At midnight, Chuikov and his personal assistants went across the Volga to Krasnaya Sloboda, where they took hot baths and relaxed with food and drink.

As the hours passed, Chuikov failed to notice the sunrise. Suddenly panic-stricken, he and his men raced out to catch the ferry back to Stalingrad. The last boat was leaving the dock and Chuikov sprinted ahead. With a running leap, he fell on board and identified himself to the startled helmsman, who returned to pick up the rest of the army staff at the dock.

Several hours later, Chuikov set up a new headquarters five miles north of the Tsaritsa Gorge. Just a trench with some boards over it, it was in an open space between the Red October and Barrikady plants. On a slope above their bunker was an oil tank farm and a concrete oil reservoir. According to everyone familiar with the area, the tanks were empty.

At Sixth Army Headquarters in Golubinka, forty miles west of Stalingrad, German newspapermen badgered Gen. Friedrich von

Paulus for permission to flash word home that the city had been taken.

Smiling cheerfully, Paulus parried their queries, saying, "Any time now, any time."

But in his stifling quarters, the general played his gramophone, smoked endless quantities of cigarettes, and tried to calm his stomach, which was churning with dysentery; he had lost most of his hopes for a quick victory.

In Germany, some newspapers printed a special edition with a banner headline: "*Stalingrad Gefallen!*" The papers were bundled for distribution, then held at the last moment while Goebbels's ministry sought confirmation from Paulus. He could not give it.

In Stalingrad's main railroad station, west of Red Square, Lt. Anton Dragan's company was enduring ferocious bombing that blew down the walls and buckled the iron girders. When the Germans surrounded him on three sides, Dragan took his men across the street to another building, the nail factory, from which he commanded a good view of the intersection leading east to the Volga.

Barely settled in a workshop, Dragan took stock of his supplies and realized he had no food, little ammunition, and no water. In a frantic search for something to quench their thirst, the Russians fired machine guns into drain pipes to see if any liquid remained. There was not a drop.

From the Tsaritsa Gorge to the slopes of Mamaev Hill, the German 295th and 71st divisions were suffering from Chuikov's renewed strength. The 71st's Division's Intelligence Chief, Col. Günter von Below, whose brother Nikolaus served Hitler as air attaché, walked through the devastation near the main railroad station and found it difficult to comprehend the enormity of the destruction. As he carefully sidestepped debris, a master sergeant came up to him and pleaded, "What am I going to do? I have only nine men left." Colonel Below sat beside the distraught man on a curb and they discussed the toll the Russians had taken of the sergeant's company in past hours. After a while, the sergeant calmed down and went back to his nine soldiers. Günter von Below remained, staring at the ruins. Thoroughly shaken, he wondered whether the Russians would collapse before his own division ran out of men.

Günter von Below's main antagonists, the soldiers of the 13th Guards Division, lay in heaps from Mamaev to Red Square. Nearly six thousand guardsmen had been killed, but they had bought the Russians several days of precious time.

One of the fortresses which had slowed the German timetable was the huge grain elevator, whose cement silos rose high on the plain just south of the Tsaritsa Gorge. For nearly a week, since September 14, a group of less than fifty able-bodied Russians had holed up in the corrugated metal side tower, and defied the guns of three Nazi divisions. Reinforced on the night of September 17 by Lt. Andrei Khoyzyanov and a platoon of marines dressed in striped shirts and navy hats, the garrison fought with renewed spirit, the men joking with each other while shells whistled through their hideout.

Once a German tank had approached and, under a white flag, an officer and interpreter cautiously asked for their surrender to the "heroic German Army." The Russians shouted, "Go to hell!" warning the intruders to leave the tank behind and get out. When the Germans tried to jump into the vehicle, the marines blew it up.

For the next three days, German artillery pounded the stronghold, set the grain on fire with incendiary shells, and riddled the tower itself with high explosives. German infantrymen broke in and crept up the stairs, but the defenders managed to drive them back with knives, fists, and bullets.

Now, on the night of September 20, the exhausted garrison

was almost out of ammunition, and the water supply had been used up completely. In a frantic search for something to drink, Lt. Khoyzyanov led his men out the tower door, across the field, a main road, and into a gully, where they stumbled on an enemy mortar battery. In the resulting melee, the startled Germans fled, leaving behind gallons of ice-cold water that the marines gulped down gratefully.

Completely dehydrated, Khoyzyanov suddenly felt faint from the water and collapsed on the ground. When he woke up, he was in a dark cellar. The shoe was gone from his right foot; his shirt was off. His head felt light and he could not move his arms and legs. Standing guard over him was a soldier from the German 14th Panzer Division. The grain elevator he had defended so heroically had passed into enemy hands. The Germans quickly put out the fires and saved most of the wheat, which would be significant in weeks to come.

A mile to the north, in another Russian strongpoint just off Red Square, Anton Dragan still occupied the nail factory. But when a Russian woman, Maria Vadeneyeva, ran through machine-gun fire to tell him the Germans were bringing up tanks, he knew his hours there were numbered.

On September 21, Dragan came under intense pressure. Enemy tanks and planes battered the building and forced a wedge between his company and the rest of the 1st Battalion of the 13th Guards, strung out across Red Square. By late afternoon, Dragan was nearly cut off from his countrymen.

At the Univermag Department Store, the Germans concentrated on battalion headquarters and killed nearly every Russian there. Dragan tried to send help, but the headquarters had been demolished and the staff annihilated. Dragan then took command of the battalion and sent a courier back to the Volga with a message for Colonel Yelin, the regimental commander. The courier died on the way, and in the 42nd Regiment bunker on the

Volga shoreline. Yelin marked the entire 1st Battalion destroyed somewhere in the area of Red Square.

But Dragan was still alive. Leading his troops from building to building, he gave ground only when the Germans set fire to his hiding places. The battle raged past the fountain with its statues of children dancing in a circle around a crocodile, past *Pravda,* the City Soviet, the theater, and the bodies hanging in the hedges around the obelisk commemorating the fallen from the Civil War of 1918. At the intersection of Krasnopiterskaya and Komsomolskaya streets, Dragan brought the remnants of his shattered battalion into the basement of a three-storey apartment house. Scattering the surviving forty men around window openings, he sat behind a heavy machine gun and waited to die.

From the far-off Urals, more reinforcements had been rushed to the beleaguered city. And from the farthest reaches of Siberia, the 284th Division, under Col. Nikolai Batyuk, came with orders to move to the Volga crossing.

A Ukrainian of medium height, slim, wih dark hair combed straight back, Batyuk suffered from a serious circulatory ailment and frequently had to be carried on the back of one of his aides. He did this only at night so his troops would not be aware of his weakness. An obviously determined man, on arrival he told Chuikov: "I came here to fight the Nazis, not for a parade."

Few in Batyuk's division wanted this battle. Mostly raw recruits, they were willing to fight the Nazis—but not at Stalingrad. Lt. Pyotr Deriabin agreed. Already badly wounded at Moscow, he had no illusions about what awaited his men in the burning city.

At Krasnofimsk, in the Urals, a hard core of veterans like Deriabin had taught their skills to eighteen- and nineteen-year-old boys, most of whom were Orientals from the Mongolian border area and had never seen a German. Then they marched and drove nearly seven hundred miles westward, chewing the roots of the *smolka* plant, a licorce-tasting substitute for gum, and gulping down whatever vodka they could find on the way. At Kamyshin they gorged on watermelon, the best grown in Russia and the pride of the town, then climbed into Studebaker trucks, which transported them the rest of the way to the Volga.

They began crossing the river on the misty morning of September 22. It was hours before the first group landed in the fiery city, and though German planes pounded them they survived the run in good shape. Deriabin tumbled into the Dolgy Ravine, and promptly fell into a troubled sleep. When he awoke, he went on to the Lazur Chemical Plant in the middle of the railroad loop between the riverbank and the slopes of Mamaev Hill, where the Germans were fighting furiously with the 13th Guards. The crest had changed hands countless times, but the Germans were still able to look down the throats of the new men from the 284th as they took position.

Alexei Petrov came across the Volga and was assigned to the northern sector near Latashanka. For ten days he had been given hurried instructions in the use of a 122-millimeter cannon, but with time running out, the exasperated instructor finally told him to teach himself. As best he could, Petrov mastered the techniques of firing the heavy weapon that had a range of nearly six miles.

The squat, wavy-haired sergeant had spent months as a construction worker in Kuibyshev before being drafted. There he unexpectedly met his brother, who told him the rest of his family—his mother, father, and sister—had been swallowed up in the Ukraine by the German advance. They had not been heard from in more than a year.

When ordered into Stalingrad, Petrov went to the dock and saw that the other shore of the Volga was a solid wall of flames. Though scared to death, he knew he would go across. But other Russians would not, and Petrov watched as NKVD guards fired in the air over the deserters, and then killed them when they ran from the landing. After Alexei climbed on board the barge, the

NKVD took no further chances. Guards lined the rails to prevent anyone from jumping overboard.

Bombers came over, seeking out the steamers and tugs. German mortars behind Mamaev reached out for them, and Petrov cursed the slowness of the voyage as the river froze in a midday tableau. Feeling trapped and vulnerable, he crouched down to hide from shrapnel singing by his ears. Men slipped off the sides to drown. Bullets thudded into flesh and soldiers sagged against neighbors and died without a word. Petrov saw the Volga water clearly. It was a swirling mixture of water and bright red blood.

His boat took nearly two hours to reach a landing site under the cliff. While the dead covered the deck, the living scrambled off. Nearly half of Petrov's regiment had died crossing the river.

Because most of his unit was already dead, he now had to fight as an infantryman. His baptism to war was brutal. Three scouts went ahead to gauge German strength. Two came back. Petrov picked up his field glasses and scanned no-man's-land for the missing man.

He was out there, spread-eagled on the ground. The Germans had thrust a bayonetted rifle into his stomach and left him face up in the open. Petrov and his squad went berserk. Screaming hoarsely, they jumped from their holes and ran forward. Bursting into a line of houses, they killed anyone who rose before them. When several Germans raised their hands in surrender, Petrov squeezed the trigger of his tommy gun and killed them all.

He came to an elderly Russian soldier, bending over a woman. Her jet black hair streaming back in a carefully arranged way, she seemed to be sleeping. The man was moaning softly: "Dear girl, dear girl, why should a young person like you have to die in such a war?"

Alexei Petrov stood beside the couple and cried bitterly as he looked down at the beautiful woman. Then he ran off to kill her tormentors.

In the hallway of a house, he listened to a German wailing in one of the downstairs rooms. The soldier prayed: "Oh God, let me live after this war." Petrov rammed the door open and saw a kneeling man who looked up at him pleadingly. Petrov fired into his face.

Wild-eyed, he went from floor to floor, smashing open doors, looking for gray green uniforms. The pounding brought Germans out of different rooms; Petrov shot three more as they ran down the stairs.

Exhausted, his anger eased. The house became very still. He stepped over the bodies on the stairway and went out the front door to find his own men.

During the afternoon of September 23, another contingent from the 284th Division set out from the far shore on barges. Twenty-year-old Tania Chernova found space at the edge of a barge and sat down with her knees against her chest for the grim ride. Some of the 150 soldiers on board pleaded with the perky blond to move into the middle of the group and share some vodka. But she tossed her head in reply and stayed where she was.

Tania had not wanted to be a soldier. As a child she had worn ballet slippers and practiced pirouettes; later, she had studied medicine. But when the Germans invaded Russia, Tania forgot her dreams of becoming a doctor, and embarked on a relentless war against the enemy, whom she always referred to as "sticks" that one broke because she refused to think of them as human beings.

As a partisan, she had broken several "sticks" in the forests of Byelorussia and the Ukraine. The experience had hardened her outlook on life, and she looked forward with enthusiasm to renewing her vendetta in Stalingrad.

The sky suddenly filled with red and orange balls of flame as the barge struggled laboriously through ugly water spouts toward a landing point somewhere near the Red October Plant. Tania started talking to two men, one about fifty and the other more her age, when a German plane dropped a bomb squarely in the center of the craft. Tania and her two comrades flew into the water and came up swimming for the Stalingrad shore. As they fought to stay afloat, the current carried them further downstream. Tania finally dragged herself onto a sandbar on the west bank of the river and ducked into a sewer outlet. The other two soldiers followed. They had no idea where they were or who controlled the land above them.

Hoping to find an exit in safe territory, the three walked on in the blackened sewer. Their footsteps echoed hollowly as they felt their way. The stench made them gag; excrement clung to their shoes and pants. When the old man fainted, Tania and her friend dragged him for a while, but exhausted and nauseous themselves, they left him lying in the filth.

Finally they climbed out of a manhole somewhere in the city. Tania saw a group of soldiers, mess tins in hand, lining up in front of a building. Famished, they got in line. A soldier turned around, his nose wrinkling in disgust, "What in God's name is that smell?" He spoke in German. Tania decided to bluff her way through. Pretending not to hear him, she kept her place.

In the mess hall, Tania and her companion sat side by side with Germans who complained bitterly about the sickening aroma. Somebody shouted, "What is that rotten stench?" Tania wrinkled her nose, too. A German officer suddenly recognized her as a Russian. Before he could react, a Russian cook rushed over to assure him she worked for the German Army. The officer ordered the two out, but the friendly cook took them into the kitchen and fed them. The German came back again and demanded they leave because they stank so badly.

Still defiant, the two pariahs calmly walked out of the mess hall and searched for the Russian lines. At nightfall they crawled through no-man's-land and met their countrymen, who gave them clean clothes, a drink, and new rifles.

The German 71st Division continued to advance slowly toward the main ferry. Only a few places like the Dragan strongpoint still held out, and they made the cost frightful.

On the morning of September 25, at the intersection of

Krasnopeterskoya Street, Dragan had ten men left. During the previous night, two of his twelve men had deserted. A lieutenant and a private slipped out, ran down to the river, and made off on a raft. Only the lieutenant reached headquarters on the other side. Anxious to cover his tracks and convinced that the 1st Battalion was doomed, he reported everyone dead and said he personally had buried Anton Dragan near the Volga.

But in his fortress, Anton Dragan was munching burned grain and waiting for the Germans to rush him. They came again and Dragan's men threw their last grenades and heaved bricks through the windows. When the sound of a tank motor suddenly was heard, Dragan sent a soldier out with an antitank rifle and the last three shells. The Germans quickly seized him.

An hour later, an enemy platoon appeared directly in front of Dragan's machine gun. Immediately assuming the captured man had told the Germans this was the defenders' blindspot, Dragan fired his last 250 bullets at the enemy. Finally out of ammunition and wounded in the hand by return fire, he propped himself up and stared numbly at the rows of dead men in the street.

Shortly afterward, the nine Russian holdouts heard some Germans calling to them from outside. When they peeked out, they saw their captured comrade being pushed onto a pile of debris. While the First Battalion looked on, a German shot him in the head.

Shaking hands and embracing, the nine Russians in the house said good-bye to each other. Dragan's orderly laboriously scratched on a wall, "Rodimtsev's guardsmen fought and died for their country here." German tanks, black and squat, came around a corner and fired directly into the building. Something hit Dragan in the head and he passed out. When he woke up it was dark and his orderly was grabbing at him.

The building had fallen down, but in the basement, the six survivors called each other's names. Buried alive, the air going fast, their only hope was to dig their way out. Their wounds aching, and their teeth caked with accumulated dust and grime, they kept clawing at the rubble. Suddenly a cool breeze hit them and they saw stars in the autumn sky.

Dragan sent a man out to reconnoiter. He returned in an hour with the news that Germans were all around, so the men cautiously left the house one by one. To their left they heard the vicious rolling gunfire on Mamaev and saw the fireworks of tracer bullets. The smell of cordite was heavy. But on Komsomolskaya Street it was relatively quiet. The Germans owned the Volga there.

When patrols nearly stumbled upon them, Dragan's group came back to the ruins. They waited again, until the moon was obscured, then, silhouetted by flames from railroad cars and houses, they edged closer to the river. Another patrol passed in front of them. When one German lingered by a truck, Dragan sent a man to kill him. The Russian buried a knife in him, put on the German's greatcoat, and approached another patrolling soldier, whom he also knifed. Suddenly the way to the river was open. The Russians scurried across the railway line and fell to the ground at the edge of the Volga. Their lips cracking from the cold water, they drank and drank.

Above them, the Germans discovered the dead bodies. While the Russians feverishly constructed a small raft from logs and sticks, the Germans fired at random toward the river. Dragan and his men finally pushed off into the current and drifted downstream. Just before dawn their raft bumped ashore on Sarpinsky Island where Russian artillerymen found them, hollow-eyed, in rags, but alive. Dragan ate his first food in three days—fish, soup, and bread—then reported the presence of the six men of his First Battalion. The rest lay dead around Red Square.

On that square, bodies sprawled grotesquely across the grass and sidewalks. Crimson puddles marked where they fell. Other trails of blood etched crazy patterns on the streets, showing where men had dragged themselves to cover.

The Univermag was desolate, smashed: Window manikins

had tumbled in awkward positions; bullets stitched paths up and down their lifeless forms. Inside, Russians and Germans huddled in death along the aisles. The store had become a morgue.

The *Pravda* building had collapsed in the bombings of August 23. The City Soviet, the Red Army Club, and the Gorki Theater were now vacant, ugly from blackened holes and gaping windows. On side streets, merchants' stores had been flattened. Rotted tomatoes and watermelon pulp splashed over the sidewalks. Fragments of bodies mixed with the vegetables. Flies swarmed over the remains.

In what once had been a fashionable restaurant just east of the mouth of Tsaritsa Gorge, Russian doctors and nurses struggled to evacuate the wounded. More than seven hundred victims had gone out the day before by boat, a motley collection of vessels that were barely seaworthy and which landed under the fire from the German 71st Division. Now nearly six hundred more victims were being carried to the shoreline.

The Germans crept closer. Their machine guns sprayed a withering fire into the masses huddled at the dock. Russian soldiers formed a defense line and held the Nazis off until the last patients crawled feebly on board. When the Germans finally broke into the restaurant, they vomited from the stench of ether and blood and of those who had died and lay unburied.

At last the main ferry had been taken. Except for isolated pockets of resistance, the German Sixth Army held the Volga shoreline for several miles north and south of the Tsaritsa Gorge. Only the factory district in northern Stalingrad remained to be conquered.

At Vinnitsa, this good news failed to stir Adolf Hitler, who sulked bitterly in his log cabin. For more than two weeks after his explosive argument with General Jodl, the Führer had refused to

German infantry advancing from the steppe toward an industrial suburb of Stalingrad.

German Lieutenant Emil Metzger and his wife, Kaethe, on their wedding day, 1940.

Lieutenant Metzger during the battle, Stalingrad, 1942.

Leaders of the Russian Sixty-second Army in command bunker near the Volga. *From left to right:* General Nikolai Krylov, Chief of Staff; General Vassili Chuikov, Commander; Kuzma Gurov, Political Commissar; General Alexander Rodimtsev, commander of the 13th Guards Division. (Note the severe eczema on Chuikov's bandaged hand, caused by nervous tension which mounted as the war progressed.)

Emil and Kaethe, reunited in Germany after the war.

Friedrich von Paulus, Commander in Chief of the German Sixth Army.

Erich von Manstein, Commander of Army Group Don.

German Panzer Lieutenant Hans Oettl in 1940.

One-armed General Hans Hube ("der Mensch") commander of the German 16th Panzer Division.

Major Josef Linden, commander of the ill-fated German Pioneers.

General Andrei Yeremenko, commander of Stalingrad front during the early months of the battle.

Russian defenders on the outskirts of Stalingrad.

Soviet Marshals Konstantin Rokossovsky *(left)* and Georgi Zhukov in conference.

Colonel Ivan Lyudnikov, tenacious division commander who held German Pioneers at bay behind the Barrikady factory.

Sacha Fillipov, the fifteen-year-old master cobbler who was hanged by the Germans for his espionage activities.

Volgograd Defense Museum

Soviet Marshal Alexander Vasilevsky, co-architect, along with Zhukov, of counter-offensive that trapped the German Sixth Army at Stalingrad.

Russian side-wheeler tugboat pulling a barge loaded with reinforcements across the Volga to Stalingrad.

The celebrated Russian sharpshooter, Vassili Zaitsev *(far right),* looks on as General Vassili Chuikov examines the lethal weapon. Commissar Kuzma Gurov is at center.

German panzer firing on workers' settlement in northern section of Stalingrad.

German troops and tanks advancing on a strongpoint in downtown Stalingrad.

Struck from the rear by a Russian sniper's bullet, a German soldier staggers and falls to the ground as a movie camera records the scene.

socialize with the men who served him. Enraged by the "insubordination" within his staff, disgusted with the lack of progress in the Caucasus and along the Volga, on September 24 he met with Franz Halder and fired him. In an icy voice, Hitler told the general that they both needed a rest, that their nerves had frayed to the point where neither could help the other. Halder bowed out gracefully and went to his quarters to pack. But before departing, he wrote a short note to his friend and pupil, Friedrich von Paulus, out on the steppe:

> 24 September 1942
>
> . . . A line to tell you that today I have resigned my appointment. Let me thank you, my dear Paulus, for your loyalty and friendship and wish you further success as the leader you have proved yourself to be.
>
> As always,
> Halder

Paulus received Halder's letter just as his soldiers raised a huge swastika over the pockmarked entrance to the Univermag Department store in the central part of the city.

But Paulus had no desire to celebrate, for he had just learned the staggering cost of the six weeks' passage from the Don to the banks of the Volga: more than seventy-seven hundred German soldiers dead; thirty-one thousand wounded. Ten percent of the Sixth Army had been lost. Moreover, he knew the worst battle had not yet been joined. North of the ferry landing, north of heavily contested Mamaev Hill, lay the key to the city—the factories. There, the Sixth Army faced the ultimate challenge. And Paulus was running out of men and ammunition.

Returning to his isolated quarters at Golubinka on the high western bank of the Don, he listened to his gramophone and tried to quell his dysentery. A tic on his cheek had become almost uncontrollable.

Paulus sent another urgent cable to Army Group B; "Rifle

strength in the city failing more rapidly than reinforcements. Unless decline halted, the battle will stretch on."

Some of Paulus's men shared his increasing gloom. One of them was Lt. Hans Oettl, who had become a forward observer on the front lines a few miles north of the tractor plant. Each day Oettl looked through his field glasses, and pinpointed Russian positions. His batteries fired barrages of shells over his head, down onto the enemy. It had gone on like this for weeks, and nothing had shaken the Russians loose. Opposite him, Russian militiamen had been replaced by seasoned troops ferried across the Volga at night. For Oettl there was a sharp awareness that the war was not ending as abruptly as he had hoped. He had also come to realize that the young officers in his division were woefully inadequate. Though many wore the Order of the Ritter Kreuz on their breast, few if any had ever received training in the art of street fighting. They were dying at an alarming rate.

During lulls in the fighting, Oettl rested in his bunker and worried about the future. Outside, his red-ribboned goat, Maedi, grazed contentedly, oblivious to the gunfire that never seemed to stop.

At Vertaichy, out on the steppe, Deputy Chief Quartermaster Karl Binder plunged into his new job, supplying the men of the 305th Division from the Lake Constance region of southern Germany. Well-fed, gregarious, a veteran of the German Army since the days of the *Freikorps* before Hitler, Binder immediately noticed the poor morale of the units in the northernmost sector held by Sixth Army. They were unwashed, discouraged, and begging for decent rations.

When Binder inquired into the reasons for their condition, he was told the enemy constantly harassed them, never giving them a chance to rest. Russian artillery dropped hundreds of shells into the German lines; Russian divisions mounted brief, small infantry attacks. Although the Russians failed to gain ground, they inflicted a mounting toll of casualties.

Binder took hold of his new job swiftly. Within days, the experienced scrounger found sausages and beer, pumpernickel, even wine for his men. In the officers' quarters, he learned more about the battle on the steppe. One of the staff, Lieutenant Colonel Codre, warned, "Stalingrad will still give the Germans the shock of their lives, because the Russians are far from beaten." Codre went on, "A nagging worry for us is the supply line back to the Ukraine. The Sixth Army requires 750 tons a day to survive, and all of it comes over a single track to the railhead at Chir." Sobered by these comments, Karl Binder began to worry more about that tenuous lifeline to the rear.

In the meantime, he wrote faithfully to his wife back in Stuttgart. He asked for his children and assured everyone that the campaign was going well. But he never mentioned Codre's pessimistic prophecy.

Capt. Gerhard Meunch was still in the same U-shaped building he had occupied on the night of September 14, just two hundred meters from the Volga. Ever since then, with less than fifty men left in his battalion, he had tried again and again to reach the riverbank. But the Russians always drove him back, and at one point, some of Rodimtsev's 13th Guards even came after him. While Meunch held the ground floor, the Russians blew a hole in the cellar and climbed in. The Germans rushed up some artillery to help the besieged captain and, after he and his men escaped by ladder, the guns smashed in the bottom of the buildings and knocked down another nearby home. Ten Russians crawled out of the wreckage and surrendered to Meunch, who went back inside what was left of the U-shaped structure to await relief.

At Sixth Army Headquarters in Golubinka, Col. Günter von Below paused to say good-bye to his friends before going to Kharkov for treatment of an acute case of jaundice. He was depressed by the cost of taking downtown Stalingrad. But as a trained intelligence officer, he was even more concerned with the overall strategic position of Sixth Army on the steppe. When he mentioned the exposed left flank to Arthur Schmidt, the chief of staff agreed with him that it was a "festering boil," and confided that both he and Paulus worried about it constantly. Leaving headquarters a short time later, Below was still convinced that Stalingrad could be taken. But since no one had been able to reassure him about the vulnerable flank, he wondered what would happen to Sixth Army should the Russians decide to counterattack in great strength.

Along that critical left flank, outside the Don River town of Akimovski, Gen. Carl Rodenburg was as anxious as Below about Russian intentions. In fact, the monocled veteran was terribly alarmed. His 76th Division had suffered such heavy casualties in fighting off persistent Russian probes that he had begun promoting wholesale lots from the noncommissioned ranks to compensate for officers killed in action. Every week, as he went to the division cemetery to pay homage to the dead, Rodenburg became increasingly pessimistic about the chances for victory at Stalingrad.

Other German soldiers were still relatively untouched by the battle. Pvt. Josef Metzler had come across the Don south of the Kalach bridge. A radio operator in an antiaircraft battery of the 29th Motorized Division, Metzler had found the summer quiet. He saw few Russians and had time to forage freely; once he even caught a pig that he and his comrades slaughtered and ate. When Metzler saw his first "slant eyes," the Kalmuks who welcomed the invaders openly, he was sure the Russians were finished. He had the feeling that he was already in Asia and that nothing could stop the German advance. Born in Furth, near Nüremberg, the private was a man of strict scruples and Christian ideals. He always comported himself correctly; never once had he picked up clothing or other belongings from a fallen soldier, either German or Russian. To Metzler, that was obscene and almost sacrilegious.

During September, promoted to private first class, he stayed on the outskirts of Stalingrad while his battery fired into the shattered city.

A former schoolteacher, Lt. Friedrich Breining went to the Volga as a sightseer, to look at the famous waterway. Commandeering a car, he drove through the safe zone afforded by the 16th Panzer Division's bridgehead and stared down at the half-mile-wide waterway. He had expected the Volga to be like his own Rhine, with steep banks on both sides as between Mainz and Coblenz. But it was entirely different, and Breining came away from it disappointed.

On the way back to his unit, he dawdled, eating watermelon from the fields and enjoying the shade of some trees which he thought to be poplars. Late in the day, he arrived at the Tartar Wall, an ancient earthworks, ten feet high, which ran for about fifteen miles along the steppe. Once the wall had protected Russian settlers from invading Mongols. Now it simply gave added cover to the German tanks and men burrowed into the ground around it. Breining went into his trench beside it and sunbathed in the lovely autumn weather. For the lieutenant, life was reasonably pleasant. His unit had suffered few casualties during the summer and few of his comrades anticipated any significant fighting during the fall.

For Pvt. Wilhelm Alter, the whole campaign was boring. A tailor in the 389th Division, he and a friend, shoemaker Emil Gehres, lived in a ravine west of Gumrak Airfield. At 4:00 A.M. each day, they got up, washed, ate breakfast, then went to work, mending clothes and repairing shoes for the combat troops. At 4:00 P.M., they stopped working, washed again, and went to supper. The food was invariably good. Alter particularly liked the goulash.

A happy-go-lucky man who smiled easily, the tailor found the war an annoyance, an interruption from wife and home. The dull rumble of shelling in Stalingrad barely intruded on his thoughts.

The same held true for Dr. Herbert Rentsch, an immaculately groomed veterinarian who had just returned after being married in Dresden. Now in charge of all animals in the 94th Division, Rentsch went out each day to inspect his herd of twelve hundred horses, forty oxen and six camels. While he arranged to send four hundred of the horses off to the Ukraine for a rest, he requisitioned enough feed from the newly captured grain elevator in the southern sector of Stalingrad to take care of the rest of his charges.

On his daily tours of the grazing grounds, forty-five miles northwest of the city and well within German lines, Rentsch always rode his own horse, Lore. At these times, he found it easy to forget the distant sounds of war. When he gave Lore her head and she cantered across the flat plain, the doctor was at peace with the world.

Lt. Emil Metzger was in a euphoric mood. While his smoothly efficient crew fired on targets reported to them by spotter planes over Stalingrad, the lieutenant savored a letter from Kaethe, who had finally forgiven him for not coming home in August. She did not tell him that the letter explaining his delay had not reached her until after she spent hours waiting at the train station. Nor did she tell him how she had gone home that day, pounded the table in frustration and screamed: "To hell with him!" Instead, she congratulated him for being so selfless in letting a friend take his place in the furlough rotation.

Emil read her letter over and over, imagining the reunion

they would have when the war was over. Still confident that Stalingrad would fall soon, he blithely ignored any conversations among fellow officers about the weak German left flank.

That weak left flank was being discussed in Moscow. On September 28, Joseph Stalin sat once more with the co-planners in Operation Uranus, Georgi Zhukov and Alexander Vasilevsky.

Stalin was relaxed, courteous, and attentive. The premier was particularly interested in the personalities of the generals commanding the various armies. He mentioned General Gordov. Both Zhukov and Vasilevsky agreed that while he was efficient, the man seemed unable to get along with his staff. Stalin suggested a change and Zhukov recommended Konstantin Konstantinovich Rokossovsky, an officer who had barely survived Stalin's purges and wore a set of stainless steel false teeth as a reminder of his imprisonment and torture by the NKVD. Stalin endorsed the promotion wholeheartedly and also agreed to changing the names of several sectors. The Stalingrad Front became the Don Front; the Southeastern Front reverted to the Stalingrad Front. Both alterations were made to conform more readily to the geography of the region.

After further discussion of Operation Uranus, Stalin told Zhukov, "You had better fly back and do everything necessary to wear down the enemy. . . ."

Before leaving, both Vasilevsky and Zhukov signed a map showing the plan for the counteroffensive. Stalin added the word, "Approved." Then he wrote his own signature.

Chapter Eleven

While Stalin was placing his personal endorsement on the plan to destroy the Sixth Army, Adolf Hitler left Vinnitsa to fly home. As the throbbing engines of his Ju-52 transport carried him across the Ukraine and then Poland, the Führer withdrew from his aides in sullen contemplation of the disastrous summer in southern Russia. His *blitzkrieg* on the steppe was foundering in the streets of Stalingrad. His thrust into the oil fields of the Caucasus was equally bogged down in the mountain foothills. But in Berlin he continued to deny these harsh realities and, on September 30, he launched into a plaintive defense of his accomplishments. Speaking at a Winter Relief Rally in the Sportspalast, he told his audience, "When Mr. Eden or some other nincompoop declares that they have a belief, we cannot talk with them, as their idea of belief seems to be different from ours. . . . They believe that Dunkirk was one of the greatest victories in the world's history. . . ."

Silhouetted by banks of spotlights, Hitler continued:

> What have we to offer? If we advance 1,000 kilometers, it is nothing. It is a veritable failure. . . . If we could cross the Don, thrust to the Volga, attack Stalingrad—and it will be

taken, you may be sure of that—then it is nothing. It is nothing if we advance to the Caucasus, occupy the Ukraine and the Donetz basin. . . .

We had three objectives: (1) To take away the last great Russian wheat territory. (2) To take away the last district of coking coal. (3) To approach the oil district, paralyze it, and at least cut it off. Our offensive then went on to the enemy's great transport artery, the Volga and Stalingrad. You may rest assured that once there, no one will push us out of that spot. . . .

In Stalingrad, "that spot" as Hitler referred to it in his speech, a few battered Russian units still managed to stymie German efforts to drive them into the Volga. In the central part of the city, Rodimtsev's 13th Guards held a tiny sliver of land along the Volga from Pensenskaya Street north to the Krutoy Gully. At some points, their salient was only two hundred yards deep.

Searching for elbow room; the 42nd Regiment's commander, Colonel Yelin, had picked out two buildings on Lenin Square that might be used for strongpoints. One was a badly damaged apartment house facing Solechnaya Street. The other building was sound. A second lieutenant named Zabolotnov took a squad to the undamaged one on the right and occupied it. The new post was labeled "Zabolotnov's House" immediately, but he died within twenty-four hours. His men maintained the position.

As for the damaged building facing Solechnaya Street, Sgt. Jacob Pavlov and three other men crawled across a courtyard, threw grenades into first-floor windows, and helped each other inside, while the few Germans not killed by the blasts scrambled away across the square. In the basement, the squat, constantly smiling Pavlov discovered a small group of Russians, both military and civilians. Some were badly wounded, and Pavlov sent a runner to report that he had taken the house, but the messenger was forced back inside when the Germans counterattacked. He finally got through the next night, September 29, taking some wounded with him, and 13th Guards Division Headquarters sent more men to `help Pavlov. The twenty men quickly organized their new home. They broke down a wall between two cellars, posted mortars and machine guns at key windows, and began to snipe at the enemy. Four more soldiers arrived, the final reinforcements from headquarters. During the breaks in the shooting, the small band of men—drawn by chance from all regions of the Soviet Union, Georgia, Kazakhstan, Uzbekistan, the Ukraine—tried to make the best of a tense situation. They found an old phonograph and one record, whose melody no one recognized. But they played it continually and it soon began to wear out.

Outside the apartment house, German tanks constantly probed for a weak spot. But "Pavlov's House" was a natural roadblock, commanding a wide field of fire and denying the enemy access to the Volga bank, only 250 yards away. Instead of bringing in planes or artillery to smash the obstacle, the Germans unaccountably continued to attack it head on and suffered the consequences.

North of Krutoy Gully, Col. Nikolai Batyuk's 284th Siberian Division clung to the southern and eastern slopes of Mamaev Hill, although the Germans held the crest and poured shells down on the zigzag network of Russian trenches. Batyuk lost three hundred soldiers on September 28 alone, but his men held their thin line and refused to allow the enemy to sweep past them to the Lazur Chemical Plant and then on to the Volga.

Lt. Pyotr Deriabin had been stationed at the yellow brick Lazur plant for a short time and from his gun position on the grounds, frequently scanned the summit of Mamaev and the two green water tanks from which the Germans watched both him and river traffic to the east. Each time he did so, Deriabin felt the Germans were looking down his throat. And they were, for his mortar batteries came under such continuous attack that regimental headquarters ordered him to pull back to the tennis racquet-shaped railroad track circling the plant. There, in a series of caves in the embankment, the lieutenant paused to write to his only brother, fighting somewhere near Voronezh. He did not know that he had been killed during the summer.

He also wrote to his girl friend back in Siberia. Desperate to tell her where he was, he enclosed clippings from the Red Army newspaper, *Red Star*, telling of the "glorious" struggle in Stalingrad. He always added: "Hello, I'm still alive." She got every letter, but from each one censors had removed the clippings.

Although Deriabin's guns had to be moved from the premises, the Lazur Chemical Plant remained in Soviet hands. In one section of the block-long building, Russian instructors now conducted an intensive course in sharpshooting. Against the wall of a long room, they painted helmets, observation slits, and outlines of human torsos. At the other end, they stood over trainees and coached them on sniper techniques. All day long, the plant echoed to rifle fire from within as the recruits practiced shooting at the targets. Those who graduated from this impromptu school went immediately to the edge of no-man's-land where they began to take a fearful toll of the enemy.

Already Russian newspapers had made the name Vassili Zaitsev famous. In but ten days' time he had killed nearly forty Germans, and correspondents gloatingly wrote of his amazing ability to destroy his enemies with a single bullet. It was a skill he had learned while shooting deer in the forests around Elininski, his home in the Ural Mountain foothills. A shepherd in the summers, Zaitsev, at the age of fifteen, went off to technical school in Magnitogorsk. Later, he served as a bookkeeper in the Soviet Far East Fleet. On September 20, 1942, the broad-faced Zaitsev came to Stalingrad with the 284th Division. Now he was a national hero, and as his fame spread across no-man's-land, the Germans took an inordinate interest in him. They called a Major Konings out from Berlin to kill him.

Unaware of the German plan, Zaitsev continued his one-man war and began to teach thirty other Russians his specialty. Blond Tania Chernova was one of his students. They also became lovers.

Tania relished her new life. Undaunted by her ordeal on the Volga and in the sewer pipe, she had become a professional soldier, living in foxholes, drinking vodka, eating with a spoon she kept in her boot. She slept curled up beside strangers; she bathed in pails of water. She also learned how to take cover in the front lines, how to track the enemy through the telescopic sight and, most importantly, how to wait for hours before firing a single shot that killed.

During her training as a sniper, she went out on a special mission ordered by 284th Division Headquarters after captured prisoners had pinpointed a German headquarters located in a building between the Stalingradski Flying School and the Red October Plant. Tania and five men were assigned to dynamite it.

Late at night they passed through Russian outposts and crawled into enemy territory. When they heard an occasional voice, or flares burst overhead, they froze. An hour later, they found their target in a half-destroyed apartment house with one entire wall missing.

The patrol tiptoed up an intact stairwell while Tania brought up the rear. When the Russians reached the second-floor landing, the five men disappeared around the corner but a noise distracted her. She whirled to see a German soldier emerging from behind a post. *"Hände hoch,"* he grunted, waving a pistol in her face. Immediately lashing out with her boot, she caught the German in the groin. He doubled over, his pistol bouncing off the stairs and into the street. Tania grabbed his helmeted head and cracked his face into her knee. In desperation he savagely bit her left thumb.

She knocked him down and twisted his right arm under his body. Pressing deep into his throat with both hands, she held on while he thrashed about violently. His helmet fell off and suddenly Tania noticed her victim had bright red hair. She leaned harder on his windpipe. When he gurgled horribly, one of her patrol came back downstairs and whispered, "Tania, are you all right? Where are you?"

Seeing her plight, the other Russian pushed her away and smashed the red-haired man in the head with his rifle butt.

Tania got up from the corpse and ran to the floor above, where the dynamite was already in place. The sergeant ordered, "You do it," and she lit the fuse. Forgetting all caution, the Russians pounded down the stairs. The noise they made alerted the Germans, who fired at the shadowy figures emerging from the building.

Racing back toward their own lines, the demolition team heard a shattering explosion and the German headquarters behind them blew apart in an orange ball of fire.

On the right flank of Tania's position, the 95th Division, under the leadership of bald-headed Col. V. A. Gorishny, occupied another part of the bomb-pitted eastern slope of Mamaev Hill. But the 95th was so badly mauled that in a matter of days it would be transferred to reserve behind new divisions now digging in at the northern factories.

There, the fresh 39th Guards had thrown up a second line of defense behind the 194th and 308th divisions, responsible for holding the western approaches to the Red October and Barrikady plants. A few miles to the north, around the tractor works, the 112th Division had just been joined by aggressive Gen. Victor Zholudev's elite 37th Guards, young marines dressed in black striped shirts and berets.

The arrival of the 37th Guards had coincided with the departure of the last civilians still working inside the plant. When the dreaded order from the Military Council finally reached them— "Get out! Go across the river!"—the employees packed their blueprints, records, and tools into trucks. German artillery shells whined into the mile-long industrial complex as the workers walked one last time through the machine shops and assembly lines.

Overwhelmed by remorse at having to leave such an integral part of their lives, they cried unashamedly.

Their convoy drove south past the statue of Felix Dzerhezinsky, Stalin's first secret police chief and, just before the tractor plant passed from view, one foreman pointed out a building near the river and said, "We can start up again there when we come back." He sounded genuinely optimistic.

Riding down the main road, the workers passed the oil-tank farm on a hillside above the primitive trench headquarters in which Vassili Chuikov sweltered and prepared for the next phase of the German offensive.

The general had just received a letter from his wife, Valentina, living in Kuibyshev almost four hundred miles northeast of Stalingrad. She told her husband she had seen him in a newsreel; she said the children were fine. Her tone was cheerful and relaxed.

But the general knew differently: His aide had learned that Chuikov's youngest daughter was suffering from acute dysentery and the family was having great difficulty getting food, clothing, and other household necessities. Lacking even soap, they used a mustard preparation to wash themselves. This distressing news only added to Chuikov's mental burden as he struggled with the daily threat of extinction. The strain was beginning to take its toll. His body was covered with eczema, which left scaly, itchy sores on his skin and forced him to bandage his hands to absorb oozing lesions on his fingers. When doctors suggested that he get some rest on the far shore, Chuikov angrily rejected their advice. With the enemy massing on the outskirts of the factories, he was afraid to leave Stalingrad even for a moment.

Fortunately, new troops were arriving via the new river crossings Chuikov had improvised after losing the downtown ferry landing. Now the Skudri Crossing serviced the area from Rynok down to the tractor works and, to this exposed mooring, boats came at night to avoid the incessant German bombardment that made daylight trips suicidal. The most vital link, however, was Crossing 62, a cluster of moorings behind the Red October and Barrikady plants where the majority of soldiers and matériel debarked under overhanging palisades. This landing site was reasonably safe as long as the Germans failed to seize the nearby factories.

The nightly voyages to Crossings 62 and Skudri were a ghastly shock to soldiers joining the battle. The sight of a city on fire, the deep rumble of thousands of guns, instinctively made them recoil. But Communist party agitators, *politrook*, were always with them, working with ferocious zeal to calm them down. The *politrook* led the way to the ferries, to tugs like the twenty-six-year-old *Abkhazets*, and there they handed out pamphlets entitled "What a Soldier Needs to Know and How to Act in City Fighting." Usually, the agitators were the first ones on board. Like sheep, the soldiers followed. Then, as the boats slowly moved out into the river, the *politrook* unobtrusively took up stations along the rails. To prevent desertions over the side they kept their hands on their pistol holsters.

From their vantage point on Mamaev Hill, the Germans always spotted these boats and called for artillery fire on them. As the shells whistled down, the political officers diverted the soldiers' attention by reading newspapers loudly, or passing out mail from home. In this way the troops were somewhat distracted. When men were hit, screamed, and died, the *politrook* worked harder to keep the rest of the group from succumbing to mob fear. Sometimes they failed, and soldiers leaped into the Volga. The *politrook* emptied their guns into these swimmers.

In this manner, nearly one hundred thousand new troops had been ferried into Stalingrad by October; an influx equalling seven full divisions and two brigades. But they were killed so quickly that Chuikov still had only fifty-three thousand troops left who were capable of bearing arms. In less than a month, the Sixty-second Army had lost more than eighty thousand men, killed, wounded, or missing.

To bring ammunition and food into the city, Chuikov had thrown together auxiliary "roads" to supplement the ferry pipeline. These footbridges, each several hundred yards long, joined

Stalingrad to Zaitsevski Island in the middle of the Volga. Two of them were blown apart several times and had to be rebuilt. The southernmost link, formed by joining wooden rafts and barrels with iron bars and steel hawsers, was relatively sturdy, but even so, the footbridge was dangerous. It swayed badly from the force of bombs exploding nearby, frequently toppling soldiers into the river. But across this unusual highway came a steady trickle of men carrying on their backs the bullets, grenades, and shells needed for daily fighting.

Now the Germans switched the focus of their attack from the downtown area of the city to the factories in the north, trying to soften the Russian defenses with nonstop artillery fire. On October 2, German shells blanketed the industrial zone and behind the Red October Plant, the supposedly empty oil tanks blew up with a shattering roar. Flaming fuel rolled swiftly down the hill to the Volga, where it became a ghastly wave. Across the river, onlookers screamed a warning to a large rowboat making for the eastern shore. But it was too far out to turn back and, when the wall of flame reached it, the oars reared up like firewings as the doomed passengers tried to beat out the fire. Through the smoke, spectators saw the sides of the boat blaze from the flaming oil. The boat's occupants stood up and jumped. Their heads bobbed briefly in the middle of the inferno, and then the flames passed relentlessly over the tragic scene.

The same fires nearly incinerated Chuikov and the entire headquarters staff. Every telephone line burned away and, when Chuikov jumped out of his dugout, he was blinded by the dense smoke.

Chief of Staff Krylov shouted, "Everyone stay where they are. Let's get to work in the dugouts that are still intact. . . . Establish contact with the troops by radio." But when he saw Chuikov, he whispered: "What do you think? Will we be able to stand it?"

"Yes, of course," Chuikov replied. "But just in case, let's clean our pistols!"

From across the river, Front Headquarters was afraid the fire had killed everyone in the dugouts. By radio, it kept asking: "Where are you, where are you?"

The answer finally crackled through, "We're where the most flames and smoke are."

The Germans were monitoring the conversation and concentrated their fire on the holocaust. Mortar shells killed men in the doorway to Chuikov's dugout, and he moved quickly, this time up the shore line, closer to the tractor factory, the complex that the Germans were preparing to attack from three sides.

In the midst of preparations by both armies for the final struggle, a sinister personal combat reached its climax in no-man's-land. The two adversaries knew each other only by reputation. Major Konings had arrived from Germany to duel Vassili Zaitsev.

The Russians first heard of Konings's presence when a prisoner revealed the major was wandering the front lines, familiarizing himself with the terrain. Upon hearing the news, Col. Nikolai Batyuk, the commander of the 284th Division, called a meeting of his sniper group to brief them on the danger.

"I think that the German supersniper from Berlin will be easy meat for us. Is that right, Zaitsev?"

"That's right, Comrade colonel," Zaitsev agreed. But first, he had "to find him, study his habits and methods and . . . wait the right moment for one, and only one well-aimed shot."

Zaitsev had no idea how his antagonist worked. He had killed many German sharpshooters, but only after watching their habits for days. In Konings's case, his camouflage, firing patterns, ruses, all these pieces of the mosaic were missing.

On the other hand, German intelligence had studied Russian leaflets describing Soviet sniper techniques, and Zaitsev's mannerisms had been bountifully illustrated by Russian propagandists. Major Konings must have absorbed this information; Zaitsev had no idea when he would strike.

For several days, Russian marksmen searched the ruins of

Stalingrad through their field glasses. They came to Zaitsev with strategies, novel and fresh, but the grim Siberian rejected their advice. He had to wait until Konings made the first move.

During this period nothing unusual occurred. Then, in rapid succession, two Soviet snipers fell victim to single rifle shots. To Zaitsev it was obvious that Major Konings had announced the beginning of their personal duel. So the Russian went looking for his foe.

He crawled to the edge of no-man's-land between Mamaev Hill and the Red October Plant and surveyed the chosen field of battle. Studying the enemy lines through binoculars, he saw no irregularity: The terrain was familiar, with trenches and bunkers in the same patterns he had memorized in past weeks.

Throughout the afternoon, Zaitsev and a friend, Nikolai Kulikov, lay behind cover, running the glasses back and forth, back and forth, searching for a clue. In the midst of the constant daily bombardment, they ignored the big war and looked for just one man.

As the sun began to set, a helmet bobbed unevenly along a German trench. Zaitsev thought of shooting, but his instincts warned him it might be a ruse, that Konings had a partner out to trap him. Exasperated, Kulikov asked: "Where can he be hiding?" But Konings had not offered a single clue as to his own position. When darkness came, the two Russians crept back to their own bunker, where they argued for a long time about the German's strategy.

Before dawn, the snipers went back to their hole at the edge of no-man's-land and studied the battlefield again; Konings remained silent. Marveling at the German's patience, Zaitsev began to admire his adversary's professional skill. Fascinated with the intensity of the drama, Kulikov talked animatedly while the sun rose to the meridian and then set behind Mamaev. As another night came suddenly, the combatants went back through their own lines to get some sleep.

The third morning, Zaitsev had a new visitor, a political

agitator named Danilov, who came along to witness the contest. At first light, the heavy guns began their normal barrage and while shells whistled over their heads, the Russians eyed the landscape for a telltale presence.

Danilov suddenly raised himself up, shouting: "There he is. I'll point him out to you." Konings shot him in the shoulder. As stretcher bearers took Danilov to the hospital, Vassili Zaitsev stayed very low.

When he put his glasses back on the battlefield, he concentrated on the sector in front of him. On the left was a disabled tank, to the right a pillbox. He ignored the tank because he felt no experienced sniper would use such an exposed target. And the firing slit in the pillbox had been sealed up.

Zaitsev's glasses continued to roam. They passed over a sheet of iron and a pile of bricks lying between the tank and the pillbox. The glasses moved on, and then came back to this odd combination. For minutes Zaitsev lingered over the metal. Trying to read Konings's thoughts, he decided the innocuous rubble was a perfect hiding place.

To test his theory, Zaitsev hung a glove on the end of a piece of wood and slowly raised it above the parapet. A rifle cracked and he pulled the glove down hurriedly. The bullet had bored a hole straight through the cloth from the front. Zaitsev had been correct; Konings was under the sheet of iron.

His friend Nikolai Kulikov agreed. "There's our viper," he whispered.

The Russians backed out of their trench to find another position. Anxious to put the German sniper in a maximum amount of blinding sunlight, they followed the irregularly curving front line until they found a spot where the afternoon sun would be at their backs.

The next morning they were settled into their new nest. To their left, to the east, the Volga ferries again struggled through enemy mortar fire. To the southeast, under the piece of iron sheeting lurked their antagonist, and Kulikov fired a blind shot to arouse the German's curiosity. Then the Russians sat back contentedly. Aware that the sun would reflect on their scopes, they waited patiently for it to go down behind them. By late afternoon, now wrapped in shade, they had Konings at a disadvantage. Zaitsev focused his telescopic sight on the German's hiding place.

A piece of glass suddenly glinted at the edge of the sheet. Zaitsev motioned to Kulikov, who slowly raised his helmet over the top of the parapet. Konings fired once and Kulikov rose, screaming convincingly. Sensing triumph, the German lifted his head slightly to see his victim. Vassili Zaitsev shot him between the eyes. Konings's head snapped back and his rifle dropped from his hands. Until the sun went down, the telescopic sight glittered and gleamed. At dusk, it winked out.

Before assaulting the factory district, Paulus insisted on eliminating a Russian salient around the town of Orlovka, three miles west of the tractor works.

The order to attack that town was sent to the 60th Motorized Division, and some of its officers complained bitterly. One of them, Lt. Heinrich Klotz, thought it absurd. At forty-three, he commanded the oldest group of men on the battlefield. One-third of them had fought in World War I in which Klotz himself had been wounded.

At a briefing, when he had asked whether tanks would support the assault, his superior answered that there were none to spare. Incensed, the aging lieutenant predicted the failure of the mission. The commanding officer angrily rebuked Klotz and told him to keep his mouth shut. Sourly, he continued, "I'm sorry, gentlemen, but we have to take Orlovka."

In the gray predawn mist, Lieutenant Klotz sat in a hole and thought: This is going to end in slaughter. But when the time came to advance, he wearily waved his arm and led the old men up a hill.

Russian planes suddenly roared over the crest and trapped Klotz's company in the open. Sticks of bombs exploded and right in front of Klotz, two stretcher-bearers simply disappeared. Lying on the ground, he stared at the huge hole where they had been, but he could not see any trace of them. Meanwhile, his troops died under bombs and machine-gun strafings. When the planes left, he shouted at his men to retreat and ran back to his own lines.

That night he went out with medics to pick up the dead and wounded. For hours he called the names of friends he had led into a massacre. Of the 120 men who had gone with him that morning, only thirty returned.

At 60th Motorized Division casualty stations the surgeons worked feverishly to save lives. Almost totally recovered from his broken upper jaw, Dr. Ottmar Kohler had moved his hospital to within a half mile of the front. Stubbornly insisting that all German aid stations treat men within minutes of their being wounded, he had fought the traditions of the German Army. Operating on the victims of the Orlovka battle, Ottmar Kohler knew his radical approach was successful. He was saving men who otherwise would have died, and recently he had been inundated with postcards from convalescent patients back in Germany. All of them thanked him for keeping them alive.

The determined Kohler planned to continue his campaign with the hierarchy until every soldier wounded at Stalingrad got an equal chance to survive.

Despite local setbacks to units like Klotz's company, the "correction" at Orlovka was successful and the Russian sector quickly collapsed. But General Paulus now faced new troubles, this time within his own ranks, when he became engaged in a feud with the Luftwaffe about how the campaign was being conducted.

Gen. Freiherr von Richthofen, the acerbic, flamboyant commander of the Fourth Air Fleet, had hinted strongly that the city would have fallen long ago were it not for the timidity of the leadership of the ground forces. Paulus resented Richthofen's insinuations, and on October 3, he and General Seydlitz-Kurzbach met with the Luftwaffe general and Albert Jeschonnek, Goering's deputy. The Luftwaffe officers lamented the loss of so many men in the streets of Stalingrad. When Paulus said prompt reinforcements would bring success, the air force men seemed sympathetic, and the generals parted on amicable terms.

But later, Richthofen gave Jeschonnek his own interpretation of the problem, "What we lack is some clear thinking and a well-defined primary objective. It's quite useless to muck about around here, there, and everywhere as we are doing. And it's doubly futile, with the inadequate forces at our disposal. One thing at a time, and then all will go well—that's obvious. But we must finish off what we've started, especially at Stalingrad. . . ."

Richthofen was now questioning not only Paulus but the Führer himself, who had "mucked about" in several directions and brought on the present crisis in southern Russia.

To get the reinforcements he needed, Paulus sent a flood of cables to Army Group Headquarters about Sixth Army's forty thousand casualties in six weeks' time. As a result, Hitler sent him the 29th Motorized Division and the 14th Panzers from Hoth's Fourth Army south of Stalingrad, plus individual replacements from the Ukraine, and these troops came as green soldiers.

Their first hours in combat were especially dangerous. They had to trust their instincts, to waken their animal senses and be alert to the slightest sound or movement. If they were slow to learn, they were soon dead. In the sector held by the 9th Flak Division, six new men entered the front line one night, and one by one their curiosity led them to look at the Russian positions. By ten the next morning, four of the six had been shot through the head.

Vassili Chuikov had organized an efficient intelligence organization to keep abreast of Paulus's plans. Reconnaissance teams regularly monitored no-man's-land, checking changes in German strength. Sometimes, select groups passed through the enemy lines to spy on troop movements in the rear, and to capture prisoners.

On October 9, a four-man commando squad found refuge in an abandoned railroad coal car on a track between Mamaev Hill and the Red October workers' settlement. The Russians stayed inside the shelter most of the day, reporting back by radio now and then on German activity. They had located dozens of artillery pieces firing on the city from behind the northern slope of Mamaev; they had seen columns of German field guns and mortars moving on rear roads toward a rendezvous on the western outskirts of Stalingrad. Behind the guns came hundreds of trucks, carrying ammunition. The squad sensed a mass movement, a buildup taking place inside Sixth Army's lines. But they needed a prisoner to confirm their hunch.

After dark, the commandos snipped a telephone cable and waited for the Germans to come and repair it. A flashlight soon appeared and when the German approached the break, the Russians shot him. One of them dressed up in his uniform and stood on the railroad embankment waiting for another German to walk the wire.

Another flashlight soon moved along the track and Pvt. Willi Brandt fell into the ambush. The Russians knocked him out and he revived to find four men standing over him, asking questions, demanding prompt answers. Terrified, Brandt gave his name, rank, and unit. Further, he told his interrogators that the German 24th Panzer Division had just been shifted toward the factories, the 94th Division had arrived from southern Stalingrad, and that Adolf Hitler had ordered the city taken by October 15.

The Russians had their answer. Warning Brandt that he had betrayed military secrets, they led him back to the railroad track and pointed out the road leading to his friends. In the darkness, the trembling Brandt expected a bullet in his back. None came and he kept walking. When he was out of range, he turned and waved, calling: *"Danke, Kamerad!"*

Vassili Chuikov added the commando team's information to his maps. Now that he knew the full weight of Sixth Army was bearing down on the factories, he ordered local attacks to push the Germans off balance, to delay the inevitable. But the Sixth Army threw the Russians back every time. They were too strong.

The Stukas came at first light on the morning of October 14, and hundreds of the black planes hovered over Stalingrad. Sirens screaming, they dove again and again. Although the day was sunny, a blanket of smoke from bomb bursts cut visibility to a hundred yards.

By 11:30 A.M., after two hundred German tanks had broken through Russian defenses around the tractor works, Gen. Erwin Jaenecke's 389th Infantry Division burst into the mile-long labyrinth of shops. The works quickly became a charnel house. Millions of shards from the enormous glass skylights in the roofs littered the concrete floors, and blood smeared the walls. Cannon shells and tracer bullets ricocheted through cafeterias, and Germans and Russians lunged at each other across chairs and tables. The eight thousand commandos of the Soviet 37th Guards Division met the Germans head-on in the factory complex and in the next forty-eight hours, five thousand of them were either killed or wounded. General Zholudev himself was a casualty. Buried in rubble to his neck by a direct hit on his command post, he waited for hours until he was rescued. Later he collapsed in shock at Chuikov's headquarters when he tried to describe the annihilation of his men.

Chuikov had little time to sympathize. His entire army was in mortal danger. All telephone lines were cut. Scattered units sent runners to the riverbank asking for directions, or whether the Sixty-second Army was still functioning. Chuikov set up an emergency radio to transmit orders across the river and then relay them to isolated forces trapped in the rubble of the factories. Chuikov told each division and regiment to hold fast.

As for himself, the commander of the Sixty-second Army wondered how long he could survive. When he asked permission to send part of his staff to the safe side of the Volga, Yeremenko refused. In the meantime, thirty men around Chuikov's bunker died from shells and bullets, and his bodyguards spent hours digging victims out of wreckage and bomb holes.

Around Mamaev Hill, Soviet troops had a bird's-eye view of the intense fighting going on north of them. From his dugout Pyotr Deriabin saw German planes repeatedly diving into the billowing clouds of smoke and flame. When their bombs exploded, whole sections of the plants pirouetted into the sky before descending with dizzying velocity onto the ground and men below.

At the northwest corner of the Barrikady Gun Factory, the Russian 308th Division was pushed inside the machine shops and its commander, tall, slender Col. L. N. Gurtiev, was cut off from his troops. Chuikov sent a small party north to reestablish contact, and General Smekhotvorov led the group up the shoreline, crawling beneath the awesome fireworks display as guns on both sides of the river fired overhead. After nearly an hour, the relief squad tumbled into Gurtiev's dugout. Old friends, the general and the colonel fell into each other's arms and wept.

Across the river, General Yeremenko worried whether or not Chuikov could hold on. Sensing an increasing discouragement in the general's radio reports, Yeremenko decided to return to the west bank for a personal assessment of the situation. Chuikov warned him not to come, but Yeremenko had been through battles before and bore scars from old wounds. On the night of October 16, he and his aides went by boat across the Volga. With shells bursting all around, they touched shore near the Red October Plant. The sky was almost as bright as day from German flares as the party walked north toward Chuikov's command post. They climbed over mountains of wreckage and watched the wounded crawling past. Yeremenko stepped over them carefully and marveled at their strength in trying to make the final yards to the landing.

He missed Chuikov, who had gone with Kuzma Gurov, a member of the Military Council, to meet him at the landing. While they paced the bank and wondered what had happened to their guest, Yeremenko had traveled nearly five miles along the riverside to Sixty-second Army Headquarters. On the way, several of his aides died from bomb and shell splinters but he arrived unhurt and sat down to wait for his host to appear.

Hours later, Chuikov returned and the two men discussed imperatives. Chuikov wanted more ammunition and men, not whole divisions but replacements for decimated units. Yeremenko promised prompt action and then spoke to individual commanders about their problems. By phone he counseled Rodimtsev and Guriev, then sat beside Gen. Victor Zholudev while that normally stolid officer tried to explain how the 37th Guards had perished at the tractor plant. In the emotion of the moment, Zholudev broke down and cried as he described the annihilation of more than five thousand of his soldiers.

After Yeremenko consoled him as best he could, the front commander said good-bye to Chuikov and reaffirmed his pledge to supply him. He also ordered him to seek a less-exposed home for Sixty-second Army Headquarters.

Just before dawn on October 17, Yeremenko returned to the far shore in a better frame of mind. Chuikov had not lost his nerve even though in three days, he had lost thirteen thousand troops, nearly one quarter of his fifty-three-thousand-man army. On the night of October 14 alone, thirty-five hundred wounded had come to the Volga moorings. As these victims of the slaughter at the factories waited for rescue tugs, the river actually frothed from shells and bullets. And when some boats finally bumped ashore, not a crewman was left alive to pull the wounded on board.

Overhead, Soviet airplanes were appearing in strength for the first time. Shuttled in from other parts of Russia in the past ten days, they began to dominate the night skies over Stalingrad.

Unused to such interference, nervous German soldiers recoiled from the new menace and complained bitterly to their superiors. At Golubinka, forty miles west of the city, a Sixth Army Headquarters duty officer noted the new peril in his daily report:

> The untouchable nightly air dominance of the Russians . . . [has] increased beyond tolerance. The troops cannot rest, their strength is used to the hilt. [Our] personnel and material losses are too much in the long run. The Army asks *Heeresgruppe* [Army Group B] to order additional attacks against enemy airports daily and nightly to assist the troops fighting in the front lines.

At the three main factories north of Mamaev Hill, the Germans attacked stubbornly, trying to crush the Russians. By October 20, they had seized all of the tractor plant's shops and broken into the mammoth breastworks of the Barrikady. Further south, they occupied the western end of the Red October Plant.

In their frenzy to hurl every Russian into the Volga, the Germans even went after Jacob Pavlov's stronghold in the relatively quiet central part of Stalingrad. Four tanks came into Lenin Square, stopped and fired pointblank into the building. But the wily Pavlov was ready for them. Because the tanks could neither elevate nor depress their cannon at such close range, he had moved some of his men to the fourth floor and others to the cellar. A single shot from his lone antitank gun put one enemy panzer out of action and machine-gun fire scattered the German infantry. As the foot soldiers bolted, the tanks skidded back to safety around the corner.

Pavlov and his group had a reunion shortly thereafter on the first floor. They had held the house now for three weeks.

Chapter Twelve

The Barrikady Gun Factory was an awful place to see. In the morning sun, track rails girdling the plant shone with dampness. The dark, towering bulk of the shops was surrounded by shattered freight cars. Heaps of coral and red slag dotted the landscape. Over them hovered the smokestacks, what few were left standing, and everywhere there were shell holes, in the concrete buildings and in the ground.

Men lived in the holes, peeking out for a brief glimpse of the enemy. They had little hope of seeing their families again, of fathering sons, of embracing their parents. At the Barrikady, they just welcomed another dawn with the dew on the rails and the sun blinding them with its malevolent intensity.

Ernst Wohlfahrt, a veteran of the French campaign, had been called up with other retired soldiers to replace losses in Russia, and the former artillery sergeant was now an infantryman with the 305th Division. Lugging a walkie-talkie, a rifle, and pistol, he picked his way through the rubble of a workers' settlement. Russian *katyusha* rockets sounded overhead and as the Germans scattered desperately to avoid the "Stalin organs," the fiery comets exploded up and down the street. Wohlfahrt hugged the ground. Next to him a man screamed "Mama!" and died.

Wohlfahrt left the body and ran ahead with his company, as Russian snipers picked off single men diving in and out of cover. Exhausted, Wohlfahrt leaned against a wall to catch his breath and a Russian climbed out of a cellar to sneak up behind him. Just as he put his rifle to Wohlfahrt's ear, a German soldier came along, shoved his gun in the assailant's back, and led him away.

Wohlfahrt stopped for the night in a vacant cellar, where he carefully arranged several wooden crates around his sleeping bag and lay down. A Soviet biplane, dubbed the "sewing machine" by the Germans because of its motor pitch, droned overhead and dropped a bomb squarely on top of his hiding place. The room disintegrated and the sergeant found himself lying twenty feet away from his bed, but unhurt. The wooden crates had saved his life.

Heinz Neist had an equally sinister introduction to the factories. The thirty-one-year-old veteran had never expected to be fighting. He had plotted diligently to avoid duty in the Wehrmacht, and for years his plan had succeeded when a friendly employer placed him on the indispensable list, subject to call only in a dire emergency. But the call finally came with the invasion of Russia, and Neist went off to basic training. Until he went into action, however, he maintained a reputation as one of the least ambitious soldiers in the army.

In combat, Neist's attitude changed. He fought hard all the way across the steppe, because it had become a matter of survival, and he won the Infantry Assault Badge. Promoted to radio specialist with Combat Group Engelke, he entered the maelstrom between the Barrikady and the tractor factory and ran through a bombed-out workers' district. With ten men he plunged into the ground floor of what had once been an industrial shop. While setting up his wireless, word filtered in that some Russians had been trapped on an upper floor. The Germans threw satchel charges up the stairs but the Russians hurled them back down, wounding several Germans. Neist and his comrades were so exhausted they decided to leave the enemy alone for awhile. That night they slept two at a time, while the rest stood watch at windows, doors, and at the staircase. Upstairs, the Russians made no sound.

In the morning the battle began again. Two Russians crept down the stairs and fired bursts from tommy guns, then retreated. The Germans tried to figure out a way to retaliate; some thought of using a freight elevator in the corner, but ruled that out as too noisy. All were afraid to go up the stairway.

When Neist tried to radio headquarters, the iron girders in the room interfered with reception. Finally he managed to get through on a walkie-talkie: "This is Sea Rose," he kept repeating, and the command post broke in to acknowledge. Neist told them, "We are in the third white house . . . and we need reinforcements urgently."

The squad waited twenty-four hours before the new men came. In the meantime the Russians upstairs had been quiet. A runner brought hot coffee to Neist and his men and promised more food later in the day. From across the street, German snipers with telescopic sights tracked the Russians through the windows. Single shots rang out and Neist heard screams from above, then silence. After a few hours, the Germans cautiously moved up the dark stairwell. Outside the door, they paused. Their breath came heavily as they counted slowly and then smashed the door in. Seven Russians lay on the floor, shot to death.

Neist went down to the cellar and fell asleep. Around him the dreadful noise of battle continued without letup.

On October 24, Lt. Wilhelm Kreiser of the 100th Division celebrated his twenty-sixth birthday. While he sat in a chair, a Russian tank fired a shell that went between his legs and on into the next room. Unhurt, Kreiser stayed low the rest of the day.

The following morning, he went into action against the Barrikady where the main line of resistance was along a railway embankment. Kreiser directed his platoons into their jumping-off sections and waited for the Stukas to prepare the way. When they arrived, their bombs fell only two hundred yards ahead and Kreiser had to fire recognition flares several times to keep the Stukas from attacking his people. Despite the pinpoint bombing, the attack failed.

After dinner, Kreiser received orders for another attack and, at 10:00 A.M. on October 26, thousands of German guns laid down a drumfire on the Russian positions. Kreiser had never heard or seen anything like it. The shelling lasted for half an hour. When it stopped, silence prevailed and in the stillness German soldiers jumped up and ran across the railroad tracks and onto the cliff. Kreiser saw tracer bullets arching up from the shore and knew his men had reached their final destination, the Volga itself. The lieutenant felt the war was over, the Russians finished at last. He miscalculated badly.

Stunned by the bombardment, Soviet soldiers had burrowed into cellars and holes and waited for the enemy to pass by. The Germans, standing on the Volga cliff, now had Russians behind them.

Kreiser moved forward with several platoons to help his men trapped on the riverbank. He came to a battered schoolhouse, put his men around it on three sides and called for artillery. But the antipersonnel shells merely bounced off the thick walls. High-explosive rounds were not available.

Assuming that headquarters would send more troops past him to the Volga, Kreiser dove into a potato cellar to set up a command post. No support came. Night fell and the Germans trapped at the Volga stood their ground, firing at shadowy figures closing in on them. Only a few lived to crawl back to their own lines.

The front froze, immobile; neither side had the strength left to win.

Quartermaster Karl Binder came to the Barrikady that day, too. He had just returned from the grain silo, where he had taken out some of the precious wheat for which so many had died in September. On his way back, he noticed how much of the city had been destroyed. Almost all the smaller houses and mud cottages had been smashed. He saw Russian civilians dragging bodies into shell holes and covering them over, and Binder sensed it was going to get worse.

At the Barrikady he peered from an observation post and saw the chaos of iron rods and semifinished gun barrels lying about the railroad yards. While he stared in fascination, a German combat group advanced across open ground to take one of the factory halls. They crawled up to the doors and the windows, threw hand grenades and ran inside. Binder waited to see what would happen, but no one came out.

When he got back to his own sector he met Lieutenant Colonel Codre, who asked him his opinion of the situation at Stalingrad.

"The same as yours," Binder grunted. He now knew, as Codre had for weeks, that what was going on in Stalingrad was totally futile.

Hersch Gurewicz would have agreed. Finally released from the hospital after his awful experience on the road to Sety in August, he had walked into Stalingrad on a footbridge and gone directly into a trench south of the tractor plant. Almost immediately the lieutenant was ordered to mount an attack, and as he ran across an open stretch of ground, a German loomed in front of him with a bayonetted rifle. Gurewicz shoved his pistol in the man's face and fired. Mortally wounded, the German fell forward and imbedded the bayonet in the palm of Gurewicz's left hand.

After what seemed a long time, the German slid to the

ground and died. Gurewicz pulled his hand off the bayonet and walked off to a field hospital for more surgery. While he recuperated there, he met a nurse, fell in love and slept with her frequently. Returned to his own company, Gurewicz met her whenever she made rounds on the battlefield. Their fragile relationship made life bearable for both of them.

He had not seen her for several days when he received an urgent summons to go to an aid station at the edge of the Volga. The nurse had been hurt and was asking for him. Gurewicz scrambled out of his trench and ran to the river.

She had stepped on a land mine and lay before him, swathed in bandages. He stared at the cot, wanting to scream but unable to make a sound. She was just a torso. Both of her arms and legs had been blown away and she was dying. For long minutes Gurewicz looked at the mummified thing he had embraced and loved. Then he turned and stumbled back to his hole near the tractor factory.

Unlike Hersch Gurewicz, some Russians in Stalingrad never paused to reflect on the daily slaughter. They regarded the appalling butchery as a punitive crusade, a purgative.

Commando captain Ignacy Changar, a curly-haired, long-nosed twenty-one-year-old, had come into the city to do the job he knew best, killing Germans. Changar was an expert guerrilla fighter and preferred to work with a knife—a technique he had perfected in the forests of the Ukraine, where he spent months during the first year of the war. There he had seen the Germans at their worst and the experience affected him deeply.

Once, at the edge of a village, he watched from a tree line while two German soldiers accosted a woman, pushed her and demanded she give up her cow. When she said that other Germans had already taken it, they shoved her again. She continued to protest and the soldiers picked up her baby, grabbed a leg each and ripped the child apart.

In the woods, the stunned Changar had cursed and raised his

rifle, but a companion knocked it down and warned him not to reveal their position. During the next months, as Changar retreated across Russia, the tormented cries of that bereaved woman followed him and, by October of 1942, he was killing Germans for the sheer pleasure of it.

For ten days now he had been involved in a bizarre contest. Ordered to occupy a half-demolished building west of the Barrikady Plant, he had led fifty men into it only to find a sizable German force entrenched in a large room across a ten-foot-wide hallway.

The corridor was impassable. No one on either side dared mount a rush, and Changar tried to estimate the size of the opposition. From the babble of voices, he judged it sufficient to hold him in check.

Days went by. Food and ammunition were passed in through the windows. Changar assumed the Germans were doing the same so he ordered special equipment: spades, shovels, and 170 pounds of dynamite.

The Russians broke through the concrete floor and started a tunnel. Digging two at a time, they slowly worked a passageway under the corridor. To mask the noise of the tools, they sang songs at the top of their voices. The Germans also burst into song from time to time, and Changar immediately figured the enemy was planning to blow him up, too.

On the eleventh day, Changar ordered a halt to further excavation. After carefully placing the dynamite at the end of the tunnel, he cut and lined a fuse along the dirt passage up into the main room.

The Germans were singing again, and someone on the other side of the hall had added a harmonica as accompaniment. While his men sang a last lusty ballad, Captain Changar lit the fuse and hollered to the two men still in the hole to "run like hell."

With the fuse sputtering, everyone tumbled out the low windows and scattered hastily across the yard, but the explosion came too quickly. It picked them up and hurled them down again with stunning force. The shaken Changar looked back to see the strongpoint rising slowly into the air. It expanded outward, then broke into hundreds of pieces. A huge ball of fire catapulted up from the debris.

He rose and called for his men. Only two had failed to get clear, the men who had been in the hole. Changar realized he had cut the fuse too short and he worried about the error until the next day, when he went back to examine his handiwork. He counted three hundred sixty legs before he lost interest and left, satisfied that the 180 dead Germans were a partial payment for his error.

Further south near the Red October Plant, sniper Vassili Zaitsev stalked the front lines. By now he had killed nearly a hundred Germans and had been decorated with the Order of Lenin. His fame was spreading to all parts of the Soviet Union.

Furthermore, his students had amassed a formidable number of victims. Men like Viktor Medvedev and Anatoli Chekhov made the Germans afraid to lift their heads during daylight hours. And sharpshooter Tania Chernova now fired a rifle with unerring accuracy. Almost forty Germans had died in her sights, victims she continued to refer to as "sticks." But Tania still had much to learn.

In the top story of a building, she settled down behind piles of bricks to monitor enemy traffic. Several other student snipers joined her as she waited for hours, tracking Germans who scurried back and forth between trenches. Tania and her squad followed each one with scopes zeroed in on heads and hearts. But no one fired, because Zaitsev had told them to wait for his approval before revealing their position.

Tania seethed at the order. Filled with disgust at having lost so many "sticks," she fidgeted at the window and cursed the delay. When a column of German infantrymen suddenly burst into the open, she screamed: "Shoot!" and the room blazed with gunfire. Tania pumped shot after shot into the gray green uniforms and counted seventeen dead men sprawled on the pavement. Exultant, she sat back and exchanged congratulations with her friends.

But they had missed some Germans, who crawled back to their lines with exact coordinates of Tania's ambush. In minutes, a succession of shellbursts blew the building in on the Russians. Tania left the dead and ran out to tell Vassili Zaitsev what had happened.

When he heard the distraught girl's story, Zaitsev slapped her across the face with all his strength, berated her for her stupidity, and told her that she alone was responsible for the deaths of her friends. Stricken with guilt and afraid of Zaitsev's wrath, Tania cried for hours.

In downtown Stalingrad, the static war continued, and outside Jacob Pavlov's stronghold, decomposing bodies attested to his ferocious defense of the apartment house he had entered a month earlier. The Germans left him alone for short periods but they always came back, so in between battles, he set up an artillery spotting post on the fourth floor, protecting it with snipers who worked during daylight hours to keep the Germans down and nervous. On all battle maps at Sixty-second Army Headquarters, the house in no-man's-land was now referred to as *"Dom Pavlov"* ("Pavlov's House"), and it had become both an integral fortification and a rallying point. Troops verified observations by saying that the Germans were seen moving two hundred yards west of Pavlov's House; German tanks were reported one hundred yards north of Pavlov's House. At General Rodimtsev's command post in a battered grain mill, one hundred yards from the Volga, his staff watched the nightly tracer duels erupting around that outpost and felt a surge of satisfaction.

Underground tunnels had been dug from several directions into the house and Pavlov, the stocky, simple peasant, felt more and more like a division commander as he radioed back information. Given the code name "Lighthouse" by Rodimtsev, he reveled in his new-found importance.

Chapter Thirteen

On October 27, at 376th Division Headquarters on the left flank of the Sixth Army, generals Paulus and Schmidt sat listening to an intense, nervous intelligence officer. They paid rapt attention, for the young lieutenant, Karl Ostarhild, was warning them of imminent disaster.

Though awed by the presence of such illustrious superiors, Ostarhild briefed them with the confidence born of a complete grasp of his subject. He had spent weeks assembling his data from snooper planes, prisoners, visual observations, and radio intercept and had no doubts about his information.

"We have seen a large number of men and material concentrated in the region of Kletskaya," Ostarhild said, outlining the danger to the north. "Our order to make reconnaissance of this concentration was fulfilled. . . . This is an attack army, armed to the teeth, and of considerable size. We have information about the units . . . their armaments, where they come from, up to the names of their commanders. We also know their attack plans, which extend to the Black Sea."

Seemingly unmoved, Paulus brusquely asked for supporting

documents. When he finished reading them, he asked: "Is this information known to my intelligence?" Advised by Schmidt that it was, though in less detail, Paulus told his worried advisers he would ask for more reserves to strengthen the defense.

After Paulus departed, the frustrated Ostarhild went back to his maps. He had done everything he could to alert the "brains" of the Sixth Army, but he wondered whether they had really grasped the enormity of the danger.

Back at Golubinka, General Paulus issued an unusual proclamation to his troops:

1. The summer and fall offensive is successfully terminated after taking Stalingrad . . . the Sixth Army has played a significant role and held the Russians in check. The actions of the leadership and the troops during the offensive will enter into history as an especially glorious page.
2. Winter is upon us . . . the Russians will take advantage of it.
3. It is unlikely that the Russians will fight with the same strength as last winter. . . .

Having heard Ostarhild's briefing, Friedrich von Paulus seemed to be whistling his way past the graveyard. Actually, he was dismayed at the bloodbath his soldiers had endured, and disgusted at himself for not having taken all of Stalingrad in September, but he continued to keep a death-grip on the ruins along the Volga, while trusting Hitler to guard his flanks.

On November 1, however, he endured another punishing attack by the Luftwaffe's self-appointed "devil's advocate" when air force general, Freiherr von Richthofen, confronted him again at Golubinka. Richthofen complained that the infantry was not taking advantage of the support given them by the Stukas and Junker bombers, and the harried Paulus argued back that he was hobbled by lack of men and ammunition.

The Luftwaffe general dismissed the rebuttal, saying he personally would use his influence to get any needed supplies, and continued with a lecture: "The real explanation is to be found in the weariness of both the troops and command and in that rigid Army conservatism, which still accepts without demur one thousand men in the front line out of a ration strength of twelve thousand, and which leads to the generals being content to merely issue orders. ¿. .."

Refusing to be drawn into a shouting match, Paulus rejected Richthofen's charge and calmly repeated his glaring deficiencies in manpower and ammunition. The self-control Paulus exhibited was a mistake, for Richthofen flew back to his own base convinced that Paulus knew he was in error but could not admit it.

North of the Don, the Russian forces continued their buildup. They moved at night, in long trains which came from the Moscow area and the Urals, carrying more than two hundred thousand troops. Heavy artillery, hundreds of tanks, nearly ten thousand cavalry horses, were being carried on flatcars of the single-track rail line running toward the Serafimovich and Kletskaya assembly points, 100 to 125 miles northwest of Stalingrad. Russian political officers worked tirelessly to infuse the troops with fanaticism. Each new soldier stood before the banners of his regiment and received his weapon in a formal ceremony. Martial songs were sung, and party officials read speeches on the need for devotion to the Motherland. Impressed by the panoply, most soldiers went back to their units "armed to the spiritual teeth."

As the men and material moved inexorably toward the front, the Germans could not fail to see their spoor. Russian deserters told astonished interrogators of the arrival of divisions and armies not only on the Don but also to the south of Stalingrad oppsite the German Fourth Tank Army, in the Beketovka and Tzatza Lake sector. Intelligence officers like Karl Ostarhild put these reports together, buttressed them with visual sightings and monitoring intercepts, and came to the obvious conclusion: The enemy was about to attack from both flanks.

Even the Axis "puppet" allies were sounding the alarm. By

the second week in October, the Rumanian Third Army had fully established itself in positions along the Sixth Army's left flank at the Don. Almost immediately, Rumanian intelligence verified what Lt. Karl Ostarhild had told Paulus. When Rumanian general Dumitrescu demanded to know what the German Army was going to do about it, the matter was forwarded to East Prussia for Adolf Hitler's response. In the meantime, the hawk-nosed Dumitrescu seethed over another matter. His army had been forced to take over some sectors formerly guarded by the Italians, and each of his seven divisions now had to cover twelve-mile-wide fronts. With meager reserves to back up these thinly stretched units, Dumitrescu felt the situation presented an intolerable risk. When he protested to the Germans, they asked him to bear with the problem.

In Stalingrad, Vassili Chuikov directed his own war from a new, invulnerable command post. The German attacks on the factories in October had forced him to leave his fourth headquarters in seven weeks. With his trench dugout reduced to smoldering timbers, he had retreated south along the Volga to the rear of the 284th Division, where engineers had just blasted a T-shaped tunnel into the cliff on the west bank to house divisional staff offices. It had been bored thirty feet deep into the rock, and was forty feet beneath the surface. He immediately requisitioned it and moved in.

If he had finally gained a sanctuary, it was his only comfort, for his army had nearly disappeared. The hand-to-hand fighting for the factories had wiped out battalions, regiments, even entire divisions. Colonel Gorishny's 95th Division had to be divided into other units. The few men from Zholudev's elite 37th Guards went into the 118th Regiment of Colonel Ivan Ilyich Lyudnikov's 138th Division. Lyudnikov also received driblets from Gurtiev's 308th Division, which was massacred at the Barrikady. From groups which had come into Stalingrad seven to eight thousand strong, only a few hundred straggled away to fight under new commanders.

From his intelligence, Chuikov knew that Paulus was planning yet another offensive against the factories. At that moment the 44th Division, the famous *Hoch und Deutschmeister* from Austria, was moving across German rear positions in a northeasterly direction. Its destination was the Barrikady. To counter the threat, Chuikov desperately reshuffled his troops, while calling across the river to ask Yeremenko for more help.

But Stalingrad Front Headquarters was busy funneling troops and supplies into the Beketovka region south of Stalingrad for the upcoming counterattack. In their conversation, General Yeremenko warned Chuikov he had to occupy the Germans in the city so that Paulus could not shift his forces to the flanks.

Yeremenko's order answered a question Chuikov had been asking himself for some time. Why had the Germans failed to support their flanks? On the right shore of the Volga, the massed Russian artillery which had backed up Chuikov's Sixty-second Army so well in recent weeks, had weakened noticeably as the Soviet High Command pulled out batteries for duty elsewhere. Since Chuikov had noticed the lessened firepower, he assumed the Germans must have, too, and therefore drawn similar conclusions about the withdrawal.

He had also noticed something else, something more disturbing. Chunks of ice, "sludge," had started to drift by on the Volga. The appearance of these floes triggered an alarm bell at Sixty-second Army Headquarters. Until the ice stopped moving and formed a solid bridge to the far shore, supply boats could not navigate through the rampaging floes. Such a situation could be disastrous for the Russians in Stalingrad.

Chapter Fourteen

The twenty-fifth anniversary of the Bolshevik Revolution fell on November 7, and Joseph Stalin spoke to his people to tell them that eight million Germans had been killed in the "Great Patriotic War." Though that figure was inflated by more than six million, another remark he made was more accurate. The premier prophesied, "Soon there will be a holiday in our streets, too."

But as the Russian people mourned the deaths of millions of relatives in the past seventeen months of war, they saw little reason to anticipate a "holiday." Hungry and exhausted, only temporarily buoyed by the fact that the Germans had not yet seized the Caucasus and Stalingrad, they dared not dream that anything would ever make them want to laugh and dance again.

In Germany, the nine-year-old Third Reich was also celebrating an anniversary. At the Löwenbräukeller in Munich, workers draped enormous swastika flags across the arches to the main hall. Massive gold eagles hung above the speaker's rostrum on the flower-banked stage. Officials stomped about, nervously supervising every arrangement for the gala event. They fretted over petty details and harangued everyone with the need for perfection. For Adolf Hitler was the guest of honor, to meet with his old friends and reminisce about the days of the Beer Hall Putsch in 1923.

His special train was rolling through the hilly country of Thuringia. It made slow time. Allied air raids had damaged the tracks, and troop trains frequently slowed its passage. During the evening of November 7, Hitler discussed the day's major news with several aides in his dining car. Agents had reported from Spain that Allied convoys were steaming past Gibraltar into the Mediterranean. No one knew their destination, but Hitler was fascinated with the bold maneuver. Almost like a disinterested party, he tried to project himself into Allied deliberations.

While dinner was served on exquisite china, the train stopped once more at a siding. A few feet away, a hospital train marked time, and from their tiered cots, wounded soldiers peered into the blazing light of the dining room where Hitler was immersed in conversation. Suddenly he looked up at the awed faces staring in at him. In great anger he ordered the curtains drawn, plunging his wounded warriors back into the darkness of their own bleak world.

All evening long, as his train traveled through the neat fields of Bavaria, Hitler kept fantasizing about the enemy's plans and concluded that if he were they, he'd occupy Rome immediately. What could stop them? But as he went to bed near dawn, American and British troops were pouring ashore in Morocco and Algeria. Their goal was a junction with Gen. Bernard Montgomery's Eighth British Army, fresh from its triumph over Rommel at El Alamein in Egypt.

The next day, Hitler ignored the disastrous news and entered the Munich Löwenbräukeller to a throaty animal roar of obeisance. Among his old beer-drinking cronies, who chanted the words to the Nazi party song, *"Horst Wessel,"* he warmed to the occasion.

Wearing the uniform of the "brownshirts," a swastika band adorning his left arm, he stood proudly on the platform and accepted the salute: "*Sieg Heil! Sieg Heil! Sieg Heil!*" Then the Führer launched into a rousing speech. He hit out at the British: "They will find out . . . that the German inventive spirit has not been idle, and they will get an answer [to air raids on Germany] which will take their breaths away." He scoffed at the landings in Africa: "The enemy moves forward and back, but what matters is the final result, and that you can leave to us."

When he spoke about Stalingrad, he became almost coquettish: "I wanted to take it—and you know we are modest—we really have it. There are only a very few small places left there. Now the others say: 'Why don't you make faster progress?' Because I don't want to create a second Verdun . . . but prefer to do the job with small shock troop units. . . ."

His cronies rocked the Löwenbräukeller with cheers.

Luftwaffe general Freiherr von Richthofen had been instrumental in getting these "small shock troop units" to Stalingrad. After his outburst against Paulus, he had intervened with General Jeschonnek and persuaded him to influence Hitler to release the elite combat engineers for the final assault. Grasping at any straw, the Führer had readily agreed to their use and had convinced himself that these reinforcements would eliminate all organized Soviet resistance along the Volga shoreline. Thus, while he traveled to meet with his cronies in Munich, the five battalions of "pioneers," as they were called, packed hurriedly for the journey to Stalingrad.

Near Voronezh, three hundred miles west of the city, cook Wilhelm Giebeler loaded his kitchen equipment onto a train. Around him, troops of the 336th Battalion grumbled loudly about their new assignment while they checked out flamethrowers, machine pistols, and satchel charges of dynamite. Giebeler had heard their griping before, on the eve of every special "dirty job." But since the pioneers were consummate professionals at street fighting, he had no worries about their morale nor doubt as to their success at the Volga.

When the 336th reached Stalingrad, Maj. Josef Linden was there to greet them. Put in charge of the operation by pioneer chief, Col. Herbert Selle, Linden had reported to Point X on November 7, at 0900 hours. Point X was just across the street from the Barrikady and, once there, the major scouted the terrain between the factory and the Volga. Never before had he seen so ghastly a setting for battle. "Loosely hanging corrugated steel panels which creaked eerily in the wind . . . a perfect mess of iron parts, gun barrels, T-beams, huge craters . . . cellars turned into strongpoints . . . over all a never-ceasing crescendo of noise from all types of guns and bombs."

Inside the Barrikady itself, Maj. Eugen Rettenmaier, recently back from a two-week furlough in Germany, checked his four companies and found only thirty-seven men left out of four hundred. To his questions about missing individuals, he got the same answers over and over: killed, wounded, presumed dead.

Within hours, one six-hundred-man battalion of the pioneers came under Rettenmaier's wing. The other four battalions spread out along the main line of resistance and prepared for a coordinated assault on the area behind the Barrikady to the Volga.

Major Rettenmaier listened intently to their extraordinary briefing. Two Russian strongpoints had to be taken: one, the Chemist's Shop on the left side of a row of partially completed houses; the other, the Commissar's House or "Red House," several hundred yards west of the Chemist's Shop and somewhat nearer the Volga bank. The Red House, a clumsy brick fortress, dominated the gently sloping terrain.

The pioneers asked questions about the buildings and the cliff along the river. They were brisk, businesslike, but when Rettenmaier and others tried to explain that the Russians in Stalingrad fought a different kind of war, that they hid in cellars and used the sewer systems to good advantage, the pioneers said they had seen the worst already, in places like Voronezh. They were prepared for such tactics.

After midnight on November 9, the combat groups assembled

in the machine shops of the Barrikady. Straining under the burden of satchel charges, shovels, grenades, and bandoliers of bullets, they shuffled through the gloom to their starting points.

In several large rooms at the eastern end of the factory, they waited for the signal to burst out onto open ground. Some men smoked furtively. Sgt. Ernst Wohlfahrt was a tense spectator. A virtual prisoner inside the Barrikady for weeks, he did not envy the pioneers their job. He himself had spent days hiding behind brick walls, afraid to raise his head. The Russians had never let him feel secure and he was pessimistic about the coming battle, despite the pioneers' cocky self-assurance.

Then a shattering explosion engulfed an adjacent room. Screams welled up and Wohlfahrt rushed in to find eighteen pioneers dead from a Russian booby trap. The survivors were suddenly subdued, fearful.

At 3:30 A.M., German artillery fire passed over and down onto Russian lines, bringing their counterfire. When the German fire lifted, the pioneers moved onto open ground, lit by eerie flashes of gunfire. Watching them go across the cratered moonscape, Major Rettenmaier silently wished them Godspeed.

The Chemist's Shop fell without trouble. But at the Commissar's House, the engineers had walked into a trap. Every opening had been sealed up by debris, and from tiny peepholes, the Russians shot with deadly accuracy. Further south, Regiment 576 quickly reached the Volga, but again the Russians held on, stealing into caves and cracks, and the engineers rolled grenades down at them. The explosives bounced harmlessly by the openings and on into the Volga.

The next morning, when pioneers of the 50th Battalion finally broke into the Commissar's House, the Russians ran into the cellars. In a frenzy, the Germans tore up the floor, threw in cans of gasoline, and ignited them. Then they lowered satchel charges and detonated them. Smoke cartridges were laid down to blind anyone surviving the blasts and flames. From the outside, the house seeped smoke. Detonations shook the ground as the cellar broke apart under the blast, and a messenger ran across the field to tell Major Rettenmaier that the Commissar's House was in German hands.

But on the edge of the Volga, the engineers who had reached the shore line the day before discovered they had won a Pyrrhic victory. Of the group on the riverbank, only one man was not wounded. A large patrol went out to give aid, and within three hours it was reduced to three men.

Col. Herbert Selle had been fully confident that his pioneers could take the last bits of contested soil in Stalingrad. Within days, however, he knew the truth. The five battalions, numbering nearly three thousand men, had lost a third of their forces. Selle gave orders to collect the remnants of the battalions and form them into one effective combat group for further attacks.

In a letter to his family he acknowledged the tragic waste: "There will be many tears in Germany. . . . Happy is he who is not responsible for these unwarranted sacrifices." For Selle, Stalingrad was no longer worth the price. He felt the battle had degenerated into a personal struggle between the egos of Stalin and Hitler.

Nevertheless, the pioneers had dealt the Russians a stunning blow. Col. Ivan Ilyich Lyudnikov's 138th Division had been trapped on the shore and held a shrinking pie-shaped slice of land only four hundred yards wide and one hundred yards deep. In front of it lay the dead of the 118th Regiment, which had met the pioneers on the open ground and in the rows of partially destroyed houses. Only six of its 250 soldiers escaped to refuge inside the wedge. Lyudnikov's forces now numbered only several hundred men and women capable of resistance, and he radioed Sixty-second Army Headquarters for help.

In Moscow, the Russian General Staff pursued its strategy. Overjoyed that the Germans continued to rivet their attention on the ruins near the Volga bank, STAVKA speeded up the movements of men and supplies to the flanks.

It also called on its espionage networks for new information:

November 11, 1942
To Dora: [Lucy Network in Switzerland]
Where are the rear defense locations of the Germans on the southwest of Stalingrad and along the Don? Are defense positions being built on sectors Stalingrad-Kletskaya and Stalingrad-Kalach? Their characteristics? . . .

The Director

Thus the Russians collected almost every scrap of intelligence they needed. Some of it came from personal observations by the mastermind, Georgi Zhukov, who cabled Stalin his impressions from the front:

Number 4657
November 11, 1942
I have just spent two days with Yeremenko. I . . . examined enemy positions facing the 51st and 57th Armies . . . I gave instructions for further reconnaissance and work on the operations plan on the basis of information obtained . . . it is urgent that the 51st and 57th Armies be provided with warm outfits and ammunition no later than November 14.

Konstantinov
[Zhukov's code name]

Finally the German High Command made a move to guard its flanks. The 48th Panzer Corps, stationed more than fifty miles southwest of the ominous Russian bridgeheads at Kletskaya and Serafimovich on the Don, received priority orders to move up to the threatened sector.

Led by Lt. Gen. Ferdinand Heim, a close friend and former aide to Paulus, the 48th clanked onto the roads and headed northeast. But only a few miles after starting out, the column ground to a halt when several tanks caught fire. In others, motors kept misfiring and finally refused to run at all. Harried mechanics swarmed over the machines and quickly found the answer. During the weeks of inactivity behind the lines, field mice had nested inside the vehicles and eaten away insulation covering the electrical systems. Days behind schedule, the 48th Corps finally limped into its new quarters. It was almost totally crippled. Out of one hundred four tanks in the 22nd Panzer Division, only forty-two were ready for combat.

No one notified Hitler about the status of his reserves.

General Richthofen was doing what he could to harass the Soviet buildup. He sent his planes to the Kletskaya and Serafimovich bridgehead areas to hit rail lines and troop concentrations. But the Russians kept coming across the thinly frozen Don on pontoon bridges, some of them laid a foot beneath the river's surface to hide them from accurate artillery fire and dive-bombers.

Discouraged and frustrated, Richthofen confided his fears to his diary:

> November 12. The Russians are resolutely carrying on with their preparations for an offensive against the Rumanians. . . . Their reserves have now been concentrated. When, I wonder, will the attack come?. . . Guns are beginning to make their appearance in artillery emplacements. I can only hope that the Russians won't tear too many big holes in the line!

On their narrow wedge of land on the Volga, the 138th Red Army Division kept in touch by radio with army headquarters further down the river. Colonel Lyudnikov talked openly, without code. Neither Chuikov nor he mentioned the other's name. Chuikov promised help but had no idea where to find it.

Lyudnikov understood his superior's predicament. He had only to look behind him at the moving ice pack coming downstream to realize that Chuikov himself was in trouble. Boats could not navigate through the floes; all footbridges had been torn away; supplies were being cut back drastically.

Burrowed into the sides of the ravine where Lyudnikov's

remnants held on, four men, known to their comrades as the Rolik group, challenged the German pioneers. When the Germans hung over the steep embankment and let down satchel charges of dynamite, the Rolik men snipped the wires dangling in front of them and the explosives dropped into the Volga. The group shot back at the Nazis as Lyudnikov's men listened intently to the sounds of the struggle. When Rolik was quiet "everyone trembled." When the shooting resumed, shouts were heard: "Rolik's firing! Rolik's firing!" The word passed from trench to trench and buoyed the Russians immensely.

On November 14, Chuikov reported to Front Headquarters: "No ships arrived at all. Deliveries of supplies have fallen through for three days running. Reinforcements have not been ferried across, and our units are feeling an acute shortage of ammunition and rations. . . . The drifting ice has completely cut communications with the left bank."

Chapter Fifteen

On November 15, the newspaper *Das Reich* carried an article by Dr. Joseph Goebbels, Hitler's minister of propaganda, that signalled a significant shift in thinking. Goebbels had decided to prepare the German people for any eventuality—including disaster in Russia.

"We have thrown the national existence into the balance," he wrote. "There is no turning back now."

Meanwhile, Marshals Zhukov and Vasilevsky shuttled back and forth between Moscow and the Stalingrad fronts. They walked the terrain, spotted artillery targets and German troop concentrations for special attention, and met with their generals to refine tactics.

During Zhukov's visit to General Vatutin's command post north of the Don River bridgeheads at Serafimovich and Kletskaya, Stalin reached him with an important telegram:

November 15, 1942
Comrade Konstantinov: *Personal*
    You can set the moving date for Federov and Ivanov [the offensives by Vatutin and Yeremenko] as you see fit, and let me know when you come back to Moscow. If you

think it necessary that either one or the other move one or two days earlier or later, I empower you to decide that question according to your own best judgment.

Vasilyev [Stalin's code name]

Zhukov and Vasilevsky checked their preparations on both fronts and agreed to begin the counterattack in the northern sector on November 19, and on the southern front a day later. Stalin approved the plan without comment.

Operation Uranus would commence within ninety-six hours.

From the Obersalzburg, where he had been resting since the Beer Hall Speech, Adolf Hitler radioed a message to Sixth Army Headquarters on the steppe:

> I know about the difficulties of the battle for Stalingrad and about the loss of troops. With the ice drifting on the Volga, however, the difficulties are even greater for the Russians. Making use of this [time] span we will avoid a bloodbath later on. I expect therefore that the Supreme Command, with all its repeatedly proven energy, and the troops, with their courage often demonstrated, will do their utmost to break through to the Volga at the metallurgical works and at the gun factory and occupy these parts of town.

In accordance with Hitler's orders, the pioneers turned right and left along the Volga and tried to roll up the fanatical defense behind the Barrikady. The battle lasted all day and on that night, two Soviet biplanes came up the river at only a fifty-foot altitude and hovered over Lyudnikov's position. A circle of bonfires lit by the trapped Russians illuminated the small area in which it was safe to drop supplies. But as the pilots prepared to unload bales of food from their open cockpits, the Germans lit another chain of bonfires to confuse them. Since the pilots were unable to gauge the extent of Lyudnikov's territory, most of the supplies they dropped fell into German lines or sank in the Volga.

At a field kitchen in the rear, west of the Barrikady, cook Wilhelm

Giebeler waited for news of his 336th Battalion. Ever since the battle for the factory district began, a friend, a dispatch runner, had kept him informed of the action at the front. The first day, he had come back and told him everything was going well; the next he had returned with snapshots, letters, and other personal effects of men Giebeler had known well. He told the cook to send them on to their next of kin. By now Giebeler had hundreds of small bundles to mail back to Germany.

Listening to the symphony of shells and grenades exploding to the east, he thumbed through the letters and pictures and waited for his friend to make his nightly visit. But the man did not appear. Giebeler never saw him again—nor any other soldiers of the 336th Battalion.

General von Richthofen had not given up his feud with Sixth Army Headquarters. In a telephone conversation with Chief of Staff Kurt Zeitzler at Rastenburg on the night of November 16, the outspoken Luftwaffe commander exploded:

"Both the command and the troops are so listless . . . we shall get nowhere. . . . Let us either fight or abandon the attack altogether. If we can't clear up the situation now, when the Volga is blocked and the Russians are in real difficulty, we shall never be able to. The days are getting shorter and the weather worse."

Zeitzler agreed.

The weather, indeed, was getting worse. It had changed dramatically, as it always does on the steppe, which knows only one extreme or the other: light or dark, abundance or famine, cruel heat or numbing cold, life or death—everything or nothing.

Warm weather had lasted through October, then it turned cold overnight. At first, drizzles drenched the plains. Then snow flurries whipped the barren land. The steppe grass turned brown, and wilted. Men caught in the open turned their collars up to ward off the chill. The sky no longer blazed with iridescent hues; it was sullen, gray, menacing. It whispered of winter.

The quartermasters of Sixth Army had learned bitter lessons from the previous year and had already dug into the many *balkas* cutting across the plain. In the sides of these deep ravines, they had stockpiled food and ammunition, and thousands of bunkers had been constructed to shield the soldiers from the icy winds. Determined not to be caught again without proper clothing and other necessities, the quartermasters requisitioned additional reserves from the German pipeline stretching back to Kharkov, nearly four hundred miles away.

Along the railroads leading to Stalingrad, ten depots had laid in stocks for both Sixth Army and the German panzer groups bogged down in the Caucasus. But moving the supplies east was difficult, for Russian partisans had received orders to impede enemy traffic to the Don and Volga. As bridges and track blew up in fiery explosions, the supply line from Kharkov to Stalingrad clogged, cleared, and clogged again.

Fortunately, the warehouses at Chir, a railhead only sixty miles west of Stalingrad bulged with appropriate items and as the first frosts touched the steppe in early November, some units of the Sixth Army received warm clothing. Convoys of trucks trailed back and forth across the steppe, bringing winter gear to German soldiers. Other convoys managed to get through with badly needed replacements for infantry regiments and battalions.

Pvt. Ekkehart Brunnert had boarded a troop train at the town of Boblingen in Germany, waved farewell to his wife, Irene, and watched her out of sight. Surrounded by fourteen comrades, the private quickly adjusted to the camaraderie of soldierly life. The train rolled eastward for endless days and, as it moved through the Ukraine, signs of war multiplied. Brunnert saw burned-out villages and railroad cars reduced to skeletal wrecks. He and his comrades decided to post guards at night, but the partisans never attacked and, weeks after leaving Boblingen, the unit arrived at Chir. There, Brunnert pitched a tent and when he got up in the morning, he saw everything covered with frost. He also saw thousands of Russian refugees headed toward Germany and labor camps. They lay in clusters on flatcars. Most wore rags; some munched sunflower seeds, their only food. In the fields around the tracks other Russians picked through garbage heaps for bits of decaying food. Brunnert was shocked at the sight.

He waited at Chir until he got orders to join a truckload of twenty-four men headed toward the front line. On all sides there was only dreary steppe country. On the eastern horizon, a deep and steady roar made the earth tremble.

To most Sixth Army soldiers, the persistent rumbling on the horizon was their only contact with the horror on the banks of the Volga. For the more than two hundred thousand men in the rear echelons, the killing was just a peripheral event they viewed in brief agonizing moments: the wounded screaming as they were manhandled out of ambulances, the stained and torn uniforms that piled up in grotesque mounds outside surgeons' tents, the thousands of crosses in regimental graveyards on the desolate prairie.

At Peskavotka Depot, forty miles northwest of Stalingrad, Karl Englehardt distributed equipment and food. He also supervised twenty *Hiwis* (Hilfsfreiwilliger), or "work volunteers," the name given to Russian defectors. Understandably, Red Army soldiers particularly hated these *Hiwis*, and invariably shot any that they caught. Englehardt, a lean, sallow-faced veteran, had collected the laborers through his kindness to their leader, a peasant named Peter, whom he had found cowering in a schoolhouse. Incredibly filthy and frightened for his life, Peter had turned to Englehardt as a savior when the German gave him a tin of water and some hot soup. From then on Peter worshipped the paymaster.

He brought other Russians in from the steppe and offered their services to Englehardt, who dressed them in German uniforms, fed them the same rations as Wehrmacht soldiers, and paid them for their labor.

Friedrich Breining went out with his unit to search abandoned dwellings for extra food, firewood, and anything else of value. When they came to a wrecked house, Breining went up to the front door and pushed it open. On the floor lay a woman, and beside her a child, a little girl. Both bodies had partially decomposed, but Breining could tell that the mother had once been quite pretty. Neither corpse bore any visible marks.

Other soldiers asked him what was wrong and the former schoolteacher pointed wordlessly to the gruesome sight on the floor. No one made a move to enter. Breining closed the door softly and left.

Veterinarian Herbert Rentsch was making plans to send another four hundred horses back to the Ukraine for rest. He had also begun substituting small Russian horses, *panjes,* for the big Belgian draft animals. Rentsch knew the native *panjes* would work better in the approaching winter.

The doctor still found time to canter his own horse, Lore, over the steppe. The mare was sleek and well groomed and Rentsch rode her every day. He found the exercise exhilarating.

Fifty miles northwest of Stalingrad, Sgt. Gottlieb Slotta returned to the 113th Division after confinement in a hospital. Weeks before, when he had spotted Russian tanks bearing down on his gun battery, he had screamed a warning to his friends. But one of them laughed derisively and yelled back: "Slotta, whenever the Russians shoot, you're afraid."

With the T-34 tanks chasing him, Slotta had run toward his comrades to urge them to take cover. The Russian shells got there first and Slotta saw his companions blown apart. Sobbing bitterly, he fell to the ground and went into shock. Unable to speak, he was taken to the rear, where he spent weeks trying to forget that nightmarish day when no one listened to him. In time, he was returned to his job as an artillery observer and now, as the chill Arctic winds tugged at him, Slotta resumed his watch for more Russian tanks.

Emil Metzger also worried about Russian tanks. Despite the lieutenant's disdain for rumors, he had begun to pay close attention to the pilots of the artillery spotter planes, who spoke to him each day. These veteran reconnaissance men told him that they had seen hundreds of Russian T-34 tanks moving along roads above the river toward the area of Kletskaya, seventy miles northwest. The aviators' genuine alarm about the enemy buildup caused Metzger to temper his optimism about a quick end to the battle and a trip home to Kaethe.

To maintain morale, Sixth Army had established a precise schedule for furloughs of twenty days, with two extra days for travel contingencies. Pvt. Franz Deifel had just finished a trip to Stuttgart, revisiting the Porsche plant where he had been a master upholsterer. His former supervisor told him that papers had already been filed to release him from the army for civilian employment. Richer by two hundred Reich marks given him by fellow workers at the factory, the elated Deifel passed through Kharkov and headed toward Chir at the Don.

Capt. Gerhard Meunch was also returning to the front. During the short visit with his wife, he had tried to forget the slaughter around the U-shaped house in the center of Stalingrad. But it was impossible, and just before leaving home, Meunch told his wife he had an insurance policy for her in case he failed to return this time from the Volga.

Under forty feet of solid earth, Gen. Vassili Chuikov still maintained his precarious hold on ten percent of Stalingrad. Behind him, ice floes made the Volga impassable and Chuikov was happy he had requisitioned twelve tons of chocolate for just such an emergency. If the Volga failed to freeze over soon, he figured a ration of half a bar a day for each man could mean their holding out two weeks longer.

While his army tried to ride out the crisis caused by the cutting of the regular supply lines, the soldiers of Batyuk's 284th Division around Mamaev Hill witnessed an extraordinary mini-war over some of those supplies. Every Russian soldier received a daily ration of one hundred grams of vodka. Most waited for it eagerly; only a few refused it. But Senior Lt. Ivan Bezditko, "Ivan the Terrible" to his men, had an incredible taste for vodka and found a way to keep a plentiful supply on hand. When troops from his mortar battalion died, Ivan reported them "present and accounted for," and pirated their daily vodka rations. In a short time, the thirsty officer amassed many gallons, which he carefully stored in his own dugout.

In a warehouse at the Volga shore, a supply officer, Major Malygin, checked his records and noticed that Bezditko's unit had borne up extremely well under weeks of bombardment. Suspicious, Malygin pursued the matter and discovered that the mortar section had actually suffered heavy casualties. He called Bezditko, told him he had exposed his petty scheme, and was going to report him to Front Headquarters. Then he added, "Your vodka ration is being canceled."

The supply officer had gone too far. Bezditko screamed, "If I don't get it, you'll get it."

Malygin hung up on him, relayed news of the crime to headquarters and shut off Ivan's liquor rations.

Enraged, Bezditko contacted the firing point for his .122-millimeter batteries, issued a precise set of coordinates, and gave the order to shoot. Three rounds dropped squarely on top of Malygin's warehouse at the riverbank, and out of the smoke and debris tottered the shaken major. Behind him hundreds of bottles of vodka had broken and spilled onto the floor. Malygin staggered to a phone and asked for headquarters. His anger rising, he shouted out what he knew to be true: Ivan the Terrible had gotten him.

The voice on the other end was patient but unsympathetic, "Next time give him his vodka. He just got the Order of the Red Star, so give it to him."

The incredulous Malygin stormed back to his warehouse and stood helplessly in the midst of the shattered rows of spirits. Within hours, Lieutenant Bezditko's liquor ration resumed and Malygin never again interfered with Ivan the Terrible's larceny.

The story went round the trenches and brought chuckles from most Russians. To them, the quest for liquor was a serious pursuit, one which sometimes assumed even more disastrous proportions. Only recently, soldiers of the 284th Division lines had found several cisterns filled with alcohol. After draining them, the Russians found one more cistern brimming with more spirits. Again they drank the well dry, but this time it was wood alcohol. Four men died and countless others went blind.

The tragedy failed to daunt the appetite of the other troops, some of whom began drinking cologne to ease the terror of living under the brow of Mamaev Hill.

Other 284th Division troops found diversion with two Russian women who had set up light housekeeping on the battlefield. The only entrance to their cellar was through a door that had to be lifted up from the ground. Beneath was a room, twelve by twelve feet square, lit by a kerosene lamp. A mattress lay on the floor with fifteen or twenty pillows ranged about it. One of the girls, a thirty-year-old brunette, had managed to find bright red lipstick, which she wore all the time. The younger one, a blonde, seemed pale and sickly.

The girls had an old gramophone in the corner and several records. The one they played for visiting soldiers was an Argentine tango and everyone who came to the cellar learned it by heart. Some soldiers found the women offensive. One was heard to say:

"Those bitches are just waiting for the Germans to arrive." But in the meantime, the girls played their Argentinian tango and entertained lines of men, who ignored shells and bullets to spend a few minutes with them.

Just a mile west of the cellar bordello, two other Russian women fought to stay alive. Natasha Kornilov and her crippled mother had been trapped in their backyard storehouse behind German lines for nearly seven weeks. Every morning the eleven-year-old girl scrounged garbage from German field kitchens. Every night she combed her mother's hair and sang lullabies to her.

Natasha's cheeks were sunken in from hunger. Her eyes bulged, and she moved slowly, heavily. But she always smiled at her mother, who lay on the concrete floor and prayed for deliverance. Mercifully, the German soldiers left the Kornilovs alone. That was the only reprieve granted the starving women.

In Dar Gova, two miles south of the Kornilov's grim hovel, another Russian youth, fifteen-year-old Sacha Fillipov, continued his dual life. Going from office to office, barracks to barracks, the young master cobbler mended hundreds of pairs of German boots. He also stole documents from officers' desks and carried them through the lines to Russian intelligence officers. Otherwise, in the hours he was not working, Sacha played hopscotch in the streets. The Germans never connected the frail boy's presence with grenade explosions that blew down soldiers' billets.

Several nights a week Sacha left home to report enemy troop movements. He always returned safely, and went to bed without giving his parents any details. Though they knew he worked for the Red Army, the Fillipovs never pressed their son for information.

One night he rushed home to warn them to get out of the house by dawn. They followed his instructions and in the morning, Russian artillery shells rained down on a German staff headquarters only a few doors away. Sacha had given his superiors the exact coordinates.

In the Beketovka Bulge, five miles south of Stalingrad, a dramatic buildup of Soviet troops and equipment had been completed. These were the southern strike armies requisitioned by Zhukov for Operation Uranus, and a small percentage of the troops had come from the holocaust in Stalingrad.

One of them was Lt. Hersch Gurewicz. He had finally left the factory area with its ceaseless noise and filth, and gone to the far shore where he ate Spam from America and for the first time, got a glimmer of hope. While munching the canned food, he realized that help was coming from outside Russia and that the "senseless" holding operation around the factories might have some meaning after all. Counting the ranks of his antitank unit, he hoped this was true. Of his one hundred men, eighty had perished in Stalingrad.

Instead of a rest period of two weeks, the lieutenant received new orders. With his company's ranks refilled, he went south on the eastern shore of the Volga and then across to the area of Beketovka. While no one mentioned an offensive, the feeling of it was in the air.

After his orgy of killing on the streets of Latashanka in September, Sgt. Alexei Petrov had returned to his .122-millimeter gun and lived in a shellhole three hundred yards west of the Volga cliff.

Like his batterymates, Petrov never washed or changed his uniform. He was infested with lice. The gray bugs nested all over his body, even in the seams of his trousers. His only diversion was lining them up on the ground on a bet to see who could field the largest army of parasites. A rumor that he was being relieved turned into a joyful reality, and Petrov crossed the Volga to a rest camp where, for days, he luxuriated in hot baths and suffered the delousing process without protest.

Refitted with winter clothing, including a white parka and

valenki (fur boots), he was propelled back into the war. Sent south of Stalingrad, the sergeant taught a new gun crew the rudiments of firing a heavy-caliber fieldpiece, while the ever-present political officers harangued them on the need for determination against the Fascists.

Petrov listened to the *politrook* and thought often about his family, somewhere beyond the western horizon. He had never received a clue to their whereabouts, and the burden of not knowing the truth preyed on his mind.

Nikita Khrushchev also appeared in the Beketovka Bulge. Clothed in a fur coat and hat, the commissar went from camp to camp, joking with soldiers and asking about their gripes. He was in an excellent mood.

His comrade, Gen. Andrei Yeremenko was not. Fidgeting at his new headquarters on the western side of the Volga, Yeremenko worried about his part in Operation Uranus. He also seethed over the slight he had experienced when Marshal Rokossovsky assumed defense of the city. Yeremenko felt he deserved better from Stalin.

The hours to Uranus rushed by, but in Stalingrad the Germans ignored reality.

Satisfied that the 48th Panzer Corps was strong enough to hold the left flank, Paulus obeyed Hitler's edict to hit the Russians hard while the river ice interrupted Chuikov's supply lines. North of the captured tractor factory, the 16th Panzer Division attempted once again to seize the suburb of Rynok, which the panzers first had entered on that lovely summer afternoon in August.

From north and south the 16th Panzers attacked, only to find the town bristling with Russian guns, a labryinth of trenches, hidden stationary tanks, and bazookas. But the German soldiers methodically moved down the streets, blowing up bunkers and pillboxes. Russian and German corpses left a ghastly trail.

A battalion led by Captain Mues cleared the area south of

town, reached the Volga, and turned north. It was Mues's intention to shake hands in the center of Rynok with German units cutting into it from other directions. Fog and a light snow began to obscure vision but the aggressive Mues pushed on. Fearless, revered by his men as "immortal," he was tracked by a Soviet sniper, who put a bullet in his brain. The attack stopped abruptly as Mues's troops gathered around the stricken officer, now unconscious and near death. They ignored the bullets and cried over the man they loved.

An officer from another regiment finally came, lifted Mues in his arms and staggered away with the heavy burden. Soldiers who had fought with the captain through Russia broke down and collapsed. Others became fearful and timid as news of his death spread like a bushfire.

The Russians continued to hold Rynok. The 16th Panzer Division was inside the suburb, but in twenty-four hours, it had occupied only five blocks.

With Uranus less than thirty-six hours away, Joseph Stalin got cold feet. Behind the blacked-out windows in his Kremlin apartment, he paced the floor, alternately sucking his pipe and running its mouthpiece through his mustache, listening all the while to Marshals Zhukov and Vasilevsky. Both men had received urgent summonses to come to the Kremlin. On the eve of H-hour, when they were most needed at the front lines, neither marshal had expected he would have to debate the merits of the operation.

But they had reckoned without the "insubordination" of one of their field commanders, Gen. Viktor T. Volsky, whose 4th Mechanized Corps was to act as right flank for the southern prong of the offensive. From his headquarters near the Tzatza lakes, south of Stalingrad, the depressed general had written a personal letter to Stalin, warning him "as an honest Communist" that lack of adequate manpower and material meant disaster for the Red Army in the coming attack.

Stalin acted quickly to protect himself and brought the marshals directly to the capital to answer the charges. Zhukov and Vasilevsky rendered a controlled, dispassionate recital of the facts. Evidently satisfied, the premier went to the phone and called Volsky. Without any show of anger, he reassured the general that the offensive had been properly conceived. While Zhukov and Vasilevsky listened in amazement, Stalin cordially accepted Volsky's apologies and hung up.

Vasilevsky received permission to fly back immediately to the Don Front, but Stalin kept Zhukov in Moscow, ostensibly to plan a diversionary attack west of the capital to throw the Germans off balance. Near the Tzatza lakes, the chagrined General Volsky tried to recover from his conversation with the premier. Sweating profusely, the pale officer pulled out a handkerchief and coughed into it. Clots of blood stained the cloth as he wiped his mouth.

For weeks Volsky had been hiding the truth from everyone. An old nemesis, tuberculosis of the throat, had returned to ravage his system. Physically and psychologically, the commander of the 4th Tank Corps was unfit to participate in an undertaking of such magnitude, but he refused to give in to the disease and go to a sanitarium. For Volsky, the road to Uranus had been filled with heartbreak and dogged determination to conquer his affliction. He had spent months in hospitals, resting, reading, and waiting for the doctor's certificate of good health. Now on the eve of the great counterstroke against the Nazis, he had no intention of relinquishing his command.

But the illness was preying on him. He had lost weight; he drank only tea and nibbled biscuits. Moreover, he suffered fits of melancholia, which tended to affect his judgment. It had been during one of those depressions that he had written his pessimistic letter to Joseph Stalin.

With his own "D day" nearing swiftly, Volsky went to bed to husband his strength.

Darkness came to the steppe before four o'clock on the afternoon of November 18. Gusty winds sprang up and drove soldiers into warm shelters. The rolling thunder of cannon never let up from the eastern horizon where sporadic bursts of flame in the blackness marked the German pioneers' stubborn attempts to dislodge Lyudnikov's men from the sandspit. Fireworks crowned the heights of Mamaev Hill; occasional necklaces of tracer bullets wove exotic patterns along the perimeters at the Lazur and Red October plants. As the Germans on the steppe noted, it was a normal night in Stalingrad.

But one hundred miles northwest of the city, along the serpentine glaze of the freezing Don, nothing was normal. Rumanian spotters had begun to phone in reports of hundreds of Soviet tank motors revving up, of the movement of thousands of artillery pieces along roads inside the bridgeheads at Serafimovich and Kletskaya. The observers added that columns of Red Army troops were assembled in marching order behind armor and ordnance.

In his advisory post at Rumanian Army Headquarters, Lt. Gerhard Stöck transmitted the ominous details back to Sixth Army Headquarters at Golubinka. Stöck, a crew-cut former Olympic medal winner in the javelin, spoke urgently to Capt. Winrich Behr, operations officer under Arthur Schmidt. After each sighting, Behr went to a map and recorded the Russian movements. They added up to what he had heard from a captured Soviet officer who, earlier in the day, had told his interrogators the long-planned offensive would begin within twenty-four hours.

Behr warned Schmidt and Paulus, who seemed extraordinarily calm. Both generals gave orders to alert the 48th Panzer Corps for immediate duty, and expressed confidence in the panzers' ability to blunt any breakthrough.

Winrich Behr was not so optimistic. He still remembered his conversation with a man he had replaced in October. The officer had taken Behr to the situation map, spread his hands over it and traced where the enemy would attack on both sides of the Sixth Army: "They will meet around here," he said, and his finger landed on Kalach, forty miles west of Stalingrad. Now, a month later, Behr recalled the prophecy and wondered about the future.

The phone kept ringing with alarming intelligence. Though

no shots had been fired, the Russian positions were alive with menacing energy. Radio traffic increased a thousandfold; coded messages filled the air. Captain Behr made notations on his map as rapidly as he could, while outside his office, light snow collected on the ground.

Just before midnight, Vassili Chuikov sat in his cliffside bunker overlooking the Volga and tried to interpret a message from front headquarters requesting him to stand by for an important announcement. Chuikov had no idea what it meant until Kuzma Gurov, his chief political commissar with the Sixty-second Army, suddenly slapped his forehead and shouted: "I know, it's the order for the big counteroffensive!"

The order came through at midnight. Chuikov felt a tremendous surge of satisfaction as he realized that the last sixty-eight days of fighting in Stalingrad had bought the time needed to prepare the counterattack. And soon he would have his vengeance against the German Sixth Army.

PART TWO

Chapter Sixteen

In the natural land bridge between the Don and the Volga to the west of Stalingrad, Paulus had concentrated practically all of his combat divisions for the purpose of capturing the city. But he had stationed most of the supply dumps needed to maintain those divisions on the far side of the Don, to the west where it makes a gigantic loop before curving southward toward the Sea of Azov. And it was this vulnerable rear area that the Russian High Command had pinpointed as a priority target for the first phase of Operation Uranus.

At 6:30 A.M. on November 19, the predawn darkness between Serafimovich and Kletskaya became a brilliant blaze of orange and red flame as thirty-five hundred Russian guns heralded the attack.

Trapped in straw-lined trenches, soldiers of the Rumanian Third Army watched the artillery bursts march precisely up and down their lines. Bunkers collapsed, suffocating hundreds; shell-shocked men screamed in fear and blocked their ears to escape the terrifying noise. When the cannonade finally stopped, the Rumanians heard the ominous sound of tank motors as the Russian Fifth and Twenty-first Tank armies burst forth from their bridgeheads.

The T-34s stormed through clinging fog and snow into the lines of bewildered Rumanians. Most succumbed to "tank fright," leapt from cover, and ran. Only a few stayed to duel the armor.

Eight miles to the south, a German weather observer, Sgt. Wolf Pelikan, stirred fitfully in his warm cot as he tried to ignore the rolling gunfire intruding on his sleep. It continued, so Pelikan slipped out of bed and dressed. Dirt cascaded on him from the ceiling and he swore as he brushed off his uniform. When the noise suddenly ceased, he finished dressing in a more leisurely manner, and his thoughts turned to breakfast and the pancakes he liked so well.

A shout brought him to the door and he recognized a company messenger, pointing frantically to the north.

"The Ivans are here! The Ivans are here!" he kept saying.

Pelikan hollered back, "You're crazy."

The commotion awakened his comrades, who poured from the bunker to laugh at the messenger. Someone even threw a shoe at him, but he kept pointing, wordlessly now, to the north.

Pelikan looked in that direction and froze. A wind had blown away the fog and he saw them clearly, huge black tanks, sitting motionless on a rise about a mile off. Pelikan's stomach churned.

At that moment the first hysterical Rumanians appeared. Weaponless, screaming, they never paused in their flight. When one of them yelled that Russian troops were right behind, the news destroyed any semblance of order in the German ranks.

Pelikan and the others forgot all discipline. Orders rang out and were as quickly countermanded. Men swept belongings into trucks, which started sluggishly in the freezing weather. The commanding officer scurried to a light plane and took off to the south.

With Russian tanks still hovering on the slope, the rest of the German unit jumped into vehicles and roared away. Bouncing

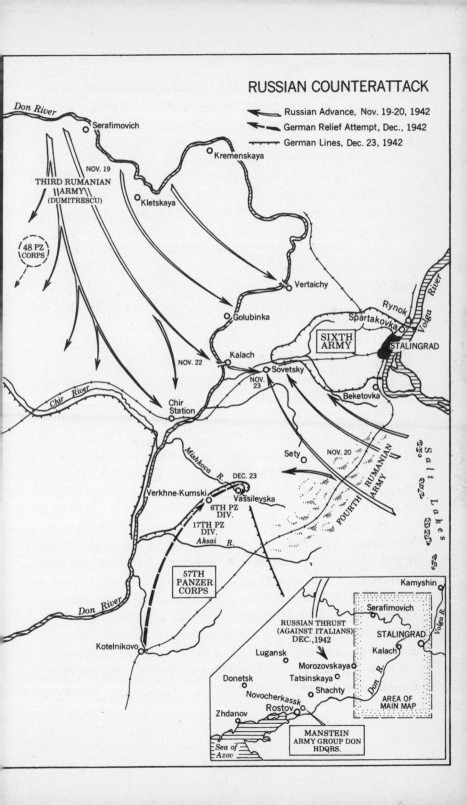

RUSSIAN COUNTERATTACK

← Russian Advance, Nov. 19-20, 1942
◄◄ German Relief Attempt, Dec., 1942
⊢⊢⊢ German Lines, Dec. 23, 1942

Don River

Serafimovich

Kremenskaya

NOV. 19

THIRD RUMANIAN
ARMY
(DUMITRESCU)

Kletskaya

48 PZ
CORPS

Vertaichy

Golubinka

Rynok

Spartakovka

SIXTH
ARMY

STALINGRAD

Volga River

NOV. 22

Kalach

Sovetsky

NOV.
23

Beketovka

Chir River

Chir
Station

Sety

NOV. 20

Salt Lakes

Mishkova R.

DEC. 23

Verkhne-Kumski

Vassilevska

6TH PZ
DIV.

17TH PZ
DIV.

Aksai R.

FOURTH RUMANIAN ARMY

57TH
PANZER
CORPS

Don River

Kotelnikovo

Kamyshin

Serafimovich

RUSSIAN THRUST
(AGAINST ITALIANS)
DEC.,1942

STALINGRAD

Kalach

Volga R.

Don R.

Lugansk

Morozovskaya

Tatsinskaya

Shachty

AREA OF
MAIN MAP

Donetsk

Novocherkassk

Rostov

Zhdanov

Sea of
Azov

MANSTEIN
ARMY GROUP DON
HDQRS.

along in a bakery truck, Pelikan silently thanked God for the chance to survive.

At Golubinka, fifty miles to the southeast, Capt. Winrich Behr heard the details of the Soviet attack from Lt. Gerhard Stöck, the liaison officer posted to the Rumanian Third Army at Kletskaya. Stöck told him the Third Army had been torn apart, was running toward Golubinka, and Behr rushed to tell Paulus and Schmidt, who took the dreadful report calmly. Amazed and pleased at their composure, Behr waited while the generals analyzed the situation. Schmidt suddenly exclaimed: "We can hold!" Paulus agreed and ordered the 48th Panzer Corps to head north, into the breach along the Don.

Thirteen hundred miles to the west of Sixth Army Headquarters, Hitler slept soundly at the *Berghof* in the Bavarian Alps. The Führer had been there for nearly two weeks, dallying in his mountain retreat. But the problems he refused to acknowledge during the past summer and fall had pursued him. In Africa, the Allies were moving to trap Rommel's legions; in Russia, his Soviet Union Intelligence expert, Col. Reinhard Gehlen, had just warned him of the extreme likelihood of a Russian counteroffensive behind Sixth Army.

Despite these reports, Hitler remained convinced that his Third Reich would endure. He was incredibly proud of the fact that his armies ruled more than three hundred million people: from the Atlantic coastline in France to the foothills of the Caucasus Mountains, from the northern capes of Norway to the bleached sands of Libya. He had reached an apogee of power. But on November 19, when the Red Army launched its massive counterattack at the Don, his Nazi empire bgan to wither imperceptibly. And though more than two years would pass before it finally collapsed, the decline would prove irreversible.

In a quiet conference room, Hitler peered intently at the latest battle maps and examined the terrain on the left flank of the Sixth Army. He showed no undue concern as he asked about the weather and Luftwaffe groups operating in the region. Unhurried, controlled, Hitler weighed the options and issued an order. It was the first of many fatal decisions he would make in the coming weeks.

That order reached Gen. Ferdinand Heim at 11:30 A.M., as he was leading his 48th Panzer Corps out to challenge the Russian Twenty-first Army rampaging south of the Don. It instructed him to change direction and speed to the sector around Blinov, where the Soviet Fifth Army had also made a serious penetration. Irritated by the confusing orders, the general skidded to a halt and redirected his columns toward the new target almost 180 degrees in the opposite direction. When the 48th Panzer Corps clumsily started up again, it was inundated with remnants of Rumanian divisions, running across the snowfields. Heim absorbed as many of these troops as he could and kept going toward his new target.

No planes interfered with the drama on the steppe, for both air forces had been grounded by the foul weather. As a result, General von Richthofen had flown south to the Caucasus, where excellent conditions permitted strikes against the Red Army. Absorbed with bombing runs along the Terek riverfront, he was stunned to hear of the massive Soviet offensive at his rear. Unable to dispatch aircraft north into the storm along the Don, he excused his impotence by saying, "once again the Russians have made masterly use of the bad weather."

That bad weather had almost caused Marshal Vasilevsky to postpone Operation Uranus. Frantic phone calls with Generals Vatutin, Christiakov, Romanenko and STAVKA in Moscow had preceded the attack. Deprived of close air support, and fearful of sending tanks into a blinding cover of fog and snow on the exposed steppe, the Russians launched Uranus with a premonition of catastrophe. But the first hours had already brought incredible success. Masses of Rumanian prisoners swarmed into Soviet lines. Red Army tank patrols quickly penetrated twenty miles southward, and by afternoon were within firing range of German Sixth Army's supply dumps.

At the town of Bolshe Nabatoff, thirty miles south of Kletskaya, Quartermaster Karl Binder was trying desperately to save his carefully hoarded rations. He had collected eight hundred cattle to feed his division during the winter and now, fearful of Russian tanks, he acted to shift his ponderous burden eastward, across the winding Don before the enemy seized the bridge at Akimovski. As he issued instructions to eight herdsmen, the first Russian shells whined into the compound and the cattle broke in terror. The herdsmen managed to turn the mass which stampeded, snorting and lowing, toward the Don miles away.

After the cattle had gone, Binder began heaving huge sacks of flour into trucks while his men filled other vehicles with bread, clothing, and blankets. Retreating Rumanian troops helped themselves to as much food as they could carry and for once, no German officer demanded receipts.

Enemy fire increased, buildings began burning furiously. Convinced he had salvaged all he could, Binder led his convoy out of Bolshe Nabatoff while behind him, the depot burned like a bright red torch.

All day long, teams of Russian tanks roamed the white steppe, shooting into headquarters detachments, supply dumps, communications centers, and then pulling back into the mist to strike again miles away. Their tactics confused and demoralized the Germans. Radio reports flooding into Golubinka placed the Russians forty miles south of the Don, then fifty miles southeast of the Don— everywhere! Hysteria marked the voices that begged Sixth Army for reinforcements and advice.

Discipline broke; unit commanders arbitrarily ordered their men to the east, toward Stalingrad. Their troops had become fearful, sullen and were openly hostile to their superiors, who ran about screaming threats of courts-martial to maintain order.

In this bedlam, Lt. Hermann Kästle shepherded his mortars to the Don. He pushed ahead on the congested roads, and held his place against repeated attempts by other officers to jockey men and equipment in front of him. Panic frequently replaced reason, and Kästle saw several arguments degenerate into fist fights as soldiers stood in the snow and smashed each other over trivial slights.

In late afternoon, Kästle neared a bridge crossing the Don. Suddenly another lieutenant appeared, waved a Luger in his face, and told him his tank held priority over Kästle's mortars. When Kästle said his guns were equally important, the lieutenant pointed the pistol at his head and told him to back away.

Kästle searched the officer's eyes, and knew he faced death if he refused. Shaking his head in disbelief, he pulled the mortars aside and watched passively as the tank commander jumped onto his machine and rode triumphantly over the river.

At Sixth Army Headquarters, Captain Behr kept the lines to Gerhard Stöck open throughout the day. Stöck had proved to be the most reliable witness to the unfolding chaos. He kept reporting the defection of Rumanian officers, who left thousands of soldiers to wander the steppe, and his account of the tragedy was distressingly accurate.

On his own maps, Behr had also watched the slow progress of General Heim's relief force. The 48th Panzer Corps finally reached Blinov in the afternoon. But the Russians had come and gone, hitting and running across the flatlands. General Heim took his panzers out of town again, seeking the elusive enemy, who was avoiding direct engagement.

In Stalingrad, ninety miles east of the fluid battleground, the city had again assumed its familiar crown of explosions and tracer bullets chasing each other through the darkening sky. On the edge of the Volga, Russian Col. Ivan Lyudnikov's trapped division still clung to its "island" under the cliff behind the Barrikady Gun Factory. Up above, German pioneers had spent another day trying to destroy them, but again they failed. Inside the Barrikady itself, Maj. Eugen Rettenmaier learned of the Russian counterattack back at the Don and sank into a deep depression. Unable to understand how his leaders had failed to prepare for the blow, he knew the situation at Stalingrad had become hopeless.

North of the Barrikady, past the shattered tractor works, the 16th Panzer Division had spent another torturous day on the outskirts of Rynok. But after dark, they received orders to turn their backs on the Volga. Mechanics labored hurriedly over tanks and trucks; soldiers received extra rations and ammunition. Then they filed out of their deep *balkas*, where they had lived since August, and went to shore up the gap in the line along the Don, ninety miles to the rear.

The weather was turning worse; a strong wind blew snow into the faces of the tankers and infantrymen. Masses of people wandered past them: Rumanians clutching their belongings, human flotsam from an unseen debacle beyond the western horizon.

At Golubinka, General Schmidt read the latest dispatches and tried to gauge the extent of the Russian penetration. Scattered rumors merged with verified reports to form a kaleidoscope of tank sightings, making it impossible to pinpoint the enemy's whereabouts.

At 10:30 P.M., Schmidt suddenly announced: "I am going to bed now," and disappeared into his quarters. As he went back to the phone and Gerhard Stöck, Captain Behr marveled again at Schmidt's coolness, a blessing in the face of the long day's discouragement.

South of Stalingrad, more Russian forces waited through the bitterly cold night to begin the second part of Operation Uranus.

From the suburb of Beketovka down to the shores of the salt lakes, Sarpa, Tzatza, and Barmantsak, the Sixty-fourth, Fifty-seventh, and Fifty-first armies were massed along a 125-mile front. Confronting them was the vastly overextended Fourth Rumanian Army, stretched thin across the wintry steppe to protect the German Sixth Army's right flank. It was the Russian High Command's intention to punch quickly through the Rumanian positions and race northwest toward the Russian armies descending from the Don.

In the early hours of November 20, shivering Red Army soldiers cleaned their weapons again, and wrote last letters to relatives in unoccupied Russia. Sgt. Alexei Petrov had no one to write; Lt. Hersch Gurewicz thought wistfully of his father and brother, but had no idea where they were.

At his headquarters cottage, General Yeremenko could not sleep. Convinced that the southern-front attack should be delayed until all the German reserves had been drawn north to meet the first phase of the Soviet offensive along the Don, he had spent hours arguing his case with STAVKA in Moscow. But STAVKA had refused his plea, and now Yeremenko brooded about the possibility of failure.

At dawn he had more worries. The weather had not changed, and a thick fog, mixed with snow, shrouded his armies. Troops had great difficulty forming into assault groups. Tanks ran into each other. Airplanes poised to the east, across the Volga, sat helplessly on runways.

Yeremenko delayed H-hour. From Moscow, STAVKA demanded the reason and Yeremenko sat at his desk and patiently explained his decision. STAVKA was not happy, but Yeremenko held his ground. For more than two hours, past nine o'clock, he waited for the weather to clear. As STAVKA came back on the BODO line to plague him, his meteorologists promised sunlight within minutes.

At 10:00 A.M., Yeremenko's artillery commenced firing and the soldiers of the Rumanian Fourth Army fled wildly in every direction. Within a few hours, the astonished Yeremenko excitedly called STAVKA to say that ten thousand prisoners had already been processed. STAVKA demanded he recheck his figures. They were correct.

Pvt. Abraham Spitkovsky had seen the prisoners coming almost as soon as the bombardment ceased. Rising from his hole when the "Urrahs" from his comrades sounded the charge, he plunged through the snow toward hundreds of black figures walking toward him with hands raised over their heads. Up and down the front beside him, Russian soldiers shot blindly into the ragged ranks and when Spitkovsky thought of the weeks and months of running, of cringing among the corpses, and of lice he, too, brought up his machine pistol and fired long bursts into their columns.

While Spitkovsky paused to reload his gun, he looked down at the rows of dead men and was completely unmoved.

One hundred twenty miles northwest of General Yeremenko's almost effortless breakthrough, the Germans were still trying to contain the Russian forces moving down from Serafimovich and Klatskaya.

At the village of Peschanyy, thirty miles south of Serafimovich, General Heim's 48th Panzer Corps finally met the enemy. His 22nd Panzer Division plunged into a firefight with T-34s, but the 22nd was already crippled; its mouse-eaten wiring had reduced tank strength to twenty.

Antitank guns acting as support helped explode twenty-six Russian tanks, but that was not enough. The Soviet armor broke away and the Germans hobbled after it. By the afternoon, the panzers were surrounded by new Russian formations and fighting for survival.

The steppe battleground resembled islands in a sea. Trapped units retreated into hedgehog defenses and lashed back at the enemy closing in around them. The Rumanians who continued to fight were almost totally isolated. A meteorological officer in the 6th Division kept a diary, later captured by the Russians:

November 20
In morning enemy opened heavy artillery fire at sector held
by 13th Pruth Division. . . . Division wiped out. . . . No
communication with higher command. . . . Currently encircled by enemy troops. In pocket are the 5th, 6th and 15th
divisions and remnants of the 13th Division.

The report spoke for the entire "puppet army."

During the night, German Quartermaster Karl Binder had crossed
and recrossed the Don, bringing out food and clothing for his
305th Division. Back again on the western side of the frozen river,
he found that his old supply depot at Bolshe Nabatoff still remained in German hands. The Russian tanks had merely burned
some of the buildings before racing off again into the fog.

Binder collected what equipment he could from the ruins,
then returned to the bridge at Akimovski to wait for his cattle.
Lost somewhere in the near blizzard of the previous night, the herd
had not been seen by anyone.

On a bluff overlooking the town, Binder stared west into the
vast steppe. Close by him, two Russian prisoners were being in-
terrogated by a German officer, who suddenly shouted something
and waved a pistol. When one of the Russians bolted, the German
shot him in the back of the head.

Horrified, Binder rushed over and begged the officer to
spare the other prisoner's life. He said he could use him as a driver.
The officer shrugged disdainfully and holstered his weapon. Binder
led the Russian back to his car, where the prisoner poured out a
torrent of thanks in fluent German. The young man explained that
he had learned the language while studying medicine in Moscow.

Russian shelling increased; dead bodies lined the roads, and
wounded men called for help. A Rumanian officer waved feebly
from a clump of bushes, and Binder and his new friend went to
him. The man had wounds in an arm and his right leg. After Binder
cut open his trousers, the Russian medical student took his knife
and skillfully picked pieces of shrapnel from the lacerations. The
Rumanian fainted.

Binder heard his cattle coming long before they showed on the horizon. With shells bursting intermittently in the town of Akimovski, he stood patiently at the bridge and listened to the sound of hooves hitting the ground. Then they appeared, a mass of animals, raising a huge cloud of snow as they ran ahead of the shouting herdsmen. Their noses dripping icicles, their eyes caked with ice and snow, they passed over the bridge into corrals in the deep *balkas* between the Don and Volga.

Satisfied with his coup, Binder dropped the Russian and wounded Rumanian officer at a dispensary and started setting up new depots for his division on the east side of the Don.

Only a few miles away, Gen. Arthur Schmidt was briefing Friedrich von Paulus at Sixth Army headquarters about the deteriorating situation. After announcing that the 24th Panzer Division was having difficulty negotiating immense snowdrifts on the way from Stalingrad to defend the vital bridge at Kalach, he added that a Russian tank column had just been reported within range of Golubinka itself.

Paulus abruptly terminated the discussion. "Well, Schmidt, I will no longer stay here. We will have to move. . . ."

Paulus suddenly seemed agitated and even Schmidt lost some of his calm. The two men said a curt good-bye to their staff and went out to pack.

They took off a short time later and flew first to Gumrak Airport, five miles west of Stalingrad. After a brief conversation there with General Seydlitz-Kurzbach, they flew southwest to the communications center of Chir, from where Paulus hoped to maintain reliable radio contact with higher headquarters.

In the meantime he acted quickly to smash the second stage of the Soviet counterattack by sending the 29th Motorized Division into battle south of Stalingrad. On alert to join General Heim's 48th Panzer Corps west of the Don, the 29th was able to move swiftly through rolling fog on the right flank of the Russian Fifty-seventh Army, which was pushing past negligible resistance from Rumanian outposts. The counterattack stunned the Russians.

Both sides suffered losses as the first tanks opened fire, and, when mounted infantry clashed, the full battle was joined. The fog lifted and German observers saw a Soviet armored train passing by to the west. Behind it several other freight trains had stopped to disgorge Red Army foot soldiers. German panzers sighted on these inviting targets and poured hundreds of shells into the packed boxcars. Through binoculars, the gunners watched countless Russian bodies cartwheeling into the air and down onto the snow.

On either side of the railroad embankment, Soviet tanks milled about, ramming each other and firing aimlessly. German batteries shot point-blank into these vehicles and the Russian 13th Mechanized Corps, ninety tanks strong, began to blaze and explode. Sensing a chance to completely seal the Russian breakthrough on the southern flank, 29th Division commander, Gen. Ernst Leyser, prepared to annihilate the burning enemy force. But as he did so an order reached him from Army Group B, more than two hundred miles away at Starobelsk, to pull back and guard the Sixth Army's rear at the Don.

In the fading afternoon light of November 21, the frustrated Leyser reluctantly broke contact and rode off to the northwest. From nearby fields, tanks started to fire over his car at unseen targets. The general suddenly had no idea whether they were friends or foes.

General Leyser's temporary victory brought a brief dividend to Paulus. News of the bloody defeat of the Russian 13th Corps quickly filtered back to Gen. Viktor Volsky's 4th Tank Corps and the tubercular general slowed his drive, now aiming for Kalach on the Don. Still spitting phlegm into his handkerchief, the cautious officer refused to go on and insisted on reinforcements against renewed German assaults. But the Germans had gone.

Agonizing over the rupture of both his flanks, General Paulus made up his mind about the future. He authorized a dispatch to Army Group B at Starobelsk and recommended the obvious: withdrawal of the Sixth Army from the Volga and Stalingrad to positions more than a hundred miles to the southwest, at the lower Don and Chir rivers.

Army Group B commander, Freiherr von Weichs, forwarded the recommendation to OKW headquarters in Rastenburg, East Prussia, with a strong endorsement. He shared Paulus's conviction that an immediate withdrawal was the only alternative to total disaster.

And disaster was close at hand. South of Stalingrad, General Yeremenko's units, after crushing the Rumanians, split "Papa" Hoth's Fourth German Tank Army in two. At a weather-beaten farmhouse outside Businovka, "Papa" Hoth sat besieged. Outside, the wind howled at the windows which were boarded over and stuffed with bits of paper and cloth. Inside, flickering candles shone on a band of weary staff officers, trying to keep in touch with their scattered combat groups on the steppe.

Messengers arrived in a stream with pleas from trapped regiments. At a solitary telephone, an officer scribbled down final words from decimated formations as they fell under Russian armor.

Hoth was helpless. With the Rumanian forces destroyed, he had too few guns and tanks to stop the enemy. It had also become apparent that the Soviet plan was breathtaking in scope. Colored arrows on the battle maps already showed a distinct arc to the northwest, around his pitiful forces, toward Kalach and its bridge over the Don. If the bridge should fall before Sixth Army pulled back from the Volga, Hoth foresaw a mass grave for the Germans in Stalingrad.

But thirteen hundred miles west of the emerging tragedy, in his Alpine *Berghof,* Hitler had a different view of the situation. Upon receiving Paulus's suggestion that Sixth Army withdraw to the southwest, he responded quickly with a sharp command to hold fast.

Radio message Number 1352
TOP SECRET .   Army Group B
Urgent!   21 November 42, 1525 hrs.
TO: *HQ Sixth Army*
Führer Order:
Sixth Army will hold positions despite threat of temporary
encirclement. . . . Keep railroad line open as long as possible.
Special orders regarding air supply will follow!

The implications of the order were stunning to consider. And
while Paulus and Schmidt pondered the message, a phone call
came in from Lt. Gen. Martin Fiebig, commander of the Eighth
Air Corps. The generals discussed the latest events and Fiebig
referred to the bridge at Kalach. Schmidt said he saw no immediate
danger there and added, "The commander in chief is thinking of
forming a hedgehog defense."

"And how do you propose to keep the army supplied?" asked
Fiebig.

"That will have to be done from the air."

Fiebig was astonished. "A whole army? It's quite impossible!
I advise you not to be so optimistic."

Fiebig hung up and immediately called his chief, General
Richthofen, who then phoned Albert Jeschonnek, Goering's deputy, and raged at him: "You've got to stop it! In the filthy weather
we have here there's not a hope of supplying an Army of 250,000
men from the air. It's stark staring madness! . . ."

On the night of November 21, the vanguard of the 16th Panzer
Division, which had left the outskirts of Stalingrad two days earlier,
arrived on the Don to act as a covering force for units fleeing out
of the great loop of the Don. But the division arrived too late to
do more than hold a few bridges open for Rumanian and German
stragglers. At the bridge he held, Lt. Eberhard von Loebbecke
commanded the rear guard as a Russian tank appeared on the
roadway. Loebbecke, who had lost his left arm to a French machine gunner in 1939, was standing upright before the T-34,

which fired one round at him. The shell ticked his empty sleeve and exploded some yards behind him. Knocked down by the explosion, the lieutenant rose almost immediately to direct return fire. In their open turret, the Soviet crew stared in amazement at the man who had apparently lost his arm to the shell and yet bounced up off the ground without any discomfort. While they hesitated, a German antitank gun put a round into the T-34, and it blew up in front of Loebbecke's eyes.

That night, relentless winds moaning over the steppe turned snow drifts into miniature mountain ranges on the flat prairie. The temperature fell below zero and the skies promised more snow. For thousands of square miles, west and east of the Don River, the land seemed lifeless.

But the steppe teemed with desperate men, skulking across the fields in small groups. Rumanian and German, they ran on frozen feet, propelled only by a common urge to survive. They fled through the night seeking food, shelter, and the protection of friendly guns.

Other men roamed the fields with different goals in mind. Lt. Col. Grigor Fillipov led the men of the Soviet 14th Motor Artillery Brigade away from the main body of Soviet troops moving down from the Don, and struck for the town of Kalach. Fillipov had no maps. He had only five tanks, supported by several trucks carrying infantry. His drivers turned on every light and sped through the darkness. Beside the road, hundreds of enemy soldiers waved to the "friendly" tankers, who ignored them and pushed on.

At 6:00 A.M. on November 22, Fillipov spied an old man, a Russian civilian, pulling a peasant cart, with two German soldiers walking beside him. The colonel issued whispered instructions and his men shot the Germans dead, then clambered down from the T-34s to talk to their terrified countryman.

"Uncle Vanya, which way to the bridge?" they asked. When he heard them speak his native tongue, the old man stopped trembling, climbed into the first tank and Fillipov waved his combat group on to the east.

In Kalach, the German garrison lived in a state of uneasy expectation. Refugees had been passing through for the past thirty-six hours, and the boom of heavy guns from the northwest sounded closer each hour. But no one in the garrison knew how badly the situation had deteriorated.

At Colonel Mikosch's Engineer Training School on the hill at the eastern edge of town, pioneers had begun another regular workday, practicing the skills of street fighting, demolition expertise, and weaponry, both German and Russian. Several captured Russian tanks were being used by pupils for firing demonstrations at the range on the west side of the Don. Each day, the tanks trundled across the bridge, up the steep west bank, and onto the steppe for gunnery lessons.

On this morning, a German Propaganda Company correspondent, Heinz Schröter, had come to film the scene. When the tanks crossed the bridge and went past him up the hill, he photographed them and then, shortly afterward, Schröter heard the usual sounds of cannon fire from the gunnery range.

At Sentry Post Number 3, a sergeant named Wiedemann dozed near his .88-millimeter antiaircraft gun. Behind him in a hut, the crew of eight slept. Wiedemann, too, had watched the tanks go by, counting them off as they roared up the slope and disappeared.

The garrison returned to a routine schedule. The snow had stopped and voices rang loudly in the clear air. Laughter echoed as soldiers threw snowballs at each other. When the tanks suddenly reappeared, the indifferent Sergeant Wiedemann watched them speed past. As the third machine rumbled onto the bridge a machine gun suddenly chattered. The tanks kept going on to the east bank where they quickly separated and turned off on either side.

Grabbing his binoculars Wiedemann screamed, "Those damn tanks are Russian!" and pounded on a piece of metal to alert his crew, which burst out of the hut. Two tanks had not yet crossed the bridge. The .88-millimeter gun fired at a three-hundred-yard range, and the T-34s ignited. The second in line teetered for a moment, then somersaulted directly onto the frozen surface of the Don below.

When the first tanks went over, cameraman Schröter had been even closer to the bridge. A lieutenant suddenly ran past him, yelling unintelligibly, and Schröter thought he had gone berserk. The officer was waving a pistol until a machine gun stuttered and he pitched to the ground.

Schröter grabbed his equipment and ran. So did most of the Germans in the immediate vicinity. In the underbrush on the east bank, Col. Grigor Fillipov radioed frantically back to the Soviet 26th Armored Brigade for help. He had won the bridge by sheer luck but he expected the Germans to react viciously.

While Colonel Fillipov dug in at Kalach, the phone rang in General Schmidt's office at Chir, fifteen miles to the south. It was Luftwaffe commander Martin Fiebig calling, and he again warned about the folly of an airlift, "Both the weather and the enemy are completely incalculable factors. . . ." But the conversation was interrupted by a group of German generals, who suddenly swept into the headquarters.

"Papa" Hoth had arrived from Businovka, where the southern flank had totally evaporated. At a loss to give a clear picture of the nightmare, Hoth listened intently while Schmidt and an old friend and school classmate, Gen. Wolfgang Pickert, debated a solution. Mimicking a former professor's manner, Schmidt said, "Pickert, decision with brief statement of reasons!"

Pickert's answer was incisive. "Get the hell out of here!"

Schmidt agreed but went on, "We cannot do that. For one thing, we don't have enough gas."

Pickert offered to help with his antiaircraft troops, who could manhandle guns across the flat land and carry ammunition by hand.

Schmidt continued, "We have, of course, considered breaking out, but to reach the Don means thirty miles of steppe without any cover. . . . No, Pickert, it could only have a Napoleonic ending. . . . The army has been ordered to hold its ground at Stalingrad. Consequently we shall fortify our positions and expect supplies from the air."

Pickert could not believe what he heard. ". . . From the air? In this weather? It's quite out of the question. You must get out, I say. Get started now!"

But Sixth Army did not get started. Even though General Paulus was convinced it should, he continued to wait for Hitler's approval. In the meantime, he put his army on alert to move quickly in case permission came.

At 2:00 P.M., after Hoth had flown west to gather together the remnants of his shattered Fourth Army, Paulus and Schmidt went back to Gumrak at the edge of Stalingrad. Flying over the bulk of their army, hemmed in between the Don and Volga, the generals saw bright fires on both sides of the aircraft as men of the Sixth Army began to burn unneeded equipment.

Warehouses filled with food and clothing were being put to the torch. At one of them, Lt. Gerhard Dietzel tried to salvage something from the flames. Seeing a cache of champagne and wine about to be consumed, he raced back and forth between the inferno and his Volkswagen with armfuls of bottles. When the car was filled, Dietzel jumped in and started the motor. A supply officer blocked his way:

"Can you pay for it?" he demanded.

Dietzel began to laugh uproariously. Pointing at the raging fires, he replied, "But, don't you see, money doesn't mean anything anymore!" He gunned the motor and raced off with his treasure.

At Kalach, Russian Colonel Fillipov unexpectedly received reinforcements when tanks of the 26th Armored Brigade charged across the bridge and joined him at the eastern edge of town. It was incredible, but with German resistance only sporadic and ineffective, the 26th Brigade then wheeled southeast out of Kalach and headed toward the village of Sovetsky, thirty miles away. And somewhere beyond Sovetsky, General Yeremenko's southern-front troops were driving up toward a junction with their comrades.

German soldiers inside the rapidly developing pocket learned of their plight in different ways.

At a field hospital, a pharmacist named Wendt was passing out morphine and bandages to medics when a soldier ran in and announced: "The Russians have closed the bridge at Kalach!" Wendt thought he was joking, but when a friend phoned headquarters and confirmed the story, Wendt refused to panic. He thought the mess would be cleaned up quickly.

A veteran sergeant, Eugen Steinhilber, learned the bitter truth when several of his comrades left by bus to go to Chir, and from there back to Germany for furlough. They were back in a few hours, saying: "We can't get over the Don. The Russians have the bridge." Since Steinhilber had been in a pocket once before and gotten out safely, the news failed to faze him. He had just written to his wife, "By December I'll be home. I'll go back to school . . . and finish my training as electrical engineer. . . ."

From his new Gumrak command post, Paulus sent another urgent cable. In it, he begged for the chance to save his Army:

HQ Sixth Army
G 3 Section

22 November 42, 1900 hours

Radio Message
To Army Group B

The Army is encircled. . . . South front still open east of the Don. Don frozen over and crossable. . . . There is little fuel left; once that is used up, tanks and heavy weapons will be immobile. Ammunition is short, provisions will last for six more days. . . . Request freedom of action. . . . Situation might compel abandonment of Stalingrad and northern front. . . .

Three hours later he received a vague answer from the Führer, "Sixth Army must know that I am doing everything to help and to relieve it. . . . I shall issue my orders in good time."

Hitler was still puzzled about how to save Paulus, but until he decided on the best course of action he intended to keep Sixth Army in position. Most of that afternoon was spent with Kurt Zeitzler and Albert Jeschonnek. Both officers had come to the *Berghof* determined to sway Hitler from the idea of an airlift; Jeschonnek pointed out the problems of weather and insufficient airfields within flying distance of Stalingrad.

Though Zeitzler felt Jeschonnek was not forceful enough in making his case, Hermann Goering thought otherwise when he heard details of the conference. He called Jeschonnek and warned him not to "put the Führer out of sorts."

That night, Hitler came down from his mountain and went by train to Leipzig, where a plane waited to fly him to Rastenburg, East Prussia. He would issue orders later.

Chapter Seventeen

In an earthen bunker just west of Gumrak Airfield, an impatient Friedrich von Paulus waited for the Führer to allow him to quit the Volga. To reinforce his argument, Paulus again reminded his immediate superiors of the perils Sixth Army faced:

23 November, 1145 hours

To Army Group B:

> Murderous attacks on all fronts. . . . Arrival of sufficient air supplies is not believed possible, even if weather should improve. The ammunition and fuel situation will render the troops defenseless in the very near future. . . .

Paulus

Once again Army Group B forwarded the message on to Hitler at Rastenburg, along with the comment by General von Weichs who agreed totally with Paulus's analysis of the situation.

On the steppe beyond the Don, General Heim's 48th Panzer Corps continued its swirling series of tank battles with marauding Soviet columns. As a result, it was impossible to link up with any

Rumanian forces still fighting on the vast plain. Russian radio-jammers even managed to convey bogus signals to any units seeking General Heim.

Between the Chir and Kletskaya at the Don, the last Rumanian outposts were about to fall. Gen. Mihail Lascar, a mustachioed strongman, had collected elements of four divisions in the midst of "burning houses and Rumanian corpses." The Russians called on him to surrender and he wired German Army Group B for authority to break out. By the time permission arrived, he was trapped. Instead of surrendering, Lascar released four thousand men and sent them to seek union, if they could do so, with Heim's 48th Panzer Corps, somewhere on the steppe. Then Lascar walked into captivity, his reputation unsullied by defeat. The battlefield he left "was a fantastic sight . . . full of dead horses . . . some horses were only half dead, standing on three frozen legs, shaking the remaining broken one. . . ."

The soldiers he had released wandered dazedly, begging food, freezing to death beside the road. A trail of bodies marked each highway, down which roared lengthening columns of Russian tanks and trucks; only a few Rumanians reached Heim, who shepherded them and his ill-fated panzers south toward freedom. Miraculously, his forces made it to the bank of the river Chir. But within hours, German military police arrested him. Hitler had accused him of dereliction of duty in not stopping the Soviet offensive with his mobile reserves. The Führer insisted that Heim had disobeyed Army High Command instructions radioed to him in the field and thus had failed to attack the enemy at crucial times in the first hours of conflict. Stunned by the charges against him, Heim went home to Germany to face a military tribunal.

During a tense, gloomy conference at Rostov, General Steflea, the Rumanian Army chief of staff, met with a German liaison officer and read field reports of Lascar's surrender. Appalled at what had happened to his Third and Fourth armies, Steflea berated his ally:

"All the warnings which for weeks I have been giving to the German authorities have passed unheeded. . . . Of the four divisions of the Fourth Rumanian Army there are only three battalions left. . . . German Army Headquarters failed to meet our requirements. And that is why two Rumanian armies have been destroyed."

The German liaison officer could not rebut the charges. Instead, he promised to pass on General Steflea's statements to higher authority.

At roadblocks outside the town of Sovetsky, fifteen miles southeast of the bridge at Kalach, Soviet T-34 tanks dueled at ten-yard range with German rear guards trying to hold the village. The din of this battle reached Russian tankers of Gen. Viktor Volsky's 4th Mechanized Corps as they cautiously probed the fields south and west of the town. Nervous because they were close to lead elements of the Russian spearheads from the northern Don offensive, they kept shooting green recognition flares to announce their own presence. Just before 4:00 P.M. on November 23, another series of green flares soared upward from the northwest and Volsky's T-34s roared ahead. Hundreds of white-clad Russians surged toward them and the two forces came together in a frenzy of shouts, embraces, and tears.

Almost hysterical with joy, the Russian soldiers danced about in the snow to celebrate an incredible triumph. In less than ninety-six hours, they had sprung a trap around the German Sixth Army. Inside that "pocket" were more than 250 thousand German troops —prisoners, isolated on a vast plain of snow.

All over Russia, radio announcers were hailing the Red Army's incredible victories. The names Kalach and Sovetsky rang through the airwaves as the Soviet people heard for the first time of the encirclement at Stalingrad.

But in Moscow, Stalin did not celebrate. The premier had

"gotten his blood up" as he sensed an even greater opportunity for his armies in the south. Looking at the maps, he saw the possibility of creating an even larger pocket. Several hundred miles below the encirclement at the Volga, German Army Group A stood immobile in the Caucasus. If the Red Army could capture the city of Rostov on the Sea of Azov, the Stalingrad trap would become just a minor phase of a greater triumph. Thus Stalin urged his generals on:

> To Comrade Dontsov [Rokossovsky] 23 November 1942
> Copy for Comrade Mikhailov [Vasilevsky] 1940 hours

> According to Mikhailov's report, the 3rd Motorized and the 16th Armored Division of the enemy are either wholly or in part transferred from your front. . . . This circumstance makes the situation favorable for all armies of your front to step up actions. Galinin is too slow. . . .
>   Also tell Zhadov to start more active operations and try to tie down the enemy.
>   Give Batov a push; he could be much more forceful in the present situation.

General Paulus was ready to break out of the newly formed pocket, a situation the Germans called "*Der Kessel*" ("The Cauldron"). In the past twenty-four hours he had assembled a battering ram of armor, artillery, and mounted infantry that would force a path to the southwest. The special group had massed around Gumrak Airfield. Lt. Hans Oettl was there; like everyone else, he was in an expectant mood. Pleased that something positive was about to happen, he watched tanks being painted white and troops receiving special white camouflage parkas.

Lt. Emil Metzger also was there, radiating enthusiasm. Since his *nebelwerfer* battery was attached to Sixth Army Headquarters, he would supply part of the firepower needed to blast a corridor through the thin Russian lines near Sovetsky. Metzger was convinced the operation would succeed.

Hours passed and Paulus did not give the order to attack.

Hitler still had not given his blessing to the maneuver. Paulus cabled Hitler again.

23 November 1942

Mein Führer,

Since receipt of your wireless signal of 22 November, the situation has developed with extreme rapidity. . . .

Ammunition and fuel are running short. . . . A timely and adequate replenishment is not possible. . . .

. . . I must forthwith withdraw all the divisions from Stalingrad itself and further considerable forces from the northern perimeter. . . .

In view of the situation, I request you to grant me complete freedom of action.

Heil, mein Führer!
Paulus
2130 hours, 23 November 1942

While this message was being transmitted, one of Paulus's generals, Seydlitz-Kurzbach, tried to trigger an unauthorized retreat from the Volga. He ordered the 94th Infantry Division to vacate its sector at the northeastern corner of the pocket. The purpose of his plan was to stampede neighboring German units into similar withdrawals which, in turn, would force Paulus to order an exodus from the *Kessel*.

Thus, on the night of November 23, Russian sentries saw giant fires blazing inside the 94th's perimeter and alerted Vassili Chuikov's command post. The flames flared again and again as ammunition dumps exploded into the black sky. In the *balkas*, German soldiers stuffed belongings into knapsacks and shouldered rifles before blowing up their bunkers with hand grenades. Important documents went into stoves. Senior officers wearing the distinctively red-striped trousers of the German General Staff took them off and burned them. At a regimental command post, where orders were given to pull back from entrenched positions, the briefing officer coldly remarked that the "planned retreat" meant the loss of one-third of "our people."

But as the 94th Division left its positions, the Soviet Sixty-second Army fell upon it. Lt. Gunter Toepke heard the Russians coming, screaming *"Urrah! Urrah!"* over and over and over. As he plunged blindly for cover, the Russians took a fearful toll. Caught in the open, and defenseless against the "steamroller" waves of Red Army attackers, the Germans died by the hundreds.

By dawn, the 94th Division "ceased to exist." Worse, General Seydlitz-Kurzbach's plan backfired. Other German units held their ground and the anticipated mass stampede to the west never took place. But the general was unrepentant. Arrogant, mulish, he insisted that his strategy was the only correct one, and that the loss of several thousand men was a small price to pay for the greater goal he had sought, the salvation of Sixth Army.

Seydlitz-Kurzbach's unilateral action reaped other unforeseen and far-reaching consequences. From inside Stalingrad, a Luftwaffe radioman wired news of the unauthorized withdrawal and destruction of the 94th Division directly to Hitler at Rastenburg. But no one bothered to tell Paulus, only a scant twenty miles away from the tragedy.

The news sent Hitler into a frenzy. Ranting at Paulus for disobeying his instructions to hold fast, he resolved to end any future insubordination once and for all. At 0838 hours on the morning of November 24, he sent a drastic message to the Sixth Army. Under the heading, *"Führerbefehl,"* the highest priority Führer Decree, it set down precise defense lines for a new fortress, or *Festung*. Warning Paulus to maintain these lines because relief was at hand, Hitler declared, "Sixth Army will adopt hedgehog defense. . . . Present Volga front and northern front to be held at all costs. . . . Supplies coming by air."

After two tense days of frantic communications, the Führer had delivered an incredible verdict. He denied Paulus any freedom of movement or decision. Further, he robbed Sixth Army of its chance to escape while the Russians were trying to strengthen their hold around the pocket.

In issuing his orders, Hitler assumed that Paulus would remain subservient to higher authority in such a grave moment. He guessed correctly. Temperamentally unsuited to reject a command from the Führer, Paulus canceled the breakout, and put his trust in the promise of an airlift.

Yet the airlift was only a topic of discussion in East Prussia. Hitler still did not know whether the Luftwaffe could support Sixth Army, and he was waiting for authoritative word on the matter. A short time later, a special train passed through concentric rings of SS watchtowers and pillboxes outside the Wolf's Lair, and the grossly overweight, bemedalled Reichmarshal of the Luftwaffe, Hermann Goering, huffed down to pay obeisance. His failure to deliver England, his failure to prevent massive bombings of the Fatherland, had eroded Goering's position in the tenuous hierarchy of the Nazi regime. Nominally he was still heir to the mantle worn by Hitler, but now he was ignored by his leader and jeered at by men such as Martin Bormann. Recently he had been living in isolation in Karinhall, his magnificent estate south of Berlin. From there he directed a hunt for art treasures through the museums of occupied Europe, and indulged in drugs which eased his sense of failure.

When the question of an airlift arose, the deflated Goering seized the opportunity to ingratiate himself with Hitler and to reverse his ebbing fortunes. He brushed aside General Jeschonnek's reservations about the inadequate airfields and bad weather in Russia, and rushed to Rastenburg, arriving in the middle of an argument. Gen. Kurt Zeitzler was warning against an extended airlift, "The Luftwaffe should muster every available aircraft and fly in fuel and ammunition *only*. That way the breakout can succeed."

When Goering appeared, Hitler asked his opinion.

Goering had his answer ready. "My Führer, I announce that the Luftwaffe will supply the Sixth Army from the air."

Zeitzler was furious. "The Luftwaffe just can't do it. Are you aware, Herr Reichsmarshal, how many daily sorties the army in Stalingrad will need?"

Goering flushed. "Not personally, but my staff knows."

"Seven hundred tons! Every day! Even assuming that every horse in the encirclement area is slaughtered, it would still leave five hundred tons." Zeitzler would not relent. "Every day five hundred tons landed from the air."

The Reichsmarshal recovered his composure. Grandly, he boasted, "I can manage that."

"It's a lie!" Zeitzler screamed.

In the sudden silence that enveloped the table, Goering turned beet red. His fists knotted as if to strike the army's chief of staff.

Hitler let his aides argue heatedly. Finally he broke in, his voice hard, devoid of sympathy for the impassioned Zeitzler, "The Reichsmarshal has made his announcement, and I am obliged to believe him. The decision is up to me."

Waiting outside the room, General Adolf Heusinger saw a beaming Goering emerge with an equally happy Hitler. To Heusinger it was apparent that an entire German Army wandering the snowfields of the Russian steppe now had to depend on Goering's promises. Heusinger felt a sense of doom.

From Rastenburg, orders flashed to *Luftflotte* 4 in Russia to fly three hundreds tons a day into Stalingrad. As soon as more planes were made available, the Luftwaffe was expected to meet Paulus's minimum demands of five hundred tons to keep his men alive. Hitler had Goering's word on it.

The Führer next turned his attention to Paulus. Still ignorant of the insubordination committed by General Seydlitz-Kurzbach, he sent another curt signal to Gumrak:

Radio message (urgent) from Army Group B

Number 1422 to HQ Sixth Army
TOP SECRET

The Führer wishes that, because of its decisive importance for the Sixth Army, the north part of the fortified area Stalingrad, . . . be placed under the command of one military commander. This commander will be responsible to the Führer that this fortified area is *held at any price*. The Führer, therefore, has charged General of the Artillery von

Seydlitz . . . with this responsibility. This does not affect the
overall responsibility of the Commander in Chief of the Sixth
Army. . . .

By order of the Führer

By now, Paulus knew the disaster Seydlitz-Kurzbach had
perpetrated, but for some inexplicable reason Paulus refused to tell
Hitler that the man he trusted actually had defied him. Instead,
Paulus took the Führer's latest order to Seydlitz-Kurzbach's
bunker and handed the document to the silver-haired officer.

When Seydlitz-Kurzbach finished reading it, Paulus asked,
"And what are you going to do now?"

Seydlitz-Kurzbach laconically replied, "I suppose there is
nothing I can do but obey."

Many German soldiers accepted the news of the canceled breakout with resignation.

Cpl. Heinz Neist could not imagine that such a large army
would be left to rot. Though briefly nagged by the thought that
nobody would be able to help, the thirty-one-year-old Neist refused to let his spirits sag. In his cellar west of the Barrikady Gun
Factory, he stayed by his radio and waited complacently for someone to come and rescue him.

Josef Metzler's commanding officer personally told him about the
aborted maneuver. When the major hastened to add that he
doubted the Russians would be able to keep Sixth Army encircled,
Metzler believed him. He was more concerned with acquiring fur
boots. Too scrupulous to steal them from Russian prisoners or
to loot them from dead bodies, he waited impatiently for the lucky
moment when he could own a pair. His feet were like ice.

Sgt. Albert Pflüger, a pugnacious veteran of the 297th Division on
the southern edge of the pocket, was not upset by the news either.

At a briefing, when an officer read an official report telling of the Russian offensive and "temporary" encirclement, Pflüger listened halfheartedly. It struck him as very funny that the words in the report seemed to rhyme.

After the meeting broke up, the sergeant waded through heavy snow toward his unit, but he lost his bearings and wandered in the freezing cold for a long time before he found his own bunker. It took him hours to get the chill from his bones.

For other German troops, the cancellation caused terrible hardship, creating disgust and doubt. These men had come from Gumrak and the southwest corner of the pocket to lead the breakout. Now they trudged back to bunkers built months before in anticipation of the Russian winter. But they found no shelter; the Russians had infiltrated during their absence and seized their shelters.

Thus, schoolteacher Friedrich Breining had to establish a series of shallow trenches in the open that were whipped by wind and drifting snow. In such exposed positions, Breining began to wonder whether he could survive for long.

Lt. Hans Oettl was in the same predicament. Disgusted with the turn of events, he raged inwardly at the German High Command. "Now we are sold out!" he muttered. But Oettl was almost alone in his opinion. Most of his men argued that the Führer would not let them down. Oettl laughed sarcastically at them.

Lt. Wilhelm Kreiser heard the news in the very potato cellar that he had seized at the end of October. "It's like a blow from a club," he told his friends. Few in Kreiser's company believed in the airlift.

The Russians in front of Kreiser were already more aggressive. While he had limited amounts of ammunition and food, the enemy lavished shells on his position. Every time Kreiser lit a fire, the Russians shot at the trail of smoke curling from the house.

To prepare for any eventuality, the lieutenant ordered a trench dug behind the command post. He wanted to be ready for the worst.

Sgt. Hubert Wirkner, a native of Upper Silesia, was too busy to analyze the future. Surrounded by smoldering vehicles, the twenty-one-year-old veteran of campaigns in Poland, France, and Crete was running for his life. His 14th Panzer Division had just been ordered east, across the Don to Stalingrad. All secret matter was to be destroyed; all vehicles not needed for combat were to be burned.

Billowing fog enveloped Wirkner and his comrades as explosions shattered the air and flaming wreckage spewed into the fields. Wirkner rode through the chaos, over the frozen Don, and into the western perimeter of the pocket around Peskovatka. The Russians did not follow closely.

At Sixth Army Headquarters, a stranger introduced himself to Paulus. Maj. Coelestin von Zitzewitz had just arrived from Rastenburg.

On the previous evening, at the Führer's headquarters, Zitzewitz had spoken with Gen. Kurt Zeitzler, who gave him an unusual set of verbal orders, "Sixth Army has been encircled. . . . You will fly out to Stalingrad with a signals section of the Operations Communications Regiment. I want you to report directly to me, as fully as possible and as quickly as possible. You will have no operational duties. We are not worried: General Paulus is managing very nicely. Any questions?"

The bewildered Zitzewitz had none.

Zeitzler went on. "Tell General Paulus that everything is being done to restore contact. . . ."

Coelestin von Zitzewitz told this to Paulus the next day. Paulus asked him how the German High Command intended to raise the siege. When Zitzewitz had no answer, Paulus spoke for a short time about the proposed airlift. He emphasized that he needed five hundred tons a day over the long run, and stressed the fact that such an amount had been promised him.

Before dismissing Zitzewitz, Paulus added that he thought Sixth Army would serve a more useful function if allowed to withdraw west from the Volga to a more defensible line near Rostov. He kept repeating that statement, saying that his generals supported this view. Zitzewitz felt a wave of sympathy for the soft-spoken general, plagued by an incessant tic which contorted his handsome face. To the major, Paulus seemed weighed down by an intolerable burden.

Zitzewitz's arrival at Sixth Army headquarters sparked comments from the staff. A few officers, notably Arthur Schmidt, wondered openly whether the major had been sent to spy on Sixth Army's leadership during the crisis.

Meanwhile, Paulus received a cable that offered unexpected hope:

Manstein to Paulus 24 November 1300 hours

Will assume command on 26 November. Shall do everything in my power to relieve you. . . . In the meantime it is imperative that Sixth Army, while holding Volga and north front in compliance with Führer orders, forms up forces in order, if necessary, to clear a supply channel toward the southwest.

Manstein

Field Marshal Erich von Manstein had first learned of this plan on November 21 when OKW had reached him at Eleventh Army Headquarters in Vitebsk, 280 miles west of Moscow. He had been appointed commander of the newly formed Army Group Don, comprising the encircled Sixth Army, "Papa" Hoth's battered Fourth Panzer Army, and the remnants of Rumanian divisions scattered on the steppe. OKW told Manstein his primary task was to carve a corridor to Sixth Army so that supplies could be sent the Germans fighting at the Volga. But at no time was the field marshal alerted to bring the Sixth Army out of the *Kessel*. He was only to "give it assistance," while working closely with both Army Groups A and B to protect the right and left flanks of the Wehrmacht in southern Russia.

Dubious about the practicality of holding on to Stalingrad, Manstein boarded a train which crossed the steppe toward Novocherkassk, just outside Rostov. As he gazed thoughtfully out the window at the unending sea of snow, he remembered that only ten years before he had traversed it as a guest of the Soviet government. That had been during the incredible era of secret cooperation between Stalin and the German Weimar Republic, when for several years, promising German officers had gone to school with their counterparts in the Red Army and, at the same time, German aviators practiced dive-bombing techniques on targets around the Don. The Western powers of World War I, sensitive to any German rearmament, had never learned of this clandestine arrangement until it was too late to stop it.

The irony of the situation struck Manstein as he stared at the forbidding hostility of the steppe. Again and again, his mind wandered to his comrades trapped at Stalingrad and he harbored few illusions about their fate. The field marshal was convinced that Paulus had already wasted any decent chance to leave safely.

On his arrival at Novocherkassk, two letters awaited him. One was from Paulus. Handwritten, plaintive, it sought to pinpoint the Sixth Army's dilemma:

> . . . Both my flanks were exposed in two days . . . the outcome is still uncertain.
> In this difficult situation, I sent the Führer a signal, asking for freedom. . . .
> I have received no direct reply to this signal. . . .
> In the very next few days the supply situation can lead to a crisis of the utmost gravity.
> I still believe, however, that the Army can hold out for a time. On the other hand—even if anything like a corridor is cut through to me—it is still not possible to tell whether the

daily increasing weakness of the Army will allow the area
around Stalingrad to be held for any length of time. . . .
. . . I should be grateful if I could be provided with more information than hitherto, in order to increase the confidence
of my men. . . .

At the bottom of the page, Paulus apologized for the poor
quality of the paper and his scrawl.

The other letter was from Marshal Ion Antonescu, the Rumanian chief of state, who was complaining bitterly of the mis-
treatment of his soldiers by German officers and troops.

Manstein was furious to receive such a letter because he
respected the Rumanians' contribution to the war effort. Also, he
already knew the shocking details of the destruction of Antonescu's
armies. Originally there had been twenty-two divisions. Nine had
been destroyed in the field; nine others had broken and fled. Only
four were fit for battle.

Nagged by these distressing messages, Manstein plunged immediately into his primary task: reaching Sixth Army. Assuming
Goering's airlift could keep Paulus's troops alive, Manstein hoped
to carve a corridor to the fortress by mounting a two-pronged
attack. One would be a diversion from the west, aimed at Kalach.
Hopefully, this diversion would draw Russian units away from the
second drive which would start from Kotelnikovo, seventy-three
mlies southwest of the pocket.

The Kotelnikovo offensive had the advantage of avoiding any
crossing of the Don. Only two of its tributaries, the Aksai and
Mishkova rivers, would hinder progress, and beyond the Mishkova were thirty miles of open steppe, reaching all the way to the
southern perimeter of the *Kessel*. When the German relief troops
reached the Mishkova River, Manstein then expected Paulus to
burst out with his army and link up with them.

But first, Manstein needed more troops and armor. Having
completed a long trip from France, the first elements of the 6th
Panzer Division were unloading from trains at Kotelnikovo. The
6th Panzers boasted 160 tanks operated by elite crews. Coming

a few days later behind the 6th was the 17th Panzer Division, at nearly full strength. For extra support, Manstein had called for the 16th Motorized Division, which was thirty miles east of his headquarters and presently filling the gap left by the demise of the Fourth Rumanian Army. Manstein also requested the 23rd Panzer Division. It had been reduced to twenty-five tanks, but he was not aware of its dilapidated condition.

To protect the flanks of the relief expedition, the field marshal had what was left of the Rumanian forces, hastily thrown together into two under-strength corps. But all his projections were doomed—unless the airlift nourished the Sixth Army, and an improvised defense force led by Col. Walter Wenck could stall the Russians on the steppe south of the Don.

Only a few days earlier, Wenck had received urgent orders to leave his post in the Caucasus and assume command of the "screening" line in front of the Russians pushing southward toward Rostov from Serafimovich and Kletskaya.

Needing troops and equipment, the colonel instituted his own set of rules. He rode the highways and dragooned stragglers into ad hoc units. He played movies at intersections and when exhausted soldiers stopped to watch, Wenck brusquely marched them back to war. One of his noncommissioned officers found an abandoned fuel dump and put up signs reading: "To the Fuel-Issuing Point." Hundreds of cars, trucks, and tanks drove into this oasis only to become part of Wenck's new army.

On November 27, when Wenck had met Manstein at Novocherkassk to discuss the situation, the field marshal bluntly reminded the colonel of his awesome responsibility:

"Wenck, you'll answer to me with your head that the Russians won't break through to Rostov. The Don-Chir front must hold. Otherwise not only the Sixth Army in Stalingrad, but the whole of Army Group A in the Caucasus will be lost."

Wenck did not need a lecture. He needed extraordinary luck.

Chapter Eighteen

"Manstein is coming, Manstein is coming," the shouts went along the frozen *balkas* in the *Kessel* between the Don and Volga. Soldiers cheered his name and repeated stories of his genius to each other: Manstein, whose plan to outflank the Maginot Line had led to the fall of France within six weeks; Manstein, who reduced the Crimean fortress city of Sevastopol within days. Listening to these stories, the men of the Sixth Army gloated over the coming of the hook-nosed, silver-haired legend and laughed at their temporary status of "mice in a mousetrap."

General Seydlitz-Kurzbach did not laugh at the army's predicament. Thoroughly cowed by Hitler's order to bear co-responsibility for defense of the pocket, he decided to avoid any blame in case the Sixth Army perished. He began writing.

FROM: Commanding General November 25, 1942
   51st Army Corps   morning

To: Commander in Chief of the Sixth Army [Paulus] I am in receipt of the army command of November 24, 1942 for the continuation of fighting. . . .

The Army is confronted with a clear alternative: break-through to the southwest in general direction of Kotelnikovo, or the annihilation of the Army within a few days. . . . The ammunition supplies have decreased considerably. The assumed action of the enemy, for whom a victory in a classic battle of annihilation is in store, is easy to assess. . . . One cannot doubt that he will continue his attacks . . . with undiminished vehemence.

The order of the High Command . . . to hold the hedge-hog position until help is near, is obviously based on unreal foundations. . . . The breakthrough must be initiated and carried through immediately.

Paulus read Seydlitz-Kurzbach's comments with the tolerance a father might show a wayward son. He needed no such analysis from Seydlitz-Kurzbach. For days he had known that retreat from the Volga was imperative. In the precious hours that had been lost, at least sixty Soviet formations were now encamped on the perimeter of the *Kessel*, their guns trained on Sixth Army. To the south and west, at least eighty other Red Army units were ready to repulse any German attempt to fight through to Paulus. By November 25, the Germans inside the *Kessel* were twenty-five miles away from the nearest friendly troops.

At the air bases closest to Stalingrad, German airmen struggled to make the airlift succeed. Gen. Martin Fiebig directed the piecemeal buildup from Tatsinskaya and Morosovskaya, which had been excellent fighter and bomber bases during balmy summer months, when weather permitted hundreds of sorties each day. But now it was wintertime, and the air units on the steppe faced enoromus difficulties. Three-motored Ju-52s, transport workhorses of the Luftwaffe, flew in from distant bases. Some were old and untrustworthy; others lacked guns and radios. Crews ranged from veterans to green graduates of training schools in Germany. Many fliers came to Russia in regular-issue clothing, without any garments suited for below-zero temperatures.

On November 25, the first planes had lifted off for Pitomnik Airfield inside the *Kessel*. For two days they struggled in and out, carrying fuel and ammunition. On the third day, November 27, the weather closed down all operations and Fiebig added up the sorry totals. In the first forty-eight hours, only 130 tons had been delivered instead of the required 600. Sadly, he wrote in his diary: "Weather atrocious. We are trying to fly, but it's impossible. Here at Tatsinskaya one snowstorm succeeds another. Situation desperate."

Marshal Richthofen agreed wholeheartedly. Despairing of the airlift, he telephoned Kurt Zeitzler and Albert Jeschonnek to warn them that Sixth Army had to fight its way out before it lost its strength to move. Richthofen begged them to submit his opinion to Hitler. They did, but Hitler refused to be swayed. He told Zeitzler the Sixth Army could hold out, must hold out. If it left Stalingrad, Hitler declared, "we'll never get it back again."

When Richthofen heard this verdict, he decided that he and other commanders were "nothing more than highly paid NCOs!" Though completely disgusted, the frustrated Luftwaffe general kept his temper in check and went back to work. His rationale was simple: "Orders are orders."

Meanwhile, the Russian High Command wrestled with its own serious problems: the success of the vast encirclement. Neither Stalin nor Vasilevsky or Zhukov had dared anticipate the dimensions of their triumph. Prepared to deal with up to one hundred thousand of the enemy, they suddenly realized that nearly three hundred thousand armed soldiers had to be contained and liquidated.

In Red Army staff schools, such an operation had never been broached. Only Zhukov had practical experience in dealing with a surrounded enemy; at Khalkin Gol in Manchuria in 1939, he had successfully eliminated a portion of the Japanese Kwantung Army in a period of eleven days. But that force had totaled only one fourth of Paulus's Sixth Army, now at bay, dangerous and defiant.

On November 28, Stalin called Zhukov to discuss the complex difficulties of dealing with the Stalingrad "fortress." Once again, the premier needed his deputy's calm analysis of an emergency. Zhukov answered with a telegram the next morning:

> The trapped German forces are not likely to try to break out without help from a relief force. . . .
> The German command will evidently attempt to hold its positions at Stalingrad. . . . It will mass a relief force for a thrust to form a corridor to supply and eventually evacuate the trapped forces. . . .
> The trapped Stalingrad group should be cut in half. . . .

But the Russians had no quick formula to achieve this goal. By now, seven Soviet armies were hugging the Sixth Army in a hostile embrace. The Sixty-sixth and Twenty-fourth pressed from the north; the Twenty-first and and Sixty-fifth barred exit to the west; the Fifty-seventh and Sixty-fourth pushed up from the south. In Stalingrad itself, Vassili Chuikov's Sixty-second Army held the Volga shoreline as it had since September.

The *Kessel* was roughly thirty miles wide by twenty miles long, its western side tapered so that it resembled the snout of a giant anteater. In its middle, five corps headquarters dotted the steppe around Paulus while on the perimeter, weary divisions faced outward.

Manning the northern front closest to the Volga were the 24th and 16th Panzer divisions. To their left, stood the depleted 60th Motorized and 113th Infantry. In the northwestern sector, the nearly destroyed 76th, 384th, and 44th divisions licked assorted wounds from their retreat across the Don. At the extreme western edge, in the "snout," the remnants of the 376th Division held a precarious foothold beside the 3rd Motorized. On the south side of the pocket, the 29th Motorized Division braced anxiously

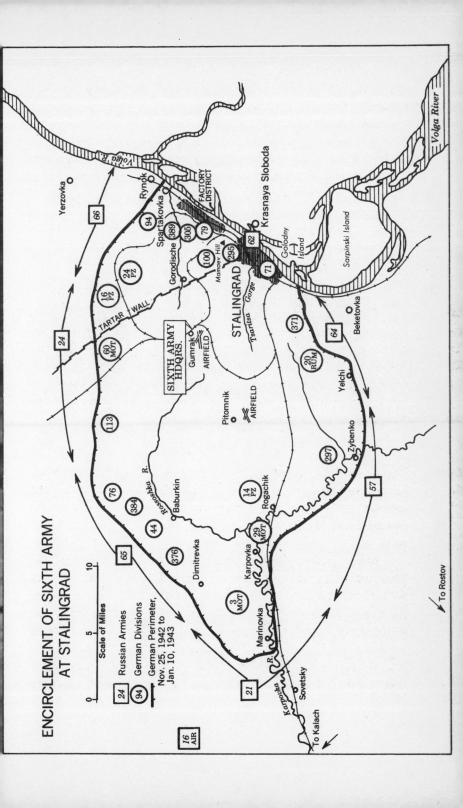

ENCIRCLEMENT OF SIXTH ARMY AT STALINGRAD

Scale of Miles

0   5   10

| 24 | Russian Armies |
| 94 | German Divisions |

German Perimeter,
Nov. 25, 1942 to
Jan. 10, 1943

Volga River

Sarpinski Island

Golodny Island

Krasnaya Sloboda

FACTORY DISTRICT

Yerzovka

Rynok

Spartakovka

Gorodische

Momaev Hill

STALINGRAD

Tsaritsa Gorge

Beketovka

Yelchi

Zybenko

Rogachik

Karpovka

Baburkin

Dimitrevka

Marinovka

Sovetsky

To Kalach

To Rostov

TARTAR WALL

SIXTH ARMY HDQRS.

Gumrak AIRFIELD

Pitomnik AIRFIELD

Rossoshka R.

Karpovka R.

94
389
305
79
100
295
62
71
24 PZ
16 PZ
60 MOT
371
20 RUM
64
113
297
14 PZ
76
384
44
376
29 MOT
3 MOT

66
24
65
21
57
16 AIR

next to the 297th and 371st divisions. The 14th Panzer and 9th Flak divisions roamed the pocket in reserve, moving from position to position depending on the threat.

Two Rumanian divisions and one regiment of Croatians fleshed out the southern line closest to Stalingrad. And in the city, six exhausted battle groups held all but five percent of the town. There, the 71st, 295th, 100th, 79th, 305th, and 389th divisions clung to the same cellars and trenches they had occupied during September and October.

At the edge of the Volga, General Chuikov stormed in and out of his cliffside bunker cursing his bad luck. His war had become static—a backwash to the drama on the steppes to the west and south—and the Volga continued to plague him. Pack ice drifted by in enormous chunks, grating against each other like knives scraping glass.

On November 27, the disgusted Chuikov radioed front head-quarters across the river: "The channel of the Volga to the east of Golodny and Sarpinski islands has been completely blocked by dense ice. . . . No ammunition has been delivered and no wounded evacuated."

The offensive on the steppe had not solved all his problems. Not only that, but he smarted under a directive that put his troops on short rations. Chuikov was furious with his superiors and he told them, ". . . with every soldier wanting with all his heart and soul to broaden the bridgehead so as to breathe more freely, such economies seemed unjustified cruelty!"

The Germans were already on half rations. Caught with most of its supplies on the wrong side of the Don, where the Russian offensive had swept the steppe, the Sixth Army had only six days' full rations for each man when the encirclement began. But Karl Binder had done his job well. The quartermaster's foresight in moving his food, clothing, and cattle east, out of the danger zone made his 305th Division one of the few "rich" ones. Then Paulus ordered an accounting of available supplies, insisting on a "balancing" of provisions among the units.

Binder was outraged. He had little sympathy for those who had failed to anticipate the calamity. Nevertheless he gave up part of his reserves: three hundred head of cattle, eighty sacks of flour, butter, honey, canned meat, sausage, clothing to destitute neighbors. Binder felt his labors for his own troops had been in vain.

Veterinarian Herbert Rentsch had a different problem. His horses, Russian *panjes* and Belgian drafts, were going to the butchers to sustain the army. The doctor was glad he had not sent four hundred animals back to the Ukraine just before the pocket closed.

He also had a personal crisis. His own horse, Lore, was showing the effects of inadequate grazing. Her rib cage showed through her winter coat. No one had yet forced him to include Lore in the list of horses to be killed, and he refused to think about that possibility.

At the western edge of the pocket, the last German regiments and companies ran across the bridges over the Don and passed through the rear guard holding the Russians in check. The last German soldier to cross the Don toward Stalingrad was a first lieutenant named Mutius. During the early morning of November 29, he looked back at the dark steppe. At 3:20 A.M., he pushed down a plunger and the bridge at Lutschinski burst into an orange ball of flame that lit the shore on both sides, illuminating a long line of German vehicles moving east, into the *Kessel*.

On November 30, forty He-111 bombers joined the Ju-52 transports on the run to Stalingrad. It took fifty minutes to cross the snowfields of the steppe and follow the radio beacon to the landing strip at Pitomnik, which was a beehive of activity. Mechanics swarmed over the planes as soon as they landed, unloading equipment swiftly, even siphoning off extra gas from wing tanks to replenish the fuel of the armored vehicles inside the pocket. On that day, almost a hundred tons of vital supplies arrived. Paulus was encouraged to believe that the Luftwaffe was about to meet his demands. It was not. Another weather front moved in and for the next two days, hardly a plane made it to Pitomnik.

Since the beginning of General Yeremenko's offensive, Lt. Hersch Gurewicz had stayed in place on the right shoulder of the breakthrough, the sector closest to the city. When Soviet armies probed the southern perimeter of the *Kessel* on December 2, he jumped into an observation plane and took off to scout the terrain.

Beneath Gurewicz, the German lines appeared as dark smudges, irregular scars. While marking the data on his map, a sudden burst of antiaircraft fire shook the aircraft, which spun wildly out of control. Gurewicz braced himself in his cramped seat and the pilot managed to pull out of the dive only to crash-land extremely hard. A tremendous explosion smashed Gurewicz unconscious. Hours later, he woke to find the cabin a shambles and the pilot dead. Gurewicz looked down at his pants, soaked through with blood. His right leg throbbed; it was bent almost at a 45-degree angle to his body.

He worked feverishly to get out of the plane, but the pilot's body kept falling over on him and Gurewicz felt a surge of panic. Finally he threw his weight against the door and fell out into a snowdrift. His leg hung by one piece of skin above the knee; he dragged it after him with his right hand. His mind fully alert, he suddenly realized that the explosion which ripped the plane apart was a mine, and that he was alone in no-man's-land, in a minefield.

He crawled very carefully, looking nervously for any telltale traces of explosives planted in the snow. When twilight came, he could not see clearly, and his breath froze in the cold wind. The leg tormented him but the freezing temperature congealed the blood around the wound, keeping him from bleeding to death.

Gurewicz struggled on. His face was caked with snow and ice had formed over his eyes and lips. By now it was completely dark, and the lieutenant lost his nerve. Afraid to move among the mines, he lay forlornly in the snowfield, shivering miserably, the pain from his wound making him want to vomit.

Somewhere in the darkness, a light wavered and Gurewicz heard men talking in low tones. The light grew stronger, hands suddenly reached out and pulled at him. When he heard musical Russian phrases, his joy at being saved released pent-up emotions. For the first time in the war, tears flooded down his face. He cried uncontrollably as his countrymen tenderly lifted him onto a stretcher.

That night, doctors cut off his right leg almost at the hip. They told him his war was over, that he would need a year to recover. Thus he went back across the Volga one last time, while behind him, the Red Army tightened its grip on the Germans in the Stalingrad pocket.

Sgt. Albert Pflüger knew it was just a matter of time before the Russians came across the sloping hills. At an outpost of the 297th Division just south of Stalingrad, he had monitored the buildup of tanks and artillery for several days. But his company was powerless to prevent it. They were running out of ammunition.

The dawn was gorgeous, a violent red sun which poked over the horizon beyond the Volga. Russian shells followed immediately and the rolling barrage drove Pflüger and his men into the ground. When the barrage lifted to pass on to the rear, Pflüger raised his head to see black Soviet T-34s approaching through a smoke screen. Three of them cautiously worked down a hillside. The first disappeared into a gully.

Pflüger waited patiently to spring a trap. He had stationed a .75-millimeter antitank gun to his right, out in no-man's-land. When the first tank crawled up from the gully, the sergeant fired a purple Very light into the sky and the .75 roared. The shell cut through the tank turret and passed on into open air before it exploded. Two Russian soldiers tumbled out of the T-34 and raced madly back up the hill. Pflüger was tracking one through his sights when he suddenly thought, My God, if you've been that lucky, who am I to shoot you now. He lowered his rifle and let the man go.

The other tanks came on. The .75-millimeter gun fired again and the second vehicle took a shell in the turret, which catapulted fifty feet in the air before crashing back down on the tank. The third T-34 was hit in the undercarriage and spun crazily for a moment before coming to a stop.

The sergeant had won the first skirmish. But the Russians regrouped. As *Katyusha* rockets sang over his head, Pflüger called for artillery support. He got only seven rounds from rear batteries which were being severely rationed.

The tanks appeared again and Pflüger's .75 went back into action. After the gun fired fifteen rounds, Pflüger received a phone call from his irate commander who screamed, "Only take sure shots." And, in the middle of the battle, the sergeant had to explain why he had been so reckless with ammunition. He was told to get his crew on the ball.

For his work in driving off yet another enemy attack, Pflüger received an official reprimand for wasting shells.

On December 4, the Russians attacked the *Kessel* from the north and northwest. The 44th Division took the main blow and the fire brigade, the 14th Panzer Division, rushed to help. Fighting swirled around foggy Hill Number 124.5 and one German regiment lost more than five hundred men. Hundreds more suffered frostbite in the frigid temperatures. Sgt. Hubert Wirkner helped take back one position that had been held by Austrian troops until the Russians ran over them with tanks. He found the defenders where they had fallen. All lay naked in the snow. All had been shot.

On the northern side of the *Kessel*, forward observer Gottlieb Slotta of the 113th Division talked quietly to Norman Stefan, an old friend from Chemnitz in eastern Germany. For several weeks Slotta and Stefan had shared their food, shelter, and innermost thoughts. Both men believed that Hitler would not leave them on the Russian steppe. When they talked of the past, Slotta often confided his reactions to the trauma he experienced in September when friends had ignored his warnings and died from shell-bursts. The memory still haunted him.

Each day he trained his binoculars on the growing numbers of Red Army units deploying in front of him. Each day he phoned this ominous evidence back to headquarters. It was a hopeless gesture. The 113th Division had barely enough ammunition to hold off one concerted attack.

Stefan was always beside him, observing the same buildup. Frequently he stood at full height and walked back and forth in the trench. Slotta joked with him about it, warning that an enemy sniper would find him irresistible.

Finally a Russian noticed Stefan, tracked his path along the the line and, as Slotta turned to give another warning, a rifle cracked. Stefan crumpled to the bottom of the shelter. That night Slotta went to the aid station and waited beside his friend for some time. But Stefan died without saying another word.

On the eastern side of the *Kessel*, at the Barrikady plant in Stalin-grad, Maj. Eugen Rettenmaier was faced with a renewed tempo in the fighting.

The commissar's house and houses 78 and 83 erupted as Red Army soldiers infiltrated them at night and fought for control of the wrecked buildings. Grenades exploded in brief flashes in the pitch-black rooms. In the morning, half-naked bodies littered the stairwells and cellars.

Major Rettenmaier sent his officers in piecemeal to hold these battered houses behind the Barrikady. They generally lasted for three days before they, too, were wounded or dead.

His reinforcements, mostly young soldiers from Austria, were used up by the end of November. House 83 had become a crucible, where most of the Germans who went in never came out again. For two days, men fought for just one room. Thick smoke billowed from it. Grenades killed friend and foe alike.

When a sergeant stumbled back to Rettenmaier's command post and demanded more grenades, a doctor looked at his bloodshot eyes and told him: "You must stay here. You may go blind." The sergeant refused to listen. "The others back there can hardly see a thing, but we must have grenades." Only when another soldier volunteered to take them did he slump into a chair and pass out from exhaustion.

Rettenmaier finally had to abandon House 83. But at the commissar's house, his troopers from the Swabian Alps held on with their characteristic "pigheadedness."

Rettenmaier also was facing an acute decline in morale. The half-rations his men ate did not alleviate their melancholy, and they missed their homeland most of all. Deprived of regular mail, they fell victim to forebodings of an inconceivable fate. Conversations dwindled to whispers in the shelters. Men sat on their bunks for hours, seeking solitude with their thoughts. They wrote letters at a feverish pace, hoping that airlift planes might carry their innermost sentiments to relatives waiting at home.

When a trickle of mail arrived at the Barrikady from Germany, the lucky few read them over and over, caressing the paper, sniffing any scent.

Cpl. Franz Deifel had returned from leave in Stuttgart two weeks earlier and each day he hoped his certificate of release from the army would arrive so he could get out of the *Kessel* and go back to work at the Porsche factory. In the meantime, he drove an ammunition truck each day to an observation post on the rear slope of Mamaev Hill. It was a boring job, made lively now and then by indiscriminate Russian shelling, so Diefel made a game of it, guessing which section of the road the enemy planned to hit. So far he had been right in his predictions.

Finally, he received a summons to regimental headquarters and ran to the bunker where a clerk handed him a slip of paper: "Here's your release."

Deifel read it slowly, and the clerk shook his head, muttering, "Damn rotten luck!" It had come too late: Only the wounded and priority cases could now leave Stalingrad.

One of the priority cases who climbed into a bomber at Pitomnik was the recipient of a premature Christmas present.

Dr. Ottmar Kohler was astounded when the staff of the 60th Motorized Division insisted he go home to see his family. Grateful for his devotion, they had rewarded the combative surgeon with ten days' leave in Germany.

When he refused the offer, he received a direct order from superiors to make the trip. Stunned by such solicitude, Kohler said his good-byes to men who had no chance of seeing their loved ones in the near future, if ever again, and promised to come back on time.

The homeland Kohler visited was uneasy because the German people had finally learned some of the truth about Stalingrad. When the Soviet Union issued a special announcement about their victory on November 23, it forced Hitler to allow some information to go out in a communique from the Army High Command. No mention was made of an encirclement, only that the Russians had broken through northwest and south of Sixth Army. The communique attributed this alarming fact to Russia's ". . . irresponsible deployment of men and material."

Because of the vagueness of the news, fear gripped the German civilian population, especially those people with relatives on the eastern front. Frau Kaethe Metzger was one of them. More and more concerned because she had not heard from Emil, she phoned the local postmaster and asked: "Is 15693 among the Stalingrad Army postal numbers?"

Though forbidden to give out such information, the man, an old friend, answered, "Just a minute."

Kaethe's heart pounded while she waited. The voice came back on the line. "Do you mean to say Emil's there?"

She could not answer.

"Hello, Kaethe, hello!"

Her eyes filled with tears, she hung up and stared blankly out the window.

Army Group Don headquarters at Novocherkassk was a gloomy place. Nothing was working as it should, and Hitler continued to "put spokes in the wheels" of Manstein's expedition to Stalingrad.

The 17th Panzer Division had failed to arrive because Hitler pulled it off trains to act as reserve for an expected Russian attack far to the west of Stalingrad. And east of Novocherkassk, the 16th Motorized Divsion stayed in place because Hitler feared another attack from that direction.

In addition, the Red Army launched a series of spoiling operations against Colonel Wenck's impromptu army, now renamed Combat Group Hollidt. This mini-offensive, known as Little Saturn, was designed to blunt the one-two punch Manstein was readying as part of Operation *Wintergewitter* ("Winter Storm"), the establishing of a corridor to the Sixth Army.

In Moscow, STAVKA was reading Manstein's mind through the Lucy spy ring in Switzerland. Thus, Zhukov and Vasilevsky had mounted Little Saturn as a stopgap measure, which delayed temporarily their more grandiose scheme, Big Saturn, the destruction of the Italian Army and the Germans in the Caucasus.

For his part, Manstein could not wait much longer to make his move. A delay of only a few days might prove fatal to Sixth Army's slim chances, so he speeded up the timetable and put his faith in the tanks assembled around Kotelnikovo. At least the 6th and 23rd Panzer divisions were ready to roll.

In spite of the encirclement, the discipline and organization of Sixth Army remained excellent. On the road network, military police directed heavy traffic and routed stragglers to lost units. The highways were always well plowed. Road signs pointed the way to divisional, corps, and regimental headquarters. Fuel and food depots handled rationed supplies in an organized, crisply efficient manner. Hospitals functioned with a minimum of confusion, despite the increasing number of casualties, approximating fifteen hundred a day. Drugs and bandages were reasonably plentiful.

At Pitomnik Airport, wounded men went out on the Ju-52s and He-111s at a rate of two hundred a day. They left in good order, under the watchful eyes of doctors who prevented malingerers from catching a ride to freedom.

Given the gravity of the situation, Sixth Army was functioning better than some might have expected. But certain signs of decay were becoming evident. On December 9, two soldiers simply fell down and died. They were the first victims of starvation.

By December 11, Paulus knew his superiors had failed him. During the first seventeen days of the airlift, a daily average of only 84.4 tons arrived at Pitomnik, less than twenty percent of what he needed to keep his men alive. Paulus was seething with frustration and when Gen. Martin Fiebig, the director of the Luftwaffe air supply, flew into the pocket to explain his difficulties, the normally polite Paulus heaped abuse on him and excoriated the German High Command.

A genuinely sympathetic Fiebig let him rant, as Paulus told him the airlift was a complete failure. He referred constantly to the promises of adequate supplies and the brutal truth that barely one-sixth that amount had actually arrived:

"With that," Paulus lamented, "my army can neither exist nor fight."

He had only one flickering hope, which he indirectly referred to as he wrote his wife, Coca, "At the moment, I've got a really difficult problem on my hands, but I hope to solve it soon. Then I shall be able to write more frequently. . . ."

Paulus knew that Manstein was about to keep *his* promise, at least, to try to save the Sixth Army.

Chapter Nineteen

From the suburbs of Kotelnikovo, the white-painted tanks and trucks of the 6th Panzer Division fanned out to the northeast and, at 5:15 A.M. on December 12, raced for Stalingrad. Operation Winter Storm, the attempt to break through to Sixth Army, had begun. "Show it to them; give it to them, boys," cheered tank expert Colonel Hunersdorff from his command vehicle. Watching the tanks' treads churn the snow, he waved his men toward the *Kessel*, seventy-three miles away.

Surprisingly, the Russian resistance was negligible. Bewildered by Manstein's accelerated timetable, their rear guards fell back after offering only token fire. The worst problem facing the Germans was the ice that covered the roads and prevented the panzers from getting ample traction.

In the village of Verkhne-Tsaritsyn, forty-five miles northeast of Kotelnikovo, worried Russian leaders converged to discuss the new German drive. Marshal Vasilevsky presided, and he and Nikita Khrushchev exchanged opinions with other generals about

German intentions. Convinced that Soviet forces were not sufficient, Vasilevsky tried to phone Stalin, but could not reach him. Increasingly alarmed by further news of German advances, he asked General Rokossovky to send the Second Guards Army from the Stalingrad front reserve to a line just north of the Mishkova River. Rokossovsky refused, citing his own needs for troops to help throttle Paulus in the pocket.

When Vasilevsky insisted, Rokossovsky held his ground. The two men argued at length and finally, Vasilevsky threatened to phone Stalin directly and placed another call to the Kremlin. But the circuits were busy and it would take hours to get a connection.

Vasilevsky paced nervously through the day while the German relief expedition gathered momentum.

During the afternoon, Hitler met with his advisors in Rastenburg. Jodl was there. So were Heusinger and Zeitzler, and six lesser aides.

Zeitzler began with a depressing report about the entire eastern front. The condition of the Italian troops defending the flanks was broached. It was agreed that, at best, they were unreliable. As to Stalingrad, the Führer agreed with Zeitzler that it was a precarious situation, but he still categorically refused to order a retreat. He felt that to do so would jeopardize "the whole meaning of the campaign" of the previous summer.

On this note, General Jodl launched a discussion of the dangers posed by the Anglo-American invasion of North Africa and the defeat of Field Marshal Erwin Rommel at El Alamein. As Jodl spoke, Hitler interrupted several times to make biting remarks about men and armies. Regarding Rommel, he declared: "He has always got to spar around with all kinds of miserable elements out there. If you do that for two years, eventually your nerves go to pieces. . . . That's the Reichsmarshal's [Goering's] impression, too. He says that Rommel has completely lost his nerve."

Going on, Hitler voiced his concern about the Italian armies in Africa and Russia, "I didn't sleep last night; that's the feeling of uncertainty. Once a unit has started to flee, the bonds of law and order quickly disappear unless an iron discipline prevails. . . . We succeed with the Germans, but not with the Italians. We won't succeed with the Italians, anywhere."

The conference went on until 3:00 P.M., adjourning after a briefing on the air supply program for Stalingrad. The figures were impressive as to number of flights attempted per day. But the statistics hid the fact that while planes were taking off for the city, their loads were not reaching troops inside the *Kessel*. Continuing bad weather forced planes to abort missions; Russian fighters had begun harassing the airlanes, and antiaircraft batteries were being reinforced. As a result, the steppe was becoming a highway of broken aircraft—a graveyard of planes.

By now Sixth Army headquarters was aware that Manstein was coming. Buoyed up, nervous, Paulus and Schmidt waited through the day for progress reports of Operation Winter Storm. They were hopeful, but each knew that time was robbing Sixth Army of its strength to break loose and meet its saviors.

That day's Sixth Army War Diary reflected the precipitate decline inside the *Kessel*:

December 12, 1942, 5:45 P.M.

Rations decreased since November 26. Another ration decrease on December 8 as a result of which the fighting power of the troops has been weakened. At the present time, only one-third of the normal rations. Losses here and there because of exhaustion.

That night, Marshal Vasilevsky finally reached Stalin to explain developments of past hours. He told the premier that the Germans had already reached the southern bank of the Aksai River, and he wanted permission to detach the Second Guards Army from the Stalingrad front and move it at all possible speed to a blocking position in front of the German panzers.

Stalin's immediate reaction was violent. He refused to go along with the proposal and assailed Vasilevsky for trying to pry troops loose from Rokossovsky without first checking with STAVKA in Moscow. Stalin warned him that he was holding him personally responsible.

In return, Vasilevsky was incensed, for he knew it was his duty to maintain the security of both fronts. His anger served no purpose. Stalin told him his request would be discussed that night at the Defense Committee meeting and rudely hung up.

At 5:00 A.M. the next morning, Stalin called back. He now agreed fully with Vasilevsky's plan; the Second Guards Army was alerted for a forced march.

The decision came none too soon. At 8:00 A.M. on December 13, bleary-eyed German tank crews crossed the Aksai River on a rickety bridge. Now only the frozen Mishkova River remained as a natural barrier to the *Kessel* around Stalingrad.

Desperate to keep abreast of the relief force's progress at Gumrak Airfield, Paulus ordered ten radio operators to monitor every wavelength for messages from the oncoming panzers. But Russian technicians constantly foiled their efforts by jamming channels and broadcasting false information.

While Paulus lingered in this limbo, he also had to contend with pressures on every sector of the *Kessel*. In the ruins of Stalingrad, the Soviet Sixty-second Army denied its own weaknesses and harassed the Germans from the tractor factory to the Tsaritsa Gorge. These aggressive tactics were totally consistent with Chuikov's military philosophy. The combative general knew of no other way to wage war.

From her home in Kuibyshev, Chuikov's wife had written recently and reminded him of that trait.

My dear Vassili:
I at times imagine you have entered into single combat with Hitler. I know you for twenty years. I know your strengths. . . . It's hard to imagine that someone like Adolf could get the better of you. This could not happen. One old lady, a neighbor, meets me every morning and says: "I pray to God for Vassili Ivanovich. . . ."

Though beset by supply problems, and disgusted with the front command for not sending enough ammunition, Chuikov continued to mount small attacks against the increasingly weary Germans. One of his storm groups concentrated on the potato cellar that Lt. Wilhelm Kreiser had held since late October. While his exhausted men slept at their guns, the Russians crawled up, then drove them outside, back to the system of trenches that Kreiser had thoughtfully prepared for just such an emergency.

Kreiser rallied his men to counterattack, but he forgot to keep low. From a nearby cottage, a Russian machine gunner put one bullet in his left shoulder, another through his arm. The lieutenant went down into the snow. Still conscious, he gave command of the company to another lieutenant and then staggered off to the rear. In minutes, his successor followed him there with a bullet through his own arm.

Kreiser radioed for reinforcements, then led a group of wounded to an aid station, where a doctor jabbed him with morphine and put him on a sled. Towed further to the rear by a *Hiwi* laborer, the drowsy Kreiser fell asleep and rolled off into the road. When the loyal *Hiwi* came back and dragged him from a snowbank, the grateful lieutenant mumbled his thanks and fell unconscious.

In the days to come, Kreiser would be one of the fortunate men flown out of the *Kessel*.

That night, another Soviet storm group crossed the German lines. Faulty Soviet intelligence reports had pinpointed General Paulus's command bunker within the city limits and the blond sniper,

Tania Chernova, and three other Russians had been sent to kill him.

Carefully picking their way past mountains of rubble, the execution squad looked for German sentries outlined against the snow. Tania was trying to control her temper because the girl ahead of her blundered frequently and made too much noise. "That cow," Tania thought as she looked at the plump figure that increasingly annoyed her.

The "cow" stumbled and a fiery explosion smashed Tania to the pavement. Unconscious, she bled into the gutter from a gaping wound in her stomach. Moments later, Vassili Zaitsey hurried to her side and tenderly lifted her limp form.

Zaitsev struggled back to his lines, to a cellar hospital where doctors worked desperately to staunch the flow of blood from Tania's wounds. For hours they despaired of saving her, but by morning she rallied and the surgeons made plans to transport her across the Volga for a major operation.

After Tania regained consciousness, her first questions were about what had happened to her patrol. Told that the woman ahead of her had stepped on a mine but survived with only superficial injuries, she listened to the details with mixed emotions. Her vendetta with the Germans was ended; she had "broken eighty sticks" in her three months of war. But the image of that "damned cow" kept intruding on her thoughts and made her furious.

On the morning of December 14, the German 6th Panzer Division charged ahead toward the *Kessel* and ran directly into Russian reinforcements of almost three hundred tanks. One platoon of panzers was chased by forty Russian T-34s, and an armored battery which went to their rescue came over a low rise to find the Russian tanks barely a thousand meters away. Painted white "just like the Germans," with black numbers on the turrets, they were surrounded by a large knot of soldiers.

For a moment, Lt. Horst Scheibert wondered whether he had stumbled on elements of the German 23rd Panzer Division that was providing support for 6th Division's drive to the pocket. Everything looked so German, then he noticed that the gun barrels seemed more stubby, and the turrets had no domes.

Still hesitant and nervous, he moved his force closer. At six hundred meters, he had not made up his mind to shoot. He trembled as the distance closed rapidly.

Suddenly the soldiers ahead jumped for their own tanks and Scheibert only had time to scream, "*Achtung!*" into the radio before two Russian tanks came at him.

Scheibert hollered again, "Fire! Russians!" But the enemy got off the first shots. At only three hundred meters, they missed completely.

German gunners were more acurate. The first two Russian tanks blew up violently, and "the rest was child's play." Reloading with tremendous speed, the Germans slamed shells through the confused enemy formation. Thirty-two curling black pillars of smoke marked the total destruction of one of the Soviet tank columns outside Verkhne-Kumski.

But other Russian armored groups still controlled the town. The Germans could not yet break through toward the Mishkova River.

While grenadiers of the 6th Panzer Division probed for a weak spot in the Russian defense, they heard and saw the Junker and Heinkel transports streaming through the sky toward Pitomnik Airfield as the Luftwaffe tried to sustain life in the *Kessel*. Paulus's tirade against Martin Fiebig on December 11, had resulted in increasing the air shipments to Stalingrad by fifty tons a day. Still it was not nearly enough.

The fault could not be charged solely to the German pilots, whose varied problems defied solution. Russian fighters and anti-aircraft were taking an ever greater toll of transports. But the most exasperating worry was the weather of southern Russia. A fulcrum for colliding maritime and continental fronts, it frustrated countless forecasts. Aircraft expecting good weather at Pitomnik frequently encountered low clouds, fog, or even blizzards that forced detours to bases hundreds of miles away. When that happened, both the cargos and planes were lost to the Stalingrad shuttle for several days at a time.

To counteract such failures, meteorologists tried to rely on eyewitness reports from observers inside the *Kessel*. But these men often failed to broadcast. There was no fuel to power the generators for their radios.

A more deadly foe was ice. It tore up engines and immobilized planes for weeks, forcing mechanics to cannibalize parts from wrecks to repair damaged motors. And the mechanics themselves had to overcome unexpected hazards. When they removed their gloves to make delicate adjustments on equipment, their fingers froze to the metal. Maintenance that should have been accomplished was left undone, with catastrophic results.

Human error led to another series of mishaps. Since the Luftwaffe refused to allow army quartermasters to supervise the loading of the transports going to Stalingrad, famished soldiers at Pitomnik frequently opened crates of utterly worthless goods. One day it was thousands of protective cellophane covers for hand grenades—but no hand grenades. Another time, it was four tons of marjoram and pepper—at a time when troops were killing mice and eating them. Again, several thousand right shoes. Most ironic of all was a shipment of millions of neatly packaged contraceptives.

While airmen braved death to carry such unusual supplies to the *Kessel*, the Germans in Stalingrad scrounged for protein.

Thirty-one-year-old Cpl. Heinz Neist met an officer, Lieutenant Till, who smiled mischievously and asked: "Want something to eat?"

Neist gratefully accepted the offer and sat down before an aluminum plate that was loaded with potatoes, meat and gravy. When he looked warily at the feast Till grinned: "Believe me, it is not a human being." Neist needed no further urging and ate everything in front of him. The meat tasted just like veal and only when he finished, did he ask what it was. Till told him it was the last of the Doberman pinschers.

Neist could not have cared less. His stomach was full for the first time in weeks.

In his snowhole at the edge of no-man's-land, Pvt. Ekkehart Brunnert could not imagine such a meal. His clothes had frozen to his body, but his worst complaint was about his stomach. It doubled him over with knifelike pains.

His main meal each day was a watery soup. More was out of the question, because whenever he held out his mess tin, his name was recorded to prevent him from getting a second helping. What really made him furious was the sight of sergeants eating from plates heaped with solid food. Afraid to speak out about the privileges of rank, the private began to wonder whether everyone in the pocket really depended on each other for survival.

Like thousands of others, he foraged for extra food where he could. Once, the head of a frozen horse provided brains for a delicious meal. Another time, a roll of medicine tablets helped assuage his hunger.

Given a break from front-line duty, he went to the rear to seek warmth and rest. Within hours, however, he faced an arms inspection. Never having been issued proper lubricants, Brunnert frantically scratched and rubbed his weapon with scissors, stones, even his fingernails, until most of the rust disppeared. But the senior corporal who inspected Brunnert's platoon used a carefully sharpened match to pry into each rifle. Disgusted with the results, he promptly placed Brunnert and the others on extra guard duty. Walking his post that night, Brunnert had barely enough strength to stand. His legs felt like rubber, and he feared the extra workload would finish him.

Forty-five miles south of the *Kessel*, at the village of Verkhne-Kumski, the 6th Panzer Division was still unable to push through

Russian opposition. The northern and eastern horizons were filled with Soviet T-34 tanks and antitank guns that poured a fountain of projectiles at the Germans.

It was like a gun duel on the ocean, but here the snowfields assumed a crazy pattern of tank treads and long black streaks left by exploding shells. In the inevitable confusion of vehicles firing and then moving quickly to new positions, Germans shot at Germans, Russians at Russians.

When T-34s entered the village, a frantic German officer radioed: "Request permission to abandon the village. . . ." It was not granted. Another formation of panzers invaded the town from the west; by noon, almost all its ammunition was spent.

Colonel Hunersdorff appeared in the midst of his weary troops. Leaning out of his tank, he screamed: "You want to be my regiment? Is this what you call attack? I am ashamed of this day!"

He kept it up, hurling invective on all sides and his soldiers reacted with cold rage. Some openly questioned his right to tell them how to fight. But Hunersdorff's motive was simply to galvanize his tankers. This he did. His tirade was followed almost immediately by another desperate call for help from the Germans inside Verkhne-Kumski. Hunersdorff gave the order to burst into the village "at maximum speed whatever the losses," and five companies formed a column with the few tanks carrying armor-piercing shells leading the way.

Still furious at Hunersdorff, the panzer crews roared ahead spraying the fields on both sides with indiscriminate machine-gun fire. The unorthodox approach terrified the Russians, who jumped up and ran wildly across the plains. Inside their Mark IVs, the Germans assumed that the Russians thought they were insane.

Verkhne-Kumski fell easily this time, but within hours an "inexhaustible supply" of Russians counterattacked and Combat Group Hunersdorff had to retreat to the west. Out of ammunition, almost out of fuel, each tank carried a load of wounded that clung desperately to the turrets. The combat groups' diary recounted in laconic fashion, "This day was connected with heavy losses."

It was also a day of heavy losses for the Russian 87th Guards Division. Jammed into a blocking position south of the Mishkova River as the result of Marshal Vasilevsky's appeal to Stalin, the Guards had marched for a day and a half without pause from the Beketovka area, just below Stalingrad.

In the vanguard of the division was Sgt. Alexei Petrov, who had just trained a new gun crew for the offensive, and he urged his men to a faster pace. Snow obscured his vision and exhaustion became the main enemy, but he allowed no one to rest. Petrov himself held on to the barrel of the gun and slept while walking. Finally they arrived at the Mishkova River—and immediate combat with the 6th Panzer Division around Verkhne-Kumski.

Petrov had never seen nor heard such heavy shelling. Hour after hour, explosions blew the ground into pillars of frozen dirt and snow, and the horizons blossomed with endless flame. To Petrov, it was worse than in Stalingrad.

On the flat plain were thousands of bodies, tossed like broken dolls onto the ground. Most were Russians, victims of German artillery and Stukas. At the height of the bombardment, Petrov saw a tiny figure, no more than three feet high, waving his arms wildly. Amazed, Petrov looked more closely and saw that it was the upper body of a Russian soldier. Beside it on the ground lay a pair of legs and hips, neatly severed by a shellburst.

The man was looking at Petrov and his mouth opened and closed, sucking air, trying to communicate one last time. Petrov gaped at the apparition until the arms stopped flailing, the mouth slackened and the eyes glazed. Somehow the soldier's torso remained upright and forlorn beside the rest of the body.

Chapter Twenty

Still unsure of the relief force's location, Paulus prepared for the crucial decision of how to link up with Manstein. After assigning the 53rd Mortar Regiment the dangerous job of leading the breakthrough, he moved armored combat groups to the southwestern corner of the pocket. But he could find only eighty tanks fit for action.

He also called on Maj. Josef Linden, whose engineer battalions had been decimated at the Barrikady Gun Factory a few weeks before, for two special assignments. The first was plowing clear the road network around the *Kessel,* a simple job on the surface, but exceptionally difficult because of the gasoline shortage.

The second task was equally vital: Two road construction battalions and a bridge company were needed to deactivate the minefields so that the German tanks and trucks could break out quickly when Paulus gave the word.

After four days of fighting, Manstein's soldiers were still on the way to Stalingrad, but the attack had slowed to a snail's pace. Combat Group Hunersdorff of the 6th Panzer Division had not yet captured Verkhne-Kumski and, supported by part of the battered 23rd Panzer Division, the replenished tankers went back to the village.

The drive bogged down again so the 6th slipped off to the west to out-flank the enemy. Around the village of Sogotskot, the Russians had prepared a vast network of rifle pits that made it impossible for tanks to advance. Nor would any of the Russians surrender. From distances of ten feet or less, the Germans shot into the trenches. "The tanks stood . . . like elephants with fully extended trunks," and when the Russians raised their heads, the "trunks" recoiled and blasted them with point-blank fire. Still the Russians held. Finally, when Soviet armor came up to help, Combat Group Hunersdorff again had to back away as the twilight of December 16 obscured the land between the Aksai and Mishkova rivers.

In Stalingrad, every Russian along the Volga shore heard a tremendous crashing noise and Vassili Chuikov bolted from his cave to witness a glorious sight: An enormous wave of ice was pushing down past Zaitsevski Island. "Smashing everything in its path, it crushed and pulverized small and large ice floes alike, and broke logs like matchwood," was how he described it later. And while the general held his breath, the monstrous ice pack slowed and, just opposite Chuikov's fortress bunker, shuddered to a halt. For minutes it groaned and heaved. Behind it, thousands more chunks of ice slammed into the jam with terrific violence. The "bridge" held.

A short time later Chuikov sent sappers across the ice to see whether it would support traffic. By 9:00 P.M. they had returned safely, and he ordered planks to build a highway to the far side.

His supply problems were over.

Just a few hundred yards west of Chuikov's jubilant cliffside headquarters, Capt. Gerhard Meunch was faced with his first case of insubordination. It had been triggered by the Führer's "Christmas

Drive," the annual fund-raising campaign for the Nazi party that reached even into the *Kessel*.

One platoon from Meunch's companies refused to make any donations. When he asked the reason, an officer said: "Captain, you will have to see for yourself what is wrong."

Meunch went to visit the platoon, reduced to six men, and inquired about the trouble. The men told him they were no longer prepared to fight. One trooper added: "Captain, I will no longer play the game. We are fed up!"

Stunned by their attitude, Meunch wisely decided to say nothing. He sent the men to the rear and waited beside their machine gun until replacements came to fill the gap. Then he went to his command post, called for the rebels and told them they could sleep at his quarters that night.

In the morning, he shared breakfast with them, and as the group sat on the floor sipping hot coffee, Meunch watched them carefully and noticed they seemed a bit more relaxed. Gingerly he brought up the previous night's difficulty. The rebels answered without hesitation.

The underlying cause of their mutiny was a letter from one of the soldier's wives, who had asked why he was at the front while several of his friends stayed at home. The soldier had been so upset that he had read the letter to his friends. It had driven them into a state of rebellion as they, too, began to wonder why they had to fight the war for malingerers in Germany.

Meunch let them talk out their bitterness, then brought them back to reality. "According to martial law, you are liable to punishment," he told them. "You know how refusal to obey an order will be punished. Are you prepared to return to your positions, and not desert or do foolish things? Can you promise that?"

They answered with a spontaneous chorus of yesses. One soldier went further, "We will fight for you as long as you command the battalion. But if you are wounded or killed, we wish to be free to make our decisions."

Meunch considered the offer briefly, then chose to compromise. "All right, confirm it by handshake," he replied. "As long as I command the battalion you will have to fight. Thereafter you may do what you want."

The men shook hands with him on the bargain.

Later that day, December 17, 150 miles to the southwest at Novocherkassk, Erich von Manstein dined with Freiherr von Richthofen. While the two men sipped wine, they ranged over their mutual problems in trying to save the Sixth Army. Richthofen had just lost two of his bomber squadrons, which OKW had transferred without notice to another sector. To Richthofen, the move was tantamount to "abandoning Sixth Army to its fate. . . ." He minced no words when he exclaimed that it was "plain murder!"

He had phoned Gen. Albert Jeschonnek back in East Prussia to make that charge. But Jeschonnek "formally disclaimed all responsibility" for the order. Now Richthofen confided this conversation to Manstein. Both men were appalled by the decisions being made from the safety of the Wolf's Lair, more than a thousand miles away.

By the time dinner ended, the two were in agreement; they were "like a couple of attendants in a lunatic asylum."

After dinner, OKW's decision to transfer the Stukas back to the upper Don suddenly became clear. Another Russian attack had routed two Italian divisions from their positions fifty miles west of Serafimovich. No one yet realized that this was the opening of Stalin's second great attack, aimed at seizing the port city of Rostov and trapping the entire German army in Southern Russia. Reports so far were sketchy, but Manstein added what fragmentary information he possessed to his pessimistic appraisal of the future. He was well aware of the disaster the news implied. If the Italian Army failed to hold, his German divisions would have to go to their rescue. The result: Sixth Army at Stalingrad would be lost.

Overwhelmed by a sense of onrushing catastrophe, the field marshal fixed his attention on the men in the *Kessel,* whose time for deliverance was at hand.

For days, Manstein had bombarded Hitler and Gen. Kurt Zeitzler about the need to issue a Führer Order for Operation *Donnerschlag* ("Thunderclap"). The order would call for the complete evacuation of the *Kessel.* It would also mean the mass movement of the Sixth Army across the steppe, during which time, the Germans would have to fight the Russians on every flank.

No matter how bloody the outcome of this retreat might be, at this stage of the battle, Manstein considered Operation Thunderclap the only practical solution. The airlift had obviously failed: Hoth's rescue force could only channel a few days' worth of supplies into the pocket.

To date, however, Hitler had agreed only to Operation Winter Storm, the physical linkup by Hoth's forces to resupply the Sixth Army. The Führer still forbade Paulus to withdraw from the *Kessel.* For Hitler, retreat from Stalingrad was out of the question, and his reasoning was typically arrogant, "Too much blood had been spilled there by Germans!"

When General Zeitzler agreed with Manstein on the need for Thunderclap, and promised to get approval from Hitler within a matter of hours, Manstein regarded Hitler's agreement as a foregone conclusion. Thus, on December 17, he briefed his intelligence chief, Major Eismann, on the situation and ordered him to fly into the *Kessel* to discuss strategy with the Sixth Army chiefs.

The next afternoon Paulus made an inspection tour of the front. It left him extremely depressed, for he saw multiplying evidence of his troops' physical decline. The men moved slowly and were indifferent to commands. Their faces had become pinched. With eyes sunken behind protruding cheekbones, many just stared into space.

Returning to Gumrak, he found Major Eismann and greeted him cordially, as did Arthur Schmidt, who had campaigned with

Eismann in France in 1940. Eismann quickly made it clear that Hoth's relief column could only continue its drive for a very limited period. He referred specifically to apparent bad news from the Italian front, and warned that Hoth's divisions might have to be shifted away from the drive to the *Kessel* in order to save that puppet army. Eismann also went on to say that even under optimum conditions, it was doubtful whether Hoth's tanks could advance more than twenty miles beyond the Mishkova River, to Businovka, where Paulus had hoped to make the linkup. He asked Paulus to extend his own drive another twenty-five kilometers south.

Paulus and Schmidt reaffirmed their intention to break out as soon as possible. But they argued that Operation Winter Storm, the linkup, was not feasible until Sixth Army received enough fuel for its tanks. There was only enough gas for a sortie of twenty kilometers, not nearly enough to reach the 6th Panzer Division at the Mishkova. Under these conditions, it was impossible to extend the drive. Both generals strongly urged that Thunderclap, the plan calling for the withdrawal of the entire Sixth Army from the Volga, had to be initiated at the same moment as Winter Storm. Then, the full weight of Sixth Army's waning power could be focused at one point. It was the sole hope for the breakout's success.

Eismann pressed them about accepting the risks of making the linkup, even on unfavorable terms. But Paulus and Schmidt steadfastly refused to begin Operation Winter Storm without more supplies. Schmidt was particularly stubborn on this point. He called the airlift the chief stumbling block to success. Half in jest, he told Eismann, "The army would hold its positions until Easter if it were supplied better."

With the situation still unresolved, the meeting adjourned. The discouraged Paulus went to his quarters, where he wrote a letter to his wife, Coca. Never one to burden her with his own troubles, he asked the usual questions about her welfare and that of his children, then closed optimistically: "Just now we are having a very hard time indeed. But we'll survive. And after the winter, there is another May to follow. . . ."

Chapter Twenty-one

For several weeks, German signal officers inside the *Kessel* had been trying to establish a reliable form of voice contact with Manstein, 150 miles to the southwest. Denied regular phone service by Russian cable cutters, they had created a minor technological miracle.

At the perimeter of the pocket they raised a 120-foot high antenna beacon that linked Gumrak with Novocherkassk by means of a radiotelephone combined with an ultra shortwave decimeter set that could not be monitored by the enemy. Constantly shelled and repaired, the beacon transmitted messages to relay stations installed in German-occupied territory. But one by one the relays fell to Russian tank columns. The radiotelephone link failed, and only a teleprinter remained to record the words produced by the decimeter machine. As the time arrived for Manstein and Paulus to make a final agonizing appraisal of their options, the chattering keys of the teleprinter became their only contact.

If the two men had been able to hear each other's voices, certain intonations or inflections might have helped resolve the crisis. But as the situation stood, Major Eismann reported to

Manstein that he did not believe Paulus would break out under prevailing conditions, and Manstein could sympathize with Paulus's reasoning. However, Manstein was beginning to wonder whether or not General Schmidt was exerting undue influence on Paulus's decision not to try a breakout without a proper quantity of fuel. To the field marshal, positive action was necessary within hours. Haggling over gasoline supplies was a luxury Sixth Army could not afford, especially since Manstein was being pressured to do something, anything, to save his own left wing.*

Unable to communicate the emotions of the moment, Paulus stood beside the teleprinter machine in the operation bunker at Gumrak shortly after midnight on December 19, and waited for its impersonal clickety-clack keyboard to begin moving. The machine hummed and leapt into life:

+++ Here Chief of Staff Army Group Don [General Schulz]. . . .

+++ General Paulus answering. . . .

+++ The field marshal [Manstein] requests your opinion regarding the following question:

What is your estimate of the possibility of a sortie toward the west in the direction of Kalach? . . . It has been ascertained the enemy is consolidating his position vis-à-vis the south front. . . .

[Confused, Paulus asked]: +++ Consolidation opposite which south front is meant? Opposite south front 6th Army or Group Hoth?

[Schulz hastened to clarify:] +++ Opposite south front 6th Army. . . .

[Paulus hesitated to give a quick answer:] +++ [I will] Reply by radio . . .

---

* The Eismann mission caused controversy among the German leaders. Field Marshal Manstein said that Eismann's report of the conference convinced him that Paulus and Schmidt did not intend to break out under existing conditions. Arthur Schmidt has dismissed this conclusion by pointing out that he and Paulus merely outlined the tremendous problems they faced without adequate air supply. Further, Schmidt believes that Manstein used the remarks of the "lowly" major to justify his own subsequent actions. Friedrich von Paulus never referred publicly to the Eismann visit, thereby creating the impression that he did not attach any particular importance to it. No stenographic record of the conference exists.

[Schulz:] +++ Any further questions?

[The teletype operator answered for Paulus:] +++ The general said no and has gone. . . .

But Paulus was back shortly with his opinion, sent on to Manstein by wireless.

Number 404   19 December 1942, 0135 hours

TOP SECRET
To Army Group Don

Sortie toward the south at present still easier, since Russians vis-à-vis south front of Army even less prepared for defense and weaker than in direction Kalach. . . . [to the west]

Paulus

Forty-five miles south of the *Kessel,* the German 17th Panzer Division rushed to position itself on the left flank of the 6th Panzer Division, trying to break through to Paulus. Finally released into action by Hitler, the 17th added the extra firepower needed to break down Russian resistance, and in the early afternoon of December 19, the German tanks went back to Verkhne-Kumski, where hundreds of Red Army men suddenly climbed from their rifle pits and raised their hands in submission. While the tankers waved these prisoners to the rear, the 6th Panzer Division received new orders: Strike quickly for the bridge at Vassilevska, fifteen miles northeast at the Mishkova River. The Stalingrad *Kessel,* its tanks and artillery readied, was only twenty-five air miles beyond that town.

As early winter darkness intruded, the rejuvenated Germans raced off on an ice-coated road. In front of them, the horizon began to blink with muzzle bursts from concealed Russian artillery emplacements.

At Novocherkassk, Erich von Manstein carefully prepared his summation on how Sixth Army might be saved. The plea was directed to Adolf Hitler.

Teletype!   19 Dec. 42, 1425 hrs.

TOP SECRET, "Chefsache," Transmittal by officers only.
To Chief of General Staff of the Army for immediate submittal to the Führer.

The situation . . . has developed in such a manner, that a relief of the Sixth Army cannot be expected in the foreseeable future.

Because of the shortage of available aircraft as well as the inclement weather, an air supply and thus the maintenance of the Army . . . are not possible—as was proven during the four weeks since the encirclement. . . . The Armored Corps alone evidently cannot clear a channel to the Sixth Army and can far less keep such a channel open. *I now believe that a sortie by the [Sixth] Army toward the southwest is the last possibility, to save at least the mass of the Army's soldiers and still mobile weapons.*

The immediate objective of the sortie will be the establishment of contact with the 57th Armored Corps [6th Panzers, etc.] approximately on the . . . Mishkova river. This can only be accomplished by fighting their way free toward the southwest, and gradually shifting the entire Army in such a manner that section by section of the fortified area in the north is given up as ground is gained in the southwest. It is imperative that, in the course of this operation, the air supply of the Army by fighter and fighter-bomber forces is ensured. . . .

In case of a further delay, before long the 57th Armored Corps will be stalled on or north of the Mishkova river and this would exclude the possibility of a simultaneous attack from within and without. Anyway, prior to assembling for the attack, the Sixth Army will need several days for regrouping and refueling.

Provisions in the pocket will last until 22 December. The men already show symptoms of debilitation. . . . According to an Army report, the mass of horses cannot be used because they are starved or else have been eaten.

Commander-in-Chief of the Army Group Don
von Manstein

Manstein was almost demanding the evacuation of the *Kessel* and the complete withdrawal from Hitler's "passion," the city of Stalingrad.

Now less than forty miles south of the *Kessel's* perimeter, the 6th Panzer Division was moving across unfamiliar terrain. Rushing ahead recklessly, it had no choice but to run a murderous gauntlet of armor-piercing shells. Tracer bullets reached out from both sides of the road and riddled the buttoned-up tanks. Inside the turrets, crewmen were dazzled by close bursts that flooded the tank interiors with intense light.

"Don't stop!" The command echoed through the formation, and the panzers rammed ahead into the night. Finally they passed through the artillery zone and were cruising steadily into the unknown. Behind them, a swarm of German tanks burned and exploded.

Now the teleprinter linking Manstein and Sixth Army began tapping out the words of another conference:

19 Dec 42, 1750 hours

[Manstein:] +++ Are you gentlemen present?
        +++ Yes, sir.
        +++ Please give me a brief comment on report Eismann.
[Paulus began a meticulous analysis of his options:] *Case 1—* Sortie [to the south] beyond Businovka with the objective of joining Hoth is possible only with armored vehicles. We are short of infantry forces and, otherwise, the defense of Stalingrad and long new flank are jeopardized.

If this solution is chosen, all reserves will leave the fortress. . . .

*Case 2—*Breakthrough without establishing contact with Hoth only in an extreme emergency. Loss of large amounts of material must be accepted. Precondition is previous arrival of sufficient air supplies [provisions and fuel] in order to improve the state of health of the troops prior to the attack. It would facilitate this solution if Hoth should be able to establish contacts temporarily in order to pour in tractors. The Infantry Divisions at present are practically immobile and more divisions are becoming so every day because we are compelled to slaughter horses continuously.

Case 3—In view of the present situation, further defense depends on supplies and sufficient reinforcements. Supplies so far were absolutely inadequate. At the present supply rate it will not be possible to hold the fortress much longer. . . .

[Manstein wanted more precise information:] +++ What would be the earliest date on which you could form up for solution 2 [Thunderclap]—the complete withdrawal from the *Kessel?*

+++ Preparatory period three to four days.

+++ How much fuel and provisions are needed? Objective Mishkova.

+++ One and a half times the normal fuel supply rate; let Chief Quartermaster Army Group Don figure it out. Reduced rations for about 10 days for 270,000 men. . . .

[Manstein was finished:] +++ . . . Greetings. Do you have any more questions?

[Paulus had two major concerns:] +++ First question: May the Corps participate in the deliberation of preparations for case 2 [Thunderclap]? Second question: How is the situation with Group Hoth [to the south]?

[Manstein was brief:] +++ To (1): Wait for tonight's conversation. To (2): . . . Hoth [the 6th Panzer Division] is attacking and advancing both sides of Verkhne-Kumski. . . .

Moments later the two generals conferred again as Manstein received permission from East Prussia to give Sixth Army a partial clearance for breakout:

+++ . . . Hello, Paulus.
Everything went all right with [6th Panzer Division] today, he gained the Mishkova section. After this conversation you will receive an order, but I want you to understand that . . . [Thunderclap] is a possible solution which becomes effective only upon special order. Eismann described the situation there to me and I am fully aware of the difficulties. . . . If you have any questions regarding the following order, let's talk again tonight. I have nothing else. +++

Paulus wanted to talk:

+++ I would like to report briefly on today's situation. Today there were combat actions with alternating success in the south part of the west front and on the southwest front. The enemy attacked with 60 to 80 tanks. On this occasion we observed a completely new tank regiment number 25. Strong enemy air support; several enemy tanks which had penetrated our lines were destroyed behind our front line. In some places there are minor breakthroughs which will yet be ironed out. . . . Today's combat actions have temporarily contained the mass of our own tanks and part of the forces of the Army, and proven that the enemy in the direction of Kalach [to the west] has particularly strong tank and artillery forces. Today, so far we have destroyed 26 enemy tanks.

[Paulus gave a grudging tribute to the Luftwaffe:] . . . For the first time, air supplies today were adequate; 128 aircraft arrived and brought in 220 tons of supplies.

+++ Congratulations to your successful defensive operations. Regards, Manstein

+++ Thank you, sir. . . . Do I get the order now?

[The teletype could not possibly convey the overwhelming emotion Paulus felt.] +++ Right away. Just a minute.

The order began to form on the teletype paper:

Teletype Nr. 60328
TOP SECRET—"Chefsache!" Transmittal by officers only
19 Dec 42, 1800 hrs.
Order!
To Sixth Army

1. 57th Armored Corps [6th and 17th Panzer Divisions] of the Fourth Armored Army has defeated the enemy in the area of Verkhne-Kumski, and reached Mishkova section. . . . Attack against strong enemy forces in the area of Kamenka and north of this area has started. Severe fighting is still expected in this area. . . .

2. Sixth Army will assemble as soon as possible for operation "Wintergewitter" [linkup]. The objective is to establish contact with 57th Armored Corps, with the aim of pouring in supplies.

3. Developments may necessitate an extension of para-

graph 2 to a breakthrough by the entire [Sixth] Army with the objective of joining . . . [6th Panzer Division] . . . on the Mishkova river. Code word "Thunderclap." In that case it would also be important to accomplish a fast breakthrough with tanks in order to establish contact . . . for the purpose of bringing in a supply convoy. The Army would then advance toward the Mishkova river, covering its flanks, . . . while giving up the fortified area by sections.

Under certain circumstances, it may become necessary to immediately follow up operation "Winter Storm" [linkup] with operation "Thunderclap," [withdrawal]. On the whole the Army will have to make do with current air supplies without stocking up notable amounts of supplies. It is important that Pitomnik airfield be kept in operational condition as long as possible.

All mobile weapons are to be taken along. . . . These items are therefore to be concentrated in the southwest part at an early date.

4. Prepare for item No. 3, [breakout] which becomes effective only upon specific order "Thunderclap."

5. Report date and time of attack as under item 2 [Winter Storm–linkup].

HQ Army Group Don, G3 Nr. 0369/42
TOP SECRET
"Chefsache," Dated 19 Dec 42,
von Manstein
Fieldmarshal General

The order left Paulus and Schmidt totally depressed. Having hoped to receive permission to combine Winter Storm and Thunderclap into one mighty operation, they had been told that all they could do was attempt a linkup with the rescue force. Once again, salvation had been denied them by Adolf Hitler.

Meanwhile, the 6th Panzer Division had begun to make excellent headway toward the *Kessel*. Their momentum toward the pocket was incredible. The night air was crisp, almost lung-searing in its frigid intensity. The moon rose slowly in a starry sky. Beneath it, the snow seemed to be fluorescent. Even when the panzers lost their way, the Russians no longer contested their passage and just after 10:00 P.M., the tankers stopped for a brief rest.

Their vehicles were strung out in a long line. Through firing slits on the right side, tankers could see a trail of telephone poles wandering off across the horizon. In front was a low chain of hills, topped by a darkened village. On the other side of the road, there appeared to be a series of tank traps and trenches.

Moments after the tanks stopped, Russian soldiers leaped out of these ditches and strolled around them. The Germans inside held their breath. Lt. Horst Scheibert first thought his eyes were playing tricks on him. When his gunner whispered that the enemy was fully armed, Scheibert warned him to be quiet since it was obvious the Russians thought they were among friends. Scheibert fingered his pistol, rummaged under his seat to pick up a hand grenade, and waited.

Lounging against the tanks, the Russians joked and laughed up at the Germans, who stood mute in the hatches. Scheibert wondered when they would realize they were not getting any answers. Sweat poured from under his helmet. As the incredible situation continued, Scheibert figured his men could kill the Russians if someone gave the order. But he felt a curious reluctance to murder these "innocents" on the road.

Suddenly, from the hill range in front, a shot rang out. It was followed immediately by a long burst of machine-gun fire. As the Russians bolted unscathed into the snow trenches, the German panzers throttled up and roared ahead.

Teletype conversation General Schmidt with General Schulz 19 Dec 42, 2040 to 2110 hrs.

+++ Here Schulz. Good evening, Schmidt.
+++ Hello, Schulz.
[Schmidt carried the conversation:] 1. Today's combat activities have contained the mass of [our] tanks and part of the infantry forces in defensive action. . . . Much fuel and ammunition was used up [from] reserves intended for the

thrust. We are certain that the Russian attack will be continued on the 20th.

We can only assemble for the attack if our forces are no longer [involved in] defensive operations. We cannot tell when this will be the case. However, preparations have been made to ensure that the troops can be assembled about 20 hours after they are free. A report can therefore only be made at a later date or shortly before assembly. The earliest date would be 22 December, provided we have received a sufficient amount of fuel and ammunition by then. We plan to start the attack at dawn.

2. A thrust beyond the Donskaya-Tsaritsa river [a stream just above the Mishkova] with infantry forces is not possible without jeopardizing the defense of the fortress. There can only be a brief sortie across the Donskaya-Tsaritsa by tank forces, with the tanks being ready to return to the fortress at a moment's notice, as a fire brigade, so-to-speak.

3. This means that—if Stalingrad is to be defended— the Army can only make a breakthrough, when it is certain that 57th Corps [6th Panzer Division] will gain Businovka and is already approaching that area.

4. You will receive our opinion regarding item 3 [Thunderclap] on the evening of the 20th, since extensive inquiries are necessary. . . .

[Schulz had no argument:] +++ Your opinion entirely agrees with ours. [Schmidt, too, seemed satisfied:] +++ O.K., no further questions.

After a brief discussion of Sixth Army's most pressing supply needs, Schulz signed off, "I have nothing else and I wish you all the best (*"Heil und Sieg"*). . . .

One-hundred-twenty-five miles to the northwest, where the second Russian offensive was aimed at Italian forces along the upper reaches of the Don, orderlies at a field hospital ran through the halls, screaming that the Russians had broken through and were just two hundred meters away. No orders were issued to retreat; none were needed. Loading his patients on trucks, Dr. Cristoforo Capone and his medical assistant hitched a ride on one of the vehicles, which navigated the snow-laden road at three miles an hour. When mortar shells bracketed them on both sides, Capone jumped out and rolled into a drift. In the next instant, the truck exploded, blowing huge pieces of metal into the sky, and killing Capone's assistant.

His mind in a ferment, the doctor wandered away from the crackling flames. Only hours before he had been prepared to leave for a Christmas furlough in Italy. Now he walked through a nightmare of dead and dying—and the living, who jostled past him with curses on their lips.

The Italian Eighth Army had broken and run.

Unaware of this new disaster, the 6th Panzer Division speeding toward the *Kessel* entered a village on the south side of the Mishkova River. In the predawn light of December 20, someone spied a Russian staff car racing toward the still-undamaged bridge leading to Vassilevska on the northern bank. A helmeted Russian officer was crouching low in the back seat of the automobile, and before anyone could stop him, the car sped over the river to safety.

But the Russians had made a grievous error. They failed to blow the span, and the German panzers rumbled into Vassilevska just before first light. They immediately formed a hedgehog defense, to wait for supply trucks with ammunition and gasoline to catch up with them.

To their front, the entire Soviet Second Guards Army was deployed across the route to Stalingrad. And while scouts of the 6th Panzer Division watched the rear for some sign of the desperately needed supplies, the Russians began to push them back. A pessimistic German officer approved the morning's report:

War Diary Tank Regiment 11–Vassilevska
December 20th–0600 hours

The gradually increasing resistance is becoming stronger every hour. . . . Our weak troops—twenty-one tanks without gasoline and two weak assault gun companies—are insufficient to widen the bridgehead. . . .

Along the upper Don, the sun rose on a ghastly scene. The bitter cold had claimed thousands of Italian soldiers who paused to sleep during the night. These victims now sat by the roads in what appeared to be comfortable positions, like bored spectators at a Roman arena, as their countrymen scurried by. Giant snowflakes began to collect on their coats and faces; soon they were covered completely. The corpses became road markers for the living.

Cristoforo Capone walked past them in a daze. Still numbed by the thought that he had barely missed his flight to freedom, he tried to grapple with the reality of the situation. The cries of a wounded soldier stopped him. Without any medical supplies, the doctor cupped the boy's head in his hands and looked sorrowfully into his eyes.

"My son, I can do nothing for you," he said softly. "You must be brave."

As the boy stared back, a shell splinter cut off the top of his head, spraying brains and blood over the doctor's face and uniform. For several long seconds, Capone held tightly to the crimson gray mask in his hands. Then the boy sagged onto the ground. Capone collapsed beside him and threw up.

When the nausea passed, the doctor rose weakly. Grazing a solid object with his hand, he grasped a bag of sugar that somehow had been hidden in the snow. Suddenly, ravenously hungry, he began to stuff handfuls of the delicacy into his mouth.

While the Italian Eighth Army collapsed, the teleprinter at Gumrak produced another frenzy of words.

20 Dec 42, afternoon.

+++ Here is General Schulz.
+++ Here is General Schmidt. Hello, Schultz.
1. As a result of the casualties of the recent days, the troop situation on the west front and in the city of Stalingrad

has become extremely tense. Penetrations can only be repulsed by those forces which are to be committed for operation *Winter Storm* [linkup]. In case of major breakthroughs we must have the Army reserves and in particular the tanks at our disposal. . . . So far the Army tanks had to be committed on the west front every second or third day, as a fire brigade, so-to-speak. This means—as was reported yesterday—that, if stronger forces of the Army advance too far away from the fortress, it becomes doubtful whether the fortress itself can be held. . . . The start of the attack will therefore depend on how far [6th Panzer Division] will presumably advance. . . . However, the Army Group may rest assured that we shall not take a one-sided view of the situation and that we shall not act selfishly. Still, we again request that we may not be ordered to form up until it is certain that Hoth's operational units will reach the area around Businovka. . . . In this connection more detailed and continual information on the situation with Hoth would be particularly important to us.

2. *The situation would be somewhat different, if it were certain that Winter Storm would be immediately followed by Thunderclap* [total withdrawal]. In this case we might put up with local penetrations on the other fronts, provided they do not endanger the retreat of the Army as a whole. We would then be much stronger for the breakthrough toward the south, because we could concentrate numerous local reserves from all fronts in the south.

It would therefore be essential for the Army to learn in time whether Thunderclap is still intended. . . .

3. In case Operation Thunderclap is put into practice, it is necessary that

(a) part of the 8,000 wounded men who are still here at present, are taken out by air. We have an additional 500 to 600 casualties per day, so that if 1,000 wounded men were taken out daily . . . 6 to 8 days would suffice to evacuate about half of them. The balance might be evacuated by truck or by air, during the operation. . . .

4. If we form up for *Winter Storm,* it must also be kept in mind, that Thunderclap can follow immediately afterwards, if we have a 5- to 6-day preparatory period. Otherwise, we are compelled to leave much material behind or destroy it. . . .

6. . . . On this side everything has been prepared in accordance with your order of yesterday, so that movements for both operations can start at short notice. Ending.

Maj. Eugen Rettenmaier left his 576th Regiment at the Barrikady Gun Factory to go on detached duty at the *Gorodische Balka,* just west of the city. It was thirty degrees below zero. Rettenmaier's nose was running and the snot froze on his lips. Walking with his orderly along a plowed road, he noticed a man sitting in the snow. It was a soldier from one of his companies.

"Are you tired?" Rettenmaier asked. The soldier nodded apathetically.

"Get up, comrade, we'll help you," and they pulled him along.

At the *balka,* a surgeon examined the man, but he died an hour later. The doctor's first comment was that he had starved to death. Then he hurriedly hedged his diagnosis to include "exhaustion or even circulatory trouble."

Rettenmaier knew better. It had been starvation, nothing else.

Chapter Twenty-two

At the upper Don, west of Serafimovich, Lt. Felice Bracci, who had come to Russia because he wanted to see the wondrous steppe country, now ran across it to save his life. He had been rudely awakened the day before by an aide shouting that most of his 3rd Bersaglieri Regiment had scattered to the south. Bracci thought he was dreaming, that the orderly was playing a joke on him, but the man's terrified eyes quickly brought him to his senses.

Grabbing a rifle, he ran to the command post, where a bewildered officer ordered him to retreat thirty miles south to a place called Kalmikoff. The officer insisted that all heavy equipment except Bracci's two antitank guns must be destroyed prior to departure.

The 5th Company of Bersaglieri moved out shortly and, after several hours, other nondescript units joined the column. Marching at the rear, Bracci personally commanded the two heavy guns. Behind him there was no one—nothing but snow and wind that cut into his back. When night came, with the temperature well below zero, Bracci's guns became harder to move. The men hauling them had deep red creases on their hands and Bracci himself felt terribly weary. But he continued to shout encouragement and helped haul, lift, or push the cannon through the drifting snow.

More and more men were losing hope. One Bersaglieri threw himself under a passing truck. Another sat down on a hump of snow and started to cry. Still clutching his submachine gun, he sobbed his torment to Bracci, who tried to get him on his feet. The man refused and sat there while the column continued on out of sight.

At nine A.M. on December 20, Bracci reached Kalmikoff, now the magnet for thousands of exhausted and frightened soldiers. The town was a tangle of guns, trucks, baggage, and excited soldiers who ran about, trying to find their friends.

Bracci soon received new orders. His regiment, now reformed, led the retreat to Meshkov, a key road junction on the road to Millerovo. The sounds of thousands of boots crunching the crisp snow lulled the marchers until the sudden roar of engines in the distance alerted them. Bracci and his men went to the front of the march and hid their guns behind some tall shrubs.

Minutes passed and Bracci felt hundreds of eyes staring at him, pleading for protection from the menacing sound. Then tanks, Soviet T-34s, appeared about a half mile ahead. Circling cautiously for a moment, as though focusing on Bracci, the tanks "sniffed the air" and finally turned away. The march to Meshkov continued.

Late that afternoon, Bracci saw the spires of a cathedral, "a fairy castle," that dominated the skyline. Spreading out in skirmish lines, the Bersaglieri approached the outskirts of Meshkov. Then a mortar shell plopped into the snow; machine guns chattered. In despair, Bracci realized the Russians had gotten there ahead of the regiment, and blocked the road south.

The beautiful stone church in the middle of town was the rallying point of the Soviet defense. Its thick walls defied destruction. In the darkness, thousands of Italians ran toward it, hollering their battle cry: "*Savoia! Savoia!*" Tracer bullets scoured a deadly pattern through them and screams echoed around the churchyard.

With a clear field of fire, Bracci shot round after round at the building, but the Russian fire never slackened. In the unnatural light, the church's basement glowed brightly from gunbursts and flames. But above the crescendo of combat, of orders being shouted and countermanded, Bracci also heard the moans and pitiful crying that marked the terrible cost of the battle.

The price was too high. Italian commanders finally called back their troops, and the Bersaglieri reformed and trudged back to Kalmikoff.

There, at a tense meeting the next morning, Bracci was told to dig in with his guns until support troops arrived; his commanding officer promised that a German task force was on the way. It was wishful thinking on his part. Mortar fire suddenly descended from surrounding hills and induced immediate panic among most of the Bersaglieri, who stampeded. Bracci crouched beside a house, which exploded and showered him with debris. Dazed but unhurt, the lieutenant staggered out to the road and jumped on the running board of a passing car, which plunged into a drift and bogged down.

At that moment, Russian horsemen appeared on the brow of the hill. While mortar shells kept exploding, the trapped Italians raised their hands in surrender. A colonel beside Bracci looked at his watch. "This is the end for us," he said mournfully. "We are prisoners."

It was 9:30 A.M. on the morning of December 21.

That same morning, intelligence officers of Manstein's Army Group Don were entertaining an important guest.

German troops had intercepted the commander of the Russian Third Guards Army, Maj. Gen. Ivan Pavlovitch Krupennikov, in an ambush the night before and, after a running gunfight, he had surrendered with most of his staff. Treating Krupennikov with the honor due his rank, the Germans fed him generously, then asked him pertinent questions about his army. In turn, he inquired about his son, Yuri, who was missing after the firefight. The Germans promised to find him, sent soldiers to bring the lieutenant to his father, and the grateful Krupennikov began to talk.

He said he was only the acting commander; his superior, General Lelyushenko, had been sick for ten days. Because he knew the Germans would soon learn it from documents captured in his briefcase, he also revealed other information: His troop strength was approximately ninety-seven thousand men. His army mustered 274 tanks and more than five hundred artillery pieces heavier than .75 caliber. But when his interrogators pressed him for other information, such as new units at the front, their makeup and purpose, he balked and cited his soldier's honor.

The interrogators switched tactics, asking the general about conditions on the Russian home front. Krupennikov told them that food shortages did exist, due mostly to transportation problems. In parts of Siberia and Central Asia, he said, surplus crops had been harvested, but the government left them there in order to keep the railroads free to carry troops and heavy equipment to the fronts.

Gratuitously, Krupennikov offered the opinion that, at one point, he had thought Russia would lose the war. However, when he had seen the pitiful condition of German prisoners near Moscow, he no longer considered the Nazis to be "supermen." Now he did not think much of German expectations of victory.

Meanwhile, his hosts had checked his son's whereabouts. Soldiers who combed the surrounding fields reported no trace of the officer, and felt he must have succumbed to wounds somewhere on the snowfields. The interrogators went back and lied to Krupennikov, telling him that Yuri was wounded, could not be transported, but was not in danger of losing his life. Greatly relieved, the Russian general continued the question and answer period.

He was explicit about Russian plans. The main Soviet strategy was to thrust to Rostov and cut off the Germans in the Caucasus. Their first attacks on November 19 and 20, between Serafimovich and Kletskaya and south of Stalingrad, had served only a limited objective, trapping the Sixth Army at the Volga. The second phase, the current attack, was intended to "break through the front of the Italian Eighth Army west of Serafimovich at the Don and fall on the back of the German troops at Morozovskaya. . . ."

The final order, to drive due south from the Don to Rostov, had not been issued as of the day Krupennikov was captured. But he believed that "due to slight losses in rolling up the Italian part of the front," such an operation was possible. This final bit of information was important enough to rush to Field Marshal von Manstein at Novocherkassk, and a typist began to write up a statement on Krupennikov's disclosures.

The interrogation room was filled with gloom. German intelligence officers could only assume that what they had learned was bound to produce an adverse effect on Army Group Don's plan to reach the Sixth Army at Stalingrad.

That plan was already in jeopardy. While the Germans questioned Krupennikov, Russian soldiers were blocking further passage to the *Kessel* by the 6th Panzer Division. Unable to move beyond Vassilevska, only forty miles south of Stalingrad, the German tankers tenaciously held to their bridgehead on the northern bank even though their supply problems had become truly desperate. They had run out of drinking water as well as gasoline. Now, almost crazed with thirst, they crammed dirty snow into their mouths while they huddled inside their immobilized Mark IV panzers. Unable to move, they were easy targets for enemy gunners and Russian infantrymen, who probed to within fifty feet of Colonel Hunersdorff's command post before he personally led a counterattack that drove them away.

So many wounded Germans lay unattended, officers wondered where they could put them in case an order came for retreat. While shells whined overhead, some of the less seriously hurt men suddenly stopped moaning and died. The subzero temperature had claimed them.

Teletype conversation General Schmidt–General Schulz:
21 Dec. 42–1605 hrs. to 1705 hrs.

+++ Here General Schmidt.

+++ Here Schulz.

[The general had vital questions for Sixth Army:] 1. What is your present fuel supply? Give the amounts of Diesel and Auto separately.

2. How many kilometers does that mean? Does this amount of fuel suffice to extend the pocket toward the south while still holding the remaining fronts?

3. If the fuel situation permits you to advance that far, can you do it in view of the available troops?

4. How much fuel is used up daily for the most urgent supply trips within the pocket? Can you answer these questions right away?

[Schmidt had the answers within minutes:] +++ 1. The presently available amount is about 130 cubic meters Auto and 10 Diesel, including today's air supply and the amounts needed for supply trips during the next few days.

2. *This amount would permit the combat troops to advance 20 km including assembly for attack.*

3. Even considering the troop situation we could make 20 km, but we cannot hold the breakthrough front [south] and the fortress for any length of time without the troops committed in the attack and, in particular, not without the armored vehicles. On the contrary, we need replacements in the fortress in the very near future, if we are supposed to hold it. Any sortie with the inevitable casualties involved will jeopardize the defense of the fortress itself.

4. The daily amount used for supply trips is 30 cubic meters.

[Schulz countered with bad news:] +++ The Supreme Command of the Army still has not given approval for *Donnerschlag* ["Thunderclap," the complete evacuation of the *Kessel*]. . . .

In view of the number of troops committed by the

enemy, it is doubtful whether a speedy advance toward the north [by Hoth's relief force] is possible, as long as the enemy does not feel the counterpressure against his forces from the pocket of the Sixth Army. It is therefore necessary that the Sixth Army starts *Wintergewitter* ["Winter Storm," the physical linkup of the relief force with the Sixth Army] as soon as possible. When can you form up for the attack?

The question was almost impossible to answer. Sixth Army was trying to form up for the attack, but Paulus's uncertainty about an actual date for the breakout, plus his worries about the lack of gasoline, caused confusion among his troops. The new recruit from Boblingen, Pvt. Ekkehart Brunnert, suffered from one of these command failures.

When his regiment was chosen to lead the attack to the south, all unneeded cars, trucks and motorcycles were quickly destroyed. For his part, Brunnert was delighted. The destruction of cumbersome equipment signaled a decisive attempt to break out, and he had noticed one special truck, filled with warm clothing sent by German civilians to men at the front. The vehicle would have to be burned, but its contents—fur boots, warm gloves, and scarfs—obviously would be distributed among the soldiers. Standing in line at the door of a huge convoy bus, Brunnert ogled the gift-filled vehicle, until a soldier poured gasoline on it and set it afire.

Brunnert could not even scream his rage as the precious cargo was consumed in the blaze. Instead, he boarded the bus, sat down heavily on his assigned seat and began to cry. Suddenly bitter, he fumed: "As long as our superiors are well clothed, nothing else seems to matter."

Outside the bus, seven Russian *Hiwis* waited for seats. When four of them found they were to be left behind, they rushed to a senior sergeant and begged for a ride. He refused. Wailing in terror, they got down on their knees and pleaded with him. The sergeant kicked one in the groin and walked away, leaving the distraught *Hiwis* huddled together at the side of the road. Their heads lowered, they tried to ignore their three comrades happily packing for the trip out of the *Kessel.*

Inside the bus, Brunnert had regained his composure and was ready to go. With his rations lying under the seat, he dismissed a momentary fear of Russian sniping and was relaxing for the first time in weeks. Suddenly an officer stuck his head inside the door and shouted: "Unpack everything!" Paulus had changed his mind again.

The disgusted Brunnert picked up his rations and walked slowly out of the bus. He had lost all hope of being saved.

Still not totally aware of the dangers posed by the collapse of the Italian Eighth Army, General Schmidt continued his tele-printer dialogue with Schulz.

> +++ If we are to form up regardless of whether the fortress can be held or not, the earliest date for such an attack would be 24 December. By then we hope to have received the neces-sary fuel to have the re-grouping for the assembly of the attack forces completed. However, the General [Paulus] is of the opinion that the fortress cannot be held if the break-through involves major casualties and loss of armored ve-hicles. If there is no prospect of relief in the near future, it would be more advisable to refrain from the sortie and, in-stead, to bring in sufficient supplies by air, so that the men may regain their strength and we may have sufficient ammuni-tion for defensive operations over a longer period. In that case we believe we can hold the fortress for some time even without relief.
>
> [Schulz replied:] +++ I shall immediately report your opinion to the Fieldmarshal and it will also be submitted to the Supreme Command of the Army. Have you any other questions regarding the situation?
>
> [Schmidt answered:] +++ Of the forces considered for the attack, we were already compelled to commit one bat-talion on the west front, since there were heavy casualties in that section during the recent days and there were already some gaps. One of these days we must also move up another

battalion to the city of Stalingrad, because the units committed there are also constantly decreasing in number and, since the Volga is covered by solid ice, that front must be manned more closely. The Russians engage in lively combat activities in the city, which cost us numerous casualties. This decrease of fighting capacity is the main reason why the General [Paulus] considers a sortie extremely dangerous, unless contact is established immediately after the breakthrough and the fortress is reinforced by additional troops. *We believe that the breakthrough is more promising if Winter Storm is immediately followed by Thunderclap since, in that case, we can withdraw the troops from the other fronts.* However, on the whole, we are of the opinion that *Thunderclap* is an emergency solution, which, if possible, should be avoided, *unless the general situation requires such a solution.* It must also be kept in mind that in view of the present physical condition of the men, long marches or major attacks would be extremely difficult.

At the Barrikady and tractor factories, the slag heaps lay under a thick blanket of snow that masked the ugly scars of war. Rusted gun barrels, twisted girders, and railroad tracks had also disappeared, along with the frozen corpses of the unburied and forgotten.

Inside the cavernous rooms, German soldiers lived as best they could. For warmth, they ripped up wood flooring and lit tiny fires. The oil-soaked wood produced a sooty smoke that turned everyone's face black.

In Tool Hall 3C at the Barrikady, an ordinary turner's lathe began to attract unusual attention from lonely Germans after someone discovered that the machine had been manufactured in a town southeast of Stuttgart. Men slipped quietly into the room to stand beside it and read the small name plate: *"Gustav Wagner, Reutlingen."* Former machinists softly caressed the metal created by German hands. Others just stared at the machine, and through it were transported home in their fantasy world of memories.

They wondered openly whether the lathe could still be used.

"Would it work again for the Russians if? . . ." Or, "Where is Reutlingen?" asked those from the Rhineland and further north.

Gustav Wagner's lathe became a shrine.

Thirteen hundred miles to the northwest, at the Wolf's Lair in East Prussia, a tragic war of nerves was being played out. Chief of Staff Gen. Kurt Zeitzler had dropped his role of sycophant as he desperately sought approval for Operation Thunderclap. Deeply committed to saving the Sixth Army, Zeitzler even insisted on reducing rations at the officers' mess as both a tribute to the beleaguered men in the *Kessel* and a reminder that it was OKW's responsibility to bring them out alive. In his daily conferences with the Führer, Zeitzler began acting like his predecessor, Franz Halder, badgering Hitler to endorse Thunderclap. When the annoyed dictator waved his entreaties aside, the frustrated Zeitzler often walked back to his office in a towering rage.

He and Manstein, at least, were of one mind on the issue, and he had promised the field marshal that Hitler would eventually relent. But when Gen. Arthur Schmidt's figures on auto and diesel supplies landed on Hitler's desk, Kurt Zeitzler lost his battle. Schmidt's report of Sixth Army's having only about 140 cubic meters of fuel, which he had given to General Schulz in the teleprinter conversation of December 21, had been forwarded quickly to East Prussia. And his statement that the Sixth Army could only move twenty kilometers (twelve miles) toward a linkup with the German relief force created a negative reaction to Zeitzler's argument for Thunderclap. For if the Führer had ever entertained any thoughts of granting Paulus permission to pull back with his entire army, Schmidt's report swept them away.

Facing the stubborn Zeitzler with the report in his hand, Hitler scornfully asked: "But what exactly do you wish me to do? Paulus can't break out and you know it!"

Zeitzler had no rebuttal. The evidence was too damning and as he left the room, he thought about the tragedy that was developing. Now, at this very moment, Hitler was correct about Sixth Army's inability to break out. But his earlier mistakes and adamant refusal to let Paulus escape when the *Kessel* was first formed thirty days earlier had created this disaster.

At Army Group Don Headquarters in Novocherkassk, Erich von Manstein prepared a final summation in hopes of changing Hitler's mind.

> Document Army Group Don 39694/5
>
> Teletype
> 22 Dec. 42
>
> TOP SECRET, "Chefsache," transmittal by officers only
> TO: Chief of General Staff of the Army
>
> 1. The development of the situation on the left flank [Italian sector] of the Army Group makes it necessary to move up forces there very soon. . . .
> 2. This measure means that the Sixth Army cannot be relieved for some time and that, as a consequence, the Army must be adequately provided with supplies for a long time. In order to maintain the physical strength of the Army through adequate nutrition and to enable the Army to engage in defensive operations, an average daily supply of at least 550 tons is required. . . . According to the opinion of Richthofen [the Luftwaffe general] in this area we can but expect an average of 200 tons, considering the long distance to be covered by the aircraft. . . . Unless adequate aerial supplies can be ensured . . . the only remaining alternative is the earliest possible breakout of the Sixth Army.

In pointing out the patent impossibility of meeting the required air supply, Manstein was reminding Hitler once again that the total withdrawal of Sixth Army from the *Kessel* was the only alternative left.

Convinced he had made the options clear, the choice obvious, the field marshal ordered the message sent to East Prussia and turned to his other problems.

Meanwhile, the teleprinter from Novocherkassk to Stalingrad

kept up a steady chatter. Its stark vocabulary failed to underline the fact that the hours left for deliverance had vanished.

Teletype: General Schmidt–General Schulz
22 Dec 42–1710 hrs. to 1945 hrs.

Here is General Schulz. Hello, Schmidt. I want to report on the situation:

Hoth's 6th and 17th Armored Divisions at Vassilevska [on the Mishkova south of the *Kessel*] were engaged all day today in repulsing strong enemy attacks from the southeast, east and north, so that the armored divisions were not able to make the intended thrust toward the north.

It is planned to make this thrust as soon as the impetus of the Russian attacks has been stopped. Developments will show whether that will already be possible tomorrow. . . . Unfortunately, during the last 24 hours weather conditions were such that no air supplies were made because of the danger of icing and fog. No air reconnaissance was possible either. We must hope for an improvement of weather conditions in the near future. The 175 "Ju" aircraft for an increase of air supplies are on their way. This much on the situation.

The field marshal requests that the following question, which is of importance for an estimate of the Army's supply situation, be clarified. According to the report of the quartermaster Sixth Army, there are still about 40,000 horses in the pocket. This report is contradicted by Major Eismann, who reported that the divisions had only about 800 horses left. Can you tell me the exact number of existing horses; if possible state number of ponies [*Panjes*] and normal-sized horses separately? This is very important, and have steps been taken on your side to ensure that the horse meat is used sparingly for the provision of the troops? . . .

Schmidt had slightly more than 23,000 horses left, only enough to feed the Army until mid-January. The general soon gave Schulz this total. He had been giving other statistics to higher headquarters all day.

. . . *Ration strength on 18 December:* 249,600 (including 13 thousand Rumanians) 19,300 auxiliary volunteers [Russian *Hiwi* laborers] and approximately 6,000 wounded.

. . . *Battle strength:* In front line . . . infantry 25,000, engineers, 3,200. . . .

. . . *Ammunition:* Stocks in Army reserve are low and include 3,000 rounds for light field howitzers, 900 rounds for heavy field howitzers, and 600 rounds for other guns. . . .

. . . *Health:* Men have been on half rations since 26 November. . . . Under present conditions they are incapable of undertaking long marches or engaging in offensive action without a large number falling out. . . .

End

At 6:30 A.M. on December 23, the 6th Panzer Division renewed its offensive to widen the bridgehead at Vassilevska on the Mishkova River south of the *Kessel.* Six hours later, at 12:30 P.M., 57th Corps commander, General Kirchner, arrived in the area "to obtain firsthand information . . ." on what was going wrong. For in the intervening time, 6th Panzer Division had been unable to move any closer to Stalingrad.

A short time later, at 1:05 P.M., the teleprinter clicked out a message from OKW in Rastenburg. Field Marshal Manstein expected it to be the answer to his plea for giving the code word Thunderclap. It was not.

PERSONAL AND IMMEDIATE

Following from Führer begins: The railway junction Morosovskaya and the two air bases at Morosovsk and Tatsinskaya will be held and kept in operation at all costs. . . . Führer agrees that units of 57th Panzer Corps be transferred across the Don. . . . Army Group Don will report measures being taken. . . .

Zeitzler

Hitler was ignoring Manstein's carefully worded warning of the dangers of leaving Paulus inside the *Kessel.* In fact, Hitler had not even alluded to Operation Thunderclap. Instead he was telling Manstein to strip combat units from Hoth's relief force and save the situation at the threatened Italian front.

Astonished that Hitler had never given Paulus a chance to

escape, Manstein dispatched a fateful order to 6th Panzer Division at the Mishkova River: "The division will be taken out of the bridgehead tonight. Trail guards will be left behind. . . ."

The order spread gloom among the staff officers of the 6th Panzer Division, but they had to agree with its logic. It had become clear that "it would be impossible to break through to Stalingrad without the assistance of added troops which were not available. . . ."

One-hundred-fifty miles northwest of Gumrak, the steppe lay under two feet of snow. The sun, reflecting off its frozen wavy crust, cast a shimmering haze. Across the bleak landscape wound a black column of prisoners, the Italian survivors of Kalmikov, Meshkov, and the Don River approaches. They shuffled painfully, haltingly through the subzero wilderness.

When patrolling Russian guards shouted, *"Davai bistre!"* ("Hurry up!"), the prisoners tried to walk a little faster. But their pace was still slow, and the men groaned constantly as the biting cold froze fingers and toes.

Felice Brazzi walked in the middle of this ragged line. He staggered on, like an automaton, one foot in front of the other, again and again. Almost unconscious from the cold, he barely heard the hoarse commands of the guards and the grim croaking of black ravens that circled overhead. One sound always brought Bracci out of his reverie: single rifle shots, which cracked loudly in the clear air as guards shot men who stumbled out of the column to seek rest. For two days, Bracci had listened to this symphony of murder. And on the trail from Kalmikov, both sides of the path were now marked by two irregular patterns of corpses. Bracci had figured out that the Italians were marching north toward the Don, because evidence of harsh fighting was everywhere. Pieces of uniforms, cases of unused bullets, submachine guns, 210-millimeter artillery, arms, legs, the wreckage of his Eighth Army littered the steppe.

Another heavy snow began to fall and it slashed the faces of the bearded soldiers and froze on their eyebrows and chins. His head tucked in like a turtle, Bracci walked on toward a village sitting precariously on the crest of a hill. He hoped the Russians would stop there to feed their captives, none of whom had eaten in at least forty-eight hours.

At dusk the Russians did halt the column, and Bracci crawled into a stable to find a place to sleep. Across the room several Italians smashed their countrymen aside in order to lie in a feeding trough filled with fresh hay.

Other remnants of the Italian Army were trying to escape through a valley near the town of Abrusovka thirty miles to the west. But on the surrounding slopes, Russian gunners had installed the awesome *Katusha* rockets, which whooshed thousands of rounds of high explosives into the writhing gray masses on the valley floor.

A small German detachment trapped at one end of the cul-de-sac managed somehow to commandeer several trucks and enough fuel to make a run through the gauntlet. A few Italian soldiers attempted to jump on the running boards, but the Germans shot them. Other Italians who clung desperately to door handles had their fingers smashed by rifle butts. Having driven their allies back, the frantic Germans pulled away and disappeared in a southerly direction.

Dr. Cristoforo Capone had been running for several days. When he came to the valley, he saw mobs of Italians rushing back and forth at the bottom of the deep gorge. Behind Capone, a Russian tank fired into the crowd, and an officer beside him suddenly gurgled as a rifle bullet went through his neck.

Capone broke away but had no place to hide as machine guns and artillery raked the valley floor. Soldiers toppled, blew into fragments, or stood resignedly, awaiting the impact of a bullet. Some officers and men raised their hands in surrender. Others refused. A surgeon Capone recognized, screamed: "They're going to kill all of us!" and ran at a Russian machine gun that cut him to pieces. For a fleeting moment, Capone thought of doing the same thing, but to his right, another group of Italians suddenly put up their hands. He joined them, and while he watched the enemy approach, several officers in the line changed their minds, pulled out pistols and shot themselves.

Another tense conversation had started between Erich von Manstein and Friedrich von Paulus on the impersonal keys of the teleprinters:

23 Dec 42, 1740 hrs. to 1820 hrs.

Good evening, Paulus—Last night you submitted for the Supreme Command of the Army a report on available fuel that would permit a 20-km advance. Zeitzler requests that you check up on that again. I personally would like to say this: It appears that the enemy [south of the *Kessel*] has constantly received reinforcements so that Hoth is forced to take defensive measures. Moreover, the situation on the left flank of the Army Group [the Italian front] makes it necessary to withdraw forces from Hoth. . . . You will be able to draw your own conclusions as to how this will affect you. I would ask you therefore to examine whether, *if there should be no other possibility,* you are prepared for Thunderclap, [complete withdrawal of the *Kessel*] provided it is possible to bring in a limited supply of fuel and provisions during the next few days. If you don't want to give me an answer right away, let's have another conversation at 2100 hrs. I must point out to you too, that an adequate supply of the Army is a very difficult problem, in particular in view of the development of the situation on the left flank of the Army Group. Please reply.

Paulus quickly pointed out the awful danger of his position:

+++ [Thunderclap] has become difficult, since for several days the enemy has dug in opposite our southwest and south front and, according to radio information, six armored brigades are drawn up behind this defensive front. I estimate we now need a preparatory period of six days for Thunderclap. . . .

From here, of course, I can't tell whether there's the slightest chance of the Army being relieved in the fairly near future, or whether we shall have to try *Thunderclap. If the latter—the sooner the better.* But it must be clearly realized that it will be a very difficult operation, unless Hoth manages to tie down really strong enemy forces outside. *Am I to take it that I am now authorized to initiate Operation Thunderclap?* Once it's launched, there'll be no turning back. Over.

The climax had been reached. Paulus was asking Manstein to give the code word that would send Sixth Army on its way to freedom—or oblivion. Acutely aware that Adolf Hitler had not actually granted permission to leave the *Kessel,* Paulus now placed his own career and the lives of thousands of his men directly into Erich von Manstein's hands. He was begging Manstein to relieve him of the onus of such a decision.

But Manstein brushed aside the plea. Unwilling to take responsibility for initiating Operation Thunderclap against Hitler's express orders, he gave an indirect answer:

+++ *I can't give you full authority today.* But I hope to get permission tomorrow. The main point is—are you confident that Sixth Army could fight its way out [to the south] and through to Hoth . . . if we come to the conclusion that adequate supplies over a long period could not be gotten to you? What do you think? Over.

[Paulus replied:] +++ *In that case, I'd have no option but to try.* Question—is the envisaged withdrawal of forces from *Kirchner's* area [the 6th Panzer Division at the Mishkova bridgehead south of the *Kessel*] going to take place? Over.

[Manstein:] +++ *Yes—today.* How much fuel and supplies would you require before launching Thunderclap and on the assumption that once the action began, further supplies to meet day-to-day requirements would reach you? Over.

[Paulus:] +++ 1,000 cubic meters [nearly 250,000 gallons of fuel] and 500 tons of food. If we get that, all my armor and motor vehicles will have enough. . . . [the fuel he

needed was almost ten times what the airlift had brought
him so far].

    [Manstein:] +++ Well, that's the lot. Good luck,
Paulus.

    [Paulus:] +++ Thank you, sir. And good luck to
you, too.

Only a few hours later, the tanks of the 6th Panzer Division holding the bridgehead at Vassilevska wheeled about and began to
recross the Mishkova River.

    Hardbitten panzer crews brushed tears from their eyes as
they turned their backs on countrymen waiting for them at Stalingrad. One officer stood in his turret hatch facing the northern
horizon, snapped his right hand to his cap in salute, then ducked
inside the Mark IV as it rumbled off to a new battle. By midnight
the last panzer had left to try and save the Italian Army and
stabilize Manstein's left flank.

    Meanwhile, German soldiers at the southern perimeter of the
Kessel were straining to hear and see the vanguards of Manstein's
relief force. But the darkness remained impenetrable. The trapped
troops shivered in their snowholes and tried to still the nagging
fear that Manstein might never arrive.

Called to a meeting of 297th Division noncommissioned officers
along the southern perimeter of the *Kessel,* Sgt. Albert Pflüger
walked gingerly along an icy path. As he neared the command
bunker, he suddenly sensed a dark form off to the right and then
a rifle shot sounded. The bullet smashed into his right arm and
broke it.

    Knocked to the ground, Pflüger gasped, "Oh, mama, now
they've got me." Then he passed out.

    Another NCO came along, wrapped him in a poncho, and
started dragging him along the bumpy path. Regaining consciousness, Pflüger insisted on walking and staggered to an aid station,

where a doctor quickly bandaged the wound and sent him on to a base hospital.

On this day, December 23, the sergeant was just one of 686 Germans killed or wounded while waiting for Hitler to approve Thunderclap.

At dawn on December 24, the great German airfield at Tatsinskaya, 180 miles west of Gumrak, came under artillery fire from the Soviet Third Guards Army. The attack had been expected ever since the Italian Army had dissolved along the Don. All week long, Generals Martin Fiebig and Freiherr von Richthofen implored Hitler for permission to move the transport planes stationed at the field out of danger. But he refused, telling them that German reserves in the area could contain the enemy.

The Führer had been wrong again, and now on this misty morning, Fiebig stood in the control tower and watched in horror as two Ju-52s blew up from enemy shellfire.

A colonel beside him begged: "Herr General, you must take action. You must give permission to take off."

But Fiebig answered: "For that I need *Luftflotte* authority. In any case, it's impossible to take off in this fog."

Standing at rigid attention, the ashen-faced colonel replied: "Either you take that risk or every unit on the field will be wiped out. All the transport units for Stalingrad, Herr General. The last hope of the surrounded Sixth Army."

When another officer agreed, that was enough for General Fiebig. With Russian shells slamming through the fog onto the runways, he ordered an immediate evacuation.

At 0530 hours, only ten minutes after the attack began, the first lumbering Ju-52s roared to life and scrambled for the sky. Incredible confusion resulted. Planes took off from all directions; two Ju-52s collided in midfield and exploded. Others ripped off their wings and tails. In the midst of this holocaust, Russian tanks appeared on the runways as twenty, thirty, forty, fifty, and more planes skimmed low over them and climbed painfully into the murky sky.

When a Russian T-34 drove past Fiebig's control tower, it prompted an aide to say: "Herr, General, it is time to go."

But he was transfixed as he watched the terrible panorama outside the window, where the last Junkers were rolling down the field, crashing against other wreckage, skidding to a halt and catching fire.

At 0607, a German tank commander rushed in to say that the enemy had completely overrun Tatsinskaya and, eight minutes later, at 0615, the dejected Fiebig's own plane lifted off the airfield and headed for Rostov.

On the ground below, fifty-six aircraft sorely needed for the Stalingrad shuttle, burned brightly through the haze. Only 124 of the airlift planes had gotten away safely.

Sixty miles north of the wreckage of Fiebig's airfleet, Lt. Felice Bracci stirred in his stable and rose to the shouts of *"Davai bistre!"* from impatient Russian guards. Behind Bracci, in the feed trough packed with straw, some of the men who had fought for space in its warmth ignored the guttural demands. They were dead, turned marble-like from the cold.

Still without food, the huge column of prisoners stumbled into another freezing morning. On the horizon, a lifeless sun peeped out at the Italians. A strange sun, Bracci thought, for those who came from a warm country. His breath quickly congealed on his overcoat collar and turned into tiny, white crystals. Above the column a cloud of vapor floated along with the soldiers, as though they were chain-smoking cigarettes.

The march continued through the morning. Bracci and another officer, Franco Fusco from Naples, walked side-by-side, saying nothing. Men fell out, rifles cracked and bodies dropped into the snow; the two found comfort in each other's presence.

In early afternoon, Bracci saw a church belfry, then a few huts. He walked over a bridge; the river underneath it had disappeared in countless snow storms. Someone called out that they had reached Boguchar, a former German headquarters, now a central assembly point for Russian divisions. Soviet cars and trucks careened past the prisoners, who halted abruptly before a large barracks. With the cold so intense that the Italians could not stand still, they jumped up and down and begged to be let inside. While they complained, a sullen crowd of Russian civilians gathered. Young, old, they muttered threats and spat on Bracci and his comrades. Some of them made gestures of beheading and strangling, then suddenly closed in and pounced on the prisoners. Like crazed wolves, the Russians stripped them of overcoats, shoes, caps, and blankets. Bracci was lucky when the Russians rejected his worn boots and ragged leggings in disgust.

The guards finally drove the villagers away, then called all doctors inside the building. Bracci was envious. He assumed the doctors' miseries had ended and they would now take care of sick and wounded in more pleasant surroundings. He wished he had studied medicine at the university.

The doctors reappeared shortly, stripped of all medical supplies and warm clothing. After a lieutenant from Rome protested their treatment, the Russians took him inside, beat him viciously and threw him back into the street. Even then his misery had not ended. When his puppy, which had faithfully trotted beside him on the march, went to nuzzle the prostrate man, the Russians kicked it to death as he watched.

The Italian finally were crowded into barracks and, in pitch darkness, fell prostrate on the floor. Bracci was one of the last to get inside. Looking for a space to rest, he found a horizontal beam three feet off the floor and straddling it, tried to sleep. His body sagged, his head drooped. Several times he lost his balance and had to brace his feet on the ground for support. When his shoe hit a small box, he picked it up and thought it seemed full of butter. He dug greedily into it with his fingers and the greasy mixture went down easily. Only later did he find that he had eaten an automotive lubricant.

Outside the barracks, very far off, the lieutenant heard the sound of bells tolling, ringing out across the icy steppe. From a church somewhere, an organ played a solemn melody. Bracci knew what the sounds meant. He had known all day. Outside, where ordinary people lived, whether in Russia or in his beloved Rome, it was a time for happiness, for family and for love. It was Christmas Eve, 1942.

Chapter Twenty-three

Vassili Chuikov was in a festive mood. Within the past twenty-four hours, Col. Ivan Lyudnikov's 138th Division finally had made contact with the rest of the Soviet Sixty-second Army. For more than a month, Lyudnikov and his men had held off both the German 305th Division and the pioneers, who had first driven them onto the Volga beach. Now replenished by food, ammunition, and recruits brought over the ice bridge from the east bank, the 138th Division surged up from the shore to the flat ground behind the factories and turned south. Sixty-second Army headquarters triumphantly recorded the success: "Direct communication with Lyudnikov's division has now been established."

His worries ended on that score, Chuikov spent most of December 24 saying good-bye to old comrades. In his tunneled-out office, he smoked his leather-holdered cigarettes and raised tumblers of vodka to toast fellow heroes of the siege, who tearfully embraced their commander. Among them were Gen. Ivan Petrovich Sologub, with whom he had fought since the summer battles on the steppe; Gen. Fedor Nikandrovich Smekhotvorov, who defended the Red October Plant almost to the last man; and Gen.

Victor Grigorievich Zholudev, whose elite commandos died at the tractor factory.

These officers had been ordered out of battle to the far side of the Volga and rest camps, taking their shattered divisions with them. Once numbering more than twenty thousand strong, the two thousand survivors now walked eastward across the ice-covered river, congested with heavy trucks and thousands of fresh infantrymen going the other way.

Only a short distance from Chuikov's farewell party for his generals, a child ran through the ruins of the suburb of Dar Gova. "Come quick!" he screamed. "They've taken Sacha!"

The Fillipovs were not surprised. They had been anticipating this awful moment for weeks, and Mrs. Fillipov quickly scooped up some food the Germans had given Sacha for his shoe repairs and rushed out into the front yard.

Accompanied by two other teenagers, one a girl, Sacha was just going by. A platoon of enemy troops hemmed in the young Russians, who were walking barefoot through the snow. Mrs. Fillipov reached past the guards and wordlessly thrust the food at her son. As he took it, a soldier pushed her out of the way, and the procession wound around the corner to a barren clump of trees on Brianskaya Street.

A small crowd of Russian civilians gathered. The Fillipovs clung to each other, staring hypnotically at lengths of rope being flung over branches of the forlorn acacias. A German looped a noose around Sacha's head and tightened the thick knot under his left ear; Mr. Fillipov moaned pathetically and broke away from his wife. Blinded by tears, he stumbled away, never looking back as the command was given for the execution. Mrs. Fillipov stood alone, facing Sacha while his tongue shot out from between his teeth and his face turned blue.

Their task accomplished, the German soldiers formed ranks and marched away. The Russian witnesses scattered silently into the gloom, and Brianskaya Street suddenly was deserted except for the three children dangling in the wind and Mrs. Fillipov, who moved to her son's body. She listened for a moment to the creaking rope, then reached up and stroked her boy's leg and spoke softly, lovingly to him.

Darkness fell. Mrs. Fillipov continued her solitary vigil, standing dutifully beside the stiffening bare feet of her master cobbler, dead by hanging at the age of fifteen.

"O Tannenbaum, O Tannenbaum, wie treu sind deine Blatter . . ." almost every German bunker rang with the melody until suddenly the night was torn apart by the simultaneous explosions of thousands of multicolored flares that flashed across the sky from Orlovka in the northeast, to Baburkin in the west, on down to Marinovka and Karpovka, and back eastward through Zybenko to the Tsaritsa Gorge at the Volga. The brilliant fireworks display lasted for several minutes. Underneath the dazzling lights, German soldiers shielded their eyes and marveled at the beauty surrounding them.

It was their salute to the Holy Season, a joyous time to every German, and for several days, German officers and men alike had prepared feverishly for the celebration. Capt. Gerhard Meunch even drafted a speech. At his command post in a cellar of the Red October Plant, he labored for hours to hone his message, then, in the early evening, he went to a nearby garage where a Christmas tree, carved from wood, adorned one corner of the cavernous room. In groups of thirty, his infantrymen appeared to sit around him as he welcomed them and distributed cigarettes, wine, or tea with rum, a piece of bread, and a slice of horse meat.

Relaxed by the liquor, the men listened attentively while Meunch spoke quietly of the need for keeping up the fight against the Russians. Still slightly unnerved by his recent brush with mutineers in the ranks, he took pains to underline a soldier's duty to orders, especially in such a dreadful situation as at Stalingrad. The pep talk seemed to appeal to the troops, who all joined in singing *"Stille Nacht"* ("Silent Night") with him. Meunch noticed that in midchorus, a number of the men were so choked with emotion they had to stop singing and wipe tears from their eyes.

After talking personally with every enlisted man, Meunch went back to the Red October Plant to drink with fellow officers. One of them, a forty-year-old captain, suddenly shouted, "What is this whole battle good for?" and pulled out his pistol.

"Let's all shoot each other!" he roared. "This is all nonsense. None of us will ever get out of here."

Stunned by the outburst, Meunch calmly replied, "Now take it easy." But the other captain kept looking wildly about him. Continuing to speak in a soothing voice, Meunch sat down with his friend to argue the merits of suicide.

Sgt. Albert Pflüger's broken arm hurt too much for him to care about the holiday. With his wound probed and dressed, and his arm in a sling, he wandered into a bunker where a rush of warm, sale air engulfed him. His head reeling, Pflüger stared at a crowd of thirteen other patients who were standing and sitting in a room meant for four. Seeing that Pflüger was about to faint, one man jumped down from a top bunk and gave his place to him.

After climbing laboriously into the cot, the sergeant promptly dozed off. Several hours later, he woke because of a terrible itch inside the cast on his right arm and, pulling back the covers, he saw a line of lice marching from the mattress over his hand, under the edge of the plaster mold. In shock and disgust, Pflüger jumped down from the bed and tore at the bugs. Grabbing a stick, he jabbed frantically at them, but they crawled deeper into the cast and hid. His arm was now a mass of gray parasites, feasting on the wound.

In thousands of bunkers in the sides of *balkas*, in concrete pill-boxes at the edge of no-man's-land, German soldiers snatched a few brief hours from the horrors of encirclement. Despite the absence of trees on the steppe, creative minds had cleverly improvised a semblance of the Christmas spirit. Iron bars, drilled with holes and filled with slivers of wood, stood as centerpieces on dirt floors; puffs of cotton snatched from medical aid stations served as ornamental bulbs. Stars made from colored paper adorned metal treetops.

At Ekkehart Brunnert's party, his comrades outdid themselves. A beautifully carved wooden Christmas tree dominated a shaky table. Someone had brought a gramophone with records and amid riotous singing, Brunnert received a bag filled with delicacies: a small cake smeared with chocolate frosting, several bars of chocolate candy, bread, biscuits, coffee, cigarettes, even three cigars. Overwhelmed by the banquet, the starving private asked where all the food had been stored for so long. No one knew. Dismissing his suspicions, Brunnert gorged himself, then lit up a cigarette. Basking in the glow of improvised Advent wreaths sparkling with candles, he momentarily forgot his anguish over the truckload of warm clothing, burned in his presence just a few days before.

Several hours later, when his turn came to stand guard, he stared into the star-filled sky and tried to imagine his parents and wife, Irene, celebrating at home in Boblingen—the tree and the presents and Irene thinking of him and perhaps crying. Pacing up and down the trench, Brunnert wanted to cry himself.

On his way to a church service, Quartermaster Karl Binder had seen mounds of unburied bodies lining the road. Shocked by this breakdown of army organization, he brooded about it for hours until he wrote a letter to his family. Now filled with a sense of foreboding about his own fate, Binder sought to prepare his wife and children for the worst:

Christmas 1942

. . . During the past weeks all of us have begun to think about the end of everything. The insignificance of everyday

life pales against this, and we have never been more grateful
for the Christmas Gospel than in these hours of hardship.
Deep in one's heart one lives with the idea of Christmas,
the meaning of Christmas. It is a feast of love, salvation and
pity on mankind. We have nothing else here but the thought
of Christmas. It must and will tide us over grievous hours. . . .
However hard it may be, we shall do our utmost to master
fate and try everything in our power to defeat the subhu-
manity that is wildly attacking us. Nothing can shake our
belief in victory, for we must win, if Germany wants to
live. . . .

I have not received any mail from you for some
time . . . there is a terrible longing for some dear words from
home at Christmas, but there are more important things at
present. We are men who know how to bear everything. The
main thing is that you and the children are all right. Don't
worry about me; nothing can happen to me any longer.
Today I have made my peace with God. . . .

I give you all my love and a thousand kisses—I love
you to my last breath.

> Yours,
>
> Karl

Affectionate kisses for the children. Be dear children and
remember your father. . . .

Oblivious to the noise in his bunker, Lt. Emil Metzger sat reading
a letter from his wife, Kaethe. It was the best Christmas present
he had ever received, and at 10:00 P.M., he quietly withdrew from
the celebration to go out—into the clear, frosty night, where a
lonely sentry walked his post. Metzger relieved the shivering man
of the responsibility and shouldered his rifle. He wanted this time
alone.

Under a bower of brilliant stars he paced back and forth,
ignoring the Russians and the war. Concentrating intensely on
Kaethe, Emil relived their life together: the first dance when they
fell in love, the exhilarating hikes through the cathedral hush of
forests, the four brief days of honeymoon they shared before he

rushed back to duty, the furlough he had given up in August because he believed the war was about to end.

For over an hour, Emil held a spiritual communion with Kaethe beneath a thousand miles of stars. It was the only gift he could give her.

While German soldiers sought escape in celebration, their generals were discussing the diminishing prospects of Sixth Army's salvation.

Teletype: General Schmidt–General Schulz

+++ Dear Schmidt, tonight the field marshal and we all are particularly thinking of the entire Sixth Army. I do not have much new information for you today.

Hoth [the German relief column south of the *Kessel*] is still engaged in defensive operations. It appears that the enemy . . . [around Vassilevska at the Mishkova] . . . has received further reinforcements. . . . As regards your situation, we still did not receive a decision from the Supreme Command of the Army. The field marshal wants you to know that you had better reconcile yourself to the idea that the solution will in all probability be "Thunderclap." [Even Field Marshal Manstein did not believe this anymore, but Schulz did not have the heart to deny Schmidt one last hope of freedom.] We are waiting for better weather so that we may commit all available airplanes to provide you with the necessary fuel and provisions. What's new on your side?

[Schmidt was querulous, demanding:] +++ Is it certain that the airplanes can start although Tatsinskaya is threatened? [Schmidt did not know that Tatsinskaya was already in Russian hands.]

[Schulz lied:] +++ Their start is ensured and alternative airfields were prepared.

[Sensing that Hoth's relief attempt from the south had already failed, Schmidt asked:] +++ Will [Hoth] . . . be able to hold the Mishkova [river] section?

[Schulz:] +++ We hope so. However, there is a possibility that he will have to narrow the present bridgehead.

[At that moment, the bridgehead had already been evacuated by the German rear guard.]

[Schmidt:] +++ Was an armored division withdrawn from . . . Hoth . . . to the west bank of the Don?

Again, General Schulz was unable to strip his friend of hope.

+++ One armored division [the 6th, which had left the previous evening] had to be withdrawn to the west bank of the Don in order to protect Morosovskaya [Airfield]. However, as of tomorrow the SS Division Viking [a fully motorized division] will be arriving in the area of Salsk by train and road. . . . Besides, we have again urgently requested considerable reinforcements from Army Group A [in the Caucasus], but we are still waiting for the decision of the Supreme Command of the Army.

I have nothing else, the Commander-in-Chief and I cordially return your Christmas greetings.

During Christmas Eve, the Stalingrad front remained alarmingly quiet. Little was heard from the Russians, except the squawking of loudspeakers urging the Germans to lay down their arms and come over to good food, shelter, and friendly Tartar girls. Crouched in their snowholes, German soldiers still listened with detached amusement to the propaganda. Most of them feared the Russians too much to trust such alluring proposals.

In the early hours of Christmas Day, a violent blizzard broke over the *Kessel*. Visibility dropped to less than ten yards; fifty-mile-an-hour gusts howled across the *balkas*, and the men of Sixth Army slept off the effects of wine, cognac, and rum. But at 5:00 A.M., the *Katyusha* rockets screamed in a multitudinous cadence as thousands of flaming missiles soared from beyond the perimeter into the *Kessel*. Heavy-throated mortars and artillery also overwhelmed the moaning wind. The ground heaved and trembled under a ferocious cannonade. "And then, out of the gray white . . . appeared tank after tank and, in between, trucks crowded with infantry. . . ."

In the sector held by the 16th Panzer Division, groggy soldiers climbed from their bunkers to fight a desperate delaying action. The attack had come too fast and Russian tanks and soldiers were suddenly among them in the swirling mist of snow. Opposing infantry fired at shadows indiscriminately; dead men heaped up in front of field guns. German .88 artillery crewmen quickly ran out of ammunition and blew up their pieces with the last shells before retreating to a second line of resistance.

As the morning of Christmas Day passed, Sixth Army intelligence officers stated positively that the Russians suffered a "frightening number of . . . casualties. . . ." But they also had to acknowledge that they too had absorbed similar "shocking" losses.

The battle blazed on into the afternoon as, on the other flanks, Russians smashed against the reeling but well-dug-in Sixth Army. The entire *Kessel* reverberated to the terrifying sounds of thousands of big and small-caliber weapons.

At his overcrowded hospital, Dr. Kurt Reuber paused in his treatment of patients to conduct friends to the door of his private quarters. When he pushed it open, they sucked in their breath at what they saw.

On the gray wall facing the door, a lamp illuminated a picture of the Virgin and Child, whose heads inclined protectively toward each other. Both were shrouded in a white cloak.

Reuber had labored secretly for days on his surprise. Perched on a stool, he had scrawled several themes on bits of paper until he remembered a verse from Saint John about light, life, and love. The words gave the doctor the ideal image, the Virgin Mary and Jesus, who best symbolized those qualities to him. Several times Russian bombardments scattered his pencils and artwork, but the doctor doggedly retrieved them and created the Madonna and Child of Stalingrad on the back of a captured Russian map.

Now, as fellow officers maintained a hushed vigil in front of the drawing, Kurt Reuber drank with his friends from his last bottle of champagne. While toasting each other, a series of trip-hammer explosions rocked the room and Reuber rushed outside to the cries of dying men.

In minutes his "chapel" became a first aid station. One of the officers who had just left Reuber's party after singing the carol *"O du Froliche"* was brought in with massive wounds. He died under the picture of Mother and Child.

At Gumrak, Arthur Schmidt was absorbed in another frustrating exchange with his friend in Novocherkassk:

25 Dec 42, 1735 hrs. to 1800 hrs.

+++ Here Major General Schulz. Is General Schmidt there?

+++ Yes sir, General Schmidt here.

+++ Good evening, Schmidt. We hope Christmas wasn't too bad for you and the entire army.

On Christmas Day, 1,280 German soldiers died in the *Kessel,* and Schulz had more disappointing news for Sixth Army:

+++ All day today . . . [Hoth, south of the *Kessel*] was compelled to ward off heavy attacks by superior enemy infantry and armored forces. . . . Major casualties were inflicted on the enemy, but there were also considerable casualties on our side. Although bridgeheads in the Aksai section were compressed, the section itself could be held. According to reconnaissance results the enemy has assembled yet another armored corps in the area and southeast of Aksai. . . . There can be no doubt that the enemy has concentrated major forces in the space between the pocket and . . . Hoth . . . . We have not yet received a decision from the Supreme Command of the Army regarding our proposals for further operations with the objective of relieving the Sixth Army. General von Richthofen told the field marshal [Manstein] today that, if the weather should improve, he will be able during the next few days, to supply the Sixth Army with 120 tons of supplies daily, and later on with 200 tons daily. The decrease in the amounts is due to the increased distance the aircraft have to cover from Novocherkassk and Salsk [new shuttle airfields]. I wished, in particular today, I could give you better news. The field marshal is still trying to get approval for armored forces and motorized infantry from Army Group A, to be brought up to 4th Armored Corps as speedily as possible, in order to facilitate "Thunderclap" for the Sixth Army.

What's the situation on your side?

Arthur Schmidt dictated the stark facts to the operator, who typed them into the teleprinter:

+++ Today we suffered fierce attacks against boundary 16th Armored Division and 60th Motorized Division on a small frontage, which temporarily led to penetration on a front of 2-km and 1-km depth. On the whole the counterattack was successful, but the Russians are still holding the frequently mentioned and important Hill 139.7. We hope to regain it early tomorrow. . . . The army's provisions and fuel have decreased dangerously. In view of an icy east wind and very low temperatures, we need a considerable increase of rations, otherwise we will have numerous men on the sick list from exhaustion and frostbite. We cannot manage with an air supply of 120 tons daily. Measures must therefore be taken to increase our supply rapidly *or else you might just as well forget about the Sixth Army right away.* Is [Hoth] still in the Mishkova section?

Schulz still refused to admit that the bridgehead over the Mishkova River had been abandoned:

+++ [Hoth] holds the Aksai section with small bridgeheads north of this area.

At this point, Schmidt indulged himself in some sarcasm:

+++ According to information we received today, some of the aircraft which were intended for our supply were again ordered to fly combat missions. In the opinion of the Commander in chief [Paulus] this is very unwise. Please do not regard our supply situation too optimistically. We suggest that the Luftwaffe should rather supply us with bread than drop a few and not always effective bombs before the Tatsin-skaya front. I have nothing else.

Schulz hastened to reassure him of Army Group's continued interest:

> + ┤ + Believe me, your supply situation is our greatest concern. I shall immediately and again report to the field marshal on the situation and he is in constant contact with Richthofen and the Supreme Command of the Army, with the aim of increasing your supplies. We are aware of your desperate situation and shall do our very best to improve it. I have nothing else. Please give my regards to the Commander in chief. Until tomorrow.
> [Schmidt:] + + + I have nothing else either, greetings—ending.

As General Schmidt signed off it was finally clear to him that the German High Command had lost control of events in southern Russia. The entry in Sixth Army's War Diary for December 25, 1942, reflected that fact: "Forty-eight hours without food supplies. Food and fuel near their end . . . the strength of the men is rapidly decreasing because of the biting cold . . . we hope for food soon . . . . No decision as yet on battle plan for the Sixth Army. . . ."

Lonely German soldiers spent the last hours of Christmas twirling radio dials to pick up shortwave broadcasts from home. On Christmas Eve, many had listened to the popular singer, Lale Anderson, as she sang special requests for the troops. Now, on Christmas night, the men of Stalingrad were treated to Propaganda Minister Joseph Goebbels's "Ring Broadcast," supposedly originating from the frontiers of the Third Reich. It was aimed primarily at the civilian population.

While Goebbels chanted the names of conquered cities, the German people toured the battlefronts.

"And now from Narvik," he announced grandly amid a rising chorus of male singers stationed at that Norwegian port. "And in

Tunisia," brought forth another strident rendition, this time of *"Stille Nacht, Heilege Nacht,"* from soldiers holding American and British troops away from Bizerte and Tunis. "And from Stalingrad!" Goebbels suddenly said. While thousands of soldiers inside the *Kessel* stared at each other in disbelief, a joyous melody burst from the radio to assure the homefront that all was well at the Volga River.

Goebbels continued with his fabricated broadcast, and his voice shrilled out the impressive boundaries of the Nazi empire. But most of his countrymen trapped on the Russian steppe had already turned off their radios.

Chapter Twenty-four

Buoyed up by the false hope that Manstein was coming, the soldiers of the Sixth Army had endured the rationing and freezing weather with a remarkable stoicism and elan. However, when Christmas brought the sobering realization that the *Kessel* was probably going to become their grave, physical and moral defenses began to crumble and the gaunt occupants of Fortress Stalingrad started to lose their ability to hold out. Drastic measures instituted by Paulus to preserve the food supply only added to the decline. The beleaguered general had no choice. Once again, the airlift had failed to step up deliveries beyond a hundred tons a day.

The teletype that night recorded the bleak facts:

+++ Today [December 26], by 5:00 P.M., we received 38 Ju and 3 He [transports], carrying seventy tons, among them food, mainly bread. We have only enough bread for two days, edible food for one day, fat is gone already. Complete food supplies must be flown in immediately, in balanced proportions, for 250,000 men. . . . We depend only on what arrives by air . . . we are also out of fuel, tomorrow we will give out the last 20 cubic meters . . . I beg you by all means to see to it that tomorrow 200 tons be flown in, 150 of which is food, 50 cubic meters in fuel. Otherwise we shall not make it.

+++ We shall do our utmost.

Colonel von Kunowski, Paulus's chief quartermaster, added a final comment: "No more from here. I never sat so deep in shit. Kind regards."

Paulus had known for several days that he would have to cut rations again. But he had waited for Christmas to pass before announcing a near-starvation diet: bread, two ounces per day per man (a piece the size of a man's thumb); soup without fat (one portion) for lunch; one can of tinned meat when available for dinner; otherwise, more watery soup.

The stringent rations struck a mortal blow at the stamina of his men. Painfully aware of that fact, Paulus, attempted once more to remind his superiors that an entire army was on the brink of extinction.

Erich von Manstein received his chilling words and passed them on to Hitler.

+++ Bloody losses, cold and inadequate supplies have recently made inroads on divisions' fighting strength. I must therefore report the following:

1. Army can continue to ward off small-scale attacks and deal with local crises for some time yet, always providing that supply improves.

2. If enemy draws off forces in any strength from Hoth's front and uses these . . . on Stalingrad Fortress, latter cannot hold out for long.

3. No longer possible to execute breakout unless corridor is cut in advance and army replenished. . . .

I therefore request representations at highest level [Hitler] to ensure energetic measures for speedy relief, *unless overall situation compels sacrifice of army. . . .*

For the first time, Paulus mentioned the nagging possibility that Sixth Army might be used as a sacrificial pawn in this maniacal game of chess in order to tie down as many Soviet units as possible while Manstein tried to stabilize his other fronts.

One of Paulus's aides, Capt. Winrich Behr, broached the same opinion in a remarkable letter to Maj. Nikolaus von Below, who was Hitler's adjutant at Rastenburg. The two men were old friends and were married to sisters. They had always been honest with each other and Behr now provided his comrade with a uniquely frank and intimate glimpse of the atmosphere at Sixth Army Headquarters in Gumrak:

> Dear Klaus :
>
> At the moment we feel somewhat betrayed and sold out. . . . To wait and to persevere is a matter which goes without saying, even if no further orders come through. I just want to tell you quite simply that there is nothing here to eat, with the exception of a few thousand horses, which may last until January, but with which one cannot alone feed an army of 250,000 men. Now there is only bread for tomorrow. . . . With my knowledge of the German soldier we have to foresee . . . that their physical resistance will be lowered so much . . . the moment will come where each man will say: "I don't give a shit about anything," and will freeze to death or be captured. The men have the desire to hold fast and it is incomprehensible how they have held so far. . . . Heating is a very big problem. Everything has to be fetched from Stalingrad, but there is no gas available for that. In other words, the cat eats its own tail all around. . . . *It may have been decided in view of the situation to give us up,* which is not unthinkable—although it is hard to fathom the consequences. If so, I will live a few days more with Eichlepp [a fellow aide], thanks to your excellent chocolate! . . .
>
> I write this to you, Klaus, so you don't think that we are griping unnecessarily. What I am telling you is based not only on my personal experience—but also on messages and daily conversations with friends at the front. It is as bad as I say it is. No miracle in the steppe can help us here, only good old Aunt Ju and the He-111 [transport planes] if they come—and come often.
>
> . . . Otherwise, the mood is and has been good here. A little running scared, but there is still hope amongst enlisted

men and officers. "Stand fast—the Führer will get you out!"
is the motto. Here at the top, especially on days like this one,
looking into an empty barrel, the responsibility lies heavy. . . .

                                                                Teddy

Like the sudden rupture of an umbilical cord, the teleprinter link
between Gumrak and Novocherkassk was torn asunder as, on
the steppe west of the pocket, Soviet armor captured the decimeter
relays maintaining the fragile semipersonal contact between
Schmidt and Schulz, Paulus and Manstein. The severed connection
left Sixth Army with a single thousand-watt transmitter, and several auxiliary sets of lesser strength, to communicate with Army
Group Don.

Some German officers inside the pocket looked on the abrupt
blackout as an augury of ominous days.

In Moscow, Stalin fumed at the delay in destroying Sixth Army.
Though his front commanders continued to relay news of heady
triumphs from other sectors of the battlefield, the premier refused
to relax.

On December 28, General Vatutin at Soviet Southwest Front
Headquarters along the upper Don contacted him with news of an
overwhelming victory; "The Italian Eighth Army's right wing had
melted away . . . sixty thousand prisoners and about the same
number . . . killed . . . their stores have been seized by our forces
. . . the pitiful remains . . . are not putting up any resistance. . . ."

Stalin absorbed this exhilarating report without much enthusiasm, and immediately pressed Vatutin on the one danger zone
in his command region. Around the great German airfield at Tatsinskaya, where Gen. Martin Fiebig had fled the wreckage of his
shuttle air force only four days previously, a Russian armored
column was temporarily trapped by lead elements of the German
panzers rushed from their aborted relief effort at the Mishkova
River.

Stalin chose this moment to lecture Vatutin on strategy:

> Your first task is to get Badanov, [commander of the en-
> circled Twenty-fourth Tank Corps] out of trouble. . . . You
> were right in allowing [him] to give up Tatsinskaya in an
> emergency. We have already given you the Second and
> Twenty-third Tank Corps to convert Little Saturn into Big
> Saturn [the drive to Rostov and the Black Sea that Russian
> general Krupennikov hinted at to his interrogators on De-
> cember 21]. . . . You should bear in mind that over very long
> distances tank corps are best launched in pairs rather than
> alone; otherwise they risk falling into a situation like Bada-
> nov's. Just remember Badanov; don't forget Badanov. Get
> him out at any cost!

With that final admonition, Stalin left Vatutin to manage his own little war between the Don and Rostov, and went on to his most perplexing situation: Paulus's Sixth Army, whose continued existence tied up seven Russian armies needed elsewhere.

Meeting with his senior generals, the premier came right to his major complaint: "Only one man should direct operations . . . the fact that there are two front commanders [around Stalingrad] is interfering with this."

When everyone at the table agreed, Stalin asked: "Who gets the assignment?"

Marshal Georgi Zhukov remained silent as someone recommended Lieutenant General Rokossovsky.

"Why don't you say anything?" Stalin prodded Zhukov.

"In my opinion, either commander is capable of doing the job. Yeremenko's feelings would be hurt, of course, if you transferred his Stalingrad front to Rokossovsky."

That point was shrugged off by Stalin. "This is not the time to worry about hurt feelings. Telephone Yeremenko and tell him about the decision. . . ."

When Zhukov called Yeremenko and explained the situation to him over a high-security line, the pugnacious general felt his professional world crumbling around him as he heard, "Transfer the Fifty-seventh, Sixty-four and Sixty-second armies from the

Stalingrad front to [Rokossovsky's control]. . . ." Yeremenko recovered enough to splutter: "What brought this on?"

Zhukov patiently explained the considerations but sensing the general's outrage and humiliation, he quietly suggested that Yeremenko call back later.

In fifteen minutes, when the phone conversation resumed, Yeremenko had not gotten control of himself. "I can't understand . . . . Please tell Stalin I want to say here until the enemy is completely destroyed."

Zhukov suggested he tell Stalin himself, and Yeremenko said he had already tried but was unable to get through Poskrebyshev, Stalin's personal secretary, who had insisted that all such matters were Zhukov's responsibility. On behalf of the shattered Yeremenko, Zhukov called Stalin immediately, but the premier remained adamant about placing Rokossovsky in charge.

Retreating to his private quarters south of Stalingrad, Andrei Yeremenko burst into tears. When Nikita Khrushchev tried to calm him, he was furious: "Comrade . . . you don't understand. You're a civilian. You forget how we thought we were doomed, how Stalin used to ask if we could hold out for three more days. We all thought the Germans would capture Stalingrad, and we would be made scapegoats. Maybe you don't foresee what will happen, but I do: The new Don Front will get all the glory for the Stalingrad victory, and our armies of the Southern Front will be forgotten."

Khrushchev could not console his friend.

The German counterattack against Russian General Badanov's Twenty-fourth Tank Corps had temporarily regained control of Moro and Tazi, the airstrips for the shuttle to Stalingrad. But the triumph proved of little consequence, for bad weather and faulty equipment continued to plague the Luftwaffe. Tonnage into the

Kessel wavered between eighty and two hundred tons daily. Hundreds of Russian antiaircraft batteries were now emplaced along the flight path, in direct line with the German radio beacon to Pitomnik, and they began to take an awesome toll of the lumbering transports. In just five weeks, nearly three hundred of them were shot down.

Pitomnik Airfield itself mirrored the mounting disaster of Sixth Army. The pulse of the *Kessel*, it lay in the middle of an arterial network of highways that drew a microcosm of despair and hope to its runways and buildings. These roads had been kept clear for weeks by Major Linden's special task force. But even his herculean efforts faltered before the terrible handicaps imposed by the winter storms. As his men worked in blizzards, the brutal winds forced them to wear gas masks to protect their faces from frostbite. When one storm ended, another began. Though snow plows moved up and down the arteries constantly, eventually the acute shortage of fuel slowed their schedule, bringing Major Linden to the brink of despair.

As the New Year approached, the roads to Pitomnik clogged again with drifts. On either side of the highways, soldiers now stuck the legs of hundreds of dead horses into the snow as trail markers for truck drivers.

Col. Lothar Rosenfeld, a former police boxing champion, monitored the field's heartbeat. Riding a small *panje* pony, he maintained rigid discipline over both the air shuttle and the hordes of wounded and couriers seeking passage from the pocket. One of his frequent visitors was Hitler's liaison officer, Maj. Coelestin von Zitzewitz, who had been suspect since the day he arrived from Supreme Headquarters as an observer.

From the beginning, Gen. Arthur Schmidt and some others had held Zitzewitz at arm's length and, shortly after his arrival, Schmidt even interfered with one of his dispatches to East Prussia. Convinced that Zitzewitz was "painting too grim a picture" at that time in early December, Schmidt insisted on altering the message to reflect a more optimistic tone.

Zitzewitz had learned his lesson. From then on, he only sent off reports after Schmidt had gone to bed. Far from being a yesman, the major wrote unvarnished accounts of the debacle he witnessed. He went everywhere: to the front-line foxholes, to hospitals, ammunition dumps, and icy ravines. In the mile long *balkas* at Baburkin, Gorodische, and Dimitrevka, he followed German troops into their dark, clammy bunkers where lack of fuel spawned colds, pneumonia, and an increased weakness to other infections. Improper sanitation in these refuges was also bringing out armies of lice.

Zitzewitz sat among hordes of mice and rats that overran the bunkers and gnawed scraps of food hoarded by Germans in knapsacks and pockets. The rodents were ravenous. He witnessed one case where they even descended on a soldier whose feet were badly frostbitten. While he slept, they chewed off two of his toes.

Above all, Zitzewitz monitored Pitomnik where the wounded crowded into hastily laid-out hospitals and waited for doctors to ease their pain while the Junkers and Heinkels circled and landed or flamed and crashed.

The major spared nothing in his attempt to alert Hitler to the whole truth. But his grim reports had an unanticipated impact at the Wolf's Lair. In discussing them, Reichmarshal Hermann Goering shook his head in disbelief. "It is impossible that any German officer could be responsible for defeatist messages of this sort," he declared. "The only possible explanation is that the enemy has captured his transmitter and has sent them himself."

Thus, Zitzewitz's reports were dismissed as Russian propaganda.

Stragglers from the Italian Eighth Army could have assured Hermann Goering that Zitzewitz's chronicles of despair were totally authentic. They were still plodding through knee-deep snow toward far-off prison camps.

Lt. Felice Bracci had continued marching in a northerly direction, across the silvery ice of the upper Don River that he once hoped to ford as a conqueror. Now he was sure it was a bewitched stream, never to succumb to an invader's boots. For several agonizing days, Bracci had kept his mind and body functioning as the "long black snake" of captives passed numerous villages where Russian women unaccountably smiled and threw crusts of bread and frozen potatoes into his outstretched hands.

Some Russians exchanged food for wedding rings, clothing or blankets. When Bracci offered a piece of adhesive tape from a roll he had saved, a villager thrust a large piece of black bread at him in payment. Bracci wolfed it down in seconds.

On December 28, Russian guards stopped the Italians at a huge barracks near a railroad station. Jammed into the dark building with hundreds of other prisoners, Bracci spent the next three days clinging to sanity. Some of his friends had contracted gangrene from frostbite and screamed without letup. Italian doctors amputated the worst limbs with homemade knives and the moans of the patients, operated on without anesthesia, drove everyone to despair.

Surrounded by bedlam, by prayers for God's mercy, Bracci and his comrades scrounged bits of wood and lit small fires in a corner of the room. The tiny blazes nourished them somewhat while the Russians subjected them to a propaganda campaign.

Two Soviet officers, one a woman, came into the barracks, and speaking fluent Italian, they asked why Bracci and his friends had come to wage war on Russia and whether the soldiers were really Fascists. The Russians told the captives that Mussolini and Hitler were finished and ended their harangue with the lie that King Victor Emmanuel had died recently of a broken heart. The woman then took out scraps of paper and pencils and asked the prisoners to write messages back to loved ones in Italy. Taking a pencil in his numbed fingers, Bracci wrote: "I am alive . . . I am well. . . ." He had no hope that his words would ever arrive in Rome.

The propaganda barrage continued into the next day, when all the Italian officers were lined up to hear a speech from a be-spectacled civilian speaking from atop a car. In flawless Italian, the man cursed the Fascist government and warned his listeners that it was extremely unlikely they would ever leave Russia alive. The cold, he claimed, would "mow them down."

Shivering in formation, Bracci wondered whether the speaker would mention starvation as a factor contributing to his imminent death, but the expatriate Italian did not. When he finished, the prisoners had to parade past a cameraman, who filmed their misery for some unknown audience.

On New Year's Eve, Bracci tried to forget his plight. Lying on the frozen barracks floor, he listened as Colonel Rosati took his comrades on a gourmet visit of Rome's best restuarants: the elegant "Zi," the Bersagliera, and on to the dining room atop the Tarpeian rock.

When the colonel recited the meal he would order in each establishment, his audience groaned. "Thursday, gnocchi," Rosati savored the words and men chewed endlessly on nothing. Spittle formed in their mouths; their stomachs churned. Someone told Rosati to shut up, but the protestor was shouted down by others desperate to hold off reality. "Saturday . . . tripe," the colonel went on and added mellow white wines to the menu.

Outside the barracks, a roaring wind blew gusts of snow through the paneless windows onto the huddled "diners." Ignoring the chill, they listened raptly: "Monday . . . cannelloni, in cream sauce. . . ."

At 10:00 P.M. on December 31, Russian artillery around the *Kessel* exploded in a frenzied acknowledgement of the holiday. Because they knew Soviet gunners were operating on Moscow time, two hours ahead of German clocks, Sixth Army troops had prepared for the deluge. Hunkered down in their holes, they rode out the fifteen-minute salvo welcoming in a year of promised glory for Soviet Russia.

Inside Stalingrad, the expectations of Russian troops ran high. The ice bridge across the Volga was the main reason for their attitude. From Acktuba and Krasnaya Sloboda, hundreds of trucks now crossed the river daily, bringing white camouflage suits to replace tattered gray brown uniforms. In the middle of the river, traffic masters waved food convoys to depots set up under the cliff. Cases of American canned goods began to litter foxholes strung along the defense line from Tsaritsa to the tractor works. Ammunition piled up to the point where Russian gunners now fired antitank shells at lone German soldiers.

On New Year's Eve, discipline in the revitalized Sixty-second Army relaxed and, along the shore, high-ranking Soviet officers held a series of parties to honor actors, musicians, and ballerinas visiting Stalingrad to entertain the troops. One of the troupe members, violinist Mikhail Goldstein, stayed away and went instead into the trenches to perform another of his one-man concerts for the soldiers.

In all the war Goldstein had never seen a battlefield quite like Stalingrad: a city so utterly broken by bombs and artillery, cluttered with skeletons of hundreds of horses, picked clean by the starving enemy. And always there were the grim police of the Russian NKVD, standing between the front line and the Volga, checking soldiers' papers and shooting suspected deserters dead.

The horrible battlefield shocked Goldstein and he played as he never played before, hour after hour for men who obviously loved his music. And while all German works had been banned by the Soviet government, Goldstein doubted that any commissar would protest on New Year's Eve. The melodies he created drifted out through loudspeakers to the German trenches and the shooting suddenly ceased. In the eerie quiet, the music flowed from Goldstein's dipping bow.

When he finished, a hushed silence hung over the Russian soldiers. From another loudspeaker, in German territory, a voice broke the spell. In halting Russian it pleaded: "Play some more Bach. We won't shoot."

Goldstein picked up his violin and started a lively Bach *Gavotte.*

At the stroke of midnight, Berlin time, a soldier of the German 24th Panzer Division at the northeastern part of the *Kessel* raised his machine pistol and fired a magazine full of tracer bullets into the sky. Others in his unit spontaneously followed his salute. The idea flared quickly along the perimeter west to the 16th Panzers, then to the 60th Motorized and on around the curve to the Marinovka "nose," through the 3rd Motorized and down to the 29th Division, eastward along the southern edge of the pocket, past the 297th and 371st to the Volga, and back to the darkened streets of Stalingrad where men poked rifles and machine guns through slits and blasted an arc of kaleidoscopic fireworks above the brooding bulk of the factories. The rainbow of fire circled the fortress for minutes as German soldiers welcomed a New Year shorn of hope.

To those standing in the middle of the steppe, around Pitomnik and Gumrak, the pyrotechnics proved only the futility of the German position. The entire horizon was a band of flame from tracer bullets. But they formed a complete circle of fire around Sixth Army.

On the first day of 1943, Adolph Hitler remembered Paulus at Stalingrad: "To you and your brave army I send, also in the name of the whole German population, my warmest New Year's wishes. I am aware of the difficulty of your responsibility. The heroic attitude of your troops is appreciated. You and your soldiers should begin the New Year with a strong faith that I and the . . . German Wehrmacht will use all strength to relieve the defenders of Stalingrad and make their long wait the highest achievement of German war history. . . ."

At an officers' mess inside the *Kessel*, blond Lt. Hans Oettl was surrounded by men wishing him a happy birthday. Seated in front of his own blue china, from which he had eaten for years, he watched a cook ladle out a huge steaming portion of goulash filled with thick chunks of meat. Astounded and delighted, Oettl began to eat.

The door suddenly burst open and a military policeman stormed in, demanding to know whether anyone had seen his watchdog. In the sudden silence, Hans Oettl looked at his companions, now staring uncomfortably at the floor, then his gaze returned slowly to the goulash and mountain of meat in front of him.

While the policeman thundered threats against anyone who might have killed his pet, the lieutenant deliberately raised his fork and chewed a portion of the policeman's German Shepherd.

Sgt. Albert Pflüger had waited patiently for a flight home, but when bad weather closed off most of the shuttle, he suddenly made up his mind to go back to his men in the 297th Division. Still drugged by pills and nearly crazed by the itching of lice under the cast on his arm, he hitched a ride to a railroad siding near Karpovka and boarded the small train that ran for a few miles toward the suburbs of Stalingrad.

In a freight car, Pflüger found company: two Rumanian enlisted men and six Rumanian officers, who stood menacingly over them. While the train moved along in fitful starts and stops, one officer told Pflüger the soldiers were prisoners who had been condemned to death for stealing food. While they talked, for some reason Pflüger could not fathom, another officer suddenly whipped the two men mercilessly.

At Peschanka, Pflüger jumped down from this depressing scene, and within hours he found his first sergeant, who greeted him exuberantly and took him to his old unit. In only a few days, six of Pflüger's men had been wounded or killed. But the survivors welcomed him and the company butcher showered him with hoarded chocolate, cigarettes, and tins of meat.

Glad to be back with his own people, Pflüger quickly dismissed the memory of missing the flight at Pitomnik.

In Novocherkassk, Field Marshal Eric von Manstein greeted the New Year in a somber mood. His attempt to save Paulus was a failure, and he knew that the fate of the Sixth Army was sealed.

But another crisis, of even greater magnitude, was at hand. Four hundred miles south of Stalingrad, Army Group A, comprising the First Panzer and Seventeenth armies, stood alone and vulnerable in the foothills of the Caucasus Mountains. Unless Manstein brought these armies north, safely through the bottleneck city of Rostov, the Russian High Command could effect the "super-Stalingrad *Kessel*" that Stalin sought.

Ever since Manstein had pulled Hermann Hoth's panzers back from the relief effort toward Stalingrad, he had phoned daily demands to East Prussia for the prompt withdrawal of the Germans in the Caucasus. And only on December 29 had Adolf Hitler authorized the retreat of the First Panzer Army.

Now, on New Year's Day, they finally turned their vehicles around and bolted for safety. As their Mark IIIs and IVs drummed northward, the tankers were praying that Manstein would hold Rostov open long enough to save their lives.

Chapter Twenty-five

From the beginning of the encirclement, German military censors outside the *Kessel* had kept careful watch on the mail flown from Pitomnik to Germany. At first, the monitors estimated that more than 90 percent of the letter writers exuded both complete confidence in their leaders and in their own ability to endure hardships caused by temporary reliance on the airlift. Also, because they had been involved in other temporary "cauldrons" in the lightning-fast panzer actions of past years, German troops had had little difficulty relating those "defeats turned to victory" to the predicament they faced at Stalingrad. Had not General Seydlitz-Kurzbach himself been involved in the rescue of a hundred thousand Germans at Demyansk in Central Russia the past winter? Thus the initial avalanche of mail to the Reich reflected an apparently unshakable conviction that the Wehrmacht was still invincible.

That conviction had held until Christmas. Between that day and the end of the year, however, censors noted a sharp decline in morale. Men began to demand better mail delivery and a speedup of parcels from home to supplement dwindling rations. They also complained openly about the cold, averaging twenty degrees below zero, and bemoaned the incessant snowfall, the lice, fleas, and rats.

Still, the majority of the Germans in the *Kessel* seemed to retain a spirit of defiance and hope, or so they told their loved ones. One man wrote: "Our weapons and our command are the best in the world." Another boasted: ". . . we gladly make every sacrifice for our country in hopes that our people will see better times than we do." A third said: "Of course we will always be the stronger ones, there can be no doubt about that."

Two enlisted men breathed both defiance and a rigid belief in the regime that had led them to the *Kessel*: On December 30, one, a corporal, APO No. 36 025 had written:

> Don't get any false ideas. The victor can only be Germany. Any battle requires sacrifices, and you should be proud to know that your son is in the very center of the decision. How pleased I will be to stand before you some day with all my medals. And to prove my valor to Uncle Willi, who always told us boys that our first goal was to become a man during combat. I remember those words all the time. We know what is at stake as far as our country is concerned. We love our country now more than ever before. Germany shall live even though we may have to die.

On December 31, the other, a private first class, APO No. 24 836 B wrote:

> The Russians are flooding us with leaflets. When I come home I shall show you some of the nonsense that they are writing. They want us to surrender. Do they really believe we are puppets for them? We will fight to the last man and the last bullet. We will never capitulate. We are in a difficult position in Stalingrad, but we are not forsaken. Our Führer will not leave us in the lurch. . . . We will receive help and we shall endure. . . . If we have a little less to eat, and if we have to do without many other things, it does not matter. We shall endure.

In their mail analysis, censors flashed a warning signal to higher authorities about what to expect when January came: "it must be expected that there will be a decline in morale as hope for relief . . . wanes. . . ." The censors' prediction proved alarmingly accurate. An abrupt, fatal change in mood occurred, and the number of farewell letters increased dramatically.

The tone of these messages reflected the sudden awareness that events were narrowing each man's prospects of survival to infinitesimal percentages. When last wills and testaments multiplied, censors tried to be delicate in their excisions of material. Using pens or pencils to match that used by the sender they smudged over words or made them illegible, as though the writer himself had made the errors.

One discouraged officer told his family, ". . . You can't starve those swine. . . . They have absolute air superiority here, day and night, nothing but those rapacious birds. I cannot imagine an end to this and that is what really gets you down."

A surgeon writing to his wife was brutally frank with her about life in the *Kessel*. He described how he had just taken off a man's leg at the thigh with a pair of scissors, and how the patient endured the hideous surgery without anesthesia.

A corporal mirrored a growing sentiment; "To tell you the truth, I would rather meet with sudden death than pine away gradually. . . ."

Quartermaster Karl Binder wrote his twenty-sixth letter from the Russian front. It was another poignant attempt to prepare his family for death:

My dearest wife,
I am still alive and alright [*sic*]. Today—Sunday—I attended the funeral of several soldiers of my bakery company. It is cruel what you witness in the cemeteries. Should I ever return home, I will never forget what I have seen. It is an epic second to none. I am sorry that I have not received any letters from you since December 5. I would be so happy to read a word of love from you for one does not know what the next hour, the next day will have in store. My dearest wife, come what may, I am prepared for everything. When the time comes I shall die a soldier . . . God is with us every

hour—these were the words of the Protestant minister at the cemetery, which is overflowing. It increases in dimension like an avalanche. But the brutal enemy is still kept under control. He will not succeed in overwhelming us, as long as I have one hand that can hold a weapon.

Time is now so short that I must concern myself about the end of everything. I have lived my life—not always a pious one—and life has always handled me roughly. There have been times when a spark of carelessness or passion controlled my heart. But I have always endeavored to be decent, a comrade, a soldier. I also tried to be a good husband to you and a good father to the children. I don't know if I was successful. Probably I was too harsh, but I had only one thing in mind: your happiness. It is too late to change anything, apart from the fact that I don't know what I could change, but I love all of you more than ever. Bring up the children for their benefit. Life has not provided me with much sunshine. Most of it came from you and the children so let me thank you here and now. . . .

With us, Death is a daily guest. He has lost all his horrors for me. . . . In case I fall, move to Schwäbisch Gmünd as soon as possible. Life is cheaper there. There are 1,900 reichsmark on my account at the post office savings bank. My belongings are in a small suitcase, a big handbag, a boot-bag and perhaps a small wooden suitcase.

I don't know if you will get these things. . . . The garrison liquidation office and the maintenance board in Stuttgart will give you information about your pension.

Throw away my uniforms. The rest is yours, . . . I wish you and the children all the best for the future. Let us hope that we shall be reunited in the other world. Don't be sad, the worst may not happen. But I feel urged to set everything in order. God's will be done. So never say die. I won't either, in spite of everything.

All my love and affectionate kisses to you. I shall love you unto death.

Karl

My love and kisses to the dear children.

Chapter Twenty-six

In the first days of January, German observation posts along the southern and western sides of the *Kessel* phoned in alarming reports of a massive Russian buildup. Observers counted hundreds of T-34 tanks churning through the snow, plus troop-carrying trucks that brazenly roared past German outposts to hidden points of concentration just over the horizon. Then there were the heavy guns, thousands of them wheeling by, from the multibarreled *Kaytusha* rocket launchers to 210-millimeter siege howitzers.

In their cramped holes, the Germans were powerless to interfere. Ammunition had to be saved for an actual attack.

Knowing their enemy was impotent, Russian soldiers set up huge field kitchens, from which the aroma of hot food wafted toward Sixth Army foxholes. This sensual torture was worse for the Germans than seeing the tanks and guns that spelled imminent disaster.

Joseph Stalin had finally put his generals in motion to crush Paulus. Artillery genius Nikolai Nikolaevich Voronov appeared at the edge of the *Kessel* to lend his authority to plans for the final offensive. On a line seven miles long, he proposed the installation of seven thousand guns, more than enough to burst through the German perimeter.

Another key part in the new Soviet offensive was delegated to Vassili Chuikov in the city of Stalingrad. Aware that Paulus still kept seven divisions along the Volga despite manpower shortages elsewhere on his flanks, STAVKA assigned his Sixty-second Army a significant tactical role in the final liquidation of the pocket.

Chuikov learned of this when a distinguished visitor, Gen. Konstantin Rokossovsky, came across the Volga to his cliffside bunker. Sitting on an earthen bench, the front commander gave Chuikov the details. While simultaneous attacks were being mounted from west, north, and south, Sixty-second Army had to ". . . attract more enemy forces in its direction, preventing them from reaching the Volga if they try to break out of encirclement. . . ."

When Rokossovsky asked whether the Sixty-second Army could contain any such desperate enemy maneuver, General Krylov, Chuikov's chief aide, answered for his superior: "If in the summer and autumn all Paulus's forces were unable to drive us into the Volga, then the hungry and frozen Germans won't even move six steps eastward."

Each day, Sixty-second Army shock troops continued to intimidate these hungry and frozen Germans, who gave ground slowly as they scurried from cellar to cellar. Firefights erupted endlessly in workshops, apartment houses, and workers' homes, all mere shells by now but filled with desperate human beings, at bay and dangerous.

Trapped for more than three months in their concrete barn behind German lines, Natasha Kornilov and her mother lay under a blanket on the icy floor and listened to a sudden flurry of grenade explosions and staccato bursts from machine guns. The eleven-year-old girl had just come back from her daily trip to garbage heaps on the streets. Once again she had failed to find any food. Since the beginning of the encirclement, Natasha had come home empty-handed most of the time and by now, she was finding it extremely difficult to gather enough strength to walk out the door. But she always did, for otherwise she knew her mother would die of starvation.

Beside her under the blanket, Mrs. Kornilov had watched her eleven-year-old daughter waste away. The child's eyes bugged out from a hollowed face. Her dress hung limply on a skeletal frame. The girl's arms were like broomsticks. Though neither dared to voice her fears to the other, each wondered how long they could go on. Each prayed that the other would not die and leave the survivor alone in the concrete barn.

Gunfire outside rose to a crescendo, bullets pinged off the walls. The door flew open and a soldier trained his rifle on the figures under the covers. Natasha heard him say something in a guttural voice, then hands reached down and someone was gruffly telling her that everything was all right. Natasha smiled weakly into the bearded face of a Russian infantryman.

Twenty-five miles to the west, Pitomnik Airport was rapidly deteriorating into a living hell. At the two main medical stations, German doctors had been overwhelmed by an influx of wounded. Patients begged for medication to stop their pain, but with drugs in short supply, medics were forced to issue them only to the worst cases. Outside the hospitals, countless bodies lay unburied. So far, however, the corpses were being stacked in neat rows for future interment.

A few of the passengers on outgoing planes looked remarkably healthy. Specialists and administrators, they had been ordered to leave the pocket to form the nucleus of new divisions. Some benefited from General Seydlitz's abortive attempt to force a retreat in November: The staff of the 94th Division boarded Junkers and embarked on a mission to rebuild that "ghost" organization.

Their division veterinarian, Herbert Rentsch, stayed behind to dispose of his livestock. His camels had just been slaughtered and now Rentsch processed the last of his twelve hundred horses for food. But he still refused to send his own horse, Lore, to the knife. Though she had lost most of her strength, when Rentsch looked at her he could not order her destruction. He rationalized his decision by thinking that one more dead horse would make little difference to the outcome of the battle.

Lt. Hans Oettl had no such problem. When he found his goat Maedi eating the documents in his files, he knew she was doomed to starvation. Bringing out his small library of books, he fed them to Maedi page by page, then handed her to the company butcher and walked away.

On the northern perimeter of the *Kessel*, some lucky German soldiers were actually having a feast. Their bonus was the gift of a grateful Dr. Ottmar Kohler who, on returning as promised from his furlough in Germany, had loaded thirty geese in the back of a Heinkel bomber as a gesture of thanks to those who had given him a brief moment with his family during the holidays.

If he had so chosen, the doctor could have stayed at home. It would have been easy for him to make an excuse, to feign illness, until too late to return. But Kohler always knew he would go back; he could not live with himself otherwise.

When he stood again in the doorway of the hospital, some of the wounded wept on seeing him, and Kohler immediately plunged back to work, trying to handle a staggering number of patients, many of whom just lay on their cots and died without a struggle. Convinced that he knew the underlying cause of their deaths, Kohler went to an autopsy to prove his case.

He joined other doctors around an operating table on which

the body of a thirty-year-old lieutenant lay stripped. There was no mark on the painfully thin corpse, but it was so frozen that attendants brought in strong lights and portable heaters to thaw it sufficiently for examination. Finally the pathologist moved to the cadaver and with swift strokes made a modified Y incision, cutting from each clavicle inward to the sternum and then straight down the torso to the pubis.

With a pair of surgical shears, the pathologist proceeded to open the rib cage. The loud snap of severed bones and cartilage accompanied his dry commentary: "Thoracic cavity, complete absence of subcutaneous fat." When he excised the heart and held it up for all to see, a murmur of surprise went around the room. The organ was shrunken to the size of a baby's fist.

The autopsy continued, the pathologist's voice droned on: "Duodenum, complete absence of subcutaneous fat; peritoneal cavity, small amount of fluid, complete absence of subcutaneous fat. . . ." To Kohler, the verdict already was obvious. He listened intently as the dissector finally straightened up and announced his diagnosis: "I cannot find any valid reason why this man is dead."

Stunned, Kohler shouted: "Shouldn't we at least offer an opinion among ourselves? The man's heart has shrunk to that of a child. There's not a bit of fat in him. He has starved to death."

His remarks were met by deadly silence, and Kohler realized that no one was about to side with him against Sixth Army Headquarters, which had banned all mention of starvation as a factor contributing to death. Disgusted with his peers, Kohler stormed from the room.

Lt. Heinrich Klotz, leader of the oldest company of men in Sixth Army, would have seconded Dr. Kohler's cry of outrage. During the past weeks, he had watched his soldiers disintegrate physically. When a doctor examined the unit, he shook his head, exclaiming: "I must say, the condition of your people is even worse than that of the Rumanians."

The men of Klotz's company died quietly. One night a forty-year-old man went to sleep and never woke up. Two other soldiers walking back from a trench-digging detail just stumbled and fell down. When the lieutenant reported their deaths, a superior demanded they be listed as "killed in action." Klotz did as he was told.

While increasing numbers of Sixth Army troops toppled into the snow from the effects of malnutrition, the distance between them and their comrades who had tried to rescue them widened perceptibly. Now, more than eighty miles southwest of the *Kessel*, General "Papa" Hoth's original relief expedition was slowly being forced backward by Russian divisions pressing in close pursuit.

Acting under Manstein's order to protect the city of Rostov as long as possible, Hoth was conducting a masterful delaying action as he feinted, ambushed, and kept the Soviet units off balance. Hoth's tactics exasperated not only the Red Army, but also Hitler, who began to complain to Manstein about this strategy of "elastic" withdrawal. When the Führer finally insisted that Hoth stop and hold every foot of ground, on January 5, Manstein abruptly offered his resignation in a curt telegram to Rastenburg: "Should . . . this headquarters continue to be tied down . . . I cannot see that any useful purpose will be served by my continuing as commander of Don Army Group."

Faced with such an outburst from Manstein, Hitler backed down and allowed General Hoth to retreat as planned.

The Russian divisions stalking Hoth were under the control of Andrei Yeremenko, who was still smarting over his recent demotion in favor of Rokossovsky. Intent on restoring his position with STAVKA and the premier, the general was pushing hard to seize Rostov and foil German Army Group A's withdrawal from the Caucasus. To that end he had already taken Kotelnikovo, fifty-two miles northeast of Rostov, and there his troops had been embraced by thousands of ecstatic Russian civilians, who blurted out a torrent of stories about Nazi oppression: three hundred boys and girls deported as slave laborers to Germany; four people shot for harboring a Russian officer. One man sorrowfully told how ". . . they burned down the public library." Another described, "a lot of rape . . ." The litany of crimes shouted out by the citizens of Kotelnikovo infuriated their rescuers.

Southwest of Kotelnikovo, Sgt. Alexei Petrov spurred his gun crew on toward Rostov. The squat artilleryman had lost count of the times he had crossed and recrossed the twisting loops of the lower Don, but he ignored his exhaustion as he pursued an enemy who had held his family in bondage for more than a year.

In the midst of this offensive, however, Petrov met a new foe. Approaching the outskirts of a steppe village, the inhabitants— men and women—ran out and attacked his unit with pitchforks and hammers. The Red Army troops withdrew from the onslaught and stumbled back with the news that their assailants were native Kazakhs, a minority violently opposed to Communist rule from Moscow.

The Kazakhs screamed insults and shouted: "We don't want any Russians here!" while bewildered Soviet soldiers milled about on the plain. Someone phoned division headquarters for advice. Within minutes a terse order came back: "Destroy them all."

In the general bombardment that followed, Petrov fired high-explosive shells into the village, which blew into thousands of pieces of mud, clay, and timber. Machine guns picked off anyone who tried to escape, and the Kazakhs were killed to the last child.

Gazing at the crackling flames, Petrov suddenly wondered why these people had such hatred for the state. What was it about Communism that made them turn on their brothers? He was plagued by a terrible guilt for killing his own brethren.

"Eins, zwei, drei, vier! Eins, zwei, drei, vier!" The harsh cadence rang across the steppe as German officers inside the *Kessel* trained

recruits for the infantry. Clerks, cooks, telephone operators, orderlies, men under company punishment for crimes—they all marched up and down the *balkas* in close-order drill. The man who taught them, Lt. Herman Kästle, did not enjoy his job. Some of the troops had been his friends for years, and he knew he was sending them to a sure death.

The soldiers he hurriedly prepared for combat were in a state of shock. Few had ever dreamed they would have to face the Russians across no-man's-land. Most had enjoyed soft assignments; almost none of them had come out of their warm bunkers during the winter.

As Kästle issued final instructions before sending them off to battle, one soldier broke down completely. Sobbing hysterically, he clutched at the lieutenant and begged to be spared. Kästle talked urgently to him, trying to quiet his fears. The man listened and then, while the column started to march off, he wiped his tears away and ran to take his place in formation.

Kästle watched him out of sight.

Pvt. Ekkehart Brunnert was already at the main line of resistance. Ever since he had de-trained from Germany, he had walked back and forth across the steppe: standing guard duty, lining up for inspections, sitting on buses which never broke out of the *Kessel*. Now he was merely two hundred meters away from the burned out hulk of a Soviet tank whose driver, charred to a "black tailor's dummy," seemed to stare back at him every day.

When he first saw the body, Brunnert had felt a brief spasm of compassion. The man must have suffered indescribable tortures trying to escape the flames. Still, Brunnert reasoned, the same thing had happened countless times to Germans in the war and that thought helped him forget the gruesome sight in front of his foxhole.

His life followed a strict pattern. He stood watch every four hours and at 5:00 P.M. every day, he crawled back to the company kitchen for rations. Otherwise he read and reread Soviet propaganda leaflets that showered down from the sky. Brunnert never once thought of defecting, but the pictures on the literature haunted him: a beautiful Christmas tree, beneath which a woman buried her face in a handkerchief. Beside her a little child sobbed her grief as they both stared at their present, the body of a soldier father. In another leaflet, a woman sang carols with her children while the figure of the dead father hovered over them like a ghost.

For over a week, Brunnert and his friend Gunter Gehlert had shared a bunker and adjusted to the presence of the enemy nearby. On January 7, just as Gunter came to relieve Brunnert at the machine gun, a shell burst only yards away. Brunnert screamed and fell face down into the trench. He stared dumbly at one of his fingers, split open like a blossoming rosebud.

His legs were hit, too, and he lay in a spreading pool of blood but remained conscious while Gunter brought a medic. In shock, Brunnert watched wordlessly as they frantically fashioned a dressing. When darkness came, Gunter put Brunnert on a sled, pressed money into his hand and asked him to give it to his own parents when he got home.

The sled rocked gently through the snow and except for his freezing feet, Brunnert enjoyed the ride to Gumrak Airfield hospital. In an operating room suffused with bright lights, he relaxed as his clothing, that filth-caked armor, was taken off. After receiving a local anesthetic, he began to dream of good food and sleep without worrying about Russians creeping up on him during the night. That thought brought back the image of poor Gunter alone at the bunker, watching now for the enemy until his eyes watered and he saw mirages on the snow. Brunnert suddenly felt very sorry for his comrade.

Still on the operating table, he turned his head. Only a few feet away, on another table, he saw the convoluted windings of a man's brain. Fascinated, he carefully examined the various folds, some pink, others grayish blue, while doctors probed his own body for pieces of metal. Shortly afterward, Ekkehart Brunnert left the *Kessel* on a plane bound for home.

"Every seven seconds, a German dies in Russia. Stalingrad is a mass grave. Every seven seconds, a German dies. . . ."

The loudspeaker's words assaulted Gunter Gehlert, alone now in his bunker without Brunnert. They assailed Gottlieb Slotta and Hubert Wirkner as they crouched in their icy holes on the steppe. The message twanged taut the nerves of two hundred thousand men trapped on the steppe. Hour by hour, the *politrook* bombarded the Germans with announcements, threats, inducements, and prophecies. In some sectors, Russian speakers even called out the names of company and battalion commanders.

Capt. Gerhard Meunch learned this when a commissar engaged him in a personal war. Near the Red October Plant, the loudspeakers blared over and over: "German soldiers, drop your weapons. It makes no sense to continue. Your Captain Meunch will also realize one day what is going on. What this 'super-Fascist' tells you isn't right anyway. He will recognize it. One day we'll seize him."

Every time the enemy mentioned his name, Meunch immediately went out and spent time with his troops. Joking about the personal comments, he watched closely for any adverse reactions from the men. But though the tactic was meant to be unnerving, they never seemed intimidated by the Russian ploy.

Less than two miles southwest of Meunch's outpost in the Red October Plant, Ignacy Changar gulped down a full ration of vodka and wondered where he could find another. The commando captain had been relying more and more on liquor to forget the daily nightmare in which he lived. His awful memories of the past had not faded and with dynamite, rifle, and knife he had blown up, shot, or stabbed more than two hundred of the enemy. Still he was not satisfied.

As a result, his one-man war had taken its toll on him. His face was drawn, the eyes haunted. His hands trembled. His only relief from inner tension was alcohol and, after finishing his vodka ration on the night of January 7, he led his men up the eastern slope of Mamaev Hill, carefully threading a path through Russian trenches and minefields to the final rolls of barbed wire. Crawling into no-man's-land, Changar tried to gauge whether the Germans sensed his approach, but the crown of Mamaev Hill remained tranquil. Reaching an open stretch where shellbursts had blown away the snow, he stood up and waited for his unit to gather around him.

Several brilliant white flares quickly popped overhead. As he screamed, "Drop!" a German shell exploded a few feet away. Changar felt a terrible pain in the right side of his head, then crumpled to the ground. His men carried him back down the slope to an aid station, where doctors worked carefully to extract the metal fragment lodged against the brain. Evacuated quickly for further surgery, the still unconscious Changar was not expected to live.

West of Mamaev Hill, at Gumrak Airfield, Paulus learned that three Red Army representatives planned to enter German lines with an ultimatum for Sixth Army. The Russians proposed a rendezvous at 10:00 A.M. Moscow time, on January 8. Though Paulus ignored the request, at the appointed hour the Russian parliamentarians walked under a white flag into German lines and delivered Marshal Rokossovsky's offer to an astonished but polite Captain Willig.

Rokossovsky offered guarantees of safety to all who "ceased to resist," plus their return at the end of the war to Germany. He also assured Paulus that all personnel might retain their "belongings and valuables, and in the case of high-ranking officers, their swords." The general went on to offer a most tempting argument to soldiers about to starve to death, "All officers . . . and men who surrender will immediately receive normal rations . . . [the] wounded, sick or frostbitten will be given medical treatment."

The Red Army ultimatum demanded an affirmative answer within twenty-four hours, or else the Germans would suffer total "destruction."

Friedrich von Paulus submitted the proposal to Hitler and asked for "freedom of action."

Rokossovsky's offer of good treatment and guarantees of safety had been voiced earlier in January by the Soviet government. In a document extraordinary for its seeming compassion during a brutal war, guidelines were laid down for the proper care of enemy captives.

TREATMENT OF POW IN THE SOVIET UNION: ORDER OF THE PEOPLES COMMISSARIAT FOR THE DEFENCE OF THE USSR
January 2, 1943   No. 001   Moscow

The manner of return-conveyance and security of POW on the front and on the way to the collection camp *shows a number of serious shortcomings:*

The POW remain too long inside the units of the Red Army. From the time of capture to the loading the prisoners have to cover 200–300 km on foot. Often they receive no food. Therefore they arrive quite exhausted and sick. . . .

In order to energetically discontinue such shortcomings while taking care of POW and to make them available as work forces . . . the following order [is issued] . . . to the commanders at the front:

. . . according to POW regulations, give timely medical attention to wounded or sick POW. . . .

Categorically discontinue sending on a march wounded, sick, exhausted or frozen prisoners . . . such prisoners are to be attended to in a field hospital and forwarded when transportation is available . . . also sick prisoners are to be fed according to regulations for these. . . .

. . . Limit the daily marching time to 25–30 km. Install stopping places for overnight stays. Give out warm food and water to the POW, and have ready a heating facility.

. . . Leave the POW their clothes, shoes, underwear, bedding and eating utensils. If a prisoner lacks any of these, it is a duty to replace the missing objects from loot, or from effects of killed or dead enemy soldiers or officers. . . .

To the chief of sanitary inspection of the Red Army:

. . . at check points have a control station· for marching POW and give medical attention to the sick . . . such POW who cannot continue the march due to illness are to be taken out of the column and sent to a field hospital close by. . . .

Forbid that POW be forwarded in cars not suitable for human transport. . . .

Sent on to Russian commanders by telegram, the document was ignored. The reasons were twofold: Hobbled by acute shortages of rail cars, medical supplies, and food, Russian officials could not cope with the enormous influx of Axis prisoners during December and January. Furthermore, the prison personnel allowed their hatred for the invaders to influence their actions. Thus, as the POWs walked and rode to internment, many Red Army officers responsible for their well-being tacitly condoned their deaths.

"*Vodi! Vodi!*" The plaintive cry for water irritated Felice Bracci as some of the thirty-five men riding in his freight car shouted their desperate plea. Bracci had no idea of their destination and, after listening to this pitiful lament for three days, he was beginning to lose his temper. Conditions were frightful enough for everyone without the constant whining from the weak.

Bracci and his fellow officers were barely alive. Twenty-four slept in shifts on the ice-covered floor, where they curled up in embraces to draw heat from each other. To pass the time, some men whispered stories of previous days and future dreams. Martini, Branco, and Giordano agreed to set up a restaurant in Rome with their savings. Franco Fusco wanted to go into business. Fasanotti talked about continuing his career as a public prosecutor.

One officer refused to talk of what might be. Instead, he announced that the trip was merely an exquisite torture conceived by the Russians, who would keep the train going endlessly until all its passengers died. It seemed that way. Just once a day, guards pulled the door open to give them a hunk of black bread and a bucket of water.

While the thirstiest howled for more than their share, Bracci and his friends carefully watched a soldier whittle the frozen bread into equal portions. The men never took their eyes off the knife as it shaved and jabbed the rock-like meal. Carefully handed out to groups of five, the bread was consumed immediately and then, in the dim light that seeped through cracks, the Italians rocked along in contemplative silence.

As the miles and days passed, each man attended to his bodily needs in a corner and a cone-shaped mound of excrement rose slowly, a daily calendar recording the length of the trip. The excrement was always gray, the color of the bread, their only sustenance.

Bracci slept as much as he could. But when he was awake, he thought often about his captors and he was torn by his feelings toward the Russian guards. In their strange dress, they looked like big wicked apes. Boisterous, crude, they showed no trace of sensitivity. Yet, Bracci knew that out on the lonely steppe of southern Russia, their women and children suffered, too. Like him, they loved and laughed, cried and bled. But the men who guarded the trail from Kalmikov and rode the train to prison camp as jailers were not the same, could not be related to those Russians who generously gave him food during the march. To these guards, the Italians were "mere objects"; not men, not slaves. They were nothing.

The prisoners' train moved due north, toward Moscow and beyond. Behind it, on the road Bracci had marched along earlier, lay thousands of frozen corpses. Some had bullet holes in the torso. Most had gunshot wounds in the back of the neck.

Baggage peculiar to the Italian Army lay on the crusted snow-trail. Crucifixes, mass cards, pictures of Jesus Christ and the saints, had fallen near the dead. One victim sat placidly in a drift. Eyes wide open, a smile creasing his face, he held a black rosary in his hands. The soldier had begun the second decade of the beads when a Russian guard shot him.

Cristoforo Capone came along this same trail several days behind Bracci. The doctor saw the ravens Bracci had noticed circling and he heard the same shouts: *"Davai bistre!" "Davai bistre!"* as Russian guards robbed the prisoners of their warm clothing and beat them when they protested. Capone, too, watched the weak fall down and winced at the sharp cracks of rifle fire as they died. Like Bracci, he huddled for many nights in below-zero weather with soldiers who screamed from the pain of frostbite or wailed to God about their cruel fate. The doctor pitied these men in their misery, but he had decided to live. Some unknown inner strength brought him to a railroad station and a section of floor in a freight car, where he now sprawled to rest.

While an Arctic wind whistled outside and the men clutched each other to transmit body heat, the train sped north. Capone began to lick the icicled walls to quench his raging thirst. Men died beside him each night and, in the morning, Russian guards opened the doors and screamed: *"Skolco kaput?"* ("How many dead?") That was all they cared about, the number of corpses they had to pull out and discard in the snow.

On the evening of January 8, Field Marshal Erich von Manstein entertained guests at Novocherkassk. Among them were Gen. Hans Hube, *"Der Mensch,"* who had just returned from East Prussia. On the way back he traveled with Col. Günter von Below, who had been invalided out of Stalingrad in September with jaundice, and was returning to duty at a time when most German soldiers were praying to leave the pocket.

During their flight, Below had learned from Hube that the Führer was planning another attempt to extricate the Sixth Army. Three panzer divisions were supposedly coming from France and would be ready to attack by the middle of February. It was apparent to Below that the aggressive Hube had succumbed to Hitler's mesmerizing personality and believed implicitly in this new rescue expedition.

At dinner that night Hube continued to talk about the promised panzers. But each time he tried to solicit Erich von Manstein's opinions, the field marshal changed the subject. Throughout the meal, in fact, Manstein avoided any comment about the army inside the *Kessel*.

Later, over drinks with staff officers of Army Group Don, Below found one reason for Manstein's negative responses when his companions told him that less than a hundred tons a day had been airlifted to Stalingrad. Without making any definite admissions about the *Kessel* being a hopeless trap, they convinced Below that he was "a condemned man having a last meal" before going to his death. The chastened colonel drank until a late hour.

The next day, January 9, he and Hube touched down at Pitomnik and went on to the crowded interior of the headquarters bunker at Gumrak, where Paulus and Schmidt awaited them. Extremely agitated, Paulus quickly told his visitors it was impossible for Sixth Army to hold out much longer. When Hube broke in to mention the tanks coming from France, Paulus merely shrugged in resignation. Still, as Hube kept insisting on the need to hold out until the panzer force arrived at the perimeter, Paulus began to show a spark of interest in the idea. A desperate man, stripped of options by the higher authority he would never disobey, Paulus had to force himself to believe in a miracle.

Only hours earlier, Hitler had again denied him the requested "freedom of action" about the Russian ultimatum of surrender. The Führer was insisting on a fight to the death, because ". . . every day the Army holds out helps the entire front. . . ."

That message had settled Paulus's mind on a basic issue. Tempted to give up the struggle, he dismissed that thought when "higher authority" declared Sixth Army's agony to be a vital necessity. Thus he now listened to Hube's ramblings about panzers coming from France and, at the same time, issued a stern warning to his troops about the Soviet peace offer: ". . . Any proposals of negotiations are . . . to be rejected, not to be answered and parliamentaries *are to be repulsed by force of weapons. . . .*"

As the ultimatum's time limit expired, an eerie quiet descended on the steppe. In their holes and trenches, German soldiers waited fearfully for Russian reaction to Paulus's order for all-out resistance.

Chapter Twenty-seven

At dawn on January 10, the forty-eighth day of the *Kessel,* a red sun poked over the horizon and shone dully on the white steppe. On both sides of the front lines, soldiers moved about in cramped foxholes, flexing their arms and legs to drive away the chill of the subzero temperature. Around them the sounds of battle were muted. Only an occasional rifle shot echoed across no-man's-land.

By 8:00 A.M., German troops standing in line for breakfast were commenting on the fact that the Russians had been unusually quiet for more than twenty-four hours. Two minutes later, as the Germans munched chunks of black bread and drank watery coffee, seven thousand Russian cannons roared in unison and the Sixth Army fortifications in the Karpovka Valley disappeared under a rainbow of fire. Along with the artillery barrage came clouds of Soviet planes, racing at low altitudes across the German lines to sow panic.

When the first monstrous thunderclap of the cannonade smashed against his reinforced shelter, Sgt. Albert Pflüger fell off his cot. Though the main bombardment was nearly five miles to the west, wave upon wave of concussive shock showered dirt on him and shook the ground as if it were "a storm-ridden sea." Dragging himself from the floor, Pflüger ran out to his headquarters command post where the phone was ringing incessantly with reports of entire units wiped out, and others reeling back from the shattered front.

Mobs of frenzied soldiers were already inundating the rear and Pflüger watched them stagger by: shell-shocked, hysterical, trickling blood from the mouth, nose, and ears. They were the survivors of General Voronov's "god of war," the heavy artillery.

Pioneer Colonel Herbert Selle was on his way to the "nose" of the pocket in the Karpovka Valley when the Soviet offensive broke over him. Switching direction, he headed instead for the headquarters of the 76th Division, which was holding a precarious position at the western side of the perimeter. There Selle met the monocled, extraordinarily calm, Gen. Carl Rodenburg, who told him the Russians had already broken through the center of his line. As they spoke, enemy shells banged into the ravine and "white- and mud-colored clouds of snow and dust rose into the air." Selle left quickly.

His car passed a wretched mob of wounded, pleading with drivers to take them along, and Selle picked up nearly a dozen of them. They tumbled inside the car, clung to the running boards or draped themselves over the hood. The strange ambulance drove on to Gumrak where the wounded helped each other into the hospital. Watching them go, Selle wondered what effect such a grisly sight would have on Gen. Kurt Zeitzler back in East Prussia. If he could see these wretches inside the *Kessel* would Zeitzler continue to parrot Hitler's orders to fight to the last bullet?

At Pitomnik, Russian shells fell on the runways and scattered personnel unloading supplies from planes. Quartermaster Karl Binder was leading a column of trucks into a nearby ration depot when explosions bracketed his vehicle and blew up ammunition dumps in the fields.

Hurrying the loading of gasoline, clothing, and cases of food, Binder hollered for the trucks to scatter. Just as he waved them off, a shellburst tossed him into a snowdrift. Unconscious, he lay there for hours until another truck driver pulled him out and sped on to Gumrak. When he revived, Binder discovered that by some miracle he had not been wounded, and that his trucks had brought back enough rations to feed the 305th Division for eighteen days— enough for nearly three weeks, if the front lines held. But the Soviet bombardment went on and on, and after two hours it had burst the German perimeter like an eggshell. Soviet T-34 tanks quickly roared through the gaps; mounted infantry followed. In the north, they punched a hole between the 113th Division and the 76th. To the west, the Austrian 44th Division vanished under a torrent of fire and steel. So did the 376th and 384th German divisions. That part of the front caved in and the village of Dimitrevka fell quickly to Russian armor. In the south, Albert Pflüger's 297th Division had broken apart in the area between Zybenko and Peschanka and the Russians smashed through with impunity.

Only in the southwest corner, at the Marinovka "nose" salient, did German resistance contain the enemy for any length of time. There, as General Schmidt had predicted earlier to Colonel Selle, the main Russian drive centered on the valley of the Karpovka River, where Sixth Army bunkers had been built into the sides of the gorge. Schmidt assumed the enemy wanted to drive the Germans from these entrenchments onto the open steppe and thus force a Napoleonic retreat eastward to Stalingrad. His analysis was almost perfect. His only error was in thinking the attack would come ten days later.

In that exposed salient, the 3rd and 29th Motorized Divisions stood side by side and tried to cling to the "nose." But within a few hours, the 3rd Motorized had its flanks beaten in, and was forced to pull back hastily to reorganize beyond the Rossoshka River. Still the 29th Division held on, and the Russians attacked it over the crest of Cossack Hill. Hundreds of tanks, crowded close

Rodion Malinovsky, Commander of the Soviet Second Guards Army that blunted Manstein's drive to relieve the men trapped in the *Kessel* in December, 1942.

Russian reinforcements being briefed by General Guriev before crossing the Volga and going into battle.

Russian skirmish line amidst wreckage of Red October Plant.

A German soldier lies dead on the frozen Volga.

Russian troops mopping u▮
former German stronghold in
apartment house in Stalingr▮

A German battalion cemetery on the bleak, snow-covered steppe inside the *Kessel,* December, 1942. After the war the Russians dug up the graves and reinterred the bodies in mass, unmarked graves.

German Quartermaster Karl Binder *(left)* and comrade celebrate Christmas Eve in bunker northwest of Stalingrad inside the *Kessel.*

General Carl Rodenburg, German commander, 76th Infantry Division.

General Arthur Schmidt, Chief of Staff, German Sixth Army.

German Sergeant Albert Pflüger of the 297th Infantry Division.

Corporal Hubert Wirkner of German 14th Panzer Division.

A street in Stalingrad after the liberation.

Field Marshal Friedrich von Paulus *(left)* after his surrender at the Univermag Department Store in Stalingrad. His adjutant, Wilhelm Adam, is at far right.

Aerial view of devastate
downtown area of Stalingrad afte
the battl

German prisoners being marched across the frozen Volga to captivity.

Russian refugees returning to their homes in Stalingrad in March of 1943.

together, led the parade and infantrymen clung to the turrets from which huge red flags flew briskly. Behind the T-34s came long columns of foot soldiers, wading through hip-deep snow. The Germans stared in awe at this massive display of might and then, with the pressure proving irresistible, gave ground.

By the end of the day, the Sixth Army was on the run toward the ruins of Stalingrad.

On January 11, the situation in the *Kessel* deteriorated further. Gen. Carl Rodenburg still wore the monocle in his right eye, but he had lost much of his quiet confidence. The day before, he possessed fifty heavy-caliber weapons in his artillery regiment. Now one of his officers rushed up to him and gasped: "General, here is the last gun." Thirty soldiers had dragged it for seven miles to the new line of resistance.

As he clasped the officer's hand and thanked him warmly for his stupendous achievement, Carl Rodenburg knew that the battle inside the *Kessel* was futile. Then the general went out to find the rest of his 76th Division. Once it had been ten thousand strong, now it was just the size of a battalion, six hundred men.

Sixth Army radio: 9:40 A.M. "Enemy broke through on a wide portion of the front line. . . . Isolated strongholds are still intact. We are trying to rally and train last available parts of supply and construction units . . . to set up a blocking line."

It was a hopeless delaying of the inevitable. Again, at 7:00 P.M., Sixth Army radio reported to Manstein: "Deep penetration east of Zybenko . . . more than six kilometers wide. Enemy had very heavy losses. . . . Our own losses were considerable. Resistance of the troops diminishing quickly because of insufficient ammunition, extreme frost, and lack of coverage against heaviest enemy fire."

Capt. Winrich Behr returned from a trip to the front lines and, in a hurried letter, described his impressions to Klaus von Below.

Behr told his friend what Sixth Army Headquarters had not mentioned in any messages to the outside world. German soldiers had begun to desert in large numbers; many officers in the field had lost the will to lead. Blankets over their heads, the men slept at sentry posts; without tanks behind them as support, terrified Germans now ran in the face of enemy assaults.

Behr said he thought the general feeling in the pocket had become one of simple self-preservation. He went on to berate leaders who directed the airlift. Bitterly he suggested that Below ". . . put some Jews or some black market operators . . ." in charge and let them run it at a profit. He closed with an appraisal of his superiors. "Paulus," he said, "means the heart" of Sixth Army. The general had "the backbone of a chief. . . ."

On the other hand, Schmidt, whom both Behr and Below had known for years through family connections, posed a special problem. Though Behr liked him, he understood why the general irritated so many high-ranking officers. Imperious, acerbic, Schmidt seldom displayed the inner qualities, the "good side" that he possessed. Behr found that a pity, since Schmidt had to work with generals now facing a situation without parallel in German military history.

In a rambling schoolhouse south of the *Kessel,* Second Guards Army Commander Rodion Yakovlevich Malinovsky took time out to entertain a group of Allied newsmen. Among them were Alexander Werth, United Press correspondent Eddy Gilmore, and Ralph Parker from *The New York Times.* Tall, with long dark hair brushed back, the ruddy-faced Malinovsky quickly admitted to his guests that Manstein's December offensive toward Stalingrad had caught the Russians napping. But then he hailed the gains of the Red Army counteroffensive and its effects on the enemy, "For the first time the Germans are showing signs of bewilderment. Trying to fill in gaps, they are throwing their troops about from one place to another. . . . The German officers we have captured are extremely disappointed in their high command and in the Führer himself. . . ."

When the reporters asked him about the drive to crush Paulus in the *Kessel*, Malinovsky was bluntly confident: "Stalingrad is an armed prisoners camp, and its position is hopeless. . . ."

Sixth Army Radio: January 12. "Continuous bombardments since 7 A.M. Cannot reply. . . . Since 8 A.M. heavy enemy attacks along all front lines with numerous tanks. . . . Army has ordered as a last means of resistance that every soldier has to fight to the last bullet at the place he is holding right now."

At Pitomnik, a single Russian T-34 tank broke through the thin perimeter defense and clanked onto the crowded runway. Its appearance induced panic among the Germans who stampeded away from the planes, the hospitals, the wounded, and ran east on the road to Gumrak and Stalingrad. The tank leisurely cruised the strip, firing at a wide choice of targets, and "the heart of the fortress" skipped several beats.

Hearing the news of the tank's appearance, Gen. Arthur Schmidt jumped to the phone and screamed his outrage at half a dozen officers responsible for protecting the field. Schmidt's anger galvanized the chagrined commanders into restoring Pitomnik to service after a short delay. But in the confusion, in one of those miraculous incidents of war, the Soviet T-34 simply disappeared in the haze and escaped.

Later that day, Paulus dispatched one of his most trusted generals for help. Wolfgang Pickert, leader of the 9th Flak Division, flew through a raging snowstorm to Novocherkassk. During the flight, he scribbled notes of his arguments on the margin of a newspaper in his own special shorthand code in case the plane was shot down. It was an unnecessary precaution. He landed safely and rushed to confer with Army Group Don about chances for a dramatic upsurge in supplies.

Inside the shrinking *Kessel,* on the road between Karpovka and Pitomnik, trucks moved carefully through congested traffic. In one of them, Sgt. Ernst Wohlfahrt rode beside the driver. Recently detached from artillery spotting inside the dread Barrikady Gun Factory, Wohlfahrt was glad to be out in the open, where he could raise his head without fearing that a sniper might take it off.

Behind him, someone shouted that Russian tanks had broken into the convoy. The driver floored the accelerator and the truck leaped ahead, straight at several wounded men scrambling frantically to get out of the way. One vehicle after another hit them and rolled their bodies under the wheels. Wohlfahrt saw arms and legs flailing madly when his truck smashed into the victims and passed on. Looking back, Wohlfahrt noticed that no one slowed down to remove the corpses.

On the western side of the pocket, curly-haired Hubert Wirkner crouched in his snowhole. His feet were frozen; flesh came off them in long strips. His right hand had been punctured by shrapnel, but he had not been able to find a doctor.

While Wirkner stoically endured the pain, a Russian T-34 tank fired a shell directly at him. Two companions took the full force of the explosion. One man's face disintegrated; the other's right arm flew into the air. Wirkner's body was a sieve. Hauled from the gory pit by friends, he was taken to Gumrak, where thousands of soldiers lay unattended. Wirkner was placed in a converted horse stable, fifty yards long, with perhaps twenty men around him on cots. A medic assured him that his chances for a flight out of the *Kessel* were good.

A short distance away from Wirkner's improvised hospital, the Gumrak message center kept up a steady stream of "life and death" chatter to Army Group Don, recording the fading pulse beat of Sixth Army.

> +++ Herr General Paulus gave permission to Ober-leutnant Georg Reymann, regiment 549, to marry Miss Lina Hauswald. Neustadt. . . . Please forward. [a proxy marriage]
> +++ Proposal of decoration General Pfeiffer sent. . . . Oberleutnant Boris received German Cross, gold.
> +++ Dead in action according to present information, Zschunke, Hegermann, Holzmann, Quadflieg, Hulsman, Roth-mann, Hahmann. . . . Losses of officers and troops not ac-countable at present, but very high. . . .

Later, Sixth Army radio: January 13, 9:30 A.M.

> +++ Ammunition is almost exhausted. For the as-sistance of the completely worn-out . . . troops, no reserves available in terms of men, tanks, antitank, and heavy weapons.

A German transport plane circled over Pitomnik and asked per-mission to land. The request was denied and Gen. Wolfgang Pickert told the pilot to go around again, until Russian gunfire lifted enough to allow a safe touchdown. The plane made several turns before the pilot warned the general he was running low on fuel. Reluctantly, Pickert ordered the aircraft back to Novocher-kassk, from where he hoped to try another flight into the pocket.

His mission to Manstein had failed. No one at Army Group Don ever offered any encouragement; no one in the Luftwaffe gave him hope, because barely seventy-five aircraft were left in running condition. More than four hundred transports had been shot down. Russian fighters ruled the skies.

At Pitomnik, ground controllers finally cleared the runways for landings. From the hospital sheds, hundreds of wounded walked or crawled to the edge of the concrete strip. When Junkers and Heinkels roared in under sporadic gunfire, the crippled rushed the opened doors and hatches. Doctors and pilots stood them off with drawn pistols while "ticketed" casualties went on board.

A major approached one pilot and offered him ten thousand reichsmarks for a seat on his plane. Before the pilot could reply, a mob of wild-eyed patients knocked the major aside and pushed into the aircraft. The pilot looked on helplessly. When he lifted off the runway a short time later, he carried a full complement of wounded. The major who offered him the bribe was left behind.

On the same day, a special courier left Pitomnik with Paulus's blessing. The general had ordered Capt. Winrich Behr to take the truth about the situation directly to Adolf Hitler. Still unable to believe that the Führer had written off his army, Paulus wanted Behr to emphasize the fact that unless the airlift brought forth a cornucopia of food and ammunition, Sixth Army would perish long before any spring offensive.

Stunned and somewhat guilty at being chosen, Behr protested loudly. But his friend "Schmidtchen," General Schmidt, convinced him to go and handed him Pass Number 7 as his key to freedom.

Carrying the War Diary of the Sixth Army under his arm, "Teddy" Behr took off at 5:00 P.M. and soared over the darkened plain, lit fitfully by shellbursts and arching tracer bullets. In an hour, the captain was safe in Novocherkassk and there he rested briefly before the long trip to East Prussia.

The plane that took Captain Behr from Pitomnik carried another batch of letters from husbands to wives, sons to parents. Though a strain of fatalism predominated, a surprisingly large percentage of them swore continued fealty to the Führer and the Fatherland.

Captain Gebhardt, APO No. 20 329, wrote to his wife

January 13, 1943

Our boss will be flown out and he will take this letter with him. . . . So far, I am still doing well in spite of all the difficulties—the grim frost and the pressure exerted by the enemy. The moon is shining outside and its blue light gives a miraculous touch to the snow crusts on the walls of the stables in the ravine where we have dug into the ground. Work never ceases day and night but comradeship is exemplary so everything is bearable. We, too, can quote Wallenstein saying: "The night must come for our stars to shine."

And you at home in our beautiful house, you can live in peace. This is our right and due and this is what makes us proud. Just as the *Winkelried* long ago, we have caused the enemy to point all of his spears at us. . . . Everything that will come from now on will be written in the book of fate. . . . They will consider "The battle without comparison," the battle of Stalingrad, to have been the highest, and we swear every day that we will bring it to a decent end, come what may come.

Captain Alt, APO No. 01 876 to his wife

January 13, 1943

I indicated to you yesterday what our position is. Today, unfortunately, our situation worsened again. In spite of all of this, we believe sincerely that we will be able to endure until they knock us out of here.

Should the end be a different one, then may the Lord give you the power to bear this heroically, as a sacrifice for our beloved Führer and our people.

Captain [illegible] APO No. 35 293 to his parents

January 13, 1943, 3:50 P.M.

. . . I should like to thank you all for the love and troubles which you have spent on my behalf. You know that I have been a passionate soldier, that I became one because of personal conviction, and on this basis I swore my military oath when I was a recruit. Many difficult weeks are now behind us, but the all-decisive hour is still ahead. . . . Come what may, we shall never capitulate. Loyal to our military oath, we shall perform our duties believing in our beloved Führer, Adolf Hitler, and believing in the final victory of our glorious Fatherland.

I shall never lament or complain. From the moment I became an officer in August 1939, I did not belong to myself any more but to my Fatherland. I do not want to become weak at this time. There is no human being who loves to die. However, if it has to be, then I have convinced myself that I want to be defeated in honest combat by superior enemy forces. With the boys I have around me, in the meantime we shall try to send as many of the Bolsheviks as we can to the happy hunting grounds. You should not be sad. . . . You should be proud during the days to come. It is still possible that a miracle will happen and that help will come in time.

Our motto is and will be during the most difficult hours: "We shall fight to the last grenade." Long live the Führer and our dearly beloved German Fatherland.

Gefr. Schwarz, 12 833, to his wife

January 13, 1943

Well, the time has come to be very honest and to write a manly letter without trying to make things look better than they are. . . . During past days I was enlightened and saw very clearly that the end will be one about which nobody has spoken so far. But now I must express myself. There will be a day when you will hear about our battle to the last. Remember that words concerning heroic action are merely words. I hope that this letter will come into your hands because it is perhaps the last letter which I can write. . . .

I am sure that you will keep me in your mind and that you will tell the children everything when the proper time has come. You should not mourn my death. Should you ever feel that fortune wants to give you a hand, do not fail to grasp it. . . . You will have to live on your own and I am sure that everything will continue. You will have to take up a job and take care of the little ones. I shall carry you over my heart till the last moment. You will be with me till I take my last breath.

I know you are a brave woman. You will overcome all this. . . . You have the children as the pledge of our joint life. . . . At some later date, perhaps you will be able to show them where we were happy together. . . . Live well with our dear children, embrace them with all of your power and love, take heart from them. They will give you strength and you will be able to take heart from them. Life will continue in the children. I wish all of you a good future with Germany, and I hope that she will end a winner.

The Russian attack continued and the "Marinovka nose" disappeared from the maps in Soviet and German intelligence centers.

The *Kessel* began to shrivel noticeably as German soldiers ran east before the enveloping arms of Russian pincers. Eight divisions— the 3rd, 44th, 60th, 76th, 113th, 297th, 376th and 384th—already had been effectively destroyed. Only the 29th Motorized Division retained any strength to combat the enemy at the western side of the pocket.

Gen. Ernst Leyser was there with his men, urging them from the houses and holes in which they cowered. He had only four tanks left but after dark, he broke cover and ran forward screaming: "Hurrah!" Hundreds of wounded and previously apathetic Germans suddenly jumped out to follow Leyser in an attack against the surprised Russians. The firefight was a confusion of men and shellbursts, dead, and more wounded crying in the bloodstained snow. Leyser had thrown the enemy off balance for a moment and he needed the time to plan another retreat. In the harsh morning light, his victory seemed Pyrrhic. But the general was delighted to find that some spirit remained in his exhausted soldiers. He hoped to find that again when he reached the last defense line—inside the city of Stalingrad.

Chapter Twenty-eight

At 9:00 P.M. on January 15, at Rastenburg, East Prussia, Capt. Winrich Behr faced the Führer of the Third Reich. When he walked into the crowded conference room, Behr was understandably nervous. He was in the presence of many illustrious men. Generals Jodl and Schmundt, Marshal Keitel, General Heusinger, even Martin Bormann stood looking skeptically at him. But when Hitler walked up and smiled warmly, Behr gathered himself to do the job Paulus had entrusted to him.

Hitler was charming, solicitous about the long flight and Behr's comfort. When he asked the captain to speak freely, Behr launched into a detailed explanation of Sixth Army's position. The captain was surprisingly blunt as he told of the dissolution of morale, the breakdown of officer leadership under pressure of Russian attacks, of starvation, and of guns blown up for lack of shells. Behr vividly described two hundred thousand men dying from official neglect.

Then Hitler spoke. With Behr listening raptly, the Führer stood over a table and swept his hand back and forth across a map. Though he admitted that mistakes had been made, he hastened to assure Behr that another expedition was going to break the

Russian ring and reach Sixth Army within weeks. In the meantime, Hitler continued, the airlift would enable Paulus to hold on. An aide broke in to assure Behr that sufficient flights were planned.

Exasperated at mention of the airlift, Behr interrupted, "But the airlift has not worked."

Hitler seemed puzzled, saying that Luftwaffe reports showed enough sorties on good flying days to keep Sixth Army at a level above starvation. As Behr shook his head, he noticed Marshal Keitel furiously wagging a finger at him—like an irate schoolmaster scolding a student for talking back to an elder. Refusing to be intimidated, the captain went on, saying that while many times aircraft took off for the pocket, many of them failed to reach their destination because of enemy fire or bad weather. And lately, the captain added, planes that dropped food bombs by parachute aimed most of them into Russian lines.

Emboldened, Behr made one final attempt to save his friends —Friedrich von Paulus, "Schmidtchen," Eichlepp, the freezing grenadiers in the foxholes at Stalingrad—and he said: "It is of paramount importance that Sixth Army should know the quantities of supplies that will be flown into the fortress. It is too late for long-term planning. Sixth Army is at the end of its resources and demands a clear decision as to whether or not it may count on assistance and support within the next forty-eight hours."

Shocked at his own impertinence, Behr waited for swift retribution. Adolf Hitler stared at him. Generals and aides were stunned into silence. Keitel's face was cherry red, almost apoplectic. Suddenly the Führer sighed deeply and shrugged. Smiling warmly at Behr, he told him he would discuss the matter immediately with his advisers.

Convinced that he had done all he could, Behr saluted stiffly and left the room.

Thirteen hundred miles to the east, the Russian ring around Pitomnik tightened as T-34 tanks moved within a quarter mile of the runways. Control-tower operators waved off further transport landings and six Messerschmitt 109 fighters roared off the strip to take refuge at the smaller, ill-equipped Gumrak Airport, a few miles to the east. On landing there, five of the fighters either overshot the runway or crashed into debris. The sixth plane circled hesitantly, then disappeared to the west, far beyond the *Kessel*. It landed eventually at Schacty and the pilot reported that Pitomnik was no longer under German control.

With Pitomnik overrun, Sixth Army had suffered a mortal wound. The end was almost at hand.

The transmitter at Gumrak relayed news of its final spasms to Army Group Don: "Composure of many troops . . . is highly commendable. Completely exhausted officers and men who have gone for days almost without food have pulled cannon for 20 kilometers through heavily snowed-in and often roadless steppes. Supply situation catastrophic. In some places troops cannot bring supplies to the front due to lack of fuel."

Field Marshal Manstein was not surprised. Threatened by Soviet tank raids himself, he had been forced to retreat another fifty miles west to Taganrog, from where he monitored the pulsebeat of his own operations. Along the upper Don, on nearly a two-hundred-mile-wide line from Pavlovsk northwest to Kasternoye, fresh Russian armies had attacked the few Italian divisions that had not been engaged in December, as well as the entire Second Hungarian Army. This latest drive quickly overwhelmed the satellite forces and opened another wide gap in Manstein's left flank.

By this time the field marshal's combat groups were practically worn out. Groups Stahel, Fretter-Pico, Mieth, Hollidt had been badly depleted in the constant leap-frogging operations, which had so far managed to keep the Russians away from Rostov. Now, thinning their lines dangerously, they sideslipped again to the west in order to slow the new Russian juggernaut moving south from the Don.

Meanwhile, Gen. Erhard Milch had arrived at Manstein's Taganrog quarters to supervise Hitler's renewed attempt to supply Paulus. From airfields all over Europe, the energetic Luftwaffe officer had collected more than a hundred extra planes and rushed them into the shuttle service to the *Kessel*. But his last-ditch activities on behalf of Sixth Army depended in good part on a hardworking, well-coordinated staff at Gumrak Airfield.

The only field capable of handling heavy traffic, Gumrak was an ugly scar across the pristine snow. A magnet to retreating troops, it drew long lines of trucks and men to it from the west, then spewed them out on the eastern side toward the Volga and Stalingrad. It had become a charnel house, a depository for the dead and dying, who littered the roads and fields around the runways.

Very few of the Germans in the *Kessel* retained any hope of rescue. Some perked up with the sound of firing to the south and wondered whether Manstein had actually arrived. Others clung to stories of mythical divisions breaking into the *Kessel* from Kalach to the west. Realists like Emil Metzger ignored such rumors. With all ammunition gone and his guns blown up to deny them to the enemy, the lieutenant had taken his men into the line of march toward Gumrak and the Volga. As he waded through the drifts, his thoughts wandered back to Kaethe in Frankfurt. He tried hard to remember every detail of her face. It seemed certain that he would die on this godforsaken plain without ever getting the chance to hold her again.

As the wind tore at him, Metzger began to toy with the thought of breaking out of the *Kessel*—all by himself if necessary.

Like Metzger, Gottlieb Slotta was determined to live. He was already at Gumrak, where he hobbled toward a trainload of wounded, parked at a siding. When a Russian plane dove and released a stick of bombs, bricks and other debris landed on Slotta's head. Shouting, "I'm not going to die like this!" he began running madly toward Stalingrad, five miles away. On both sides of the road, he saw heaps of men who had given up and died. But Slotta had no intention of relinquishing his fragile hold on life that way.

Cpl. Franz Deifel was not sure life was worth fighting for anymore. Until this moment, he had been one of the few Germans inside the *Kessel* who pursued a relatively normal routine. He still hauled ammunition up the back slopes of Mamaev Hill and though his load was limited to only a few shells, he went up the hill almost every day.

By late January, Russian planes had begun to stalk individual trucks and men, and they finally found Deifel as he drove back to the ammunition dump outside the city. A bomb landed twenty feet away; shrapnel sprayed the vehicle and tore into his legs. He fell out of the cab and crawled into a house, where he pulled off his pants and tried to staunch the flow of blood. Another bomb exploded and the walls fell out, so he ran to a nearby trench, hid until dark, then stole back to the truck. By some miracle the engine started on the first try and heavy shellfire followed him down the road until he stopped at a dispensary.

Ordered on to a hospital, Deifel found it to be a dimly lit bunker. At the entrance, he froze in horror at a pyramid of bodies which blocked the door. Nauseated, he broke away and limped back to his own quarters.

A general withdrawal had been ordered, and Deifel hitched a ride on a truck headed back to Stalingrad. Just as the convoy started up, Russian shells exploded on the lead vehicles and blew them apart. Horns blared and drivers raged at the delay while Deifel wandered down the road. Dazed and frustrated, he sank down heavily on the corpse of a comrade and muttered: "Kiss my ass." For the first time in his life, he thought of committing suicide.

Behind the utterly depressed corporal, Gumrak Airport had become bedlam. On January 18, two days after Pitomnik had fallen, it was crammed with thousands of wounded from all around the *Kessel*. Doctors worked eighteen-hour tours of duty treating patients lying on cots, on floors, and outside in the snow. Delirious and pain-wracked soldiers bellowed in torment as medics jabbed needles into arms crawling with gray lice, then stripped the patients for surgery.

Trucks bulging with torn and mutilated men pulled up at the hospitals but when drivers were waved off because of lack of space, they left their cargoes unattended. The temperature fell to twenty degrees below zero and the wounded cried feebly for help. When no one responded, they froze to death within a few yards of the operating table.

At his bunker a mile away, Gen. Friedrich von Paulus filled the airwaves with messages to Manstein: "Airfield at Gumrak usable since the 15th of January, landing ground available for night landings. . . . Request quickest possible intervention. Gravest danger."

The Luftwaffe rejected Paulus's claim about Gumrak. Declaring the field almost totally unfit for use, it insisted that adequate safety measures were needed to insure proper deliveries.

Paulus was furious: "Objections raised by Luftwaffe regarded here as mere excuses. . . . Landing ground has been substantially extended. Fully competent ground organization with all necessary installations. . . . Commander in chief has directly requested the Führer to intervene. . . ."

The reality of the situation, however, was that neither Paulus nor Schmidt understood that there was an almost total operational breakdown at the airport. The so-called "fully competent ground organization," which had performed admirably at Pitomnik, was no longer a cohesive group. Though Col. Lothar Rosenfeld now tried to clear Gumrak for an intensive shuttle service, he was working with men exhausted beyond recall.

When a Luftwaffe officer landed in Gumrak on the morning of January 19, he recognized these symptoms immediately. Major Thiel, who had come to the *Kessel* to reconcile differences between Sixth Army and the Luftwaffe, was appalled at the condition of the runways. The wrecks of thirteen planes littered the landing cross, forcing incoming pilots to touch down within a tight eighty-yard radius. Bomb craters pocked the concrete. Newly fallen snow had not yet been cleared.

Thiel descended into the cramped, brightly lit command bunker where he was quickly surrounded by Generals Schmidt, Paulus, Heitz, and other aides, all of whom began to insult him about the Luftwaffe.

"If your aircraft cannot land, my army is doomed," roared Paulus, who was particularly bitter as he unleashed his fury on the startled Thiel. "Every machine that does so can save the lives of one thousand men. An air drop is no use at all. Many of the canisters are never found because the men are too weak to look for them and we have no fuel to collect them. I cannot even withdraw my lines a few miles because the men would fall out from exhaustion. It is four days since they have had anything to eat. . . . The last horses have been eaten up."

While Thiel stood mute, someone else shouted, "Can you imagine what it is like to see soldiers fall on an old carcass, beat open the head and swallow the brains raw?"

Paulus picked up the conversation again, "What should I, as commander in chief of an army, say when a simple soldier comes up to me and begs, 'Herr General Oberst, can you spare me one piece of bread?' "

"Why on earth did the Luftwaffe ever promise to keep us supplied? Who is the man responsible for declaring that it was possible? Had someone told me it was not possible, I should not have held it against the Luftwaffe. I could have broken out. When I was strong enough to do so. Now it is too late. . . ."

In his frustration and sorrow, Paulus ignored the fact that in November, his Luftwaffe friends Richthofen and Fiebig had warned him that the air force could not supply him. But now it was January, and the commanding general of Sixth Army needed to blame someone, so Major Thiel bore the brunt of his rage.

"The Führer gave me his firm assurance that he and the whole German people felt responsible for this army and now the annals of German arms are besmirched by this fearful tragedy, just because the Luftwaffe has let us down. . . ." Disdainfully waving aside Thiel's attempts to explain the Luftwaffe's terrible difficulties, Paulus continued, "We already speak from a different world than yours, for you are talking to dead men. From now on our only existence will be in the history books. . . ."

That night Major Thiel went back to his plane and found proof for the Luftwaffe's charge that Gumrak was not "efficiently managed." No one had unloaded the supplies from the Heinkel bomber, even though it had been on the ground for nine hours. Thiel left the *Kessel* to report his conviction that Sixth Army was beyond help.

West and north of Gumrak, German detachments paused in their flight to hold back Soviet T-34 tanks that were close enough to shell the airfield's runways. At the Gumrak railroad station, thousands of weary troops asked for information about their units. Almost everyone received the same answer: "Go into Stalingrad. You'll find them there."

Sgt. Ernst Wohlfahrt wandered through this uproar in a mood of suppressed anger. He had just found an abandoned corps headquarters and inside the bunkers he picked through empty champagne and cognac bottles, plus canned meat delicacies which he had never dreamed were available during the encirclement.

Wohlfahrt seethed at the thought that his leaders had been eating well while he starved.

A short time later, he passed a half-burned shed. In disbelief, he counted huge stocks of new uniforms, overcoats, felt boots, and meat rations stacked from floor to ceiling. Wohlfahrt was now almost sick with rage. Besides his own need for warm clothing, he had seen hundreds of men clutching shawls or thin blankets to protect their shivering bodies from the cruel winds. Yet German quartermasters still guarded the supply depots with criminal disregard for the suffering around them. No German soldier was allowed to touch a single item.

Private First Class Josef Metzler had already taken matters into his own hands. For weeks he had begged for warm footwear, and for weeks he had been told none was available. When his toes began to burn fiercely from frostbite, he stole a pair of felt boots from a hospital and ran off. A scrupulous man, who never before had stolen anything, Metzler felt no remorse. He was now desperate, and desperation encouraged rationalization for his misdeeds.

Intent on survival, Metzler stopped at another field station to seek some food and treatment for his feet. Meeting a soldier carrying two mess tins, he asked him for one. When the man refused, Metzler waited patiently until his antagonist's attention was diverted, then stole a tin and walked away. Unrepentant, the righteous Metzler stayed on at the hospital to care for his feet.

One mile west of Gumrak, beneath timbered roofs and tons of snow, the staff of Sixth Army worked in semi-isolation from the procession of death moving past them into Stalingrad. Radio operators in the underground bunkers maintained close communications with Manstein at Taganrog over the single thousand-watt transmitter. Their commentary recorded the now commonplace mention of heroic deeds, and the transfer of key men:

Oberst Dingler flew out yesterday, report arrival.

Have left: Sickenius, Major Seidel, . . . Obertleutnant Langkeit. . . .

Proposal of knight's cross Oberstleutnant Spangenburg. Spangenburg held on own initiative from 10 to 15 January the flank of the Seventy-sixth Inf[antry] Division against the great enemy attack at Baburkin. . . .

Proposal of knight's cross, iron, to Oberleutnant Sascha. . . . Sascha repelled enemy attacks repeatedly on January 16 with only four usable tanks . . . in spite of heavy enemy fire Sascha left his vehicle to make the infantry get back into position without regard to his personal safety. . . . without his positive action an enemy entry into Gumrak would have been unavoidable. Signed Deboi [general]

And the radio operators recorded other indications of behavior: "Oberleutnant Billert missing in action. . . . Later: Oberleutnant Billert left without permission by air. Request court martialling procedures."

Beside the few officers who abdicated their responsibilities, some of the wounded flying out of the *Kessel* did so under false pretenses. They had shot themselves in order to reach safety and surgeons who operated on them failed to detect evidence of their self-inflicted injuries. The reasons were twofold. First, the malingerers had fired through a loaf of bread to eliminate close-range powder burns. Secondly, none of them followed patterns normally associated with such cases. Instead of aiming into a leg or arm, areas less dangerous as well as less painful, these men blasted holes in their stomachs and chests to guarantee a successful escape. Since no doctor dared accuse a man of inflicting so grievous a wound on himself, the offenders flew unpunished from Gumrak to hospital beds and a hero's welcome at home.

Knowing that each transport touching down at Gumrak might be the last, the walking wounded thronging the runways eyed each other suspiciously and jockeyed for elbowroom in anticipation of where the aircraft would roll to a stop. The ensuing rush to hatch doors brought death to many who were trampled by half-crazed men.

Now, with time at a premium, Paulus was stepping up the evacuation of specialists, ordering them out to form new divisions for the Wehrmacht. Armed with passes, this elite filtered through the wounded, who glared at them in open hostility.

Gen. Hans Hube left; so did Maj. Coelestin von Zitzewitz, carrying some of Paulus's medals. Gen. Erwin Jaenecke, commander of the Fourth Corps, departed with sixteen shrapnel holes in his body. Capt. Eberhard Wagemann flew out clutching General Schmidt's last will and testament. From each division came officers and hand-picked enlisted men to form the cadre of a new Sixth Army that would fight again someday, somewhere.

On the morning of January 21, Gerhard Meunch answered the field telephone in the basement of a house near the bread factory, and was told to go immediately to 51st Corps Headquarters.

Puzzled by the summons, the captain reported to Colonel Clausius, General Seydlitz-Kurzbach's chief of staff and heard the incredible words, "Captain Meunch, you will fly out this day."

"This cannot be true. I cannot leave my soldiers in the lurch," he protested, but Clausius stopped him, saying that because he was a specialist in infantry tactics he was needed elsewhere. Then the colonel brusquely said good-bye.

Meunch rushed to the airfield where an officer standing beside a car shook his head vehemently and told him that no more aircraft were going out that day. "Get in," he shouted, "or else you will stay here. I am going to the city."

Exhausted from the tension and hunger of previous days, Meunch sagged into the car and rode on to the tiny auxiliary airstrip at Stalingradski, on the outskirts of Stalingrad itself, where he spent the night in the company of hundreds of soldiers, pacing through the snow.

At 7:00 A.M. on January 22, a lone Heinkel 111 flew over several times, dropped food bombs into the fields, but would not land. The hours passed and the wounded had eyes only for the western horizon, where suddenly three specks appeared—Ju-52s. The "old reliables" grew bigger, circled, and came in for landings.

Moments later, Meunch saw a sight he would never forget: The wounded rose from the snow to rush the doors of the taxiing aircraft. Clawing at each other, they kicked the weak to the bottom of the pile and hoisted themselves into the empty cabins.

Meunch walked slowly up to a pilot and showed his special pass. The pilot shook his head:

"You don't intend to get in there?" he said, pointing to the "animals" at the side of the plane. "You won't make it. Get in with me through the cockpit."

While Meunch clambered into the plane, Russian shrapnel sprayed the crowd. The pilot quickly gunned the motors and tried to lift off. He could not. Looking out the window Meunch saw nearly fifty men lying on the wings, holding on to anything they could with blue-cold hands as the Ju-52 picked up speed and raced down the strip. One by one, the riders fell off and tumbled back in the slipstream from the propellers. Shorn of its added burden, the plane rose swiftly into the bright sky and turned away from the Volga. Meunch tried hard to calm himself. For the first time in more than two months, he could not hear the sound of guns.

Radio message: 22 Jan. 43, 1602 hours
To Army Group Don

. . . For submittal to the Führer and to commander in chief, Army Group Don. . . . The Russians are advancing on a six-kilometer frontage both sides of Voporonovo toward the east, [toward Stalingrad] in part with flying colors. There is no possibility to close the gap . . . All provisions are used up. Over twelve thousand unattended [wounded] men in the pocket. What orders am I to issue to the troops, who have no ammunition left? . . .

Immediate decision is required, since symptoms of disintegration are noted in some places. However, the troops still have faith in their commanders.

Paulus

East Prussia had the answer ready within hours.

Capitulation impossible.
The troops will defend their positions to the last. . . . The Sixth Army has thus made a historic contribution in the most gigantic war effort in German history.

Adolf Hitler

"A historic contribution," Hitler had declared, so Paulus stopped trying to convince his superiors that further resistance was simply mass murder. Blocking out the reality of the men dying around him, he chose instead to be overwhelmed by the natural course of events, and he left Gumrak for a cellar in Stalingrad.

In an anteroom just off Adolf Hitler's conference room, Maj. Coelestin von Zitzewitz waited nervously for an audience. Snatched from the *Kessel* by direct orders from East Prussia, he had flown to the Wolf's Lair to echo Capt. Winrich Behr's graphic description of conditions at Stalingrad.

When the door opened, Zitzewitz strode in and came to attention. Hitler walked forward and covered Zitzewitz's right hand with both of his. Shaking his head, he said: "You've come from a deplorable situation." And he waved his guest to a high stool beside a table.

Zitzewitz tried to adjust his eyes to the dim half-light in the room. A huge map of the Russian front framed one wall. A fireplace dominated another. He noticed Generals Zeitzler and Schmundt sitting back in the shadows.

Hitler opened the discussion. Pointing frequently to maps on the table, he spoke of German tanks striking across the Don and breaking into the *Kessel* with supplies. A battalion of them, he thought, could crush Russian resistance and reach Sixth Army.

Zitzewitz listened in growing disbelief. When his chance came to speak, he rattled off statistics and comments he had jotted down on a piece of paper: casualty rates, ammunition stocks, food supplies, death, disease, frostbite, morale. The figures were catastrophic, irreversible, and damning. While Hitler stared in surprise, Zitzewitz summed up. "My Führer, permit me to state that the troops at Stalingrad can no longer be ordered to fight to their last round because they are no longer physically capable of fighting, and because they no longer have a last round."

Hitler looked right through Zitzewitz. Dismissing the shocked major, the Führer mumbled: "Man recovers very quickly."

The railroad station at Gumrak burned brightly against the snow. Russian artillery fire had blown the structure apart and ignited the corpses that had been stacked against its walls up to the level of the second-storey windows. The frozen bodies became a gruesome bonfire that Sgt. Hubert Wirkner witnessed as he was carried to the edge of the runway and a last opportunity to get away from the *Kessel*.

Completely disabled by his arm and leg wounds which were complicated with frostbite, Wirkner lay unattended on a stretcher for hours while twenty-four transports screeched in, unloaded and took off with hundreds of soldiers. In disgust he watched some of the lesser wounded "play possum" in the snow until the doors of the planes opened, then leap into the aircraft before harassed officials could see them. Too weak and proud to consider doing such a thing himself, Wirkner felt only pity for those who stole seats from their comrades.

One more plane glided in through the foggy mist and settled on the runway. From his prone position, Wirkner stared in disappointment as hundreds of ambulatory patients crowded around it and blocked access to the more seriously wounded.

At one of the doors, Col. Herbert Selle helped check ongoing passengers. An engineering specialist, the colonel had received orders earlier that day to leave and train another unit for another battle. Surprised by the unexpected reprieve, he stifled his momentary guilt feelings and reported to General Paulus for a few last words.

Paulus's appearance shocked Selle. The general was unshaven, bedraggled. His blue eyes, formerly so sparkling, "had become lifeless."

The general had a brief but bitter message for Selle. "Tell them," he said mournfully, "wherever you think it is advisable, that the Sixth Army has been betrayed by the Supreme Command."

Selle had left the pathetic figure of his commander in chief and gone to Gumrak where he waited through the foggy night until the last Ju-52 landed. While the pilot kept the motors running, Selle counted "cases" into the plane. His orderly, who had accompanied him to the field in hopes of a free ride, hovered nearby. The colonel nodded his head and winked him into the rear section. Beside the runway, Hubert Wirkner craned his neck and watched the Ju-52 depart.

Resigned to being left to die, Wirkner began to crawl on hands and knees in the general direction of the gutted railroad station. He passed an officer who stared incredulously at him and then begged Wirkner to go back to the hospital. The sergeant ignored him and pushed on into a snowfield. The wind tore at him, ice formed on his face, and he breathed torturously as his mouth filled with lumps of snow.

He dragged his dead legs for nearly a mile, reached the main road to Stalingrad, and collapsed alongside the stream of traffic. When he tried to climb into the back of a truck, his legs collapsed and he fell down. With a final burst of strength, Wirkner rose once more to clutch a howitzer with his frozen hands. Grunting from the pain, he pulled himself over the gun barrel and dangled precariously, his head hanging down on one side, his feet on the other.

The howitzer crept toward the city. With his face inches from the ground, his eyes bulging and his head pounding from blood draining into it, Wirkner drifted in and out of consciousness. The sounds of speeding cars washed over him and he heard the mournful prayers of soldiers lying on the ice. Screams, machine-gun fire, and curses came at him from all sides. He fainted again and when he woke up, he was surrounded by Germans sitting beside the road. When he called weakly for help, they failed to respond. Wirkner heard the wind and gunfire but nothing from his companions. They were all dead.

The lights of a truck flashed over him and he tensed for a terrible blow, but the driver had seen him move and stopped to pick him up. Wirkner rode the rest of the way into Stalingrad, where, again on all fours, he dragged himself into a dark cellar and "switched off his mind."

At Gumrak, Russian tanks were rolling over the runways and firing point-blank into hospital bunkers. Hundreds of German wounded died where they lay, abandoned by countrymen now stampeding into Stalingrad. Along the main road into the city, a long line of trucks and cars roared through the fog, while in the fields beside the highway, a thin line of troops sat in hip-deep snow as a rear guard protecting the disorderly retreat. Panicked at the thought of being left alone to face Soviet armor, some of them swiveled their guns around and fired into the vehicles. When a driver was hit and his truck stopped, the gunners ran to the road, pulled their victim from the front seat and drove off themselves.

On the morning of January 24, the "Road of Death" as the truckers called it, was a five-mile stretch of snow coated with frozen blood left by the passage of Sixth Army to its final positions. By now more than a hundred thousand Germans had plunged into the black basements of Stalingrad.

Cpl. Heinz Neist rode into the city on a sleigh dragged by friends. Totally exhausted, Neist shivered under a thin blanket while Russian artillery knocked down what buildings were left standing. To Neist it seemed that "everything had been annihilated." The world was dead. He was in a state of despair.

Quartermaster Karl Binder had burrowed into the *Schnellhefter Block*, a series of workers' houses just west of the tractor factory. Still the efficient organizer, Binder was trying to establish a food-sharing program in his sector, but his problems defied solution. Although the Ju-52s and He-111s still were dropping supplies by parachute, most of them drifted inside Russian lines and were lost. The few that landed among the Germans were supposed to be brought immediately to central points for equal distribution, but the soldiers frequently hid them away for their own use. German military police held summary courts-martial for those found stealing and executed the offenders.

A few hundreds yards away from Binder's refuge, in the tangled wreckage of the tractor works, tailor Wilhelm Alter was busy working on a "thing of beauty." With a piece of brown cloth and fur from a coat collar, he was making a Cossack hat for an officer who was looking ahead to the rigors of captivity. Besides having the chance to pass the time doing something creative, Alter was especially pleased about the payment due for his labor. The officer had promised him an extra piece of bread.

In the same sector, veterinarian Herbert Rentsch had assumed command of a machine-gun company. He had also made a heart-rending decision about his horse, Lore. Forced out of a *balka* toward the city, Rentsch went to the black mare, led her into a tunnelled-out bunker and tied her to a post. As Lore stood patiently beside her master, Rentsch patted her neck and gently stroked her emaciated flanks. When she turned her head to nuzzle his hand for food, he choked back a sob and ran away. His one hope was that the Russians would find her quickly and treat her with tenderness.

In central Stalingrad, Sgt. Albert Pflüger, despite his broken arm, set up a machine gun to interdict some side streets, then sat back to think about the future. Fully aware that the Russians had already won the battle, he conjured up the possibility that Hitler and Stalin had reached an agreement on the humane treatment of prisoners of war. Pflüger also "dreamed" that the Americans were going to intervene with Stalin to prevent the mass killings of captives.

These delusions helped immensely as he prepared himself for the ordeal he knew was coming.

"Hold out for the next few days? For what?" asked an increasing number of German officers and men as they scurried for shelter in the broken-down houses of Stalingrad. They had finally begun to question the purpose of fighting for a thousand cellars at the edge of Asia.

With the fall of Pitomnik and Gumrak, all but a tiny hard core of Nazis faced the ghastly truth. Stalingrad would be their tomb. Abandoned to a miserable fate, they vented their rage in their letters, and one of the last planes leaving the *Kessel* carried seven sacks of mail scribbled on toilet paper, maps, anything that passed for stationery.

At Taganrog, German military censors analyzed the letters, sorted them into appropriate categories and forwarded a report on to Berlin and the Propaganda Ministry, where Dr. Joseph Goebbels read the findings.

1. In favor of the way the war was being
   conducted   2.1 percent
2. Dubious   4.4 percent
3. Skeptical, deprecatory   57.1 percent
4. Actively against   3.4 percent
5. No opinion, indifferent   33.0 percent

Nearly two out of every three writers now complained bitterly against Hitler and the High Command. But their protest was tardy and irrelevant. Fearful of the effect of these letters on the German population, Goebbels ordered the letters destroyed.*

Meanwhile, Erich von Manstein read a wireless from Stalingrad that convinced him the Sixth Army was finished.

---

* A few were saved and published after the war.

Attacks in undiminished violence . . . Frightful conditions in the city area proper where about 20,000 unattended wounded are seeking shelter among the ruins. With them are about the same number of starved and frostbitten men, and stragglers, mostly without weapons. . . . Heavy artillery pounding the whole city. . . . Tractor works may possibly hold out a little longer. . . .

Positive that Paulus had done all he could ever do, Manstein called Hitler and recommended that Sixth Army be allowed to surrender. Hitler would not consider the idea. Manstein argued that "the Army's sufferings would bear no relation to any advantage derived from continuing to tie down the enemy's forces . . .", but the Führer repeated his claim that each hour that Paulus continued to fight helped the entire front. Then he charged that capitulation was futile. The men at Stalingrad would have no chance to survive since "the Russians never keep any agreements. . . ."

That thought was uppermost in the minds of more than one hundred thousand Germans penned up like cattle at Stalingrad to await their executioner. Unable to control their destinies, they succumbed to the malignancy of fear, which centered around one question: "Will the Russians kill us outright or send us into slavery at some terrible Siberian prison camp?"

Few expected decent treatment. Too many had seen the butchered remains of German prisoners left on the battlefield by retreating Soviet troops. They also knew what their own countrymen had done to Russian soldiers and civilians during the occupation of the Soviet Union.

The retribution the Germans feared was real. It was taking its toll among soldiers of the puppet armies already in captivity. At the monastery town of Susdal, northeast of Moscow, Felice Bracci and Cristoforo Capone shivered in windowless barracks and waited for their captors to increase the food ration to a bare subsistence level. They waited in vain. At Susdal, men died at the rate of two hundred a day from starvation.

At Oranki Prison, Rumanian troops staggered into camps from a hundred-mile forced march and pressed their hands on lighted stoves to take away the pain of frostbite. When they pulled back their fingers, the flesh remained on the stoves and the stench made them retch. Amidst screams of torment, many fell dead. The change of temperature from the steppe to warm rooms had brought on massive heart attacks. More than a hundred bodies were hauled out of the barracks feet first. The thump, thump, thump of their heads striking the stairs kept other soldiers awake for hours.

In a camp at Tambov, north of the Don, Italian soldiers crowded around a gate as Russian troops dumped cabbages from a truck onto the snow. Then thirty thousand prisoners rioted and fought each other for the food. Guards shot those they caught in the act of murder.

Chapter Twenty-nine

From January 24 on, the fighting in Stalingrad was spasmodic. Trapped in their frozen, dark cellars, German troops listened fearfully for the footfalls of Russian soldiers. Even the Russians took their time now, moving carefully in squads, in platoons, over the mounds of snow-covered wreckage. In countless minor engagements in the side streets of the city, the command *"Raus! Raus!"* echoed when the shooting stopped, and Germans climbed out of their holes with hands held high. The Russians kicked a few, punched others, but led most prisoners away without further incident.

Germans who witnessed these surrenders took heart. A network of runners carried the message that the enemy did not kill their captives and the news soothed many who were close to hysteria. For the moment they forgot their fear of capture while they fought another deadly struggle, the endless war with lice.

The gray parasites now dominated everyone's life. Multiplying rapidly in the incredible filth, they swarmed from head to ankles in a voracious quest for food. Ravenous, relentless, they drove their hosts to the verge of insanity. Wherever they feasted, they left giant red welts. Worse, they infected their victims with disease.

In the wall of a *balka*, just south of the Tsaritsa Gorge, more than two thousand German wounded had been jammed into a Russian air raid shelter, known as the Timoshenko Bunker. Tunneled into the side of the ravine like a giant anthill, the bunker's tiered galleries were nearly two and a half miles long. The "hospital" once had contained electric lights, ventilation, even proper drainage facilities, but those conveniences had long since been destroyed. Now it was a fetid morgue, where only the patients' body heat brought any warmth to the damp chambers. The air was foul, heavy with sickness and rot.

Doctors who ministered to the rows of wounded noticed an alarming increase of fevers ranging from 102 to 104 degrees. Some men died raving. Chills and a tendency to lung congestion were added symptoms which pointed inexorably to a damning medical diagnosis. Unchecked, it could now complete the extermination of the Sixth Army, which had never been adequately vaccinated against typhus.

In his cellar home to the north of Railroad Station Number One, Sgt. Hubert Wirkner lay among fifty other wounded soldiers and groaned from the fever wracking his frail body. His head ached; his eyes were bloodshot. Blood dripped through the bandages on his legs and arms. He had soiled himself repeatedly and hated the smell that clung to him.

Along the walls of the cellar, a collection of manikins stared unwaveringly at the wounded Germans. Marked in ink with the outlines of female reproductive organs, they had obviously been used in a maternity training program for nurses and interns. How ironic, Wirkner thought, that he and his comrades were in a former Soviet hospital but had no doctors to care for them.

Near the Tsaritsa Gorge, the grim black walls of the NKVD prison enclosed what was left of the German Fourteenth Corps, plus the 3rd and 29th Motorized Divisions. Most of the jail itself was gutted, but on the first floor enlisted men mounted guard at the windows. From there they monitored the huge yard, in which scores of wounded soldiers lay unattended in the snow. Though these men begged for help, no one paid any attention to their pleas.

In the bowels of the prison, a group of German generals lived with a retinue of aides. One of them, Edler von Daniels had not been sober for days. Gloriously drunk, he weaved back and forth among troops lying on the damp floors. "Boys," he shouted, "who of you is against bringing this to an end?" When nobody objected to surrender, von Daniels showered them with packs of cigarettes.

The general was one of several plotting mutiny. Generals Schlömer, Pfeiffer, Korfes, and Seydlitz had been unable to convince Paulus that further resistance was futile. Increasingly annoyed at his constant refrain: "Orders are orders," they centered their wrath on Arthur Schmidt, the éminence grise behind the throne. Convinced that Schmidt was the culprit who insisted on insane continuation of the fighting, they were planning to end the chief of staff's domination and force Paulus to surrender.

Arthur Schmidt was indeed assuming active leadership of Sixth Army. Paulus seemed dazed by the calamity that had overtaken him. "Sorrow and grief lined his face. His complexion was the color of ashes. His posture, so upright otherwise, was now slightly stooped. . . ." The tic on the right side of his face now extended from jaw to eyebrow.

Schmidt, on the other hand, was a bulwark of strength, bullying defeatist officers with blunt commands, abusing protesters by phone, threatening malcontents with the firing squad. Where Paulus wilted under the enormity of the disaster, Schmidt shone in adversity.

In the early morning of January 24, General von Hartmann, commander of the 71st Division, had put down the book he was reading and said to General Pfeiffer: "As seen from Sirius, Goethe's works will be mere dust in a thousand years' time, and the Sixth Army an illegible name, incomprehensible to all." With his mind settled as to his own course of action, Hartmann led a small band of men out to a railway embankment. Standing upright in full view of Russians across the snowfields, he shouted: "Commence firing!" and shot a clip of bullets from his carbine.

Col. Günter von Below hurried from Paulus's cellar with the order to "stop this nonsense." But Hartmann ignored him and continued to fire at the enemy. Within moments, a Russian bullet tore into his brain.

A short time later, another German general settled his own affairs. Hearing that his son, a lieutenant, had been killed while trying to lead some men out of the city toward far-off German lines, General Stempel took out a pistol and shot himself in the head.*

Only hours after Generals Hartmann and Stempel died, the 297th Division Commander, General Drebber, stood on a street near the grain elevator and saluted a Russian colonel, who politely asked: "Where are your regiments?" Drebber shrugged and replied: "Do I have to tell you where my regiments are?" Accompanied by several aides, he marched off to Soviet lines.

Just before 9:00 A.M. that morning, Friedrich von Paulus was handed a letter sent through the lines by Drebber. As he started to open it, a bomb exploded outside the basement window and showered both him and his adjutant, Col. Wilhelm Adam, with shards of glass and rock. Shaken and bleeding, the two men submitted to medical attention before Paulus sat down again to read the note.

In a moment, the general uttered a surprised cry: "It is not believable! Drebber states that he and his men have been well received by the Red Army soldiers. They were treated correctly. We all were victims of Goebbel's lying propaganda. Drebber

---

* Though badly wounded in the escape attempt, his son survived.

urges me to give up '. . . useless resistance and . . . capitulate with the entire Army.' " Paulus put the letter down and stared at Adam in wonder.

At that moment Arthur Schmidt entered and when Paulus told him what Drebber had written, Schmidt's face darkened.

"Never has von Drebber written this letter voluntarily," he stated. "He was under compulsion. . . ."

The chief of staff was furious at the defection of a senior officer. But Paulus was merely confused. Had he been wrong about the Russians? Was it possible they would treat every German fairly?

Just north of Mamaev Hill, behind the Red October workers' settlement, tanks from General Batov's Sixty-fifth Army smashed through scattered German resistance to meet troops of General Rodimtsev's 13th Guards. The linkup on January 26 marked the first time that Vassili Chuikov's divisions inside Stalingrad had established physical contact with another Russian army since September 10, 138 days earlier.

Rodimtsev, who had thrown his cannon-fodder division into Stalingrad on September 14 to hold the Germans between Mamaev and the Tsaritsa Gorge, spied tanker captain Usenko and cried: "Tell your commander that this is a happy day for us. . . ." More than eight thousand guardsmen under his command had died in the last four months. Embracing, the general and captain wept together.

A few hours later, Sixth Army Headquarters moved abruptly to the hulking Univermag Department Store on Red Square. The buildings around the square were just shells—windowless, pocked with gaping holes. The building housing *Pravda* was gutted; so were those of the City Soviet and the post office. The theater had fallen in.

Paulus went past these ruins, down a broad ramp in the Univermag courtyard, and into the basement warehouse. While aides set up a radio room for last transmissions to Manstein, the general retired to a curtained cubicle containing a cot and chair, and sagged down to rest. A barred window cast a pale light on his haggard, bearded face.

Later in the day, Arthur Schmidt stormed into Paulus's room to announce: "Sir, the Fourteenth Armored Corps is considering capitulation. Muller [the Fourteenth Corps chief of staff] said that the troops had reached the end of their strength and that they had no ammunition left. I told him that we are aware of the situation, but that the order to continue combat was still valid and a capitulation was out of the question. Nevertheless, sir, I would suggest that you visit those generals and talk to them."

At the NKVD prison, "those generals" were holding a meeting. "Paulus will refuse to sign a capitulation, we all know that," stated General Schlömer, commander of the Fourteenth Corps. "But we cannot let this mass murder continue. I ask for your approval to get hold of Paulus, whereafter I shall bring the negotiations to an end acting as the new commander in chief."

At this remark, the mercurial General Seydlitz-Kurzbach jumped up and shouted: "By God, gentlemen, this is treason!" As his astounded colleagues stared in amazement, he reached for his hat and put his hand on the doorknob to leave.

Suddenly the door opened from the other side and Paulus walked in to face his adversaries. His lips tightly pressed together, and the tic on his cheek noticeably aggravated, he glanced coldly at the mutineers and in that brief instant assumed complete command of the men who had followed him to the Volga and disaster.

"Schlömer, you will go back to your duties. Seydlitz," he gestured at the Fifty-first Corps commander, "you will resume your responsibilities. And the others will do the same."

A babble of protest broke out, centering on Arthur Schmidt's insistence on fighting to the last bullet. Refusing to be drawn into an argument, Paulus turned and walked out of the building. Behind him, the rebellious generals gathered their belongings and left the room. No one mentioned mutiny again.

On January 28, the Russians divided the city into three sectors: the Eleventh Corps was isolated around the tractor plant; the Eighth and Fifty-first corps around an engineering school west of Mamaev Hill; the remainders of the Fourteenth and Fourth corps were in the downtown area around the Univermag.

At the *Schnellhefter* Block across from the tractor plant, Dr. Ottmar Kohler had run out of morphine. Wallowing in filth and blood, he operated under flickering lights and in incredible cold. Outside the building, lines of soldiers crowded the entrance, looking for a place to sleep. An officer went to the door and begged them to go away because there was no room, but they said they would wait until morning.

At sunrise, the visitors were still there, huddled together against the below-zero temperature. During the night they had all died from exposure.

At the central military garrison post, now a hospital a mile north of the Univermag, three thousand wounded lay under a merciless wind that whipped through the building's shattered walls. Without enough medicine to care for everyone, doctors placed gravely ill soldiers at the edge of the crowd so they would die first from the cold.

Ringing the huge building on four sides was a stack of bodies six feet high. When soldiers stopped at the garrison to ask for food, they earned it by arranging corpses in neat piles, like railroad ties. After stacking their quota of bodies, cooks splashed soup into their outstretched mess tins and they shuffled away from the cordwood cemetery.

Batteries of Russian mortars zeroed in on the Central garrison and set it afire. While medics screamed for the wounded to get up and run, flames fanned by the gale winds raced through the cavernous hallways. In the courtyard, onlookers saw the building billow into a fire that flashed out of every opening on the upper floors. When fiery bodies hurtled out of the inferno, they sizzled in the snow for minutes.

The hospital walls turned cherry red in color and became almost transparent. Finally they bulged outward and whole sections crumpled into the streets. Through the breaks, horrified witnesses saw patients tearing at burning bandages in frantic dervish dances.

After the ceilings crashed down and the violent whoosh of flames subsided, rescuers pushed in to save as many as they could. They found every stairway clogged by a chain of corpses.

With the last hours at hand, wounded German soldiers in countless cellars asked for pistols, placed them to their temples and fired. The lice that had lived on them for weeks quickly left the cooling bodies and moved like gray blankets to other beds.

At the bottom of a ravine west of Mamaev Hill, General Seydlitz-Kurzbach debated suicide with his companions. Once again, the chameleon-like general had changed his attitude toward Paulus and Hitler. Only a short time before he had told his comrades they were plotting treason; he now spent hours cursing the Nazis and Hitler's insanity, and openly advocated a revolt of the masses against the Third Reich.

His companions tended to agree with him. White-haired General Pfeiffer goaded Seydlitz-Kurzbach on, shouting that he owed no subservience to "a Bohemian corporal skunk." General Otto Korfes vacillated between calling for a *Gotterdammerung* and cursing the leaders of the Nazi regime. Colonel Crome withdrew into a careful reading of the Bible; General Heitz ignored the seditious talk around him. Totally loyal to Paulus, he mounted guns at the entrance to the bunker and said, "I will shoot the first man who deserts."

While Seydlitz-Kurbach openly discussed taking his own life, his orderly, an elderly man, blew himself up with a hand grenade.

At the Univermag, Arthur Schmidt had intercepted a colonel named Steidle who wanted to plead with Paulus to capitulate. Raging at the man, Schmidt threatened him with the firing squad.

In public Schmidt showed a tenacious will to resist to the final bullet but in secret, he was having conversations with two officers, one a Colonel Beaulieu, who had spent some years in Russia in the twenties and the other, Capt. Boris von Neidhardt, a Balt and former czarist officer. Both men spoke fluent Russian and were knowledgeable about life in the Soviet Union. Schmidt spent hours with each man, asking probing questions about their experiences.

Col. Wilhelm Adam, Paulus's adjutant, intercepted Beaulieu after one of these talks and asked what was going on behind Schmidt's closed door. Beaulieu was candid, "Schmidt asked me to tell him about the Red Army. He was particularly interested to learn what one had to expect of their soldiers and officers. I didn't know that your chief of staff could be so friendly."

The suspicious Adam checked with Neidhardt and found that Schmidt had quizzed him on the same topics.

On the evening of January 29, Adam received further proof that Schmidt had no intention of fighting to the last breath. Schmidt's orderly suddenly pulled Adam into the chief of staff's room, and pointing to a suitcase in the corner, whispered, "To all his subordinates he says 'you must hold out, there will be no capitulation,' but he himself gets ready for captivity."

Seething with hatred, Adam went back to his cot and brooded.

From his basement window just off Red Square, Sgt. Albert Pflüger looked past his machine gun at a water fountain on the intersection. For days it had been the focal point of firefights, and

Pflüger had killed a number of Russians trying to reach it. There was also a line of dead Germans around it, cut down as they crawled across the ice with empty canteens.

With his war now reduced to fighting for a sip of water, Pflüger was ready to surrender. But first he wanted to hear a speech being given by Adolf Hitler on January 30, celebrating the tenth anniversary of the Third Reich. At noon, he stood with others beside the radio and waited for the Führer's voice to flood into the cellar. It did not. The announcer said that Hermann Goering would speak instead, and the Reichsmarshal was his bombastic self:

> . . . What herculean labors our Führer has performed . . . out of this pulp, this human pulp . . . to forge a nation as hard as steel. The enemy is tough, but the German soldier has grown tougher. . . . We have taken away the Russians' coal and iron, and without that they can no longer make armaments on a large scale. . . . Rising above all these gigantic battles like a mighty monument is Stalingrad. . . . One day this will be recognized as the greatest battle in our history, a battle of heroes. . . . We have a mighty epic of an incomparable struggle, the struggle of the Nibelungs. They, too, stood to the last. . . .

In Pflüger's cellar, men groaned and someone cursed the "fat man" in Berlin.

Goering continued ". . . My soldiers, thousands of years have passed, and thousands of years ago in a tiny pass in Greece stood a tremendously brave and bold man with three hundred soldiers, Leonidas with his three hundred Spartans. . . . Then the last man fell . . . and now only the inscription stands: 'Wanderer, if you should come to Sparta, go tell the Spartans you found us lying here as the law bade us.' . . . Someday men will read: 'If you come to Germany, go tell the Germans you saw us lying in Stalingrad, as the law bade us. . . .' "

It was suddenly clear to Pflüger and thousands of Germans standing by shortwave radios that Hitler already considered them dead.

After Goering's speech ended, the German national anthem was played, and Pflüger joined hands with his comrades to sing: *"Deutschland, Deutschland, über alles."* He sobbed unashamedly at the beautiful words. When the anthem was followed by *"Horst Wessel,"* the Nazi party song, someone in the room lashed out with his gun butt and broke the radio to pieces.

To the last, however, Paulus publicly worshipped at the feet of the Führer:

> January 30th:
> On the tenth anniversary of your assumption of power, the Sixth Army hails its "Führer." The swastika flag is still flying above Stalingrad. May our battle be an example to the present and coming generations, that they must never capitulate even in a hopeless situation, for then Germany will come out victorious.
>
> > Hail my Führer
> > Paulus, Generaloberst

At a railroad embankment near the engineering school, Gen. Carl Rodenburg sighted his rifle and carefully squeezed off a shot. Then he turned and asked his aide to find another target. The monocled general had come to the "range" as he called it, to have a last crack at the enemy. He fired for over an hour while the aide, newly promoted to captain, chose his targets. As the general turned once more to speak to the young officer, a Russian bullet tore into the man's head, killing him instantly. The sorrowful Rodenburg left the body in the snow and went back to his bunker to await the end. It was some consolation to him that at least the captain's family in Germany would get a bigger pension because of his new rank.

Inside the NKVD prison, several hundred German officers and men waited for the confrontation with Russian soldiers. Some drank heavily, and in an upstairs room, one officer enjoyed pan-cakes cooked for him by a pleasant Russian woman, who had magically appeared in anticipation of victory.

Other soldiers prepared by dressing in clothing taken from corpses: extra underwear, two shirts, double socks, sweaters—anything they could find to ward off the cold weather they knew awaited them on the march to internment.

Shots rang out in one of the cells and several soldiers rushed to the open door to find a sergeant standing over three officers sprawled in death. Behind the sergeant, a blond lieutenant sat at a table and stared intently at a girl's picture, framed by the light of two candles. The lieutenant seemed completely oblivious to the scene around him.

Hearing the commotion at the door, the sergeant whirled on the spectators and shouted; "Goddamn you, go away or you'll get the next one!"

As they retreated from the doorway, the sounds of two more shots rocketed off the walls and when they looked in again, the blond lieutenant had fallen face down on the floor. His head was a mass of blood.

The sergeant was there, too, with a self-inflicted bullet wound in the mouth. He had carried out the suicide pact exactly as ordered.

At the southeastern side of Red Square, Col. Gunter Ludwig held the cellar of an office building beside the Gorki Theater. His post was also the last defense line the Germans manned in front of the Univermag. On the evening of the thirtieth, a military po-liceman arrived and told the colonel that General Schmidt wanted to see him. Ludwig was suddenly fearful, for during the day he had been talking to Russian officers about surrender. Knowing Schmidt's threats of a firing squad for those who quit the battle, he walked to the department store feeling like a condemned man.

Schmidt greeted him sternly and asked about his position on the lower part of the square. After Ludwig told him his men were

still deployed there, Schmidt offered him a seat and said, "Listen,
I just heard that you negotiated with the Russians today."

Ludwig admitted he had, and justified his actions by describing the woeful condition of his troops. As he spoke, Ludwig
watched Schmidt carefully, trying to gauge his reaction. The general paced the room, then whirled, "You mean you just went to
the Russians and negotiated capitulation, and no one even thinks
of coming to us, to army headquarters?"

The stunned colonel had trouble getting the point: Schmidt,
the martinet, also wanted to surrender! Then he recovered enough
to say: "If that is all you want, sir, I believe I can promise you
that a parliamentarian will report here in front of the basement
tomorrow morning at about 0900 hours."

Schmidt was suddenly gentle, "All right, Ludwig, you see to
that—good night now."

Minutes later, the 71st Division commander, General Roske,
went to Paulus and said, "The division is no longer capable of
rendering resistance. Russian tanks are approaching the department store building. The end has come."

Paulus smiled at his aide, "Thank you for everything, Roske.
Convey my gratitude also to your officers and men. Schmidt has
already asked Ludwig to take up negotiations with the Red Army."

Paulus went back to his cot where Colonel Adam sat across
from him. A small candle flickered between them; neither spoke
for a while. Finally Adam said, "Sir, you must go to sleep now.
Otherwise you will not be able to stand up to tomorrow's trials.
It will cost us the rest of our nervous strength."

Shortly after midnight, Paulus stretched out to nap, and
Adam went to Roske and asked if there were any new developments. Roske gave him a cigarette, lit one for himself, and said:
"A Red tank is standing quite close in a side street, its guns aimed
at us. I immediately reported to Schmidt on the matter. He said
the tank must be prevented from firing at all costs. . . . The interpreter should go to the tank commander with a white flag and
offer negotiations. . . ."

Adam went back to his own cot from where he stared across

the room at his sleeping commander. His relationship with Paulus had become almost worshipful and Adam could no longer see the flaws in Paulus's character: his failure to comprehend the destructive alliance that existed between Hitler's ambitions and the Wehrmacht's apolitical generals, or Paulus's unwillingness to shoulder the burden of independent command. What a handsome man, Adam thought as he pondered the events that had overwhelmed such a brilliant military career. Decent and honorable, Paulus had subordinated himself completely to Hitler's demands and in so doing, had lost control of his destiny.

While the commander in chief of the Sixth Army rested, the Führer employed one last device to salvage something from the disaster. He ordered a shower of promotions on Sixth Army's senior officers, most notably one that made Paulus a field marshal. Knowing that no German field marshal had ever surrendered, Hitler hoped that Paulus would take the hint and commit suicide.

Paulus did not. Before dawn, his interpreter, Boris von Neidhardt, went out through the darkened square to the Russian tank, where a young Soviet lieutenant, Fyodor Yelchenko, stood in the turret. When Neidhardt waved to him, Yelchenko jumped down and Neidhardt said, "Our big chief wants to talk to your big chief."

Yelchenko shook his head and answered: "Look here, our big chief has other things to do. He isn't available. You'll just have to deal with me." Suddenly apprehensive because of nearby shelling and the presence of the enemy, Yelchenko called for reinforcements and fourteen Russian soldiers appeared with their guns ready.

Neidhardt was disgusted. "No, no, our chief asks that only one or two of you come in."

"Nuts to that," Yelchenko said. "I am not going by myself." The lieutenant with the turned-up nose and boyish smile had no intention of going alone into the enemy camp. After agreeing on three Russian representatives, the group went into the cellar of the Univermag where hundreds of Germans had gathered. Yelchenko had a difficult time deciding who was in command. Though Roske spoke to him and then Arthur Schmidt, he did not see Paulus.

After Roske explained that he and Schmidt were empowered to speak for the commander and negotiate a surrender, Schmidt asked as a special favor that the Russians treat Paulus as a private person and escort him away in an automobile to protect him from vengeful Red Army soldiers. Laughing gaily, Yelchenko agreed. "Okay," he said, and then they took him down the corridor to a green-curtained cubicle. Yelchenko stepped in and confronted Friedrich von Paulus, unshaved, but immaculate in his full-dress uniform.

Yelchenko wasted no time on formalities. "Well, that finishes it," he offered in greeting. The forlorn field marshal looked into his eyes and nodded miserably.

A short time later, after conversations with more Soviet officers, Paulus and Schmidt walked out of the fetid depths of the Univermag and stepped into a Russian staff car. It took them south over the Tsaritsa Gorge, past the grain elevator, through the ruins of Dar Gova, and on to the suburb of Beketovka where, in a wooden farmhouse, they were ushered into the presence of Gen. Mikhail Shumilov, commander of the Soviet Sixty-fourth Army. Surrounded by cameramen, Shumilov greeted his guests correctly and asked for identification. When Paulus produced his paybook, the Russian pretended to read German and grunted his acceptance.

The Russians offered the Germans food from a tremendous buffet but Paulus balked, insisting that he first receive a guarantee that his men be given proper rations and medical care. Reassured on that point by Shumilov, Paulus and Schmidt finally picked lightly at the feast spread before them.

The primary antagonists of the battle for Stalingrad never got to meet. Deprived by jealous commanders of the chance to capture Paulus himself, Vassili Chuikov had to content himself with lesser fry.* Dressed in a fur jacket, Chuikov sat behind a big desk in his Volga bunker, and glared at the first German to come through the door.

"Are you Seydlitz?" he asked. The officer was Lt. Philip Humbert, Seydlitz's aide. To cover his error, the flustered Russian interpreter introduced Humbert as a lieutenant colonel, and then brought the rest of the Germans into Chuikov's presence.

Chuikov was suddenly expansive. "Be glad, general," he said to Seydlitz, "that you are with us. Stalin will have his parade in Berlin on the first of May. We shall then make peace, and we shall work together with you."

His questions then came fast. "Why do you look so bad? Why did they not fly you out?" General Krylov broke in to say that he had been flown out of Sevastopol when that city was doomed.

At this point, General Korfes became a talkative spokesman for the German officer corps. "It is the tragic point of world history that the two greatest men of our times, Hitler and Stalin . . . have been unable to find common grounds so as to beat the mutual enemy, the capitalist world."

Even Chuikov seemed startled by this declaration. Seydlitz grabbed Korfes's arm and cried: "Why don't you stop talking?"

Korfes could not be stilled. "After all, I feel entitled to say this because it is the truth."

Seydlitz-Kurzbach and General Pfeiffer lapsed into a fretful silence, marred by each man's occasional weeping. Chuikov tried to make his prisoners more comfortable by ordering food and tea, which they gratefully accepted. After more polite conversation, the Germans were escorted to the Volga shore and a battered Ford which took them across the ice to captivity. Behind them, their German troops faced a mixed reception from the Russian captors.

On the summit of Mamaev Hill, Lt. Pyotr Deriabin led a company

---

* The honor of capturing Paulus caused bitter rivalry among Red Army officers. In postwar reminiscences, several lesser generals and colonels claimed that they had received Paulus's surrender in the Univermag cellar. In almost all these accounts, Lt. Fyodor Yelchenko's role was dismissed.

of soldiers into German trenches. Intent on looting, the Soviet troops shot at random into men who raised their hands in surrender, then stripped the bodies of watches and other valuables.

At the edge of Red Square, Sgt. Albert Pflüger packed a few pieces of bread and sausage while the Russians tiptoed down the cellar stairs. In the corner of the room, three *Hiwis* dressed in German uniforms crouched nervously. As the Russians began to seize rings and watches, the terrified *Hiwis* bolted from the basement into the street. The Russians chased them for a block and shot them dead.

At the NKVD prison, the surrender was orderly. From the catacomb of cells, the Germans poured into the courtyard, ringed with piles of corpses. In the middle of the assembly area, a German cook, incongruously attired in a spotless white apron, stood by a stove. As Russian guards circulated among the prisoners and shared cigarettes with them, the cook continued to ladle out mugs of hot coffee both for his men and their new masters.

Further north, Cpl. Heinz Neist heard the Russians pounding down into his cellar. One of them confronted him and pointed at the wedding ring on his hand. When Neist used sign language to explain that it was difficult to pull off, the Russian whipped out a knife and made a motion to slice the finger away.

At that moment, the corporal heard a voice shouting, "All nice young Germans, goddamn Hitler," and Neist beckoned the speaker over to help him with the irate looter. But the officer just shook his head and said: "Give the ring, give everything you have, save your life." Struggling frantically with the wedding band, Neist finally loosened it and handed the treasure to the happy Russian who then left him alone.

That same day, January 31, hundreds of wounded German troops were killed where they lay.

In his cellar north of Red Square, the desperately ill Hubert Wirkner heard a noise and turned to see a Russian soldier pouring gasoline in through the window. Summoning all his strength, he lunged from his bed and crawled on his deadened arms and legs toward the stairs.

Behind him the Russian lit a match and tossed it onto the fuel. The cellar exploded in a violent orange cloud and turned fifty men into human torches. As some of the flaming bodies clutched frantically at the window bars the Russians pounded their hands with rifle butts.

At the bottom of the stairs, Wirkner dumped a pail of water over himself and groped upward toward fresh air. Clouds of smoke choked him and the awful screams of the burning patients followed him as he fell out the door into the snow. On all fours, he crouched like a dog while a Soviet officer came up to him, cocked his pistol and shoved it in Wirkner's ear. While he waited to die, another voice broke in, "Comrade Stalin wouldn't like that." Wirkner's executioner pulled the pistol away and stalked off. Safe for the moment, Wirkner dragged himself across the street to find another sanctuary.

On February 1, at the Wolf's Lair in East Prussia, Adolf Hitler had not taken the news of surrender calmly.

Sitting before the huge map of Russia in the main conference room, he spoke with Zeitzler, Keitel, and others about the debacle: "They have surrendered there formally and absolutely. Otherwise they would have closed ranks, formed a hedgehog and shot themselves with their last bullet. . . ."

Zeitzler agreed: "I can't understand it either. I'm still of the opinion that it might not be true; perhaps he [Paulus] is lying there badly wounded."

"No, it is true," Hitler said. "They'll be brought to Moscow, to the GPU right away, and they'll blurt out orders for the northern pocket to surrender, too. That Schmidt will sign anything. A man who doesn't have the courage, in such a time, to take the road that every man has to take sometime, doesn't have the strength to withstand that sort of thing . . . He will suffer torture in his soul. In Germany there has been too much emphasis on training the intellect and not enough on strength of character. . . ."

The conversation droned on.

Zeitzler said, "One can't understand this type of man."

Hitler was disgusted: "Don't say that. I saw a letter. . . . It was addressed to Below [Nikolaus von Below, Winrich Behr's close friend]. I can show it to you. An officer in Stalingrad wrote, 'I have come to the following conclusions about these people— Paulus, question mark; Seydlitz, should be shot; Schmidt, should be shot.' "

"I have also heard bad reports about Seydlitz," Zeitzler offered.

"One could say that it would have been better to leave Hube in there and bring out the others," Hitler added. "But since the value of men is not immaterial, and since we need men in the entire war, I am definitely of the opinion that it was right to bring Hube out. In peacetime, in Germany, about eighteen or twenty thousand people a year chose to commit suicide, even without being in such a position. Here is a man [Paulus], who sees fifty or sixty thousand of his soldiers die defending themselves bravely to the end. How can he surrender himself to the Bolshevists? . . . That is something one can't understand at all."

"But I had my doubts before," Hitler continued. "That was at the moment when I received the report that he was asking me what he should do [about the Russian ultimatum to surrender]. How could he ever ask about such a thing? . . ."

"There is no excuse," declared Zeitzler. "When his nerves threaten to break down, then he must kill himself."

Hitler nodded, "When the nerves break down, there is nothing left but to admit that one can't handle the situation and to shoot oneself. . . ." Hitler stared at Zeitzler, who replied: "I still think they may have done that and that the Russians are only claiming to have captured them all."

"No . . ." said the Führer vehemently. "In this war, no more field marshals will be made. . . . I won't go on counting my chickens before they are hatched. . . ."

Zeitzler shrugged: "We were so completely sure how it would end, that granting him a final satisfaction. . . ."

"We had to assume that it would end heroically."

Zeitzler agreed, "How could one imagine anything else? . . ."

Hitler sounded depressed: "This hurts me so much because the heroism of so many soldiers is nullified by one single characterless weakling. . . ."

In the northern part of Stalingrad, Eleventh Corps commander, General Strecker, held out for another forty-eight hours in a futile gesture of defiance.

On the morning of February 2, all the Russian artillery concentrated on this area, and for two hours, shells rained down on the pitiful survivors of the Sixth Army. Then the barrage was over and thousands of Russian troops rushed the cellars while German machine-gunners fired their last belts of ammunition. Enraged at the fanatic resistance, the Russians pulled prisoners out of foxholes and beat them savagely. With clubs and fists they pummeled the die-hards, cursing the "Nazi swine" who continued the bloodshed long after Paulus had quit the field and stopped the killing.

Suddenly white flags popped out of windows up and down the side streets across from the factories. The stronghold began to collapse.

While Hans Oettl paused to urinate outside his building, a

Russian sergeant poked a gun in his back and demanded in broken German that he call everyone out of the cellar to surrender. Oettl refused and stared into the silver-toothed grin of his captor, who made a motion with his weapon as if to kill him. When Oettl still refused, the sergeant shouted *"Raus!"* into the stairwell and Oettl's companions streamed into the brilliant sunlight with their hands over their heads.

Across the main road from Oettl's basement, the Russians poured into the tractor factory assembly rooms where hundreds of wounded lay on shelves against the walls. Other Germans dangled grotesquely from belts hooked onto stanchions. Unwilling to endure captivity, they had taken their own lives during the hours before dawn. Just before the Eleventh Corps command post was overrun, General Strecker issued a last message to the Fatherland: "Eleventh Corps and its divisions have fought to the last man against vastly superior forces. Long live Germany!"

At 12:35 P.M. that afternoon, Army Group Don at Taganrog logged the final words from Sixth Army at Stalingrad when a weather team filed its daily report: "Cloud base fifteen thousand feet, visibility seven miles, clear sky, occasional scattered nimbus clouds, temperature minus thirty-one degrees centigrade, over Stalingrad fog and red haze. Meteorological station now closing down. Greetings to the homeland."

Reacting to Soviet proclamations about their stupendous triumph, the Nazi government reluctantly told the German people of the loss of the entire Sixth Army. For an unprecedented three days, all radio broadcasts were suspended. Funeral music droned into thousands of homes across the Third Reich. Restaurants, theaters, cinemas, all places of entertainment were shut down, and the trauma of defeat gripped the population.

In Berlin, Goebbels began to draft a speech calling for a realization that Germany must prepare for "total war."

Chapter Thirty

Two days after organized resistance ended, on February 4, A. S. Chuyanov of the City Soviet Committee phoned across the Volga to a foreman from the tractor factory. "It's time to come back," he said, and the workers who had waited months for that message packed their equipment and started home. They drove across the ice, past traffic masters directing long lines of Germans out of the city, and the jubilant Russians snickered at the wretched state of their enemies, many of them wrapped in shawls and women's clothing to ward off the cold.

In five months of fighting and bombings, 99 percent of the city had been reduced to rubble. More than forty-one thousand homes, three hundred factories, 113 hospitals and schools had been destroyed. A quick census revealed that out of more than five hundred thousand inhabitants of the previous summer, only 1,515 civilians remained. Most of them had either died in the first days or left the city for temporary homes in Siberia and Asia. No one knew how many had been killed, but the estimates were staggering.

In Dar Gova, the Fillipovs remained to mourn the irreparable loss of their cobbler son, Sacha. And behind General Rodimtsev's grain mill headquarters on the Volga bank, Mrs. Karmanova and her son, Genn, celebrated their freedom after months of hiding in trenches and snowholes. On Red Square, two little girls, separated since September, hopped over corpses to meet in a joyful embrace. Their innocent laughter, carrying far in the still air, brought smiles to Russian soldiers, who were tossing dead Germans onto a roaring bonfire.

The Russian Sixty-second Army began to leave the city for a well-earned rest on the eastern side of the Volga. Within weeks, the rejuvenated troops would follow Vassili Chuikov to other battlefields. But behind them, in hospitals across Russia, they left thousands of comrades from the darkest days in Stalingrad who would be fighting another kind of war, the struggle toward physical and mental recovery.

In a hospital bed at Tashkent, the tiny blond sniper Tania Chernova, was slowly recuperating from the stomach wound that had nearly taken her life. She had borne well the news that the operation she had endured would prevent her from ever bearing a child. She had obeyed the doctors' orders to the letter and looked forward to a speedy release from confinement. But when she received a letter from a friend in the Sixty-second Army, her world fell apart.

The friend wrote that her lover, Vassili Zaitsev, a Hero of the Soviet Union, had died in an explosion during the final weeks of fighting around the Red October Plant. The news drove Tania into acute depression. As days passed, her physical strength improved greatly but doctors noticed that she rarely exhibited interest in anything around her. Instead she just stared for hours into space as though trying to recapture a lost moment.

At another hospital, Lt. Hersch Gurewicz clumped about on his artificial leg and tried to get a new assignment in the Red Army. Told that he would have to be discharged for medical reasons, Gurewicz wrote directly to Stalin, begging for reconsideration. The letter won a reprieve and Gurewicz found himself a mail censor with a Polish contingent heading west toward the Ukraine. Glee-fully, the lieutenant packed an extra wooden leg and headed back to war.

Several hundred miles to the north, guards at a railroad station in the Ural city of Novosibirsk gently wrapped their arms around the bandaged figure of Commando Capt. Ignacy Changar as he stood singing on the station platform. Transferred from a hospital in Moscow, Changar had gotten so drunk on the train ride that he had no idea where he was supposed to be.

Admitted to a military hospital, Changar began to flirt with the nurses, particularly one young girl who came from Kiev. When he asked repeatedly for her, she went to him wondering why such an old man would be interested in her. She had no idea that Ignacy was just twenty-one, because he now had snow-white hair.

What of the German Sixth Army? Swallowed up on the steppe, it had disappeared into the wastes of Russia and no one in the German High Command had witnessed its going. In the last days of the battle, Paulus had allowed several squads of men to make a break toward the west. But they all had been captured or killed by alert Red Army units.

Other Germans had also left on their own. Quartermaster Karl Binder took a group with him as far as Karpovka, thirty miles west of Stalingrad before the enemy surrounded him and forced his surrender.

Lt. Emil Metzger hid in a bunker in the vain hope that the Russians would leave the area and allow him to slip off at night toward the Don. But the Russians fired bullets down a ventilation pipe and wounded Emil in the right heel. Finally driven into the open by grenades, he walked off to prison camp with blood slosh-ing around in his boot.

Two Germans actually reached friendly lines. In late Feb-ruary, a Corporal Neiwig staggered into a command post of Army Group Don nearly 150 miles west of the *Kessel*. The sole survivor of a twenty-man group of escapees who had succumbed to the freezing cold, Neiwig knew little about the fate of the rest of his army. Within hours, as he tried to regain his strength from the trip, a Soviet mortar shell landed nearby and blew him to bits.

On March 1, Pvt. Michael Horvath walked into German positions near Voronezh, far to the west of Stalingrad. Captured on January 31, he had been shipped off to another front as an interpreter for Russian intelligence officers. Therefore, Horvath could add little information to what was known about the Sixth Army since the day of its capitulation. The German High Command and the German people were unable to tell how Paulus and his troops were faring in Russian hands.

The field marshal and his generals were, at that moment, living in relatively comfortable quarters near Moscow. But the men Paulus believed would be guaranteed food and medical care were dying in great numbers on the icy steppes.

Thirty miles northwest of Stalingrad, at Kotluban, a group of Russian nurses heard the German prisoners coming long before they saw them. They listened in astonishment to the mournful groaning as lines of soldiers crept over the horizon and shuffled through snowdrifts toward them. Lowing like cattle, the Germans were a procession of rags and dilapidated earmuffs, blanket-wrapped feet, and faces blackened by beard and frost. Almost all of them were crying, and the nurses felt an instinctive wave of sympathy for them. Then the Russian guards hoisted rifles and fired indiscriminately into the columns. As the victims fell down and died, the rest of the Germans plodded along, at a half mile an hour, and the nurses shook their fists in outrage at their own soldiers.

Quartermaster Karl Binder was in another of these processions. Marching toward Vertaichy on the Don he flinched at every shot, and at each dull whack of a rifle butt crashing down on a skull. Hundreds of bodies lay beside the trail, freshly killed Germans,

Russian women and children dead for weeks, Soviet and German troops mutilated in months-old battles.

At villages along the march, civilians broke into the lines to rob the prisoners of lighters, fountain pens, and fieldpacks. His hands blue from the cold, Binder plunged on and tried to distract himself by thinking of his family safe at home in Germany.

Emil Metzger had already walked more than a hundred miles to a train that took him to the foothills of the Urals in Siberia. Besides the bullet still in his heel, Metzger had fallen victim to typhus and, by the time he reached a straw cot in a primitive barracks, was close to death. Handing his pictures of Kaethe to a chaplain he said: "Give these to my wife if you get back." Then he lay down to die.

In the morning, Emil woke to an unreal silence. Nearly everyone in his barracks had perished during the night. Suddenly ashamed of his own willingness to give up the struggle, the lieutenant vowed he would survive. From that moment on, he ignored his fever and ate anything the Russians offered, though the food "was like eating his own gall."

The German Sixth Army was scattered to more than twenty camps stretching from the Arctic Circle to the southern deserts.

One train carried thousands of Germans from the Volga to Uzbekistan, in Central Asia. Inside each car, stuffed with one hundred or more prisoners, a macabre death struggle ensued as the Germans killed each other for bits of food tossed to them every two days. Those closest to the door were set upon by ravenous soldiers in the rear; only the strongest men survived the weeks-long trip. By the time the train reached the Pamir Mountains, almost half its passengers were dead.

Other Germans remained in Stalingrad to help reconstruct the city they had devastated. Typhus swept their ranks and in March, the

Russians dug a ditch at Beketovka and dumped nearly forty thousand German bodies into a mass grave.

Cpl. Franz Deifel, who had thought of killing himself in January, survived the plague and now picked up the bricks of Stalingrad. In March, Deifel heard a whistle from the tractor factory as the Russians ran the first train around that massive plant's convoluted rail system. Later that month, Deifel also saw his first butterfly of the spring. A blaze of yellow and orange, it flitted nervously from ruin to ruin in the glorious sunlight of a cloudless day.

But for more than five hundred thousand other Germans, Italians, Hungarians, and Rumanians, the Russian winter had been a harsh, unfair struggle. During a single, three-month span—February, March, and April of 1943—more than four hundred thousand of them had perished.

In many cases, the Russians let them starve to death. Every third day, Red Army trucks unloaded heads of cabbage, loaves of frozen bread, even garbage for the prisoners to eat. At Tambov, Krinovaya, Yelabuga, Oranki, Susdal, Vladimir, and other camps, the inmates fell upon the food and beat each other to death for scraps.

Other prisoners, more intent on survival, took matters into their own hands, especially in camps where military self-discipline had broken down. At Susdal, Felice Bracci first noticed it when he saw corpses without arms or legs. And Dr. Cristoforo Capone found human heads with the brains scooped out, or torsos minus livers and kidneys. Cannibalism had begun.

The cannibals were furtive at first, stealing among the dead to hack off a limb and eat it raw. But their tastes quickly matured and they searched for the newly dead, those just turning cold, and thus more tender. Finally they roamed in packs, defying anyone to stop them. They even helped the dying to die.

Hunting day and night, their lust for human flesh turned

them into crazed animals and, by late February, they reached a savage peak of barbarism. At Krinovaya, an Italian Alpini soldier raced across the compound to find his priest, Don Guido Turla.

"Come quickly, Father," he begged. "They want to eat my cousin!"

The startled Turla followed the distraught man across the compound, past quartered stomachs, headless cadavers, arms and legs stripped of flesh and meat. He arrived at the barracks door to see madmen smashing at it with their fists. Inside was their quarry, shot and mortally wounded by a Russian guard. The cannibals had followed the trail of warm blood to the door and now tried to pound it down to get at the terrified man.

The sickened Turla screamed at the cannibals, telling them theirs was a heinous crime, a blot on their consciences, and that God would never forgive them. The flesh-eaters slunk back from the door; a few begged the priest for forgiveness. Father Turla went inside to the dying soldier and heard his last confession. When the boy begged the priest to save him from the cannibals, Turla sat beside him in his final moments. The cannibals left his corpse alone. They had thousands more to choose from.

In another barracks at Krinovaya, two Italian brothers had sworn to protect each other from cannibals in case death separated them. When one brother succumbed to illness, the cannibals crowded around the fresh corpse. The other brother straddled the dead man's cot, and warned off the jackals hovering around the bed. During the long night he stood guard while the cannibals urged him to let them take care of the victim.

As dawn approached, they increased their verbal assault, telling the brother it was pointless for him to stay any longer. They even offered to bury the body for him. As he weakened, they moved closer to the bed and gently picked up the corpse he had sworn to defend. Exhausted from his vigil, the surviving brother threw himself on the floor and began to howl hysterically. The experience had driven him insane.

The Russians shot every cannibal they caught, but faced with the task of hunting down so many man-eaters they had to enlist the aid of "anticannibalism teams," drawn from the ranks of captive officers. The Russians equipped these squads with crowbars and demanded they kill every cannibal they found. The teams prowled at night, looking for telltale flickers of flame from small fires where the predators were preparing their meals.

Dr. Vincenzo Pugliese went on patrol frequently and, one night, he turned a corner and surprised a cannibal roasting something on the end of a stick. At first it looked like an oversized sausage, but then Pugliese's trained eye noticed the accordion-like pleats on the object and with a sickening start, he realized that the man was cooking a human trachea.

Prisoners who refused to eat human flesh used other tricks to survive. At Krinovaya, a group of Italian entrepreneurs retrieved excrement from huge latrine ditches and with bare hands picked out undigested corn and millet, which they washed and ate. German prisoners swiftly improved the process. Setting up an assembly line of sieve-like tin cups, they strained the feces through them and trapped so much grain that they started a black market in it.

At Susdal, Dr. Cristoforo Capone employed his fertile imagination to save himself and his comrades. Still a charming rogue who found humor in the darkest moments, he devised truly elaborate schemes. When a truck filled with cabbages parked outside the fence, Capone organized a group that stole the load and hid it under beds, in latrines and mattresses. While his friends ate voraciously, Capone then spread a trail of cabbage leaves from the empty truck to a nearby Rumanian barracks. The theft was finally discovered, and the Russians followed the trail and fell upon the Rumanians with clubs. Meanwhile, Capone's friends ate every other piece of evidence.

The inventive doctor found yet another macabre way to sustain life. Divided into fifteen-men squads, the Italian POWs lived in ice-cold rooms where they walked incessantly to keep from freezing. Each morning a Russian guard entered, counted the men present and left rations for that exact number. As men began to waste away and die, Capone decided their corpses could serve a better purpose than being thrown onto the pile of bodies in the yard. From then on Capone propped bodies upright in their chairs and when the Russian guard made his daily count, he and his companions engaged them in spirited conversation. The guard always left the fifteen rations; soon Capone and his companions were looking better, feeling better.

Because the frigid temperature kept the corpses from decomposing, the doctor kept them for weeks. When his own room was "bursting with protein," he felt compelled to help neighboring prisoners so he instituted a form of "lend-lease." Each day, he carried the petrified bodies back and forth to different rooms, dropping them off wherever increased rations were needed.

By May of 1943, the Russians began to feed the prisoners better. As one captive explained, "They wanted some soldiers to go home after the war." Doctors and nurses moved in to care for the survivors; political agitators roved the camps, seeking candidates for anti-Fascist training. After several months of indoctrination, one German exclaimed, "I never knew there were so many Communists in the Wehrmacht!" In most cases, those who turned on Hitler and Mussolini had a specific goal in mind. Cooperation meant extra food.

Thousands of German families still waited for word of their loved ones at Stalingrad. In Frankfurt on the Main, Kaethe Metzger watched while American planes leveled the city in 1944. When Allied armies crossed the Rhine in 1945, she fled to the suburbs and, after Frankfurt fell, she returned to her old neighborhood several times to see if anyone had heard news of Emil. Kaethe never doubted that she would see him again, even though each time she asked her friends if her husband had contacted any of them, they shook their heads and turned away.

After the war, Frankfurt slowly surged with life as the rubble was carted away and the city became headquarters for the Allied Army of Occupation. When construction began on apartment houses and stores in the downtown area, Kaethe found a small flat for Emil and herself. Through the years of the cold war she waited—the Berlin airlift in 1948 and the first trickle of prisoners to return from behind the Iron Curtain. Kaethe refused to give up hope. On July 7, 1949, a yellow telegram arrived from Frankfort on the Oder, inside the Russian zone of East Germany. It said simply, "*Ich komme,* Emil."

Kaethe cried all that day. Then she began to worry about what to wear when she met Emil at the train station. Like a schoolgirl, she prepared for her husband's return.

Peering nervously through a train window, Emil Metzger was traveling across his fallen nation. Passing lush farmlands, he recalled the terrible devastation he had seen in Russia and the six years he had spent in a Siberian prison camp. How long, he wondered, would Germany remain divided, bankrupt, a pariah in the family of nations. Would there be any place in the new world for a man who had served so discredited a cause?

The train slowed and pulled into the enormous yards at Frankfurt. His heart pounding, Emil rose and stretched. His right foot throbbed painfully from the bullet still imbedded in his heel, but he paid no attention to it as he descended to the platform and was carried along by the frantic rush of fellow passengers. Suddenly he was in the midst of a screaming, hysterical group of civilians. Someone shouted his name and he nodded absently at an old friend thrusting a bouquet of flowers at him.

Then he saw her, standing quietly apart from the crowd. Pushing through the people in front of him, he never took his eyes off Kaethe, looking radiant in a colorful print dress. He reached out, their hands touched and then they were together, sobbing and clinging desperately to each other. But as he smothered his wife with kisses, Emil was suddenly afraid. The woman he held was almost a total stranger. Although he had never spent an hour in prison camp without thinking about her—about her smile and laughter and how much he wanted to be with her—it struck him forcibly that, in their nine years of marriage, this was only their fifth day together as man and wife.

Epilogue: Among the Survivors

Col. Wilhelm Adam. Paulus's adjutant surrendered with him at the Univermag Department Store. In prison camp, he joined the Communist-inspired Bund Deutsche Offiziere, an "anti-Fascist" group that broadcast appeals to the citizens of the Third Reich against the Hitler regime. After the war, Adam returned home to East Germany and became an official in the Communist government of the German Democratic Republic.

Col. Nikolai Batyuk. The arthritic commander of the Soviet 284th Division on Mamaev Hill was promoted to general and later died in another battle in western Russia.

Capt. Winrich Behr. Today "Teddy" Behr is an executive with a West German telephone company. He still maintains close contact with Nikolaus von Below and Arthur Schmidt, his confidants from the days of the *Kessel*.

Col. Günter von Below. Kept in captivity until 1955 with a "hard-core" group of Sixth Army officers, Below lives in retirement at Bad Godesburg, West Germany. His affection and respect for Friedrich von Paulus remain constant.

Q.M. Karl Binder. He survived the death march and in 1948 went home to Swäbisch-Gmund, southeast of Stuttgart. In his modest apartment, the ever-efficient pensioner keeps an unofficial roster of those Germans who came back from Soviet prisons. Out of 107,000 Sixth Army soldiers herded into prison camps in 1943, he has found less than five thousand survivors.

Lt. Felice Bracci. Now an employee of the Banco Nazionale del Lavore in Rome, the adventurous Bracci recently realized another of his life's ambitions. In 1969, he saw the Pyramids that he had forsaken in 1942 in order to explore the steppe country of Russia.

Pvt. Ekkehart Brunnert. After a long recuperation from wounds suffered at Stalingrad, Brunnert went into the front lines around Berlin in 1945. Wounded a second time, he escaped capture by the Red Army and returned home to Boblingen.

Lt. Cristoforo Capone. When the "rogue" arrived home in 1946 as an emaciated stranger, his daughter Guiliana shrank back, screaming: "Mommy, who is this man? Send him away." Along with a brilliant career as a heart specialist, Capone enjoys a legendary reputation for his courage, according to the comrades who endured privation with him in prison. More than one hundred thousand Italian soldiers went into captivity with the doctor but only twelve thousand ever saw sunny Italy again.

Capt. Ignacy Changar. After recovering from massive head wounds in the Novosibirsk Hospital, the commando leader married the nurse who had been so shocked by his prematurely white hair. Today Changar lives in Tel Aviv, Israel, where he solemnly raised tumblers of vodka with the author to the memory of his fallen comrades at Stalingrad.

Sgt. Tania Chernova. More than a quarter century after her vendetta against the enemy, the graying sniper still refers to the Germans she killed as "sticks" that she broke. For many years after the war she believed that Vassili Zaitsev, her lover, had died from grievous wounds. Only in 1969, did she learn that he had recovered and married someone else. The news stunned her for she still loved him.

Gen. Vassili Chuikov. The great leader of the Sixty-second Army, renamed the Eighth Guards, led it on to the glorious triumph at Berlin in May 1945. Rewarded with the highest decorations and honors, he eventually became commander of all Russian land forces in the postwar period. In 1969, the semiretired marshal flew to Washington to represent the Soviet Union at Dwight D. Eisenhower's funeral. Chuikov spends most of his time now at his country *dacha* outside Moscow.

Lt. Pyotr Deriabin. Recruited into the Soviet Secret Police, Deriabin defected in 1954, and exposed some of the KGB European espionage network to CIA officials.

Lt. Anton Dragan. After the war he wrote Chuikov a letter explaining that he had been the commander of the 1st Battalion, 42nd Regiment, 13th Guards Division. It was the first proof Chuikov had that anyone had survived from the heroic group that fought the Germans from the main railroad station to the edge of the Volga. In 1958, Chuikov spent part of his vacation with his old comrade. In Dragan's home in the village of Likovitsa, they reconstructed the gruesome details of the firefight that gained precious hours and days for the Sixty-second Army in September 1942.

Mikhail Goldstein. The violinist fled to the West during a tour of Eastern European countries in the 1960s. When the author visited with him, he was still performing occasional concerts and lecturing to students at conservatories.

Capt. Hersch Gurewicz. While working as an army mail censor, the one-legged officer intercepted a letter written by his father and traced him to Berlin. When Gurewicz stood before him, his father collapsed in tears for he thought Hersch had died during the war. Several years later, he told his son that the Gurewicz family was Jewish, a fact he had hidden to spare them from virulent anti-Semitism in the Soviet Union. Gurewicz emigrated to Israel, where he recently suffered one more war wound: an Arab sniper shot him in the arm.

The nurse he loved at Stalingrad did not die. Miraculously recovered from the loss of all her limbs, she married and bore several children.

Gen. Franz Halder. Driven into retirement by Hitler, Halder joined the abortive coup against the Führer's life. Sentenced to death, he was rescued by Allied soldiers in the last weeks of the war. For years afterward, he helped American historians write the history of the Wehrmacht in World War II.

Gen. Ferdinand Heim.   Ordered to stand trial for dereliction of duty, the commander of the 48th Panzer Corps spent months in Moabit Prison awaiting punishment. Only when Marshal Keitel interceded for him with Hitler was Heim released. He now lives in the city of Ulm, West Germany.

Gen. Hermann Hoth.   In postwar comments, "Papa" Hoth stated that Paulus should have broken out of the *Kessel* in December 1942 and reached the oncoming German relief column. Ailing for years, the 85-year-old panzer leader is now confined to his home in Goslar, West Germany.

Dr. Ottmar Kohler.   Packed to leave prison in Russia in 1949, the doctor listened in amazement while a Soviet NKVD officer sentenced him to a further twenty-five years in jail for espionage. Finally repatriated in 1955 with the last contingent of Stalingrad prisoners, Kohler received a hero's welcome in West Germany. The Bonn government decorated him for his extraordinary labors on behalf of fellow captives and he became known as "The Angel of Stalingrad." He is now a practicing surgeon in the town of Idar-Oberstein, West Germany.

Lt. Wilhelm Kreiser.   Wounded in the potato cellar he had occupied near the Barrikady Gun Factory, Kreiser gained a reprieve from death when a Heinkel transport landed next to him on a snowfield and carried him away to safety. The lieutenant's home is in Ulm, West Germany.

Political Commissar Nikita Khrushchev.   After Stalin's death in 1953, Khrushchev eventually assumed ultimate power of the Communist state. Deposed in 1964, he revealed later in his memoirs what no Soviet official had ever admitted: that at Stalingrad, large numbers of German prisoners had been shot to death by Russian guards.

Gen. Nikolai Krylov.   Chuikov's chief of staff during the darkest days at Stalingrad later rose swiftly in the Red Army hierarchy. In the 1960s, the marshal commanded all Soviet strategic missile forces. He died in 1972.

Col. Ivan Lyudnikov. The defender of the pie-shaped slice of land behind the Barrikady Gun Factory was acclaimed a Hero of the Soviet Union for his tenacious resistance. In 1968, the retired general returned to the site of his victory as an honored guest of the city of Stalingrad.

Gen. Rodion Malinovsky. When Khrushchev became premier, he appointed the beefy Malinovsky as defense minister. In May 1960, at a press conference in Paris, the two men boisterously denounced President Eisenhower for Francis Gary Powers's ill-fated U-2 flight; the pending summit meeting never took place. Malinovsky died in 1967.

Field Marshal Erich von Manstein. Foiled in his attempt to rescue the Sixth Army, Manstein performed a miracle by holding the port city of Rostov open until mid-February 1943, allowing most of German Army Group A in the Caucasus to escape entrapment. Sacked by Hitler in 1944 for differences of opinion on grand strategy, Manstein faced war-crimes charges for permitting *Einsatzgruppen* to exterminate Jews within his territorial command. Exonerated, he wrote a controversial memoir in which he blamed Paulus for not breaking out of the *Kessel* in December 1942. However, Manstein ignored the fact that he never issued the code word "Thunderclap," which Paulus had been told was a prerequisite for launching the operation.

Lt. Emil Metzger. With the bullet from Stalingrad still imbedded in his right heel more than twenty years later, Emil and his wife, Kaethe, live in Frankfurt on a government pension. A constant visitor to their apartment is the son of the officer who took Emil's place in the furlough rotation so that he could get married. The man died in a Siberian prison camp and never saw his child, now a lawyer.

Capt. Gerhard Meunch. After serving as a general staff officer in the German Armed Forces High Command, Meunch spent many postwar years in school and business. Returning to the newly created West German army, the *Bundeswehr*, in 1956, he now holds the rank of general.

Lt. Hans Oettl. Released to his home in 1949, Oettl married and resumed his post with the city administration in Munich, where he continues to live.

Field Marshal Friedrich von Paulus. Except for a brief visit to Nuremburg to testify against the Nazi leaders, Paulus spent the rest of his life behind the Iron Curtain. He lived in Russia until 1952, then went to Dresden, in the Communist East Zone of Germany. He never saw his wife Coca again. Because he had lent his name to the "anti-Fascist" officers group in Soviet prisons, the Gestapo imprisoned her. Rescued from an Alpine detention center by American soldiers, she died at Baden-Baden in 1949.

Paulus's final years were bitter ones. Reviled by some critics for his subservience to Hitler, stung by histories and memoirs that accused him of timidity, he wrote copious rebuttals to these charges. His son Ernst visited him several times; his other son, Alexander, had been killed at Anzio in 1944. Paulus believed that communism was the best hope for postwar Europe, and Ernst noted sadly that his father "had gone over to the other side."

The field marshal died in 1957 after a lingering illness. In 1970, his son Ernst committed suicide. He was fifty-two, his father's age when he surrendered his Sixth Army at Stalingrad.

Sgt. Jacob Pavlov. A Hero of the Soviet Union for his fifty-eight-day defense of the apartment building at Solechnaya Street, Pavlov fought on to Berlin. To this day he is known to countless admirers as the "Houseowner" for his incredible achievement.

Sgt. Alexei Petrov. In the spring of 1943, Petrov finally heard dreadful news about his family. A sister-in-law wrote that his entire family had been reported killed by Nazi occupation troops. The information was correct; Petrov never found any trace of his relatives.

Sgt. Albert Pflüger. His wounded arm still crawling with lice, Pflüger marched off to prison, where he later contracted typhoid fever. Invalided home in 1949, he now makes his home in a suburb of Stuttgart, West Germany.

Gen. Carl Rodenburg. One of the "incorrigibles" whom the Russian government kept in jail until 1955, the monocled Rodenburg now lives in Lubeck, West Germany.

Gen. Alexander Rodimtsev. For his gallant leadership of the illustrious 13th Guards Division, the youthful general was named a Hero of the Soviet Union for the second time. Retired from active service in 1966, he now lives in Kiev.

Gen. Konstantin Rokossovsky. Stalingrad was just one of many victories for the Polish-born general as he traveled the long road to Berlin. Later elevated to marshal, he died of cancer in 1968.

Rudolph Rossler. On January 16, 1943, the director of Soviet espionage at the center in Moscow radioed congratulations to the "Lucy" network in Switzerland for its help in defeating the Germans around Stalingrad. Finally exposed as a spy by Swiss police, Rossler served a short term in jail and died in 1958 without ever revealing his sources within the German High Command.

Gen. Arthur Schmidt. The man who Hitler said would "sign anything" in captivity proved to be one of the most stubborn prisoners the Russians held. Sentenced to solitary confinement for long periods and physically abused, the dogged Schmidt always refused to cooperate with Soviet authorities who were anxious to use his name against the Nazi government. In October 1955, he returned to Hamburg, where he still resides. For years the general has continued as a highly controversial figure. His many detractors claim that he dominated Paulus and kept the battle going far beyond humane limits. Schmidt vehemently denies that he unduly influenced Paulus and claims that they rarely, if ever, argued about decisions. On one point, however, there is no doubt: that in the last weeks inside the *Kessel,* Schmidt's determination to continue fighting far exceeded Paulus's apathetic acceptance of disaster.

Col. Herbert Selle. Flown out of the *Kessel* in January, Selle became vocal in his opposition to the Nazi party. His associations with men who later tried to kill Hitler nearly cost him his life. Like Schmidt, he lives today in Hamburg, West Germany.

Gen. Walther Seydlitz-Kurzbach. A prime mover in the *Bund Deutsche Offiziere* that broadcast against Hitler, Seydlitz reaped bitter fruit. The Nazi government forced his wife to divorce him. His name became anathema to patriotic Germans, and when he declined a position in the Communist East German government, the Russians sentenced him to twenty-five years at hard labor. Repatriated in 1955 to West Germany, he faced a stony silence from former friends and the mass of German people. Now in his eighties, he has only slightly refurbished his image. In the recent wave of revulsion against Hitler's tyranny, Seydlitz's strong denunciations of the Nazi rulers have earned him some favor with the younger generation.

Maj. Nikolai Tomskuschin. The officer who dismissed the thought of suicide so that he might live to see his son Vladimir, never went home to Russia. Sent to Germany as a slave laborer, he survived brutal imprisonment. But after the war, like many Russians, Tomskuschin feared reprisals from suspicious Kremlin leaders and refused to board a train bound for the Soviet Union. His fears were justified. Thousands of former prisoners went home to face execution or prison terms for various misdeeds, real or imagined: collaboration, dereliction of duty in the field, or simply contamination by Western ideas.

Sgt. Hubert Wirkner. Burned, frostbitten, and aching with typhoid fever, Wirkner huddled for nearly two weeks in a Stalingrad cellar until kindly Russian soldiers carried him out to captivity. Declared unfit for labor, he received a release from prison camp in 1945. Today he lives in Karlsruhe, West Germany, is married, and the father of two children.

Gen. Andrei Yeremenko. He published a trilogy about the Russo-German War in which he condemned Stalin's mishandling of strategy during the first year of the war. Never given full credit for his initial defensive tactics against General Hoth's onrushing panzers south of Stalingrad in August 1942, he nevertheless enjoyed nationwide acclaim for his participation in the battle. Yeremenko died in 1971.

Lt. Vassili Zaitsev. The supersniper was credited with killing 242

Germans at Stalingrad before a land mine's explosion temporarily blinded him. Hailed as a Hero of the Soviet Union, he married and settled in Kiev as the director of an engineering school.

Marshal Georgi Zhukov.   The architect of the counteroffensive at Stalingrad failed to get proper recognition for that feat until after Khrushchev fell from power in 1964. Forced into retirement after a clash with the premier, Zhukov was rehabilited by Brezhnev and Kosygin and allowed to publish his version of the struggle for Stalingrad and other battles. Zhukov lives in a country home near Moscow.

Maj. Coelestin von Zitzewitz.   The controversial "observer" inside the *Kessel* went into business in Hannover, West Germany, after the war. He always denied that he had been Hitler's spy, put there because of the Führer's lack of faith in the Sixth Army command. Zitzewitz died in 1962.

Acknowledgments

During the past four years many people have contributed their time and knowledge to this book. They have also shown great hospitality and kindness to a stranger. My sincere gratitude is extended to the following:

Alexander Akimov, Guiseppe Aleandri, Wilhelm Alter, Max Aust, Helmut Bangert, Herbert Barber, Dora Barskaya, Raya Barskaya, Shura Barskaya, Heinrich Bartels, Eugen Baumann, Winrich Behr, Günter von Below, Luba Bessanova, Karl Binder, Felice Bracci, Hans Bräunlein, Friedrich Breining, Franz Brendgen, Franz Bröder, Mikhail Bruk, Ekkehart Brunnert, Cristoforo Capone, Horst Caspari, Ignacy Changar, Leo Checkver, Tania Chernova, Mrs. David Dallin, Franz Deifel, Gregori Denisov, Pyotr Deriabin, Fritz Dieckmann, Gerhard Dietzel, Karl Englehardt, Berthold Englert, Paul Epple, Clemens Erny, Isabella Feige, Karl Floeck, Georg Frey, Karl Geist, Werner Gerlach, Wilhelm Giebeler, Heinz Giessel, Jacob Grubner, Hersch Gurewicz, Mrs. Kurt Hahnke, W. Averell Harriman, Gerhard Hässler, Adolf Heusinger, Otto von der Heyde, R.M.A. Hirst, Mrs. Hermann Hoth, Georgi Isachenko, Donat Ismaev, Lucy Jarvis, Vasile Jirjea, Hans Jülich, Dionys Kaiser, Leah Kalei, Anton Kappler, Hermann Kästle, Liora Keren, Fritz Kliem, Heinrich Klotz, Herbert Kreiner, Wilhelm Kreiser, Ottmar Kohler, Vadim Komolov, August Kronmüller, Joseph Lapide, Heinz Lieber, Josef Linden, Eberhard von Loebbecke, Alexander Makarov, Veniero Marsan, Xaver Marx, Emil Metzger, Josef Metzler, Gerhard Meunch, Heinz Neist, Hans Oettl, Karl Ostarhild, Vittorio Paolozzi, Ernst Paulus, Wolf Pelikan, Alexei Petrov, Albert Pflüger, Boris Pishchik,

Wilhelm Plass, Rudi Pothmann, Mesten Pover, Vincenzo Pugliese, Ugo Rampelli, Enrico Reginato, Herbert Rentsch, Carl Rodenburg, Manfred Rohde, Stelio Sansone, Kirill Sazykin, Arthur Schmidt, Albert Schön, Heinz Schröter, Hans Schueler, Kurt Siol, Gottlieb Slotta, Abraham Spitkovsky, Oskar Stange, Eugene Steinhilber, Giorlamo Stovali, Friedrich Syndicus, Rudolf Taufer, Nikolai Tomskuschin, Andrea Valletta, Siegfried Wendt, Hubert Wirkner, Ernst Wohlfahrt, Pyotr Zabavskikh.

There were others whose generous assistance greatly eased my journey across three continents and 50,000 miles: Konrad Ahlers, William E. Andersen, Ronay Arlt, James Atwater, Charles E. Bohlen, Patricia Carey, Edward Craig, Anatoly Dobrynin, Virginia Gough, Donald Irwin, Siegfried Kaiser, Eugene King, Joseph Kolarek, David Laor, Renata Libner, Prof. Edward A. McCormick, Neville Nordness, Charles E. Northrop, Doris Orgel, A. A. Pishchotkin, P. Ramroth, Prof. John Roche, Eugenie Schneider, Joseph Skobel, G. Sosin, Malcolm Tarlov, Prof. Peter Viereck, Lucien Weisbrod, Hans Willee.

Archives and archivists have been of tremendous value to my research:

In the United States: Office, Chief of Military History, Washington, D. C. —Charles MacDonald, Hannah Zeidlik, Earl Ziemke; The Federal Records Center, Alexandria, Virginia—Wilbur Nigh and Lois Aldridge; the National Archives, Washington, D. C.—Joseph Bauer, Thomas Hohmann and John Taylor; The Library of Congress; The New York Public Library, Main Branch; Columbia University, Butler Library and International Affairs Library; Yale University, Sterling Memorial Library; Harvard University, Widener Library; Westport, Connecticut Public Library.

In Europe: *Freiburg:* The Research Center for Military History—Messrs. Arenz, Hermann and Stahl; *Munich:* The Commission for History of German Prisoners of War—Dr. Erich Maschke; The Institute for the Study of the USSR—Leon Barat, Peter Krushin; The Institute for World History; *Nuremberg:* The Club for Former Stalingrad Fighters.

In Israel: *Jerusalem:* Yad Vashem Documentation Center.

In Russia: Volgograd: The Volgograd Defense Museum—Colonel Gregori Denisov.

And finally, special thanks to those most intimately connected with my project:

To the Reader's Digest offices in Stuttgart: Frau Morike, Brigitte Berg, Annalise Gekeler, and, in particular, the late Arno Alexy; in Rome and Milan: Doctors Fiocca and Polla; in Washington: Julie Morgan; in New York: Jo Ann Schuman.

To Conrad Sponholz and the staff of the MacDowell Colony in Peterboro, New Hampshire, for giving me a chance to collect my thoughts.

To Richard Baron, who helped carry the burden for a long time.

To my agent Don Congdon, who so patiently listened and advised.

To Mrs. Dora Israel, a brilliant researcher, who diligently located and translated most of the Russian material.

To Kenneth Wilson, a gracious man whose faith and support meant so much to me.

To editor Nancy Kelly, whose deep sensitivity to the story and the author profoundly influenced the final draft.

And most particularly, to Bruce Lee, managing editor of the Reader's Digest Press, whose constant encouragement and astute editorial judgment contributed immeasurably to the manuscript. From the very first day, he, more than anyone, understood the complexities and magnitude of the effort. I am deeply grateful to him.

Selected Bibliography

Accoce, Pierre, and Quet, Pierre. *The Lucy Ring.* London: 1967.

Adam, Wilhelm. *The Hard Decision.* E. Berlin: 1967.

Afanasyev, I. F. *House of the Soldiers' Fame.* 2d ed. Volgograd: 1966.

Agapov, B. *After the Battle—Stalingrad Sketches.* London: 1943.

Armstrong, J. A., ed. *Soviet Partisans in World War II.* Madison, Wis.: 1964.

Bachurin, A. P. *Front Line Memoirs.* Moscow: 1962.

Baldwin, Hanson W. *Battles Lost and Won.* London: 1968.

Batov, P. I. *In Campaigns and Battles.* Moscow: 1962.

Bekker, Cajus. *The Luftwaffe War Diaries.* New York: 1968.

Belov, K. S. *From the Volga to Prague.* Moscow: 1966.

Bergschicker, Heinz. *Stalingrad: Battle on the Volga.* E. Berlin: 1960.

Biryukov, N. I. *Battle for Stalingrad.* Volgograd: 1962.

———. *Two Hundred Days in Battle.* Volgograd: 1963.

Biryusov, S. S. *Rough Years.* Moscow: 1966.

———. *When the Cannons Thundered.* Moscow: 1962.

Carell, Paul. *Hitler Moves East 1941–43.* Boston: 1965.

Cassidy, Henry. *Moscow Dateline.* Boston: 1943.

Chuikov, V. I. *The Army of Mass Heroism.* Moscow: 1958.

———. *The Battle for Stalingrad.* New York: 1964.

———. *Heroism Without Precedent.* Moscow: 1965.

———. *One Hundred Eighty Days in Battle Fire.* Moscow: 1962.

Churchill, Winston. *The Second World War.* 6 vols. London: 1948–54.

Chuyanov, A. S. *Stalingrad Is Reviving.* Moscow: 1944.

Clark, Alan. *Barbarossa*. London: 1965.

Conquest, Robert. *The Great Terror*. London: 1968.

Dahms, Hellmuth. *History of the Second World War*. Tubingen: 1965.

Dallin, Alexander. *German Rule in Russia, 1941–45*. London: 1957.

Deriabin, Peter, and Gibney, Frank. *The Secret World*. London: 1960.

Dibold, Hans. *Doctor at Stalingrad*. London, 1958.

von Dieckhoff, Gerhard. *The Third Infantry Division (Motorized)*. Gottingen: 1960.

Doerr, Hans. *The Campaign to Stalingrad*. Darmstadt: 1955.

Druzhinin, D. V. *Two Hundred Fiery Days*. Moscow: 1968.

Epic Story of Stalingrad, The. (Collection). London: 1943.

Erickson, John. *The Soviet High Command*. London: 1962.

Fight for Stalingrad, The. (Collection). Volgograd: 1969.

Filimonov, B. V. *The Immortals*. Volgograd: 1965.

Filippov, N. *Northwest of Stalingrad*. Moscow: 1952.

Freidin, Seymour, and Richardson, William, eds. *The Fatal Decisions*. New York: 1956.

Gehlen, Reinhard. *The Service*. New York: 1972.

Genkina, E. *Heroic Stalingrad*. Moscow: 1943.

Gerasimov, E. *The Stalingradians*. Moscow: 1950.

Gerlach, Heinrich. *The Forsaken Army*. Munich: 1957.

Gilbert, Felix, ed. *Hitler Directs His War*. New York: 1950.

Glukhovsky, S. D. *Lyudnikov's Island*. Moscow: 1963.

Goerlitz, Walter. *Paulus and Stalingrad*. New York: 1963.

Gorbatov, A. V. *Years and Wars*. Moscow: 1965.

Grams, Rolf. *The Fourteenth Panzer Division, 1940–45*. Bad Nauheim: 1957.

Grossman, V. I. *Stalingrad Hits Back*. Moscow: 1942.

Gummer, I., and Harin, Y. *Heroes of the Big Battle*. Volgograd: 1962.

Hart, B. H. Liddell. *The German Generals Talk*. New York: 1948.

Heiber, Helmut, ed. *Hitler's Strategy Talks*. Stuttgart: 1962.

Heusinger, Adolf. *Hitler and the Army High Command 1923–1945*. Paris: 1952.

Hindus, Maurice. *Mother Russia*. New York: 1943.

Ingor, M. *Siberians—The Heroes of Stalingrad*. Moscow: 1954.

Jacobsen, H. A. *The Second World War in Chronicle and Document*. Darmstadt: 1960.

———, and Rohwer, J. *Battles of the Second World War*. Frankfurt: 1960.

Jukes, Geoffrey. *Stalingrad: The Turning Point*. London: 1969.

Kantor, A., and Tazurin, A. *The Volgarians in the Battles Around Stalingrad*. Stalingrad: 1961.

Kazakov, V. I. *The Turning Point*. Moscow: 1962.

Khrushchev, N. S. *Khrushchev Remembers*. Boston: 1970.

Killen, John. *A History of the Luftwaffe, 1915–1945*. London: 1967.

Kluge, Alexander. *The Battle.* New York: 1967.

Kolesnik, A. D. *The Great Victory on the Volga, 1942–1943.* Moscow: 1958.

Konsalik, Heinz G. *Stalingrad.* Bayreuth: 1968.

Koren, L. P. *There Is a Cliff on the Volga.* Moscow: 1969.

Korets, L. B. *The Soviet Air Force in the Battle of Stalingrad.* Moscow: 1959.

Koroteev, V. *I Saw It.* Moscow: 1962.

———. *Stalingrad Miracle.* Moscow: 1966.

———. *Stalingrad Sketches.* Moscow: 1954.

Lentchevsky, V. E. *Eighty Days Under Fire: Recollections of a Scout.* Moscow: 1961.

———. *Trial by Fire: Recollections of an Intelligence Officer.* Volgograd: 1964.

Lenz, Friedrich. *Stalingrad—The Lost Victory.* Heidelberg: 1956.

Levin, Nora. *The Holocaust.* New York: 1968.

Lochner, Louis, ed. *The Goebbels Diaries.* New York: 1948.

Loginov, I. M. *The Militia in the Battle for Its Homeland.* Volgograd: 1963.

von Manstein, Erich. *Lost Victories.* Chicago: 1958.

von Mellenthin, Friedrich W. *Panzer Battles.* London: 1955.

Menshikov, M. P. *The Stalingrad Battle.* Stalingrad: 1953.

Morozov, I. K. *The Fight for the Volga.* 2d ed. Volgograd: 1962.

———. *The Regiments Fought Like Guards.* Volgograd: 1962.

Morzik, Fritz. *The German Transport Command in the Second World War.* Frankfurt: 1966.

Nekrassov, V. P. *Front Line Stalingrad.* London: 1962.

Paderin, I. *In the Main Direction.* Moscow: 1959.

Pavlov, F. D. *In Stalingrad 1942—Front Notes.* Stalingrad: 1951.

Perrault, Gilles. *The Red Orchestra.* London: 1969.

Philippi, Alfred, and Heim, Ferdinand. *The Campaign Against Soviet Russia 1941–45.* Stuttgart: 1962.

Plievier, Theodor. *Stalingrad.* Translated from German by Richard and Clara Winston. New York: 1948.

Pollack, E. *Children of Stalingrad.* New York: 1944.

Reginato, Enrico. *Twelve Years as a Prisoner in Russia.* Milan: 1955.

Reitlinger, Gerald. *The House Built on Sand.* New York: 1964.

Rodimtsev, A. I. *On the Banks of the Mandanares and Volga.* Petrozavodsk: 1966.

———. *On the Last Frontier.* Volgograd: 1964.

———. *People of Legendary Heroism.* Moscow: 1964.

von Rohden, H. *The Luftwaffe Struggle for Stalingrad.* Wiesbaden: 1950.

Röhricht, Edgar. *Problems of the Battle of Encirclement.* Karlsruhe: 1958.

Rokossovsky, K. K. *The Soldier's Duty.* Moscow: 1968.

Rooney, Andrew A. *The Fortunes of War.* Boston: 1962.

Salisbury, Harrison. *The 900 Days.* New York: 1969.

Salvatores, Umberto. *Bersaglieri on the Don.* Bologna: 1966.

Samchuk, I. A. *The Thirteenth Guards.* Moscow: 1971.

Samsonov, A. M., ed. *Stalingrad Epopeya.* Moscow: 1968.

————. *The Stalingrad Battle.* Moscow: 1960, 2d ed.: 1968.

————. *Under the Walls of Stalingrad.* Moscow: 1953.

Sanzhara, A. *The Heroism of the Thirty-Three.* Vladivostok: 1964.

Scheibert, Horst. *Relief Operation Stalingrad.* Neckargemund: 1968.

————. *To Stalingrad—48 Kilometers.* Neckargemund: 1956.

Schneider, Franz, and Gullans, Charles, trans. *Last Letters from Stalingrad.* New York: 1962.

Schramm, Percy Ernst., ed. *War Diary of the Army High Command.* Frankfurt: 1961.

Schröter, Heinz. *Stalingrad.* Translated by Constantine Fitzgibbon. New York: 1958.

Selishchev, I. P. *The Volga in Flames.* Moscow: 1963.

Selle, Herbert. *The Tragedy of Stalingrad.* Hannover: 1948.

Semin, I. A. *Stalingrad Tales.* Moscow: 1961.

Seth, Ronald. *Stalingrad: Point of Return.* London: 1959.

Shirer, William L. *The Rise and Fall of the Third Reich.* New York: 1959.

Simonov, K. *Days and Nights.* New York: 1945.

Stalingrad: An Eyewitness Account by Soviet Correspondents and Red Army Commanders. London: 1943.

Stupov, A. D., and Kokunov, V. L. *The Sixty-Second Army in the Stalingrad Battles.* 2d ed. Moscow: 1953.

von Telpuhovsky, B. S. *The Soviet History of the Great Fatherland War 1941–45.* Frankfurt: 1961.

von Tippelskirch, Kurt. *History of the Second World War.* Bonn: 1951.

Toepke, Gunter. *Stalingrad: How It Really Was.* Stade: 1949.

Turla, Don Guido. *Seven Rubles to the Chaplain.* Milan: 1970.

Umansky, R. G. *At the Battle Frontiers.* Moscow: 1960.

Valori, Aldo. *The Campaign in Russia.* Rome: 1950.

Vasilyev, A. V. *The Great Victory on the Volga.* Moscow: 1965.

————. *In the Days of the Great Fight.* Stalingrad: 1958.

Vinokur, L. *The Seventh Guards.* Volgograd: 1962.

Vodolagin, M. A. *The Defense of Stalingrad.* Stalingrad: 1948.

————. *Outline of the History of Volgograd.* Moscow: 1968.

————. *Stalingrad in the Great Patriotic War, 1941–43.* Stalingrad: 1949.

————. *Under the Walls of Stalingrad.* Moscow: 1960.

Voronov, N. N. *Service in War.* Moscow: 1963.

Warlimont, Walter. *Inside Hitler's Headquarters, 1939–45.* London: 1964.

Weinert, Erich. *Memento Stalingrad.* E. Berlin: 1951.

Werth, Alexander. *Russia at War 1941–45.* London: 1970.

————. *The Year of Stalingrad.* London: 1946.

Werthen, Wolfgang. *History of the Sixteenth Panzer Division*. Bad Nauheim: 1958.

Wieder, Joachim. *Stalingrad: How It Really Was*. Munich: 1962.

———. *The Tragedy of Stalingrad*. Deggendorf: 1955.

Wilmot, Chester. *The Struggle for Europe*. New York: 1952.

Wolfe, Bertram. *Three Who Made a Revolution*. New York: 1948.

Yeremenko, A. I. *Stalingrad*. Moscow: 1961.

Yevgeniev, P. *Yerzovka*. Kazan: 1966.

Yuriev, V. *The Great Victory in Stalingrad*. Moscow: 1943.

Zaitsev, V. *Notes of a Sniper*. Vladivostok: 1956.

Zamyatin, N. M. et al. *The Fight for Stalingrad*. Moscow: 1943.

Zarubina, A. D. *Women in the Defense of Stalingrad*. Stalingrad: 1958.

Zelma, G. *Stalingrad: July 1942–February 1943*. Moscow: 1966.

Zhematis, F. R. *The Stalingrad Battle*. Moscow: 1953.

Zhilin, P. A. *The Principle Operations of the Great Fatherland War, 1941–45*. Moscow: 1956.

Zhukov, G. K. *Marshal Zhukov's Greatest Battles*. New York: 1969.

———. *The Memoirs of Marshal Zhukov*. New York: 1971.

Ziemke, Earl. *Stalingrad to Berlin—The German Campaign in Russia 1942–1945*. Washington, D. C.: 1968.

Documents

Freiburg Archives and National Archives, Washington, D.C.:

Ia. Situation Maps, War Diary 12, Russland. Situation maps for the southern sector of the Russian front. May–July 1942.

Ia, Ic/AO, Volume of Appendices, War Diary 12, Russland. Reports and teletype messages concerning the tactical situation and operations of Sixth Army units in the Izyum and Volchansk areas, and Operation "Wilhelm" and "Blau"; intelligence reports on enemy operations, troop identification, movement, and losses; and maps (1:300,000) showing the tactical grouping of enemy units in the Stary Oskol and Belgorod areas. June 20–24, 1942.

Ia, Ic, Volume of Appendices, War Diary 12, Russland. Reports, orders, and teletype messages concerning the tactical situation and operations of Sixth Army units in the Voronezh, Voronovka, Krasnoye, and Pavlovsk areas; intelligence reports on enemy operations, troop identification and movements; and captured booty and prisoners of war. July 7–11, 1942.

Ia, Ic/AO, Volume of Appendices, War Diary 13, Russland. Reports, orders, and teletype messages concerning the tactical situation and operations and ammunition and fuel supply situation of Sixth Army units in the Don River Bend area west of Stalingrad; intelligence reports on enemy operations and troop identification and movements; and a map showing the tactical grouping of enemy units in the Serafimovich area. August 8–13, 1942.

Ia, Ic, Volume of Appendices, War Diary 13, Russland. Reports, orders, and teletype messages pertaining to the tactical situation and operations, chain of command, and combat readiness of Sixth Army units in the Don River area; intelligence reports on enemy operations and troop identification and movements; and a map showing the tactical grouping of the Eighth Flieger Korps in the Don River area. August 14–19, 1942.

Ia, Ic, Volume of Appendices, War Diary 13, Russland. Reports and teletype messages concerning the tactical situation and operations, subordination, and combat readiness of Sixth Army units in the Don-Volga River area; and intelligence reports on enemy operations, troop movements, and identification. August 20–25, 1942.

Ia, Ic/AO, Volume of Appendices, War Diary 13, Russland. Reports and teletype messages concerning the tactical situation and operations and order of battle of Sixth Army units in the Don-Volga area; intelligence reports on enemy operations and troop movements; and an enemy information bulletin "Stalingrad," giving an appraisal of the enemy situation, tactics, and combat readiness of Soviet divisions and the defenses for Stalingrad, including a map (1:300,000) showing the tactical disposition of the Soviet armies in the area around Stalingrad. August 25–30, 1942.

Ia, Ic, Volume of Appendices, War Diary 13, Russland. Reports and teletype messages concerning the tactical situation and operations of Sixth Army units in the Don River area and intelligence reports on enemy tactical operations and troop movements and identification. July 24–29, 1942.

Ia, Ic, Volume of Appendices, War Diary 13, Russland. Reports and teletype messages concerning the tactical situation and armored and antitank weapons situation of Sixth Army units in the Stalingrad area; intelligence reports on enemy operations, troop identification, movement, and losses, and Soviet fortifications around Stalingrad. September 12–17, 1942.

Ia, Ic, Volume of Appendices, War Diary 13, Russland. Reports and teletype messages concerning tactical operations, training, combat readiness, and losses of Sixth Army units in the Stalingrad area; a report on conditions in Stalingrad; intelligence reports on enemy tactical operations and troop identification and movements; and an overlay showing the tactical grouping of the Ninth Flakdivision in the area between the Don and Volga Rivers. September 17–21, 1942.

Ia, Ic/AO, Volume of Appendices, War Diary 13, Russland. Reports and teletype messages concerning the tactical operations and subordination of Sixth Army units in the Stalingrad area; intelligence reports on enemy operations and troop identification and movements; enemy information bulletin "Stalingrad," pertaining to the tactical situation in and the defenses of Stalingrad and the combat readiness and order of battle of Soviet forces participating at Stalingrad; and a map (1:300,000) showing the disposition of Soviet units in and north of Stalingrad. September 20–26, 1942.

Ia, Ic, Volume of Appendices, War Diary 13, Russland. Reports, orders, and teletype messages pertaining to tactical operations, subordination, combat readiness, and strength of Sixth Army units in the Stalingrad area; survey of the supply needs of the Rumanian Fifth Army Corps; and intelligence reports on enemy operations and troop identification and movements. September 27–October 3, 1942.

Ia, Ic, Volume of Appendices, War Diary 13, Russland. Reports and teletype messages concerning tactical operations, combat readiness, and activation of winter mobile units of Sixth Army, intelligence reports on enemy operations and troop identification and losses. October 3–5, 1942.

Ia, Ic, Volume of Appendices, War Diary 14, Appendices 1–174, Russland. Reports and messages pertaining to own and enemy tactical situation, activity, losses, and order of battle in the Orlovka, Beketovka, and Chalchuta areas. Also included are a situation map (1:300,000) indicating disposition of Soviet forces in the Stalingrad area and an order of battle chart of Soviet units on the Stalingrad front. October 6–13, 1942.

Ia, Ic, Volume of Appendices, War Diary 14, Appendices 175–334, Russland. Reports and messages pertaining to own and enemy tactical situation, activity, losses, and order of battle in Stalingrad, Rossoshka, Kamyshin, and Leninsk areas. Also included are reports pertaining to transportation and training matters, increasing of combat strength on the Stalingrad Front, air reconnaissance, and a chart showing assignment of construction troops of the Sixth Army. October 13–21, 1942.

Ia, Ic, Volume of Appendices, War Diary 14, Appendices 335–468, Russland. Reports and messages pertaining to own and enemy tactical situation, activity, and losses in the Stalingrad, Leninsk, and Beketovka areas. Also included are a list of alert units subordinate to the Sixth Army, enemy information bulletin No. 11 "Stalingrad," order of battle charts of own and enemy units in the Stalingrad area, and a situation map (1:300,000) indicating disposition of Soviet units in the Stalingrad front. October 21–28, 1942.

Ia, Ic, Volume of Appendices, War Diary 14, Appendices 468a–588, Russland. Reports and messages pertaining to own and enemy tactical situation, activity, losses, and order of battle in the Stalingrad, Gratshi, and Repin areas. Also included are orders governing combat during the winter of 1942–43, relating to mission, assignment, combat from winter positions, training, and security and Führer directives concerning defensive combat. October 29–November 3, 1942.

Ia, Ic, Volume of Appendices, War Diary 14, Appendices 589–751, Russland. Reports and messages pertaining to own and enemy tactical situation, activities, losses, and order of battle in the Stalingrad area. Also included are a survey concerning status and utilization possibilities of Turkish battalions and march reports of engineering battalions concerning units designations, strength, weapons, date of arrival, and mission. November 4–12, 1942.

Ia, Zweitschrift des War Diary 13, Part 1. Copy of war journal relating to daily activities and tactical situation along the Sixth Army front in the area of Stalingrad, Frolovo, Sarepta, and Kletskaya. Also included are three situation maps (1:1,000,000) indicating disposition of Soviet and German forces in the area west of Stalingrad. July 20–August 26, 1942.

Ia, Zweitschrift des War Diary 13, Part 2. Copy of war journal regarding daily activities and tactical situation along the Sixth Army front in the area of Stalingrad, Sarepta, Belshoi, and Olchovka. Also included is a situation map (1:1,000,000) indicating disposition of Soviet and German forces in the Stalingrad area. August 26–October 5, 1942.

Ia, Zweitschrift des War Diary 14, Part 1. Copy of war journal containing chronological entries pertaining to daily activities and tactical situation along the Sixth Army front in the area of Stalingrad-Golubinka. October 6–November 11, 1942.

Ia, Angriff "Nordwind," Russland. Reports, orders, and maps (1:100,000 and 1:300,000) concerning Operation "Nordwind" (plans to destroy the Soviet forces between the Don and Volga rivers northwest of Stalingrad). September 3–15, 1942.

Ia, Volume of Appendices, War Diary 13, Lichtbilder. Photographs depicting the march of Sixth Army units to the Don River and the thrust to the Volga River and Stalingrad, and a study of Sixth Army combat operations from Kharkov to Stalingrad. May 21–October 26, 1942.

Ia, War Diary 14, Russland. War diary pertaining to tactical operations of Sixth Army units in the Stalingrad area. October 6–November 19, 1942.

Ia, Appendix, War Diary 14, Russland, Situation Maps. Maps (1:20,000 and 1:100,000) concerning enemy situations, attack on Stalingrad North; city plans of Stalingrad; and Sixth Army check points. October–November 1942.

IIa, Volume of Appendices, Report, Russland. Reports concerning the granting of leave, awarding of decorations, casualties of Sixth Army personnel, and billeting and weather conditions in the Sixth Army sector; and a letter from General Paulus to corps and divisions adjutants concerning an army retraining course. June 13–October 28, 1942.

Ic, Report. Intelligence Branch activity reports. January 1–March 31, 1943.

Ia, War Diaries 15 and 16, "Festung Stalingrad." War journals 15 and 16 containing chronological entries pertaining to the situation and activities of the Sixth Army around Stalingrad. December 23, 1942–January 9, 1943.

Ia, Documents, War Diary 16, "Festung Stalingrad." Reports, orders, and directives concerning the German attack on Stalingrad; German casualties between November 21 and December 26, 1942; supplying of the army by air; and the German and Russian tactical situation. December 1942.

Ia, Documents, War Diary 16, "Festung Stalingrad." Data concerning German activity in the Stalingrad area, ration situation, German casualties and artillery losses, ammunition supply situation, and Russian tanks destroyed or disabled. November 1942.

Ia, Documents, War Diary 16, "Festung Stalingrad." Reports pertaining to the tactical situation and activities of Sixth Army units in the area around Stalingrad. November 1942–January 1943.

Ia, Documents, War Diary 16, "Festung Stalingrad." Reports pertaining to the tactical situation and activities of Sixth Army and operations, order of battle, and combat readiness of Sixth Army units in the Stalingrad area, and intelligence reports on enemy operations and troop identification and movements. August 30–September 3, 1942.

Ia, Ic, Volume of Appendices, War Diary 13, Russland. Reports and teletype messages concerning the tactical situation and operations, combat readiness, and subordination of Sixth Army units in the Stalingrad area, and intelligence reports on enemy operations and troop movements and identification. September 3–8, 1942.

Ia, Ic, Volume of Appendices, War Diary 13, Russland. Reports, orders, and teletype messages concerning the tactical situation, operations, and losses of Sixth Army units in the Stalingrad area; intelligence reports on enemy operations and troop identification and movements; enemy information bulletin pertaining to an appraisal of the enemy situation, defenses of Stalingrad, and order of battle and combat readiness of enemy units facing the Sixth Army; and maps (1:100,000 and 1:300,000) showing operational plans for the destruction of Soviet forces between the Don and Volga Rivers north of Stalingrad and the tactical grouping of Soviet forces around and north of Stalingrad. September 9–11, 1942.

Ia, Ic, Volume of Appendices, War Diary 13, Russland. Reports and teletype messages concerning tactical operations, training, combat readiness, and losses, and ammunition and operations, combat readiness, and ammunition and fuel supply situation of Sixth Army units in the Don River Bend area west of Stalingrad; intelligence reports on enemy operations and troop identification, movements, and losses; and enemy information bulletin "Stalingrad" giving an appraisal of the enemy situation, defenses, and organization of Soviet forces around Stalingrad. July 29–August 3, 1942.

Ia, Ic, Volume of Appendices, War Diary 13, Russland, Reports and teletype messages concerning the tactical situation and operations and subordination of Sixth Army units in the Don River Bend area west of Stalingrad; intelligence reports on enemy tactical operations and troop movements and identification; and a captured order of the People's Commissariat of Defense of the USSR, July 28, 1942. August 3–8, 1942.

War Diary 8a, "Festung Stalingrad." War journal containing reports on increasing supply difficulties, greater reliance on air supply, and finally, on January 17, the breakdown of all supply routes. The last few entries describe the increasing Soviet pressure and depleted supplies of munitions and food. November 22, 1942–January 21, 1943.

Ia, Ic, Volume of Appendices, War Diary 13, Russland. Reports and teletype messages pertaining to the tactical situation units at Stalingrad, a map (1:10,000) showing German antitank defenses, and a note from the Red Army High Command to General Paulus demanding the capitulation of German forces encircled at Stalingrad. December 1942–January 1943.

Ia, Documents, War Diary 16, "Festung Stalingrad." Daily reports pertaining to the tactical situation and activities of Sixth Army units in the area of Stalingrad. November–December 1942.

Ia, Various Documents, War Diary 16, "Festung Stalingrad." Daily reports pertaining to the tactical situation and activities of Sixth Army units in the Stalingrad area and a list of subordinate General Headquarters troops. January 1943.

Ia, Documents, War Diary 16, "Festung Stalingrad." Daily reports pertaining to the tactical situation and activities of Sixth Army units in the Stalingrad area. December 1, 1942–January 11, 1943.

Ia, Various Documents, War Diary 16, "Festung Stalingrad." Daily reports pertaining to the tactical situation and activities of Sixth Army units in the Stalingrad area, a map showing disposition of German units, and a report concerning Operation "Donnerschlag." December 1, 1942–January 13, 1943.

Ia, Volume of Appendices, War Diary, Russland. Orders and daily reports concerning the defense of and counter-attacks along the Don, Donets-Rostov, and Stalingrad fronts, tactical mission, ground and air operations, commitments, transportation, march movements, combat readiness, losses, and air reconnaissance, and the destruction of railroad bridges by Army Group Don, Sixth Army, Fourth Panzer Army, Armee-Abteilung Hollidt, and Air Fleet 4 units; and enemy order of battle, tactical mission, operations, and situation. Reports pertaining to air transportation of supplies to "Fortress Stalingrad," and armored, antitank, and assault gun situations. Also, combat reports of Seventh and Eleventh Rumanian Divisions and special directives for signal communication. January 4–12, 1943.

Ia, Volume of Appendices, War Diary, Russland. Orders and daily reports concerning the defense of and counter-attacks along the Don, Donets-Rostov, Volga, and Stalingrad fronts by Army Group Don, Sixth Army, Fourth Panzer Army, Third Rumanian Army, Armee-Abteilung Fretter-Pico, and Hollidt and Air Fleet 4 units; and enemy order of battle, tactical mission, operations, and situation. Reports pertaining to the construction of the "Mius" position in the Donets area, morale of the Rumanian forces, and experience gained during defense against major Russian attacks in Army Group Don Mitte sector. Also, special directives for air reconnaissance and report on preparations for the defense of Rostov, including maps (1:25,000) showing disposition of units defending the city. January 13–20, 1943.

Ia, Appendix, War Diary 1, "Armee-Abteilung Hollidt." File of the German staff attached to the Third Rumanian Army containing reports, orders and messages on the situation and activities in the Third Army area northeast of Rostov. Also operational and combat reports with map overlays (1:100,000) indicating disposition of Third Army units in the area around Oblivskaya. November 23–December 29, 1942.

Ia, War Diary 1, "Armee-Abteilung Hollidt." War journal of the German staff attached to the Third Rumanian Army (northeast of Rostov) containing daily battle and operation reports. November 23–December 31, 1942.

Ia, Appendix, War Diary 1, "Armee-Abteilung Hollidt." File of the German staff attached to Third Rumanian Army containing reports on the situation, activities and mission of the Third Rumanian Army in the Gusinka-Parchin-Ostrov-Golaya-Artenoff-Rytschon area. November 27–December 31, 1942.

Ia, Appendix, War Diary 1, "Armee-Abteilung Hollidt." Order of battle charts of components of the Third Rumanian Army. December 1942.

Ia, Appendix, War Diary 1, "Armee-Abteilung Hollidt." Order of battle chart of "Armee-Abteilung Hollidt." Twenty-six sketches (1:300,000) of situations of units at the front (southeast of Boguchar). November 1942.

Ia, Appendix, War Diary 1, "Armee-Abteilung Hollidt." Eight situation maps (1:300,000 and 1:100,000) of German and Soviet Forces on the Don-Chir front. December 1942.

Ic, Report, Rum. AOK 3. Intelligence and battle reports of the German staff attached to the Third Rumanian Army. December 5–31, 1942.

Ia, Situation of Army Group Don. Maps (1:100,000) showing the daily tactical disposition of Army Group Don, First and Fourth Panzer Armies, and Armee-Abteilung Fretter-Pico and Hollidt in the Don, Donets, Rostov, Kalitva, Ssal, Derkul, Ssalsk, and Asov areas and the steadily diminishing territory held by the encircled Sixth Army at Stalingrad, until captured or destroyed by January 31, 1943.

Selected messages from Sixth Army to Headquarters Group South NAFU.

Daily Reports of Ia Army Group Don November 1942–January 1943.

Daily Situation Reports, Sixth Army to Army Group Don, January 1943.

Records of Headquarters, German Army High Command, Part III, including correspondence, memoranda pertaining to plans regarding campaign in Russia . . . high level data, usually marked "Chefsache" 1942; statements of Russian POWs concerning Rumanian resistance northwest of Stalingrad, November 30, 1942 on.

Film T-78–Roll 574: Soviet directives to camp commanders on the treatment of German prisoners of war and deserters. Roll 576: Informants' reports and Russian POW statements concerning Soviet recruiting; also reports on the utilization of women in the Red Army, August 1942–August 1943. Roll 581: Russian POW statements. Roll 587: Maps showing presumed Red Army operational intentions along the entire Eastern Front, November 6, 1942–January 1943. Roll 276: Original Russian Military Orders; Treatment of POWs; Interrogation Lists, 1941–42. Roll 1374: Russian writers during the war; Collection of letters written by enlisted men and officers of Red Army to Soviet writers during World War II. Roll 1379: Collection of Stalin's speeches; Stalin's orders to various front commanders, 1943.

National Archives Microfilm Numbers T-78/39; T-84/188; T-84/262; T-175/264; T-311/268, 270, 292.

In the Days of the Great Battle—Collection of Documents on Stalingrad. Stalingrad, 1958.

Dossiers on Russian and German generals (from U.S. Army Counter Intelligence Corps).

Sbornik (Collection of materials for the study of war experiences), published by the Red Army General Staff in 1943 (not intended for circulation outside the Soviet Union).

"A Visit to the Don-Stalingrad Front" from *Military Reports on the United Nations*, No. 4, March 15, 1943.

Guide to Foreign Military Studies, U.S. Army, Europe, 1954. Ms. #T-14—Army Group Don: Reverses on the Southern Wing, 1942–1943. Ms. #T-15—Sixth Army: Airlift to Stalingrad, November 1942–February 1943. Ms. #D-036—The Fighting Qualities of the Russian Soldier. Ms. #P-137—Espionage Activities of the USSR. Ms. #D-271—Stalingrad, signal communications. Ms. #C-065—Greiner diaries (notes on conferences and decisions in the OKW, 1939–1943). Ms. #P-060g—Sixth Panzer Division, enroute to Stalingrad.

Newspapers: *Berliner Lokal—Anzeiger; Das Reich; Deutsche Allgemeine Zeitung* (Berlin Issue); *Essener Allgemeine*.

For other periodicals and newspapers, as well as diaries, letters, and miscellaneous documents, see Chapter Notes.

Chapter Notes

Certain books and documents have proved extremely helpful as references for almost every chapter. To avoid needless repetition I will mention these works only once; this is not to minimize their importance.

Istoriya Velikoi Otechestvennoi Voiny Sovetskogo Soyuza 1941–1945 (History of the Great Patriotic War of the Soviet Union), 6 vols., Moscow, 1961; also, a one volume version of this work, *Velikaya Otechestvennaya Voina Sovetskogo Soyuza.*

Vtoraya Mirovaya, Voina, 1939–45 by S. P. Platonov and others; Moscow, 1958.

War Diary, German Sixth Army and related material (see Documents).

War Diary, German Army High Command (see Bibliography).

The Italian Eighth Army in the Second Defensive Battle of the Don: December 11, 1942–January 31, 1943. Rome, 1946.

Nazi Conspiracy and Aggression. 10 vols., Washington, D.C., 1946–48.

Trials of War Criminals Before the Nuremberg Military Tribunals. 15 vols., Washington, D.C., 1951–52.

Chapter One

GERMAN SIXTH ARMY MARCH ACROSS THE STEPPE

From interviews with Helmut Bangert, Friedrich Breining, Franz Deifel, Karl Englehardt, Werner Gerlach, Hans Jülich, Dionys Kaiser, Emil

Metzger, and Kurt Siol. Also Wolfgang Werthen's *History of the Sixteenth Panzer Division* and Rolf Gram's *The Fourteenth Panzer Division, 1940–45*.

OPERATION BLUE OBJECTIVES

From OKW Directives 43 and 45. Also Franz Halder diary.

FRIEDRICH VON PAULUS

Interview with his son Ernst Paulus; Field Marshal Paulus's private papers; and Walter Goerlitz's *Paulus and Stalingrad*.

THE SATELLITE ARMIES

Interviews with Giuseppe Aleandri, Felice Bracci, Cristoforo Capone, Veniero Marsan, Ugo Rampelli, and Enrico Reginato; Records of German Military Mission to Rumania (see Documents).

Chapter Two

HITLER'S HEADQUARTERS AT VINNITSA

From interview with Adolf Heusinger; Halder diary. Also Albert Speer's *Inside the Third Reich* and Walter Warlimont's *Inside Hitler's Headquarters 1939–45*. In the D Papers (see Documents) the Director of Espionage in Moscow asked the Lucy network to pinpoint Hitler's headquarters during the summer of 1942. Lucy did.

Chapter Three

STALIN

From an interview with Governor W. Averell Harriman, who spent more time with him than any other Western diplomat. Also Robert Conquest's *The Great Terror* and Bertram Wolfe's *Three Who Made a Revolution*.

RUDOLF ROSSLER AND LEONARD TREPPER

From an interview with Mrs. David Dallin; the D Papers, a collection of messages transmitted between the Director in Moscow and the Lucy network in Switzerland. Also Accoce's and Quet's *The Lucy Ring* and Gilles Perrault's *The Red Orchestra*.

Just before Operation Blue commenced in June, 1942, a German officer named Reichel crashed behind Russian lines. Since he carried plans for the initial phase of the attack on Voronezh, German Intelligence assumed the Russians' later moves to bolster the defense of that city were based on

Reichel's maps and data. It is far more likely that STAVKA made its decisions from Lucy's radio reports. The Reichel affair drove Hitler into a rage at his field commanders; he sacked several and reaffirmed his own growing mistrust of senior officers in the Wehrmacht.

Chapter Four

THE HISTORY OF TSARITSYN–STALINGRAD–VOLGOGRAD

From Maurice Hindus's *Mother Russia* and M. A. Vodolagin's *Outline of the History of Volgograd.*

STALINGRAD'S TOPOGRAPHY

From interviews with Luba Bessanova, Tania Chernova and the author's own impressions during a battlefield tour. Also Victor Nekrassov's *Front Line Stalingrad* and Yeremenko's *Stalingrad.*

PREPARATIONS FOR THE DEFENSE OF STALINGRAD

From A. D. Kolesnik's *The Great Victory on the Volga, 1942–1943;* V. Koroteev's *Stalingrad Sketches* and *I Saw It;* A. M. Samsonov's *The Stalingrad Battle* and *Stalingrad Epopeya;* M. A. Vodolagin's *The Defense of Stalingrad* and *Stalingrad in the Great Patriotic War;* Kantor and Tazurin's *The Volgarians in the Battles Around Stalingrad;* Yeremenko's *Stalingrad.*

Chapter Five

THE ROUT OF THE RUSSIAN ARMIES WEST OF THE DON

From interviews with Ignacy Changar, Jacob Grubner, Hersch Gurewicz, Nikolai Tomskuschin, and a former Red Army colonel who asked to remain anonymous.

THE FIGHT FOR KALACH

From interviews with Josef Linden and Gerhard Meunch. From Pyotr Ilyin's reminiscences in *Voyenno-Istoricheskii Zhurnal* (hereinafter referred to as *V.I.Z.*), no. 10. 1961.. Also *Das Kleeblatt,* the German Seventy-first Division Magazine, and Paul Carell's *Hitler Moves East 1941–43.*

THE GERMAN BREAKTHROUGH TO THE VOLGA

From interviews with Friedrich Breining, Franz Bröder, Hans Jülich, Ottmar Kohler, Hans Oettl, Arthur Schmidt. From statements by Franz

Brendgen. Also Werthen's *History of the Sixteenth Panzer Division* and Gerhard von Dieckhoff's *The Third Infantry Division (Motorized)*. Also Y. Chepurin's "The Fire Frontier," *Izvestia*, February 2, 1963; S. Dyhne's Ruben's "Drops of Blood," *Voyennyi Vestnik*, no. 2, 1968; and N. Melnikov's "Let Us Fraternize," *Krasnaya Zvezda*, February 2, 1963. Also Yeremenko's *Stalingrad*. Ruben Ibarruri was the son of Dolores Ibarruri, La Passionaria of Spanish Civil War fame. Ruben died trying to hold the Germans at the approaches to Stalingrad.

Chapter Six

THE BOMBING OF STALINGRAD AND ITS EFFECTS

From interviews with Alexander Akimov, Gregori Denisov, Kirill Sazykin, Pyotr Zabarskikh and recollections of Mrs. K. Karmanova, Mrs. V. N. Kliagina, V. Nekrassov, P. Nerozia, C. Viskov, and M. Vodolagin in Agapov's *After The Battle;* E. Genkina's *Heroic Stalingrad;* E. Gerasimov's *The Stalingradians;* V. Koroteev's *I Saw It;* V. Nekrassov's *Front Line Stalingrad;* I. Paderin's *In the Main Direction,* and M. A. Vodolagin's *The Defense of Stalingrad* and *Under the Walls of Stalingrad.* Also Nikita Khrushchev's *Khrushchev Remembers;* Yeremenko's *Stalingrad;* and A. Zarubina's *Women in the Defense of Stalingrad;* also *The Epic Story of Stalingrad* (Collection).

Chapter Seven

GERMAN CORRIDOR TO THE VOLGA

From interviews with Franz Bröder, Ottmar Kohler, Hans Oettl; statements by Franz Brendgen and Otto von der Heyde; also Werthen's *History of the Sixteenth Panzer Division* and Dieckhoff's *The Third Infantry Division (Motorized)*.

RUSSIAN DEFENSE

From interviews with Alexander Akimov, Gregori Denisov, Jacob Grubner. Also E. Genkina's *Heroic Stalingrad;* E. Gerasimov's *The Stalingradians;* A. D. Kolesnik's *The Great Victory on the Volga;* L. P. Koren's *There Is a Cliff on the Volga;* V. Koroteev's *Stalingrad Sketches* and *I Saw It;* I. M. Loginov's *The Militia in the Battle for Its Homeland.* Also Red Army Front Newspaper, August 31, 1942. Also Samsonov's *The Stalingrad Battle* and *Stalingrad Epopeya;* Yeremenko's *Stalingrad; The Epic Story of Stalingrad* (collection); and *The Fight for Stalingrad* (collection).

Chapter Eight

STALIN AND ZHUKOV

From Zhukov's *Marshal Zhukov's Greatest Battles* and *The Memoirs of Marshal Zhukov;* also Zhukov and Vasilevsky in *Stalingrad Epopeya.*

HITLER, HALDER, JODL

From an interview with Adolf Heusinger plus Halder's diary. Also William L. Shirer's *The Rise and Fall of the Third Reich* and Speer's *Inside the Third Reich.*

FOURTH PANZER ARMY ADVANCE

From interviews with Fritz Dieckmann and Hubert Wirkner; Han Schüler's diary; plus German Twenty-ninth Motorized Division History; also V. Chuikov's *The Battle for Stalingrad;* plus Paul Carell's *Hitler Moves East.*

KHRUSHCHEV'S CONVERSATION WITH STALIN

From Khrushchev's *Khrushchev Remembers.*

Chapter Nine

VASSILI CHUIKOV'S ASSUMPTION OF COMMAND

From N. I. Krylov in *Stalingrad Epopeya;* Chuikov's *The Battle for Stalingrad* and Yeremenko's *Stalingrad.*

THE MEETINGS AT THE KREMLIN

From A. M. Vasilevsky in *Stalingrad Epopeya* and Zhukov's *Marshal Zhukov's Greatest Battles* and *The Memoirs of Marshal Zhukov.*

THE ENTRY OF GERMAN INFANTRY INTO CENTRAL STALINGRAD

From interviews with Günter von Below, Gerhard Dietzel, Gerhard Meunch, Arthur Schmidt; statement by Hans Schüler. Also Werner Halle's diary in Twenty-ninth Division history.

RUSSIAN COUNTERMOVES (this and next two chapters)

Chuikov's *The Battle for Stalingrad;* A. S. Chuyanov's "From the Stalingrad Diary," *Oktyaber* no. 2, 1968; E. Kriger's article in *Izvestia,* Feb. 3, 1970; Ivan Paderin's "Infantryman of the Party," *Krasnaya Zvedza,* Feb. 2, 1963, and his *In the Main Direction;* Colonels Petrakov and Yelin's recollections in *The Fight for Stalingrad;* A. I. Rodimtsev's "Stormy Days and Nights," *Yunost,* no. 2, 1968; his *On the Banks of the Mandanares and Volga* and *On the Last Frontier,* and his excerpted diary in *Sovetskaya Rossiya,* Feb. 1, 1970; K. K. Rokossovsky's "The Stalingrad Epopeya," *Sputnik,* no. 2, 1968; I. Samchuk's *The Thirteenth Guards;* M. Vavilova's "A Severe Existence" in *Krasnaya Zvezda,* Feb. 1, 1963; Samsonov's *The Stalingrad Battle* and *Stalingrad Epopeya.*

Chapter Ten

SOVIET CIVILIANS

From B. V. Druzhinin (collection) *Two Hundred Fiery Days;* Genkina, Gerasimov, Grossman and Koroteev (works previously cited); Vodolagin's *Under the Walls of Stalingrad.*

THE GERMAN SEVENTY-FIRST DIVISION

From interviews with Gunter von Below and Gerhard Meunch; also daily reports of the Seventy-first Infantry Division.

THE VOLGA CROSSING BY SOVIET REINFORCEMENTS
FOR THE SIXTY-SECOND ARMY

From interviews with Tania Chernova, Pyotr Deriabin and Alexei Petrov. Also Chuikov's *The Battle for Stalingrad,* Genkina's *Heroic Stalingrad;* Gerasimov's *The Stalingradians;* V. I. Grossman's *Stalingrad Hits Back*; M. Ingor's *Siberians—The Heroes of Stalingrad*; V. Koroteev's *Stalingrad Sketches* and *I Saw It*; Samsonov's *Stalingrad Epopeya* and *The Stalingrad Battle.*

ATTITUDE OF GERMAN SOLDIERS IN LATE SEPTEMBER

From interviews with Wilhelm Alter, Karl Binder, Friedrich Breining, Emil Metzger, Josef Metzler, Hans Oettl, Herbert Rentsch, Carl Rodenburg; also Paul Epple, Georg Frey, Karl Geist, Anton Kappler, Oskar Stange.

OPERATION URANUS TALKS

Zhukov's memoirs previously cited. Vasilevsky's "Unforgettable Days," *V.I.Z.,* 1965. Also Samsonov's *The Stalingrad Battle* and *Stalingrad Epopeya.*

Chapter Eleven

PAVLOV'S HOUSE

From I. F. Afanasyev's *House of The Soldier's Fame,* and his article in *Krasnaya Zvedza,* Feb. 2, 1963. Also I. Gummer and Y. Harin's *Heroes of The Big Battle*; V. Gurkin's "The Pavlov House," *V.I.Z.*, no. 2, 1963. L. Savelyev's "I Am From the House of Pavlov," *Sovetskaya Rossiya*, Feb. 2, 1963. Also Ronald Seth's *Stalingrad: Point of Return.*

SNIPING AND ZAITSEV'S DUEL WITH MAJOR KONINGS
From an interview with Tania Chernova. Also V. Zaitsev's *Notes of a Sniper* and V. Yuriev's *The Great Victory of Stalingrad; V.I.Z.*, no. 8, 1966; Chuikov's *The Battle for Stalingrad.*

GERMAN BUILDUP AND ATTACK ON FACTORY DISTRICT
From interviews with Wilhelm Alter, Eugen Bäumann, Karl Binder, Franz Deifel, Heinz Giessel, Heinrich Klotz, Ottmar Kohler, Heinz Neist, Arthur Schmidt, and Rudolf Taufer. Also Sixth Army records, October 6–30 (see Documents).

SOVIET INTELLIGENCE OPERATIONS AND AIR STRENGTH
From Chuikov's *The Battle for Stalingrad*; N. Denisov's "On Airports Near the Volga," *Aviatska I. Kosmonavtika*, no. 1, 1968. I. Dynin's "Smoky Sky," *Krasnaya Zvezda*, Feb. 2, 1968; N. E. Lentchevsky's *Trial by Fire;* A. Vladimirov's "Air Force in the Battle of Stalingrad" in *Vestnik Vozduznoge Flota*, May 1943.

RUSSIAN DEFENSE OF THE FACTORIES
From interviews with Alexander Akimov, Pyotr Deriabin, Hersch Gurewicz, Alexei Petrov, and Pyotr Zabavkiksh. Also Boris Filimonov's *The Immortals;* V. Gartchinko's "Tempered in the Fire," *Krasnaya Zvezda*, Feb. 2, 1968; Genkina's *Heroic Stalingrad;* Gerasimov's *The Stalingradians;* A. Kolesnik's *The Great Battle on the Volga;* I. Lyudnikov's "Soldiers on the Barricades," *Ogonyok*, no. 5, 1968; I. Paderin's *In the Main Direction;* E. T. Siserov in *The Fight for Stalingrad;* I. Semin's *Stalingrad Tales.*

Chapter Twelve

FIGHTING AROUND THE BARRIKADY AND RED OCTOBER PLANT
From interviews with Ignacy Changar, Tania Chernova, Hersch Gurewicz, Heinz Neist, Alexei Petrov, Ernst Wohlfahrt and from diaries of Karl Binder and Wilhelm Kreiser. Also German Seventy-ninth Division History—*The Way of the Seventy-ninth Infantry Division, 1939–1945*, and a series of orders to German 305th Division regiments on seizing the factory district, plus K. S. Belov's *From the Volga to Prague;* N. I. Biryukov's *Two Hundred Days in Battle;* A. D. Kolesnik's *The Great Victory on the Volga;* A. D. Stupov's *The Sixty-second Army in the Stalingrad Battles;* and Samsonov's *The Stalingrad Battle* and *Stalingrad Epopeya.*

Chapter Thirteen

RUSSIAN BUILDUP AND GERMAN REACTION

From interviews with Winrich Behr, Gregori Denisov, Hersch Gurewicz, Alexei Petrov, Emil Metzger, Arthur Schmidt, Wolf Pelikan; a statement by Karl Ostarhild (see Second Television Company, Wiesbaden, Germany, documentary film on twenty-fifth anniversary of Battle of Stalingrad); and a report by German Intelligence East, September–November, 1942. Also Reinhard Gehlen's *The Service* and Goerlitz's *Paulus and Stalingrad*. For statements by Batov, Kazakov, Lelyushenko, Popov, Rokossovsky, Telegin, Vasilevsky, Zheltov, Zhukov, etc., see Samsonov's *Stalingrad Epopeya* and *The Stalingrad Battle*, as well as Freiherr von Richthofen's diary.

Chapter Fourteen

HITLER'S SPEECH IN MUNICH

From Speer's *Inside the Third Reich*. The author also visited the Löwenbräukeller and inspected the stage where Hitler accepted his cronies' applause.

THE PIONEERS AND LYUDNIKOV

From interviews with Karl Binder, Wilhelm Giebeler, Josef Linden, Ernst Wohlfahrt; also Linden monograph, Eugen Rettenmaier's diary and Herbert Selle's *The Tragedy of Stalingrad;* Lyudnikov's "There Is A Cliff on The Volga" from Druzhinin's *Two Hundred Fiery Days;* Lyudnikov's article in *Ogonyok*, no. 5, Jan. 1968; S. Glukhovsky's *Lyudnikov's Island*.

SOVIET BUILDUP

The D papers (previously mentioned).

Chapter Fifteen

CONDITIONS IN THE STEPPE

From interviews with Friedrich Breining, Karl Binder, Ekkehart Brunnert, Karl Englehardt, Herbert Rentsch, Gottlieb Slotta; also Herbert Selle's *The Tragedy of Stalingrad*.

SOVIET SOLDIERS LIFE BEHIND THE FRONT LINES

From interviews with Alexander Akimov, Ignacy Changar, Tania Chernova, Pyotr Deriabin, Hersch Gurewicz, and Alexei Petrov. Also Genkina's *Heroic Stalingrad* and Gerasimov's *The Stalingradians;* Grossman's *Stalingrad Hits Back*.

STALIN–VOLSKY

From Vasilevsky and Zhukov in *Stalingrad Epopeya.* Also Zhukov's own memoirs (previously mentioned), and V. T. Volsky's story in *V.I.Z.*, no. 10, 1965.

THE APPROACH TO ZERO HOUR

Interviews with Winrich Behr, Hermann Kästle, Wolf Pelikan, Alexei Petrov, and Abraham Spitkovsky. Also Werthen's *History of the Sixteenth Panzer Division.*

Chapter Sixteen

RUSSIAN OFFENSIVE (November 19–27, Chapters Sixteen and Seventeen.)

From interviews with Wilhelm Altar, Winrich Behr, Karl Binder, Horst Caspari, Franz Deifel, Pyotr Deriabin, Gerhard Dietzel, Isabella Feige, Karl Geist, Heinz Giessel, Gerhard Hässler, Herman Kästle, Dionys Kaiser, Leah Kalei, Heinz Lieber, Josef Linden, Xaver Marx, Wolf Pelikan, Albert Pflüger, Wilhelm Plass, Carl Rodenburg, Arthur Schmidt, Abraham Spitkovsky, Eugen Steinhilber, Siegfried Wendt, and statements by Karl Ostarhild (television documentary mentioned previously). Also, Heinz Schröter's *Stalingrad;* Herbert Selle's *The Tragedy of Stalingrad;* German Motorized Twenty-ninth Division history; Gram's *The Fourteenth Panzer Division;* Werthen's *History of the Sixteenth Panzer Division;* and *The 384th Infantry Division* (privately published); and Alex Buchner's Combat Report of Second Battalion, Sixty-fourth Armored Infantry Regiment. Also, the War Diary of the Seventy-sixth Infantry Division and Karl Binder diary; Rumanian Army Records (see Documents for this period); plus Goerlitz's *Paulus and Stalingrad;* Carell's *Hitler Moves East,* and Philippi and Heim's *The Campaign Against Soviet Russia 1941–1945.* Also, P. I. Batov's *In Campaigns and Battles;* Michael Bragin's "Stalingrad—Uranus, Saturn and Tanks," *Moscva,* no. 2, 1968; M. Popov's "South of Stalingrad," *V.I.Z.,* no. 2, 1961; Rokossovsky's "Victory on The Volga," *V.I.Z.,* no. 2, 1968; A. Telegin's "Between Volga and Don," *Voyenny Vestnik,* no. 2, 1963; A. Zheltov's "The Southwest Front of the Counterattack of Stalingrad," *V.I.Z.,* no. 11, 1967; P. Zhidkov's "How the Ring Around the German Sixth Army Was Closed," *V.I.Z.,* no. 3, 1962; also A. P. Bachurin's *Front Memoirs;* Chuikov's *The Battle for Stalingrad;* Khrushchev's memoir; Koroteev's *Stalingrad Miracle;* K. Morozov's *The Regiments Fought Like Guards* and *The Fight for the Volga;* and various participants' recollections in Samsonov's *Stalingrad Epopeya;* and Yeremenko and Zhukov books previously cited.

Contrary to many Western accounts, the vital bridge at Kalach fell on November 22, not November 21.

Chapter Seventeen

COLLAPSE OF RUMANIAN ARMIES AND REPERCUSSIONS

From Winrich Behr diary; records of German military mission to Rumania (see Documents); Frank Capra's documentary movie *The Battle for Russia;* Henry Cassidy's *Moscow Dateline;* Erich von Manstein's *Lost Victories;* General Platon Chirnoaga's monograph on unfairness of Germans to their Rumanian allies.

EAST PRUSSIAN CONFERENCES

From interview with Adolf Heusinger; Kurt Zeitzler's remarks in *The Fatal Decisions;* Cajus Bekker's *The Luftwaffe War Diaries;* also Carell's *Hitler Moves East, 1941–1943.*

NEWLY FORMED KESSEL

From interviews with Karl Binder, Hermann Kästle, Emil Metzger, Heinz Neist, Hans Oettl, Albert Pflüger, Arthur Schmidt; Schüler diaries; Günter Toepke's book; also Wilhelm Kreiser diary.

Chapter Eighteen

THE AIRLIFT

From Paulus' private papers and Richthofen diary; Cajus Bekker's *The Luftwaffe War Diaries;* Goerlitz's *Paulus and Stalingrad;* Fritz Morjik's *The German Transport Command in the Second World War;* H. von Rohden's *The Luftwaffe Struggle for Stalingrad;* also Carell's *Hitler Moves East 1941–1943.*

THE KESSEL AND RUSSIAN ATTACKS

From interviews with Karl Binder, plus Binder diary; Franz Deifel, Hersch Gurewicz, Anton Kappler, Heinrich Klotz, Heinz Lieber, Albert Pflüger, Friedrich Syndicus, Hubert Wirkner; also statements by Wilhelm Plass and Rudi Pothmann; Eugen Rettenmaier diary. Also von Dieckhoff's *The Twenty-ninth Motorized Division History;* A. D. Kolesnik's *The Great Victory on the Volga* and V. Koroteev's, *Stalingrad Miracle, Stalingrad Sketches* and *I Saw it.*

Chapter Nineteen

OPERATION WINTER STORM

From interview with Alexei Petrov. From War Diary Tank Regiment Eleven, Sixth Panzer Division (see Horst Schiebert's *Relief Operation—*

Stalingrad); also Manstein's *Lost Victories;* Ms. number P-060g; Sixth
Panzer Division, en route to Stalingrad, December 1942 (see Documents);
A. M. Vasilevsky's "Unforgettable Days" *V.I.Z.*, no. 3, 1966; also Felix
Gilbert's *Hitler Directs His War.* Also Manstein's *Lost Victories,* Paulus'
private papers; Arthur Schmidt's critique (unpublished).

KESSEL
From interviews with Ekkehart Brunnert, Tania Chernova, Ignacy
Changar, and Heinz Neist; plus diary of Wilhelm Kreiser and Eugen Retten-
maier; also Koroteev's *Stalingrad Miracle;* I. Paderin's *In the Main Direction.*

Chapter Twenty

RELIEF ATTEMPT
From interviews with Josef Linden, Gerhard Meunch, Alexei Petrov,
and Arthur Schmidt; also Schmidt's unpublished manuscript on details of
relief operations through December 25 (see next two chapers). From
Goerlitz's *Paulus and Stalingrad;* and Manstein's *Lost Victories;* also Friedrich Paulus's private papers.

Chapter Twenty-One

ARMY GROUP DON—SIXTH ARMY CONVERSATIONS
From interviews with Winrich Behr and Arthur Schmidt; Schmidt
manuscript and communications log between both groups (see Documents
for appropriate dates). Also Sixth Panzer Division manuscript referred to
in previous chapter notes and Horst Scheibert's *Relief Operation-Stalingrad;*
plus Carell's *Hitler Moves East;* Goerlitz's *Paulus and Stalingrad* and
Schröter's *Stalingrad.*

THE ITALIAN EIGHTH ARMY
From interviews with Giuseppe Aleandri, Felice Bracci, Cristoforo Capone, Stelio Sansone. Also Umberto Salvatore's *Bersaglieri on the Don.*

Chapter Twenty-Two

THE CONTINUING ROUT OF THE ITALIAN EIGHTH ARMY
From interviews as noted in preceding chapter. German communications between Gumrak and Novocherkassk (see Documents as noted in
previous chapters).

SIXTH PANZER DIVISION ADVANCE
(see previous citations.)

SITUATION INSIDE KESSEL

From interviews with Ekkehart Brunnert, Albert Pflüger, Ernst Wohlfahrt; Karl Binder diary.

AIRLIFT BREAKDOWN

From Bekker's *The Luftwaffe War Diaries;* Carell's *Hitler Moves East;* and Morzik's *The German Transport Command in the Second World War.*

Chapter Twenty-Three

THE CHRISTMAS SEASON (also in next chapter)

From interviews with Hans Bräunlein, Karl Binder, Ekkehart Brunnert, Mikhail Goldstein, Emil Metzger, Gerhard Meunch, Hans Oettl and Albert Pflüger. Also Sacha Fillipov in *The Great Victory in Stalingrad,* Moscow: 1950; plus previously mentioned works by Gerasimov and Koroteev. Also Koroteev's *I Saw It;* Schröter's *Stalingrad;* and Werthen's *History of the Sixteenth Panzer Division.* The author listened to the Ring Broadcast, played during the twenty-fifth anniversary documentary on German television.

TELETYPE

See previous chapter notes.

Chapter Twenty-Four

TEDDY–KLAUS EXCHANGE

From von Below family papers (microfilm in National Archives, Washington, D.C.).

KREMLIN MEETING

From Yeremenko's *Stalingrad;* Zhukov's memoirs; and Khrushchev's memoir.

ITALIANS

From interview with Felice Bracci and his unpublished manuscript, a harrowing story.

Chapter Twenty-Five

MAIL

From unpublished letters on file in German archives at Freiburg. Also Karl Binder's letters to his wife.

Chapter Twenty-Six

DETERIORATION OF GERMAN TROOPS

From interviews with Günter von Below, Ekkehart Brunnert, Ignacy Changar, Hermann Kästle, Heinrich Klotz, Ottmar Kohler, Gerhard Meunch, Hans Oettl, Alexei Petrov.

ITALIANS

From interviews with Felice Bracci, Cristoforo Capone, and Veniero Marsan. Also Bracci's manuscript and Enrico Reginato's *Twelve Years of Prison in the USSR.*

Chapter Twenty-Seven

THE COLLAPSE OF THE POCKET (January 10–20)

From interviews with Eugen Baumann, Winrich Behr, Karl Binder, Hans Bräunlein, Franz Bröder, Horst Caspari, Pyotr Deriabin, Fritz Dieckman, Georg Frey, Werner Gerlach, Anton Kappler, Emil Metzger, Albert Pflüger, Carl Rodenburg, Gottlieb Slotta, and Hubert Wirkner. Also statements by Wilhelm Plass and Rudi Pothmann; Selle's *The Tragedy of Stalingrad;* and Third Motorized; Twenty-ninth Motorized, and 384th Division histories. Also Ninth Flak Division war diaries; and Valeriu Campianu's *The Stalingrad Siege,* written in Bucharest in 1945; N. N. Voronov article in *Krasnaya Zvezda,* Feb. 1, 1963.

MALINOVSKY

From *The New York Times* dispatch. Also *The Red Army* by Walter Kerr and Alexander Werth's *The Year of Stalingrad.*

Chapter Twenty-Eight

EAST PRUSSIA MEETINGS

From interview with Winrich Behr and statement by Coelestin von Zitzewitz. Also Carell's *Hitler Moves East,* and Goerlitz' *Paulus and Stalingrad.*

LOSS OF PITOMNIK AND GUMRAK

From interviews with Wilhelm Alter, Franz Deifel, Ottmar Kohler, Emil Metzger, Josef Metzler, Gerhard Meunch, Heinz Neist, Albert Pflüger,

Gottlieb Slotta, and Hubert Wirkner. Also Selle's *The Tragedy of Stalingrad;* Joachim Wieder's *Stalingrad: How It Really Was.* Sixth Army radio traffic (see Documents for appropriate dates).

The Luftwaffe lost 488 planes on the shuttle to the Kessel. A pilot named Wieser was the last to fly from the pocket (January 25).

In his book, Colonel Adam mentions the wide-spread rumor among Sixth Army officers that General Schmidt kept a light plane at the airport for an escape from the *Kessel*. In my conversations with Schmidt, he admits that he planned to fly out, but only long enough to plead for more help from Hitler.

Paulus refused to let him go.

Chapter Twenty-Nine

SURRENDER AND AFTERMATH

From interviews with Wilhelm Alter, Helmut Bangert, Eugen Baumann, Günter von Below, Karl Binder, Hans Bräunlein, Friedrich Breining, Franz Bröder, Horst Caspari, Franz Deifel, Gregori Denisov, Pyotr Deriabin, Fritz Dieckmann, Gerhard Dietzel, Karl Englehardt, Paul Epple, Isabella Feige, Karl Floeck, George Frey, Karl Geist, Wilhelm Giebeler, Werner Gerlach, Heinz Giessel, Adolf Heusinger, Hans Jülich, Dionys Kaiser, Anton Kappler, Hermann Kästle, Herbert Kreiner, Heinrich Klotz, Ottmar Kohler, Heinz Lieber, Josef Linden, Emil Metzger, Josef Metzler, Heinz Neist, Hans Oettl, Alexei Petrov, Ernst Paulus, Albert Pflüger, Mesten Pover, Herbert Rentsch, Carl Rodenburg, Arthur Schmidt, Albert Schön, Kurt Siol, Gottlieb Slotta, Oscar Stange, Eugen Steinhilber, Friedrich Syndicus, Rudolf Taufer, Siegfried Wendt, Hubert Wirkner, Ernst Wohlfahrt, and Pyotr Zabavskikh. Also statements by Franz Brendgen, Berthold Englert, August Kronmüller, Xaver Marx, Hans Schüler and unpublished monograph by Arthur Schmidt on last days. Also Professor Jay Baird's "The Myth of Stalingrad" in *Institute of Contemporary History*, vol. 4, no. 3, July 1969.

German works dealing extensively with the end of the battle include: Wilhelm Adam's *The Hard Decision;* Hans Dibold's *Doctor at Stalingrad;* Philip Humbert's article in *Der Spiegel*, no. 5, 1949; Theodor Plievier's *Stalingrad* and Wieder's *Stalingrad.* (see Ludwig affidavit). Among many Russian books and periodicals on the surrender are P. Batov's *In Campaigns and Battles;* V. Grinevsky's "The Last Days," *Krasnaya Zvezda*, Feb. 2, 1963; I. Laskin's "Once More on the Capture of General Field Marshal Paulus," *V.I.Z.* 1961; I. Morozov's *The Fight for the Volga;* K. K. Rokossovsky's "The Morning of Our Victory," *Izvestia*, Feb. 1, 1968; M. S. Shumilov in *Komsomolskaya Pravda*, Feb. 1, 1963; L. A. Vinokur's "In Those Days," *Sovetskaya Rossiya*, Feb. 2, 1958; P. Vladimirov's "The Encounter," *Krasnaya Zvezda*, Feb. 2, 1963. Also: Rokossovsky, Shumilov and Voronov in Samsonov's *Stalingrad Epopeya*.

Others: Agapov's *After the Battle;* Chuikov's *The Battle for Stalingrad;* Druzhinin's *Two Hundred Fiery Days;* A. Werth's *Russia At War, 1941–1945.*

Chapter Thirty

THE WRECKAGE OF WAR

From interviews with Ignacy Changar, Tania Chernova, Hersch Gurewicz. Also A. S. Chuyanov's *Stalingrad Is Reviving*, written in 1944; and A. M. Samsonov's *The Stalingrad Battle*, the best analysis of destruction in the city.

PRISON CAMPS AND CANNIBALISM

From interviews with Germans listed in preceding chapter and with Felice Bracci and Cristoforo Capone. Also Bracci's diary; Reginato's *Twelve Years of Prison in the USSR;* Don Guido Turla's *Seven Rubles to the Chaplain;* and a report by Guiseppe Aleandri on the treatment accorded the Axis POWs in Russia.

After Twelve Years

In September 1955, Konrad Adenauer, Chancellor of the new West German government, flew to Moscow to meet the leaders of the USSR. During their discussions, Adenauer broached a sensitive topic:

". . . Let me start with the question of the release of those Germans who are still imprisoned within the area or sphere of influence of the Soviet Union, or who are otherwise prevented from leaving this area. It is on purpose that I put this problem at the beginning, as this is a question that leaves no German family unconcerned. I wish with all my heart that you do understand in which spirit I want to treat this problem. For me only the human point is at stake. The thought is unbearable that—more than ten years after the end of the war—there are still men who are separated from their families, homeland, and their normal, peaceful work—men who were involved—in whatever way—in the maelstrom of war. You must not find any provocation in my saying: It is out of the question to establish 'normal' relations between our states as long as this question is unsolved. It is normalization itself of which I am talking. Let us make a clean break with a matter which is a daily source of remembrance of sorrowful and separating past."

Mr. Bulganin answered:

"The Federal Chancellor, Mr. Adenauer, raised as first question that of the prisoners of war. In our opinion there is a definite misunderstanding. There are no German prisoners of war at all in the Soviet Union. All German prisoners of war were released and repatriated. In the Soviet Union there are only war criminals of the former Hitler armies—criminals that were convicted by a Soviet court for especially grave crimes against the Soviet people, against peace and against humanity. In fact, 9,626 men have been retained up to September 1. (Some 2,000 actually fought at Stalingrad.) But these are men who must be kept in prison as criminals, according to the most humane standards and rules. They are men who have lost the human countenance; they are men guilty of atrocity, of arson, of murder committed against women, children and old people. They were duly sentenced by a Soviet court and cannot be regarded as prisoners of war.

"The Soviet people cannot forget the capital crimes committed by these criminal elements, as, for instance, the shooting of 70,000 men in Kiev on the Babi Yar. We cannot forget these million people who were killed, gassed and burned to death. Can anyone ever forget the tons of hair that were cut off (and stapled) from women who were tortured to death. Those present on our side have witnessed all that happened in Maidanek. In the Maidanek and Auschwitz camps more than five and a half million people, all innocent, were murdered. The Ukrainian people will never forget those innocent people murdered in Kharkov, where thousands were shot or gassed. I could name the concentration camps in Smolensk, Krasnodar, Stavropol, Lov, Poltava, Novgorod, Orel, Rovno, Kaunas, Riga—and many others—where hundreds of thousands of Soviet citizens were tortured to death by the Hitler fascists. We cannot forget those innocent people, murdered, gassed and buried alive; we cannot forget the scorched towns and villages, the killed women, juveniles and children. And those 9,626 men I mentioned are criminals who committed these monstrous crimes . . ."

Adenauer was quick to respond:

"Then, Mr. Prime Minister, you talked about the prisoners of war. May I be permitted to draw your attention to the fact that in my yesterday's statements the words 'prisoners of war' were not at all mentioned. I avoided this expression on purpose. If you closely examine my statements, you will find that I rather spoke of 'persons who were retained.' You talked of 'war criminals' and of sentences passed by Soviet courts. We have similar facts also in our relation to the U.S.A., Great Britain and France. But these states came to understand that the sentences passed by the courts of these countries in the first postwar period were not free from emotions, from the atmosphere of that specific time . . .

"Much evil was done.

"This much is true: German troops invaded Russia. And this much is true: Much evil was done. But this is true, too: Russian armies invaded

Germany—in defense, I admit without hesitation—and many horrible things also happened in Germany during the war. I think, if we enter into a new period of our relations—and this we want seriously—we should not take too close a look into the past, for then we only start putting up obstacles."

Premier Nikita Khrushchev vehemently attacked Adenauer's position:

"Mr. Chancellor, you said at the end of your declaration that the Soviet troops, when they crossed the Soviet borders and penetrated deeper into your country, also committed crimes; I refuse this categorically, as this was not the case and the German party cannot submit any evidence as to this (author's note—here Khrushchev ignored the truth). The Soviet troops drove away the others from this country and persecuted them, as they did not surrender. If we had left these troops alone, they could have prepared for another invasion. We could not stop halfway, but had to destroy the enemy who dared to raise his weapons against us. That is why the Soviet soldiers fulfilled their holy duty toward their homeland by continuing this war and sacrificing their lives. Are these horrors? If any troops had invaded Germany and Germany had defended herself and destroyed the enemy—would you call that horrors? It would be Germany's holy duty. For these reasons, I am of the opinion that an insulting remark has been made as to the Soviet troops. And this forced me to make such a statement."

On September 14, Adenauer held a press conference in Moscow:

". . . The Soviet Government—Mr. Bulganin and Mr. Khrushchev—expressly declared during the negotiations that the Soviet Union has no longer any German prisoners of war, but only 9,626 convicted war criminals —as they put it.

"All of them will leave the Soviet Union in the near future. They will partly be amnestied and released; as far as the Soviet Union believes that really serious crimes were committed they will be extradited to Germany to be treated according to the laws of our land. I think this will ease a lot of grief—not only of those nearly 10,000 people here in the Soviet Union but also of the numerous relatives in our home country. Now I may also inform you that Prime Minister Bulganin said to me—and he authorized me to tell you this—that the entire action will be under way even before we have arrived in Bonn . . ."

In this manner, the last of the Stalingrad prisoners began their final journey home from Soviet prison camps.

INDEX

Index

READ MORE IN PENGUIN

In every corner of the world, on every subject under the sun, Penguin represents quality and variety – the very best in publishing today.

For complete information about books available from Penguin – including Puffins, Penguin Classics and Arkana – and how to order them, write to us at the appropriate address below. Please note that for copyright reasons the selection of books varies from country to country:

In the United Kingdom: Please write to *Dept. EP, Penguin Books Ltd, Bath Road, Harmondsworth, West Drayton, Middlesex UB7 0DA*

In the United States: Please write to *Consumer Sales, Penguin Putnam Inc., P.O. Box 12289 Dept. B, Newark, New Jersey 07101-5289*. VISA and MasterCard holders call 1-800-788-6262 to order Penguin titles

In Canada: Please write to *Penguin Books Canada Ltd, 10 Alcorn Avenue, Suite 300, Toronto, Ontario M4V 3B2*

In Australia: Please write to *Penguin Books Australia Ltd, P.O. Box 257, Ringwood, Victoria 3134*

In New Zealand: Please write to *Penguin Books (NZ) Ltd, Private Bag 102902, North Shore Mail Centre, Auckland 10*

In India: Please write to *Penguin Books India Pvt Ltd, 11 Community Centre, Panchsheel Park, New Delhi 110017*

In the Netherlands: Please write to *Penguin Books Netherlands bv, Postbus 3507, NL-1001 AH Amsterdam*

In Germany: Please write to *Penguin Books Deutschland GmbH, Metzlerstrasse 26, 60594 Frankfurt am Main*

In Spain: Please write to *Penguin Books S. A., Bravo Murillo 19, 1° B, 28015 Madrid*

In Italy: Please write to *Penguin Italia s.r.l., Via Benedetto Croce 2, 20094 Corsico, Milano*

In France: Please write to *Penguin France, Le Carré Wilson, 62 rue Benjamin Baillaud, 31500 Toulouse*

In Japan: Please write to *Penguin Books Japan Ltd, Kaneko Building, 2-3-25 Koraku, Bunkyo-Ku, Tokyo 112*

In South Africa: Please write to *Penguin Books South Africa (Pty) Ltd, Private Bag X14, Parkview, 2122 Johannesburg*

INSPECTION COPY REQUESTS

Lecturers in the United Kingdom and Ireland wishing to apply for inspection copies of Classic Penguin titles for student group adoptions are invited to apply to:

Inspection Copy Department
Penguin Press Marketing
80 Strand
LONDON
WC2R 0RL

Fax: 020 7010 6701

E-mail: academic@penguin.co.uk

Inspection copies may also be requested via our website at:
www.penguinclassics.com

Please include in your request the author, title and the ISBN of the book(s) in which you are interested, the name of the course on which the books will be used and the expected student numbers.

It is essential that you include with your request your title, first name, surname, position, department name, college or university address, telephone and fax numbers and your e-mail address.

Lecturers outside the United Kingdom and Ireland should address their applications to their local Penguin office.

Inspection copies are supplied at the discretion of Penguin Books

READ MORE IN PENGUIN

HISTORY

A History of Twentieth-Century Russia Robert Service

'A remarkable work of scholarship and synthesis . . . [it] demands to be read' *Spectator*. 'A fine book . . . It is a dizzying tale and Service tells it well; he has none of the ideological baggage that has so often bedevilled Western histories of Russia . . . A balanced, dispassionate and painstaking account' *Sunday Times*

A Monarchy Transformed: Britain 1603–1714 Mark Kishlansky

'Kishlansky's century saw one king executed, another exiled, the House of Lords abolished, and the Church of England reconstructed along Presbyterian lines . . . A masterly narrative, shot through with the shrewdness that comes from profound scholarship' *Spectator*

American Frontiers Gregory H. Nobles

'At last someone has written a narrative of America's frontier experience with sensitivity and insight. This is a book which will appeal to both the specialist and the novice' James M. McPherson, Princeton University

The Pleasures of the Past David Cannadine

'This is almost everything you ever wanted to know about the past but were too scared to ask . . . A fascinating book and one to strike up arguments in the pub' *Daily Mail*. 'He is erudite and rigorous, yet always fun. I can imagine no better introduction to historical study than this collection' *Observer*

Prague in Black and Gold Peter Demetz

'A dramatic and compelling history of a city Demetz admits to loving and hating . . . He embraces myth, economics, sociology, linguistics and cultural history . . . His reflections on visiting Prague after almost a half-century are a moving elegy on a world lost through revolutions, velvet or otherwise' *Literary Review*

READ MORE IN PENGUIN

HISTORY

The Vikings Else Roesdahl

Far from being just 'wild, barbaric, axe-wielding pirates', the Vikings created complex social institutions, oversaw the coming of Christianity to Scandinavia and made a major impact on European history through trade, travel and far-flung colonization. This study is a rich and compelling picture of an extraordinary civilization.

A Short History of Byzantium John Julius Norwich

In this abridgement of his celebrated trilogy, John Julius Norwich has created a definitive overview of 'the strange, savage, yet endlessly fascinating world of Byzantium'. 'A real life epic of love and war, accessible to anyone' *Independent on Sunday*

The Eastern Front 1914–1917 Norman Stone

'Without question one of the classics of post-war historical scholarship' Niall Ferguson. 'Fills an enormous gap in our knowledge and understanding of the Great War' *Sunday Telegraph*

The Idea of India Sunil Khilnani

'Many books about India will be published this year; I doubt if any will be wiser and more illuminating about its modern condition than this' *Observer*. 'Sunil Khilnani's meditation on India since Independence is a *tour de force*' *Sunday Telegraph*

The Penguin History of Europe J. M. Roberts

'J. M. Roberts has managed to tell the rich and remarkable tale of European history in fewer than 700 fascinating, well-written pages ... few would ever be able to match this achievement' *The New York Times Book Review*. 'The best single-volume history of Europe' *The Times Literary Supplement*

READ MORE IN PENGUIN

HISTORY

Hope and Glory: Britain 1900–1990 Peter Clarke

'Splendid ... If you want a text book for the century, this is it'
Independent. 'Clarke has written one of the classic works of modern
history. His erudition is encyclopaedic, yet lightly and wittily borne.
He writes memorably, with an eye for the telling detail, an ear for
aphorism, and an instinct for irony' *Sunday Telegraph*

Instruments of Darkness: Witchcraft in England 1550–1750
James Sharpe

'Learned and enthralling ... Time and again, as I read this scrupu-
lously balanced work of scholarship, I was reminded of contemporary
parallels' Jan Morris, *Independent*

A Social History of England Asa Briggs

Asa Briggs's magnificent exploration of English society has been
totally revised and brought right up to the present day. 'A treasure
house of scholarly knowledge ... beautifully written, and full of the
author's love of his country, its people and its landscape' *Sunday
Times*

Hatchepsut: The Female Pharaoh Joyce Tyldesley

Queen – or, as she would prefer to be remembered king – Hatchepsut
was an astonishing woman. Defying tradition, she became the female
embodiment of a male role, dressing in men's clothes and even wearing
a false beard. Joyce Tyldesley's dazzling piece of detection strips away
the myths and restores the female pharaoh to her rightful place.

Fifty Years of Europe: An Album Jan Morris

'A highly insightful kaleidoscopic encyclopedia of European life ...
Jan Morris writes beautifully ... Like a good vintage wine [*Fifty
Years*] has to be sipped and savoured rather than gulped. Then it will
keep warming your soul for many years to come' *Observer*

READ MORE IN PENGUIN

PENGUIN CLASSIC BIOGRAPHY

Highly readable and enjoyable biographies and autobiographies from leading biographers and autobiographers. The series provides a vital background to the increasing interest in history, historical subjects and people who mattered. The periods and subjects covered include the Roman Empire, Tudor England, the English Civil Wars, the Victorian Era, and characters as diverse Joan of Arc, Jane Austen, Robert Burns and George Melly. Essential reading for everyone interested in the great figures of the past.

Published or forthcoming:

E. F. Benson	**As We Were**
Ernle Bradford	**Cleopatra**
David Cecil	**A Portrait of Jane Austen**
Roger Fulford	**Royal Dukes**
Christopher Hibbert	**Charles I**
	The Making of Charles Dickens
Christopher Hill	**God's Englishman: Oliver Cromwell**
Marion Johnson	**The Borgias**
James Lees-Milne	**Earls of Creation**
Edward Lucie-Smith	**Joan of Arc**
Philip Magnus	**Gladstone**
John Masters	**Casanova**
Elizabeth Mavor	**The Ladies of Llangollen**
Ian McIntyre	**Robert Burns**
George Melly	**Owning Up: The Trilogy**
Raymond Postgate	**That Devil Wilkes**
Peter Quennell	**Byron: The Years of Fame**
Lytton Strachey	**Queen Victoria**
	Elizabeth and Essex
Gaius Suetonius	**Lives of the Twelve Caesars**
	translated by Robert Graves
Alan Villiers	**Captain Cook**

READ MORE IN PENGUIN

PENGUIN CLASSIC HISTORY

 Well written narrative history from leading historians such as Paul Kennedy, Alan Moorehead, J. B. Priestley, A. L. Rowse and G. M. Trevelyan. From the Ancient World to the decline of British naval mastery, from twelfth-century France to the Victorian Underworld, the series captures the great turning points in history and chronicles the lives of ordinary people at different times. Penguin Classic History will be enjoyed and valued by everyone who loves the past.

Published or forthcoming:

Leslie Alcock	**Arthur's Britain**
John Belchem/Richard Price	**A Dictionary of 19th-Century History**
Jeremy Black/Roy Porter	**A Dictionary of 18th-Century History**
Ernle Bradford	**The Mediterranean**
Anthony Burton	**Remains of a Revolution**
Robert Darnton	**The Great Cat Massacre**
Jean Froissart	**Froissart's Chronicles**
Johan Huizinga	**The Waning of the Middle Ages**
Aldous Huxley	**The Devils of Loudun**
Paul M. Kennedy	**The Rise and Fall of British Naval Mastery**
Margaret Wade Labarge	**Women in Medieval Life**
Alan Moorehead	**Fatal Impact**
Samuel Pepys	**Illustrated Pepys**
J. H. Plumb	**The First Four Georges**
J. B. Priestley	**The Edwardians**
Philippa Pullar	**Consuming Passions**
A. L. Rowse	**The Elizabethan Renaissance**
John Ruskin	**The Stones of Venice**
G. M. Trevelyan	**English Social History**
Philip Warner	**The Medieval Castle**
T. H. White	**The Age of Scandal**
Lawrence Wright	**Clean and Decent**
Hans Zinsser	**Rats, Lice and History**

READ MORE IN PENGUIN

PENGUIN CLASSIC MILITARY HISTORY

 This series acknowledges the profound and enduring interest in military history, and the causes and consequences of human conflict. Penguin Classic Military History covers warfare from the earliest times to the age of electronics and encompasses subjects as diverse as classic examples of grand strategy and the precision tactics of Britain's crack SAS Regiment. The series will be enjoyed and valued by students of military history and all who hope to learn from the often disturbing lessons of the past.

Published or forthcoming:

Correlli Barnett	**Engage the Enemy More Closely**
	The Great War
David G. Chandler	**The Art of Warfare on Land**
	Marlborough as Military Commander
William Craig	**Enemy at the Gates**
Carlo D'Este	**Decision in Normandy**
Michael Glover	**The Peninsular War**
	Wellington as Military Commander
Winston Graham	**The Spanish Armadas**
Heinz Guderian	**Panzer Leader**
Christopher Hibbert	**Redcoats and Rebels**
Heinz Höhne	**The Order of the Death's Head**
Anthony Kemp	**The SAS at War**
Ronald Lewin	**Ultra Goes to War**
Martin Middlebrook	**The Falklands War**
	The First Day on the Somme
	The Kaiser's Battle
Desmond Seward	**Henry V**
John Toland	**Infamy**
Philip Warner	**Sieges of the Middle Ages**
Leon Wolff	**In Flanders Fields**
Cecil Woodham-Smith	**The Reason Why**